AISLIN'S SHENANIGANS

...and other recent cartoons

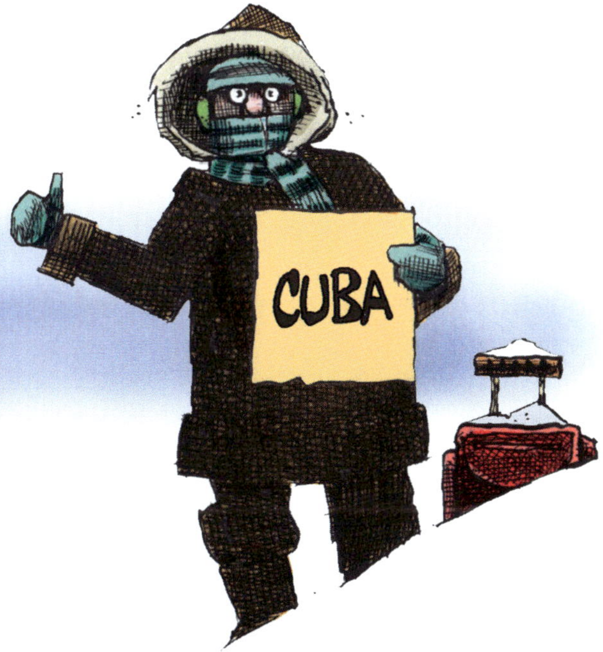
CUBA

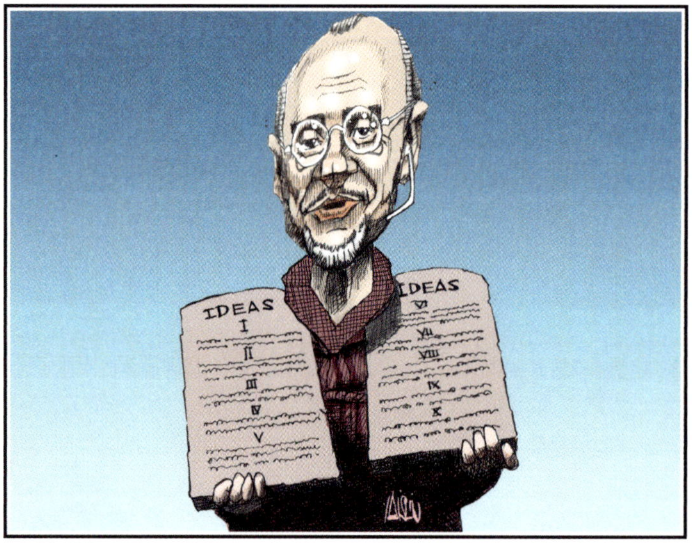
IDEAS
IDEAS

This book is dedicated to Moses, another one of those former Montrealers.

Thanks to all involved:
Mary Hughson, Janet Hughson, Andrew Phillips, Brian Kappler, Michael Goldbloom, Jack Rabinovitch and Pat Duggan.
Thanks as always to Kim McArthur and the terrific team at McArthur & Company.

AISLIN'S SHENANIGANS

...and other recent cartoons

Nice!
Who knew?
AISLIN 09
MONTREAL
THE GAZETTE

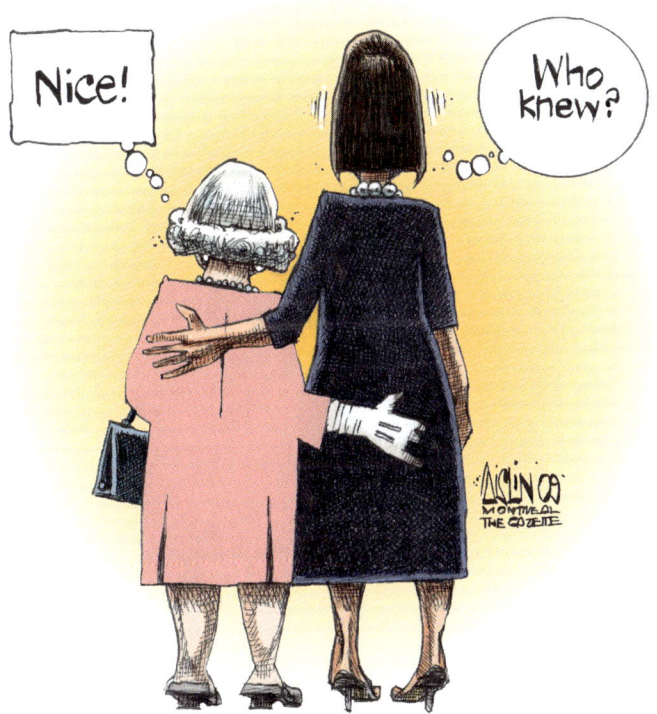

With an introduction by Jack Rabinovitch

Text by Terry Mosher

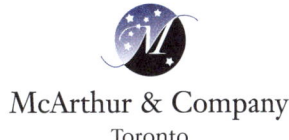

McArthur & Company
Toronto

First published in Canada in 2009 by
McArthur & Company
322 King Street West, Suite 402
Toronto, Ontario
M5V 1J2
www.mcarthur-co.com

Copyright © 2009 Terry Mosher

All rights reserved. The use of any part of this publication reproduced, transmitted in any form or by any means, electronic, mechanical, photocopying, recording or otherwise stored in a retrieval system, without the expressed written consent of the publisher, is an infringement of the copyright law.

Library and Archives Canada Cataloguing in Publication

Aislin
    Shenanigans : and other recent cartoons / Aislin ; introduction by Jack Rabinovitch.

ISBN 978-1-55278-807-3

1. Canada--Politics and government--2009- --Caricatures and cartoons. 2. Canadian wit and humor, Pictorial. I. Title.

NC1449.A37A4 2009   971.07'30207   C2009-903943-5

Cover illustration by AISLIN
Layout, design and electronic imaging by Mary Hughson
Printed and bound in Canada by Transcontinental Printing

The publisher would like to acknowledge the financial support of the Government of Canada through the Book Publishing Industry Development Program (BPIDP) and the Canada Council for our publishing activities. The publisher further wishes to acknowledge the financial support of the Ontario Arts Council and the OMDC for our publishing program.

10 9 8 7 6 5 4 3 2 1

CONTENTS

Introduction by Jack Rabinovitch /6

1 From Bush to Obama /9

2 Oh, Canada! /39

3 I'm a Quebecaholic /83

4 Festival Montréal /115

5 And So It Goes /141

6 Aislin's Travels /161

Introduction

I inherited Terry Mosher, better known as Aislin, from my late wife Doris Giller. In the 70's and early 80's, Terry, Doris, Mordecai Richler and Nick Auf Der Maur were drinking buddies and were single-handedly responsible for keeping the Press Club in Montreal financially viable. I was the designated driver.

Terry and Doris were close friends at the now defunct Montreal Star and later at the Montreal Gazette. They shared a common characteristic. They both liked to take the "mickey" out of pompous people; she with verbal wit Terry with an acid pen.

At the beginning, Aislin, our Canadian troublemaker, was born in 1942 within sight of Canada's Parliament buildings, and his wicked, artistic eye has never strayed far from that target.

One of his early shenanigans however took place in Quebec City when he applied to the Ecole des beaux-arts. After reviewing his art portfolio he was admitted, conditional upon providing a high school leaving certificate. Although he had attended 14 different schools in his checkered youth, he had failed to graduate from any high school. Undaunted by this minor omission, Terry went home and drew a high school leaving certificate. Eventually, he graduated from this distinguished art school with honors.

Terry referred to the above episode when he received his honorary degree at McGill University, thereby encouraging all the graduates to use chicanery and deception in their future endeavors.

Audacious and outrageous, even with friends, Aislin has become Canada's premier political cartoonist. His satirical pen respects no one. In the finest tradition of political fun-poking, his name is now a legend. For verification just ask some of our former Prime Ministers.

One of Terry's friends, Josh Freed, put it aptly when Terry received his Order of Canada; "How refreshing! Terry won the Order of Canada for NOT being nice."

Others have referred to him as an "irritating genius" and "wickedly funny".

Read the cartoons in this book and decide for yourself. They represent some of Aislin's latest and best.

Jack Rabinovitch
Terry's friend and admirer
and also Founder of the Scotiabank Giller Prize

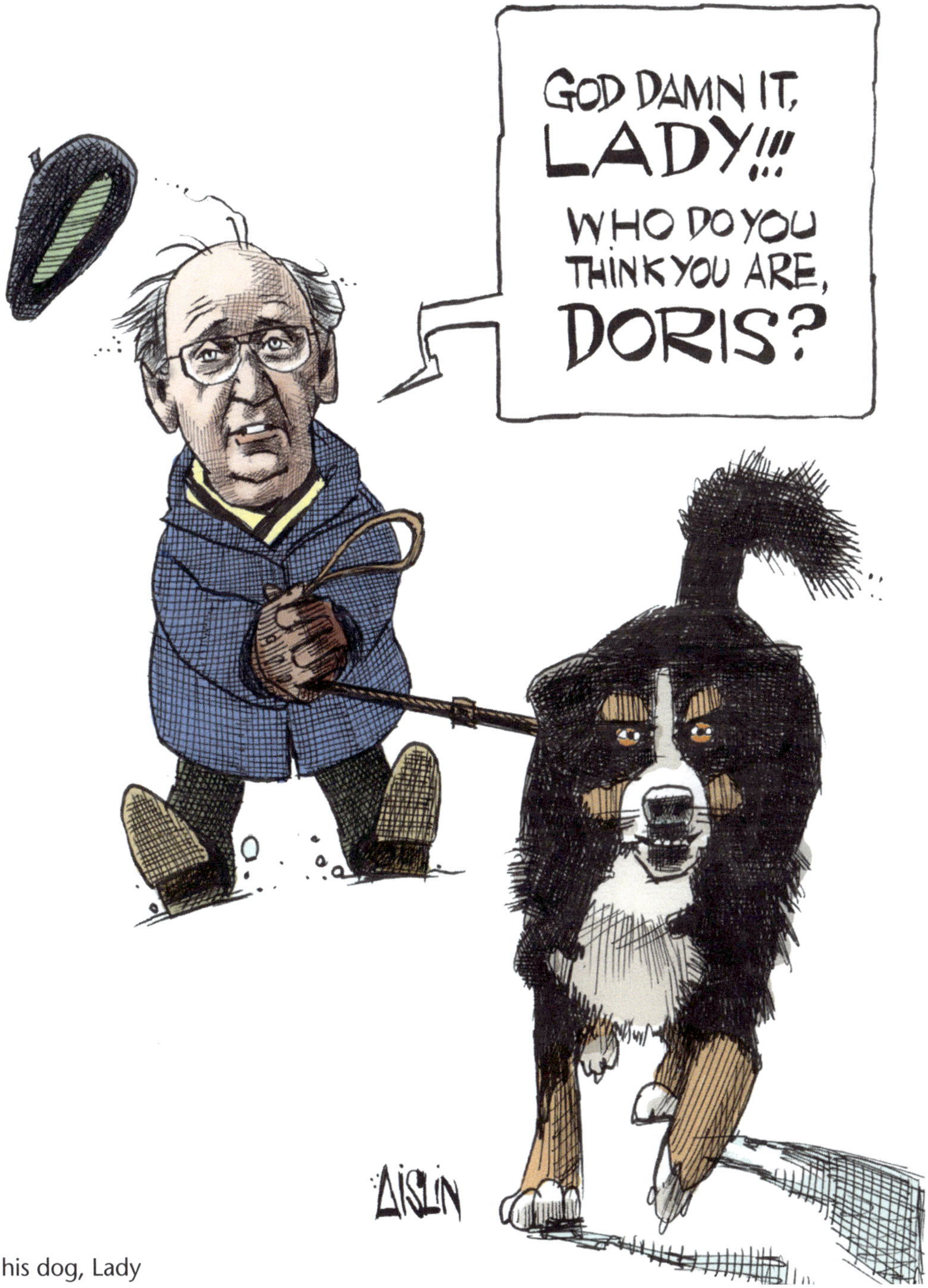
GOD DAMN IT, LADY!!!
WHO DO YOU THINK YOU ARE, DORIS?
AISLIN

Jack walking his dog, Lady

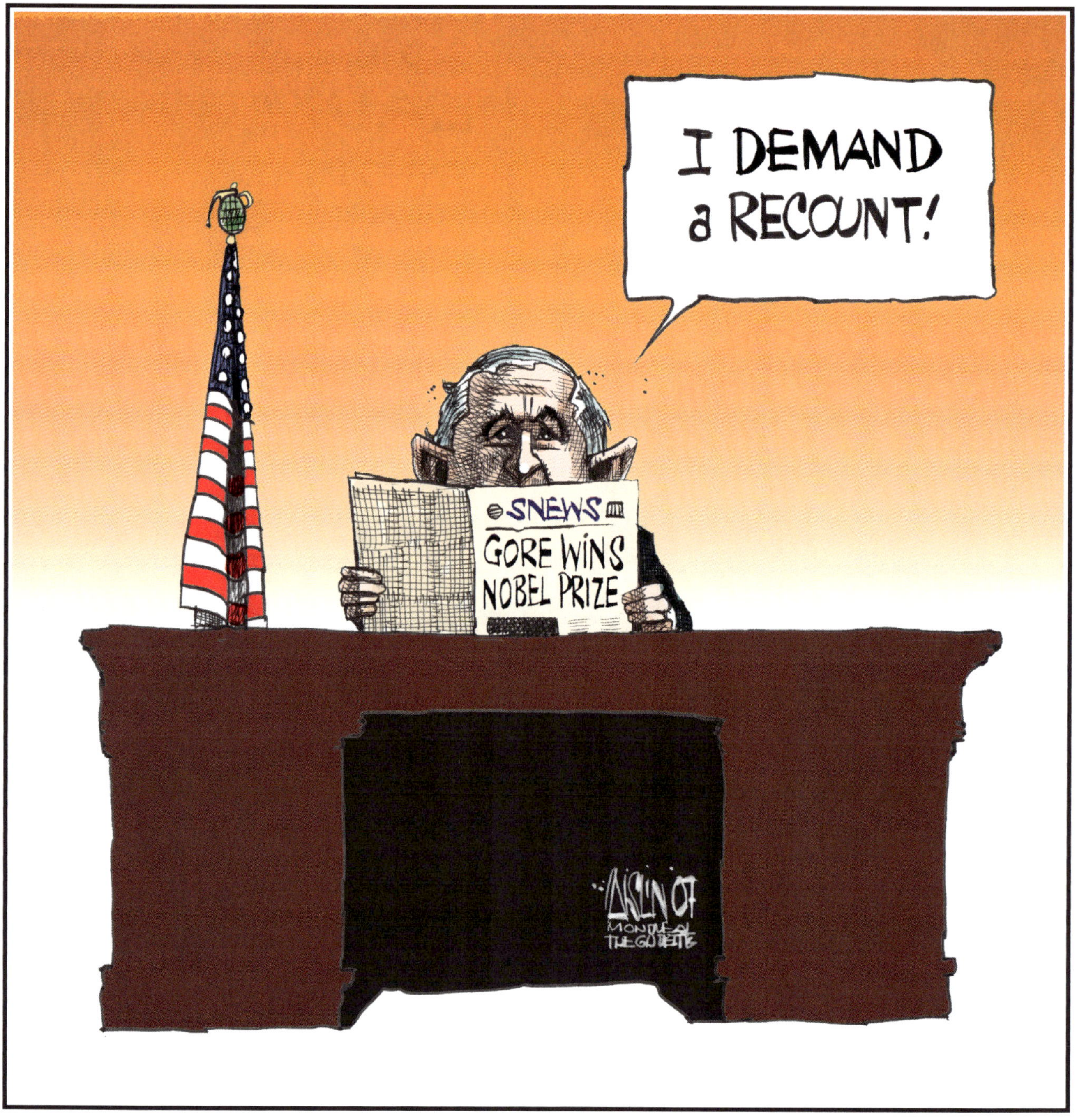
I DEMAND a RECOUNT!
SNEWS
GORE WINS NOBEL PRIZE

CHAPTER 1
From Bush to Obama

George W. Bush is gone.

Not to worry. Many of the same nefarious characters who appeared in my 2006 collection "What Next?" still tread the world's stage for our amusement or outrage.

For your consideration: Kim Jong Il of North Korea, once described as "your average madman – armed with nuclear weapons"; newly re-elected Iranian President Mahmoud Ahmadinejad, reportedly in possession of enough fission material to build a nuclear bomb and eagerly cracking down on election protests; and lest we forget... Osama bin Laden, probably still hiding out somewhere in mountainous northern Pakistan.

Though their effectiveness has been diminished, the Taliban continue to plague Afghanistan. Canadian soldiers have been on the ground there since 2002. The plan is for us to withdraw in 2011, but could the U.S.'s growing commitment to the war threaten that timetable?

The complex, volatile nature of the Middle East's political and religious mix poses seemingly insurmountable challenges for peacemakers. Many of the world's conflicts are deeply rooted in religious and sectarian differences. Is it any wonder we often look askance at religious spokespeople?

But back to the good news... George W. and his crew have left the building and the war in Iraq seems to be winding down. However, we will be burdened with the effects of the war and other Bush policy choices for many years to come. Remember the Iraqi journalist who threw a shoe at Bush during his final press conference? If only we could throw a shoe at the economic mess we inherited from the previous U.S. administration and make it all better. Instead, new American President Barack Obama is throwing money – a lot of money – at the problem, hoping some of it will stick.

Throughout the marathon run-up to the Presidency, Obama demonstrated superior strategic abilities, first eliminating the heavily favoured Hillary Clinton for the Democratic nomination and then handily defeating his Republican opponent, Arizona

Senator John McCain, for the Presidency. In the end, the latter seemed a less formidable opponent: who can fathom his baffling choice of Sarah Palin as his running mate?

Barack Obama has proven to be one of the most engaging politicians in recent memory, inspiring an almost religious fervour among his supporters. During the first months of his presidency, he pitched a number of unpalatable policy choices to the American public without in the least denting his popularity. The honeymoon period is drawing to a close, but whether at home or abroad, he remains an extremely popular American president, if for no other reason than he is not George W. Bush.

Obama's first state visit, in February 2009, was to Canada.

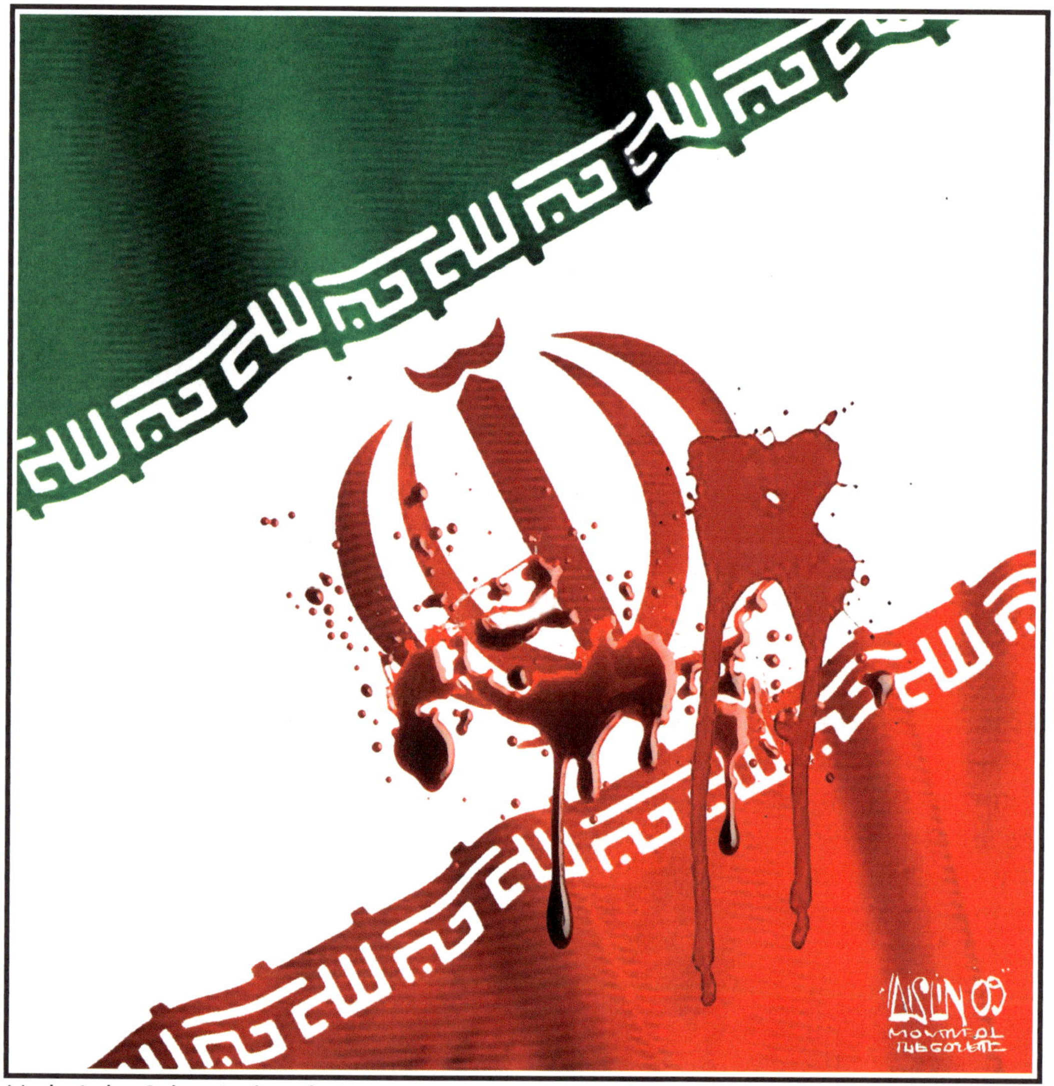

Neda Agha-Soltan is shot during protests over Iranian elections

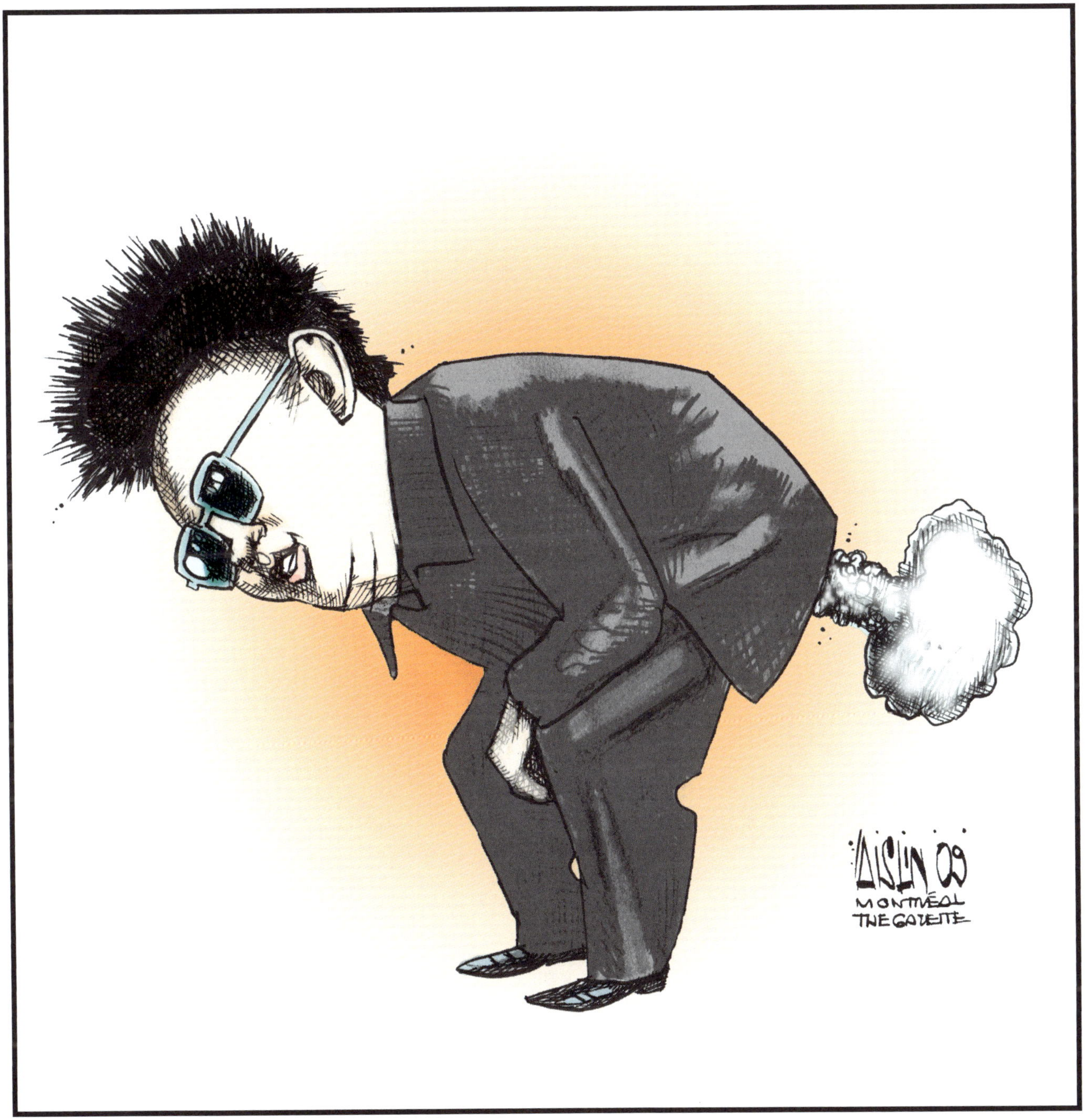
AISLIN 09
MONTRÉAL
THE GAZETTE

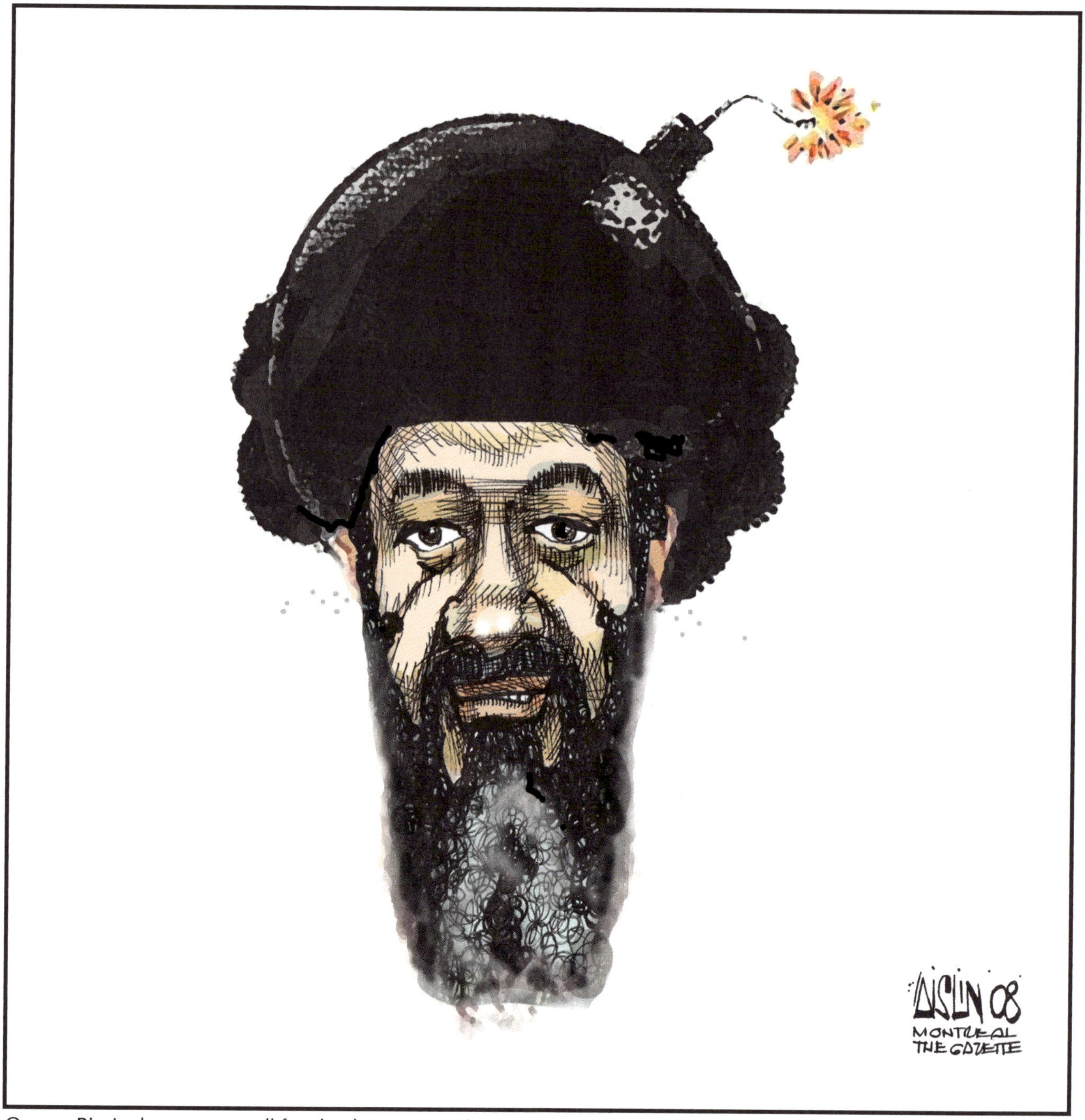
AISLIN 08
MONTREAL THE GAZETTE
Osama Bin Laden renews call for death to cartoonists

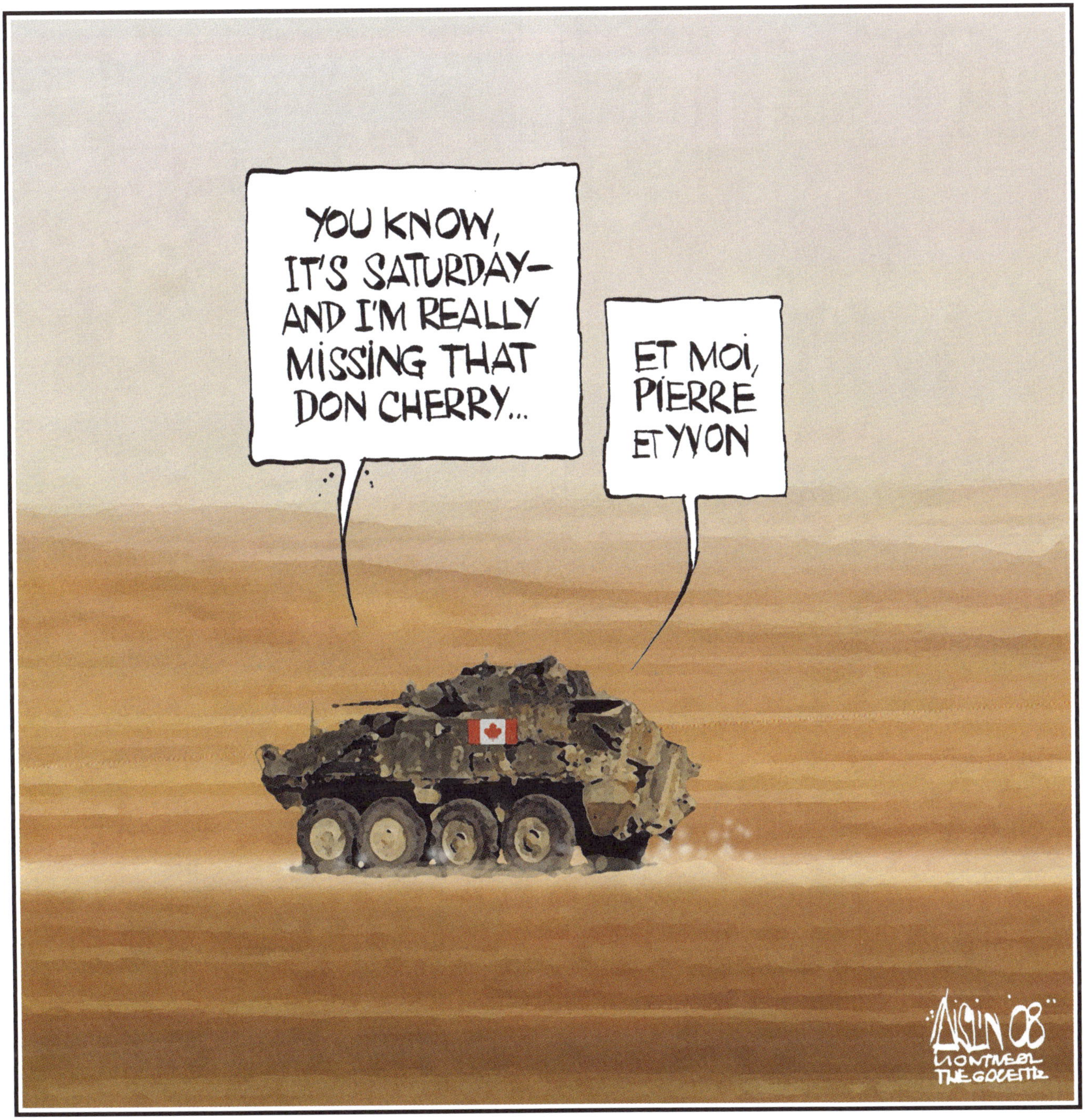
YOU KNOW, IT'S SATURDAY- AND I'M REALLY MISSING THAT DON CHERRY...
ET MOI, PIERRE ET YVON
AISLIN 08
MONTREAL THE GAZETTE

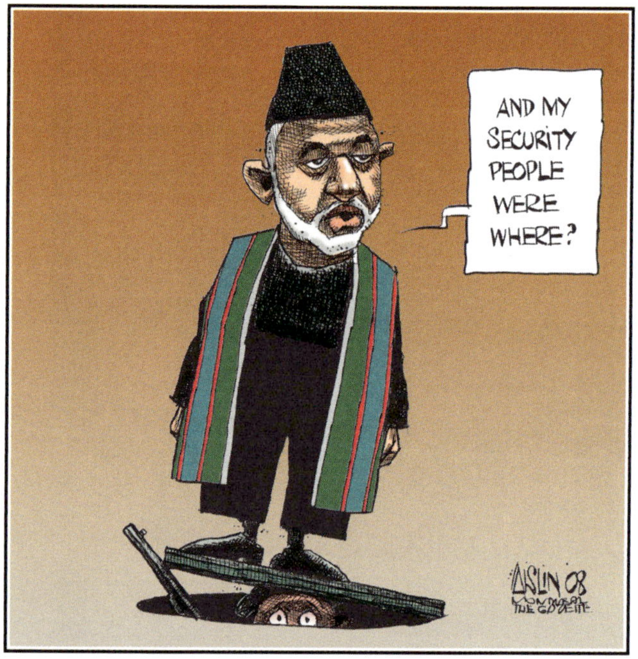
AND MY SECURITY PEOPLE WERE WHERE?
AISLIN 08 MONTREAL THE GAZETTE

Assassination attempt on Hamid Karzai

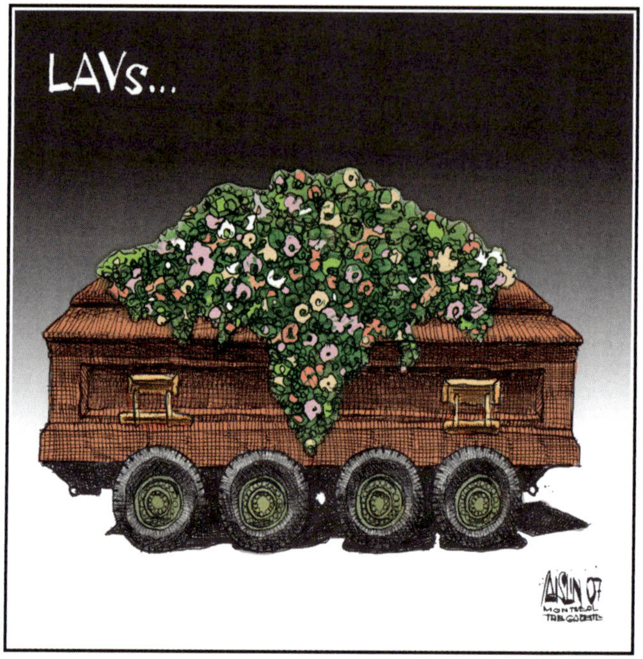
LAVs...
AISLIN 07 MONTREAL THE GAZETTE

Canadian casualties escalate in Afghanistan

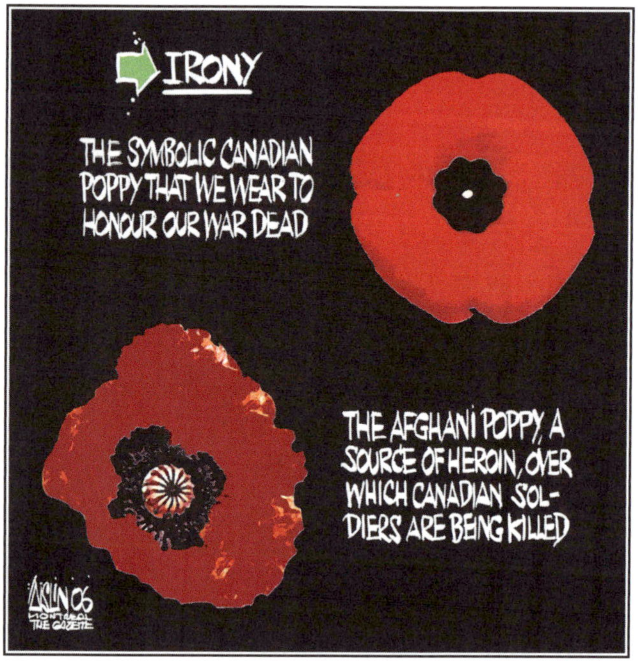
IRONY
THE SYMBOLIC CANADIAN POPPY THAT WE WEAR TO HONOUR OUR WAR DEAD
THE AFGHANI POPPY, A SOURCE OF HEROIN, OVER WHICH CANADIAN SOL-DIERS ARE BEING KILLED
AISLIN 06 MONTREAL THE GAZETTE

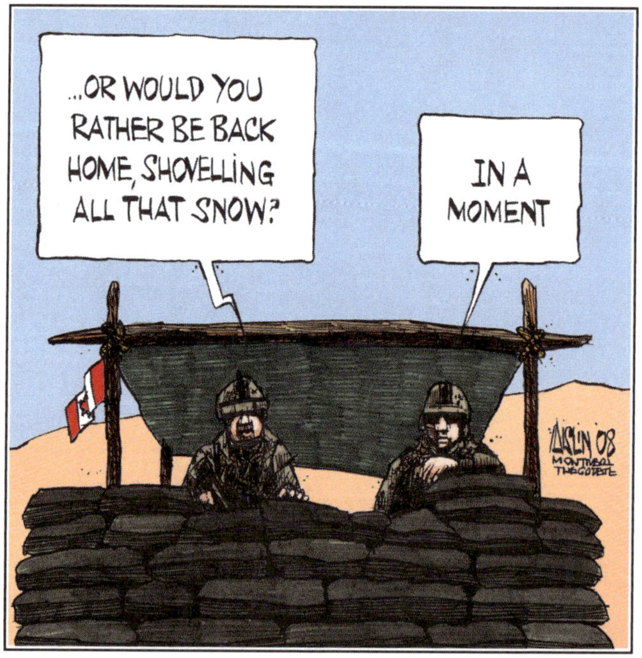
...OR WOULD YOU RATHER BE BACK HOME, SHOVELLING ALL THAT SNOW?
IN A MOMENT
AISLIN 08 MONTREAL THE GAZETTE

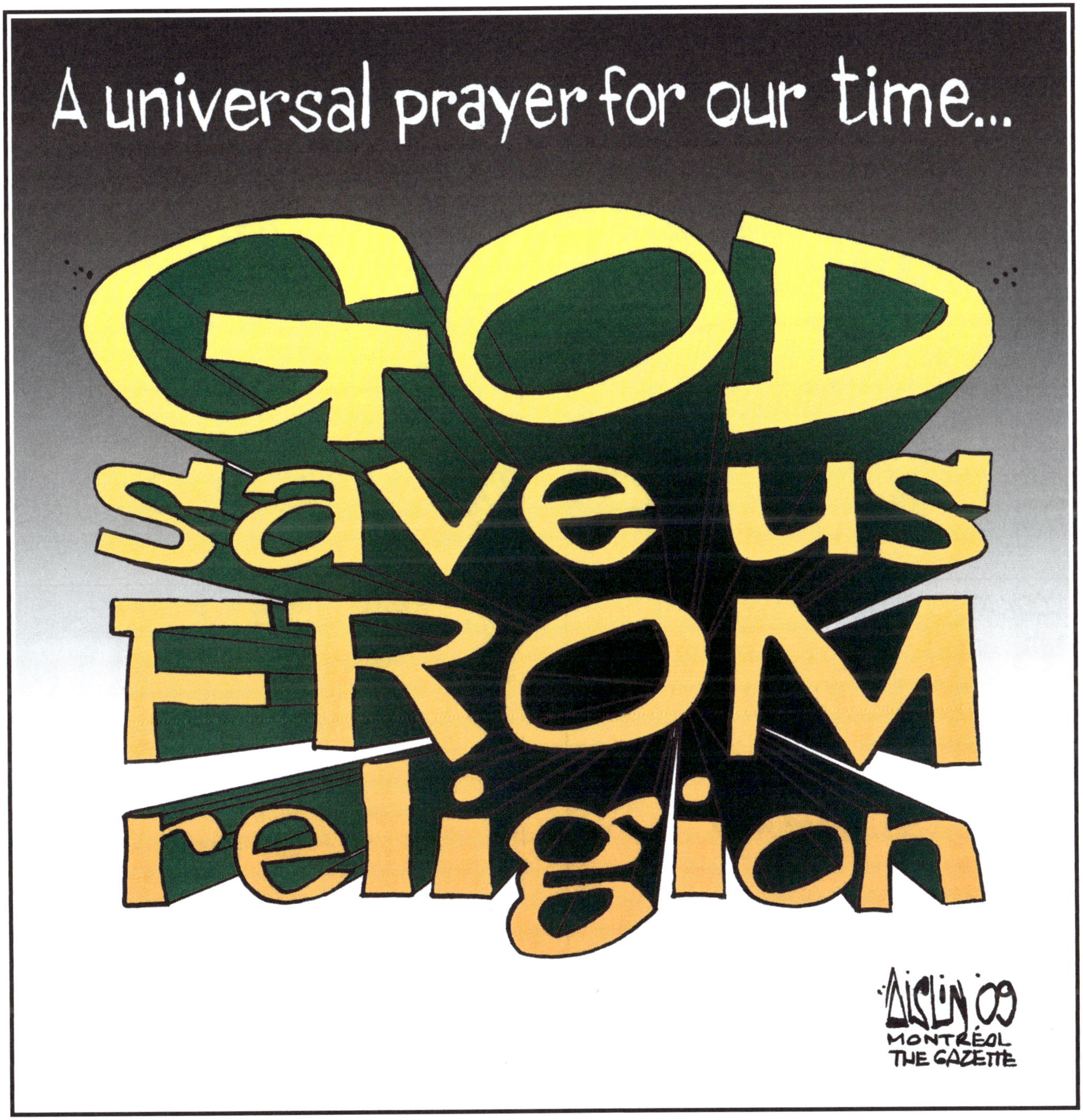
A universal prayer for our time...
GOD
save us
FROM
religion
AISLIN '09
MONTRÉAL
THE GAZETTE

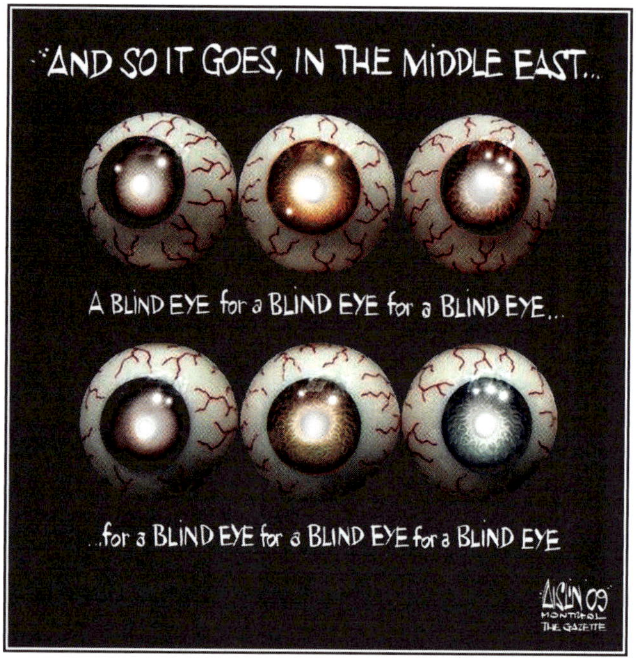

"AND SO IT GOES, IN THE MIDDLE EAST...
A BLIND EYE for a BLIND EYE for a BLIND EYE...
...for a BLIND EYE for a BLIND EYE for a BLIND EYE
AISLIN 09
MONTREAL THE GAZETTE

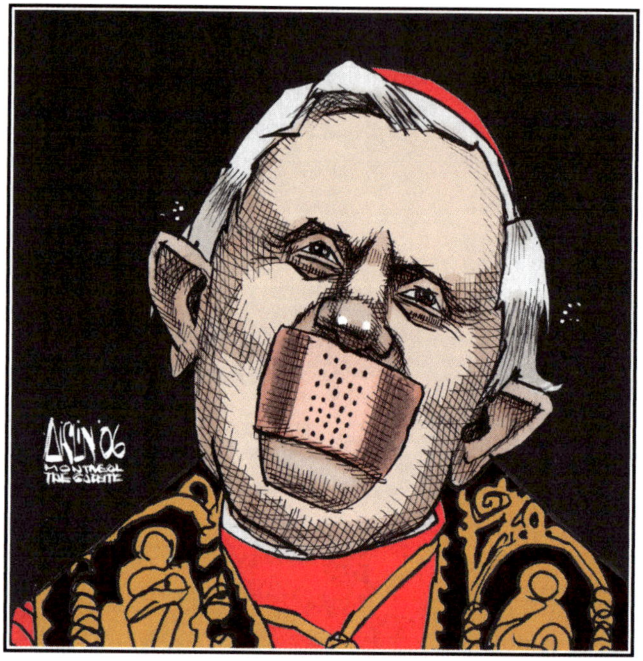

AISLIN '06
MONTREAL THE GAZETTE

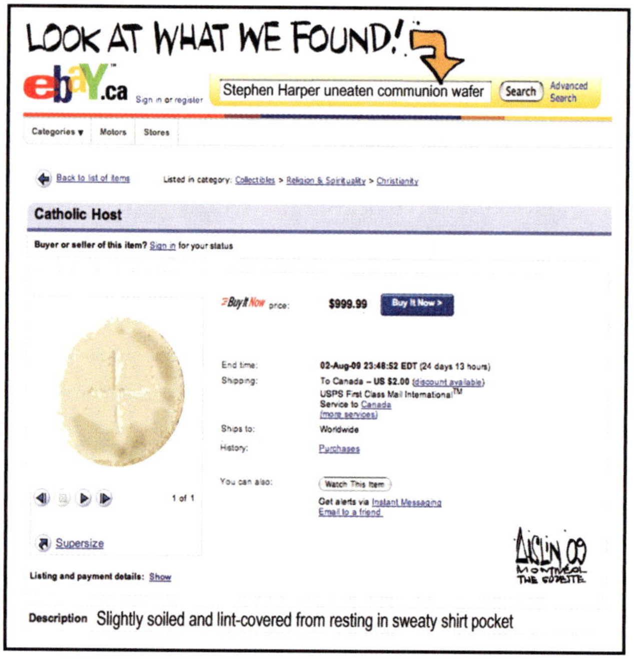

LOOK AT WHAT WE FOUND!
ebay.ca
Sign in or register
Stephen Harper uneaten communion wafer
Search
Advanced Search
Categories ▾
Motors
Stores
Back to list of items
Listed in category: Collectibles > Religion & Spirituality > Christianity
Catholic Host
Buyer or seller of this item? Sign in for your status
Buy It Now price:
$999.99
Buy It Now >
End time:
02-Aug-09 23:48:52 EDT (24 days 13 hours)
Shipping:
To Canada – US $2.00 (discount available)
USPS First Class Mail International™
Service to Canada
(more services)
Ships to:
Worldwide
History:
Purchases
You can also:
Watch This Item
Get alerts via Instant Messaging
Email to a friend
1 of 1
Supersize
Listing and payment details: Show
AISLIN 09
MONTREAL THE GAZETTE
Description Slightly soiled and lint-covered from resting in sweaty shirt pocket

Did Stephen Harper swallow the communion wafer?

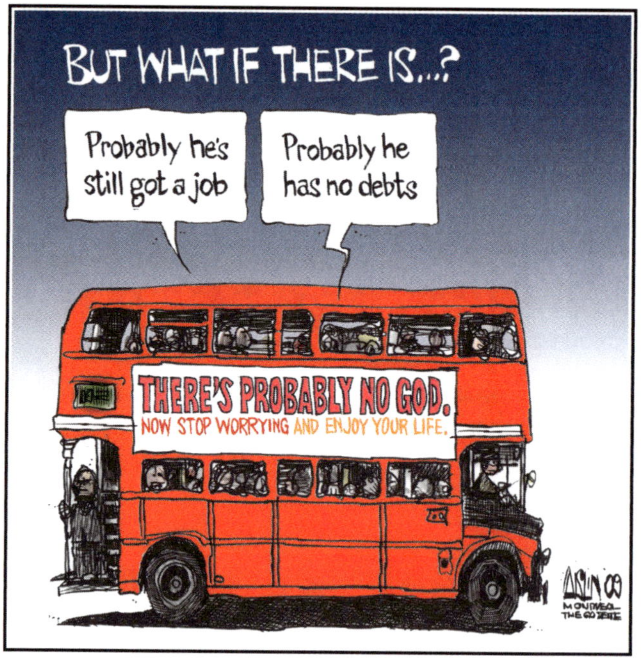

BUT WHAT IF THERE IS...?
Probably he's still got a job
Probably he has no debts
THERE'S PROBABLY NO GOD.
NOW STOP WORRYING AND ENJOY YOUR LIFE.
AISLIN 09
MONTREAL THE GAZETTE

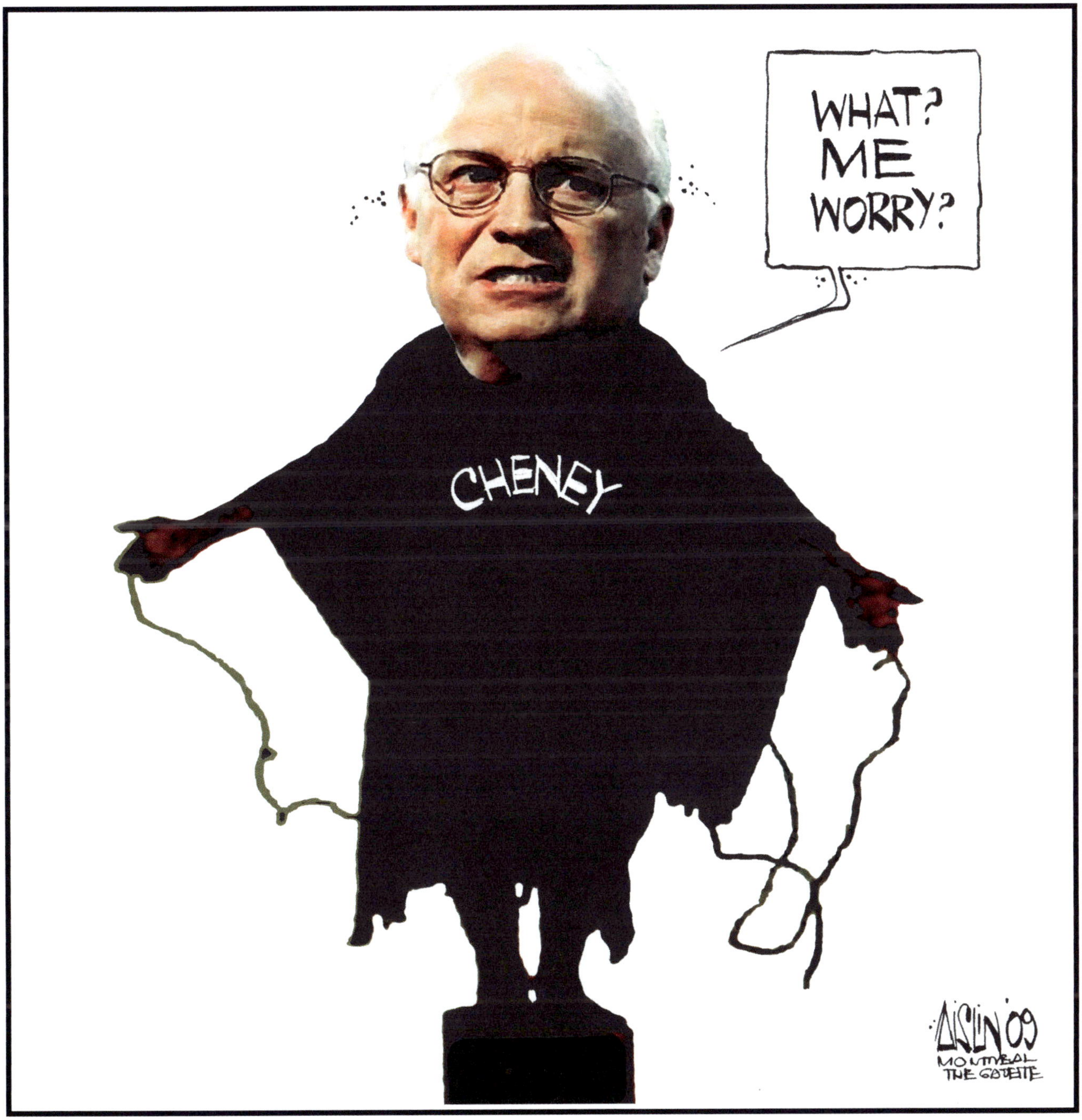
WHAT? ME WORRY?
CHENEY
AISLIN '09
MONTREAL THE GAZETTE

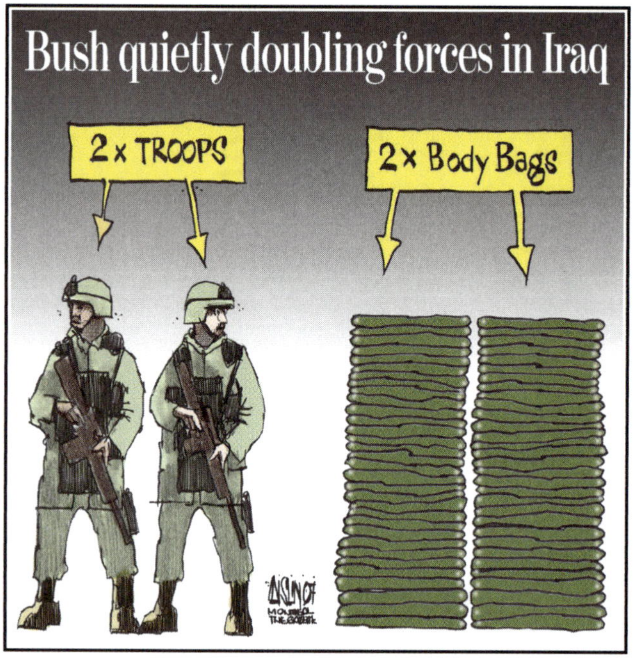
Bush quietly doubling forces in Iraq
2 x TROOPS
2 x Body Bags

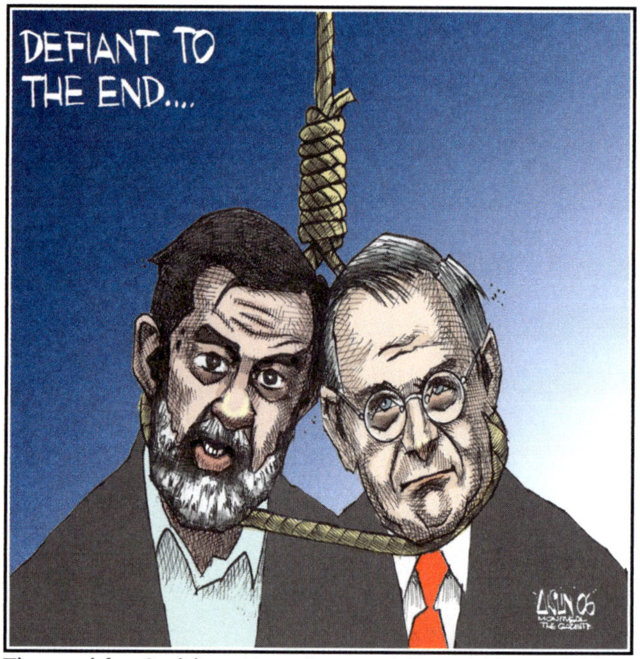
DEFIANT TO THE END....

The end for Saddam Hussein – and Donald Rumsfeld

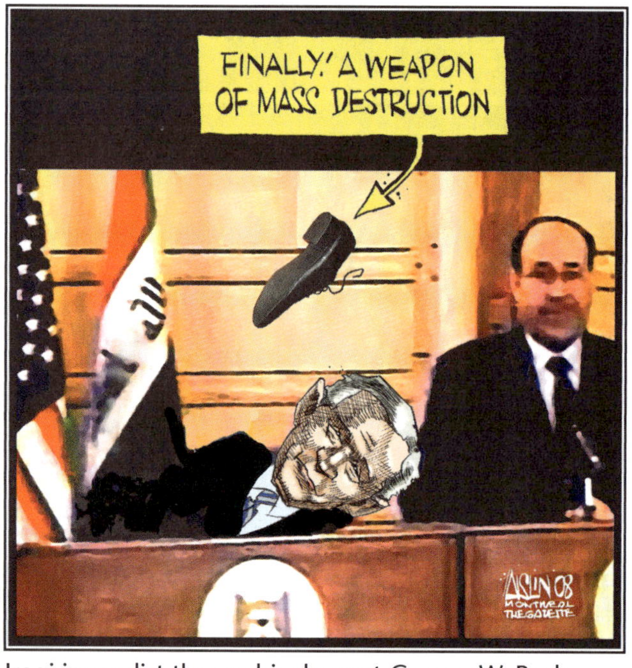
FINALLY! A WEAPON OF MASS DESTRUCTION

Iraqi journalist throws his show at George W. Bush

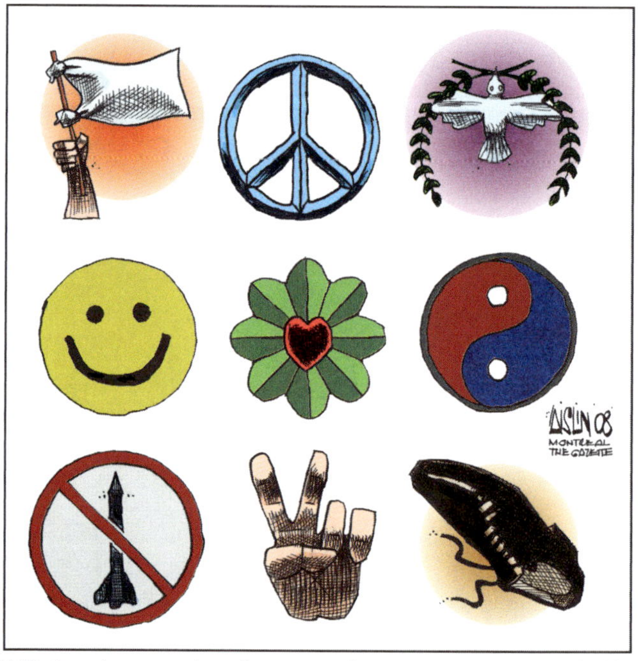

Will the thrown shoe become the next protest symbol?

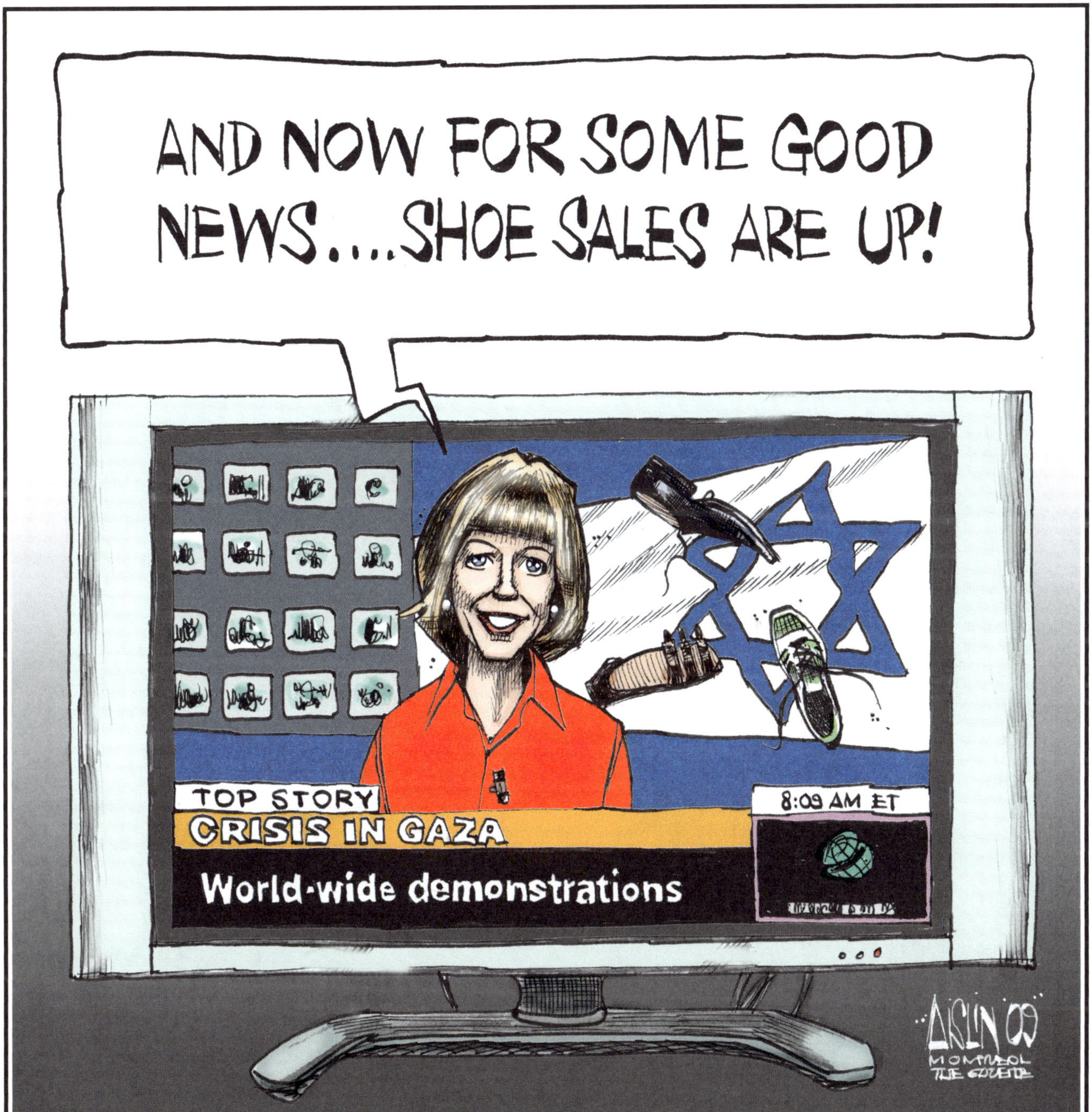
AND NOW FOR SOME GOOD NEWS....SHOE SALES ARE UP!
TOP STORY
CRISIS IN GAZA
World-wide demonstrations
8:09 AM ET
AISLIN 09
MONTREAL THE GAZETTE

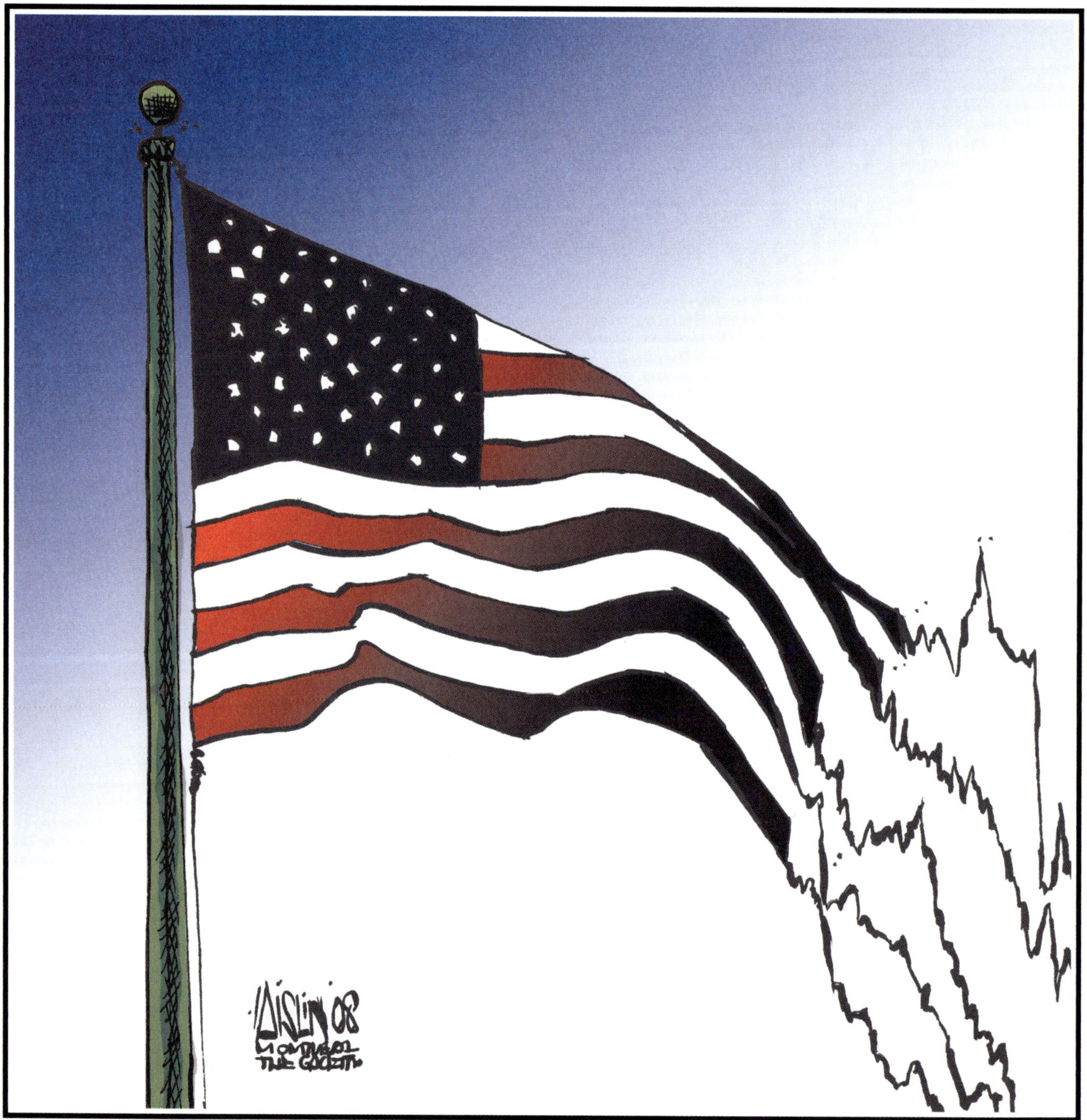
AISLIN 08

American economy falters sending the world's stock markets into a tail-spin

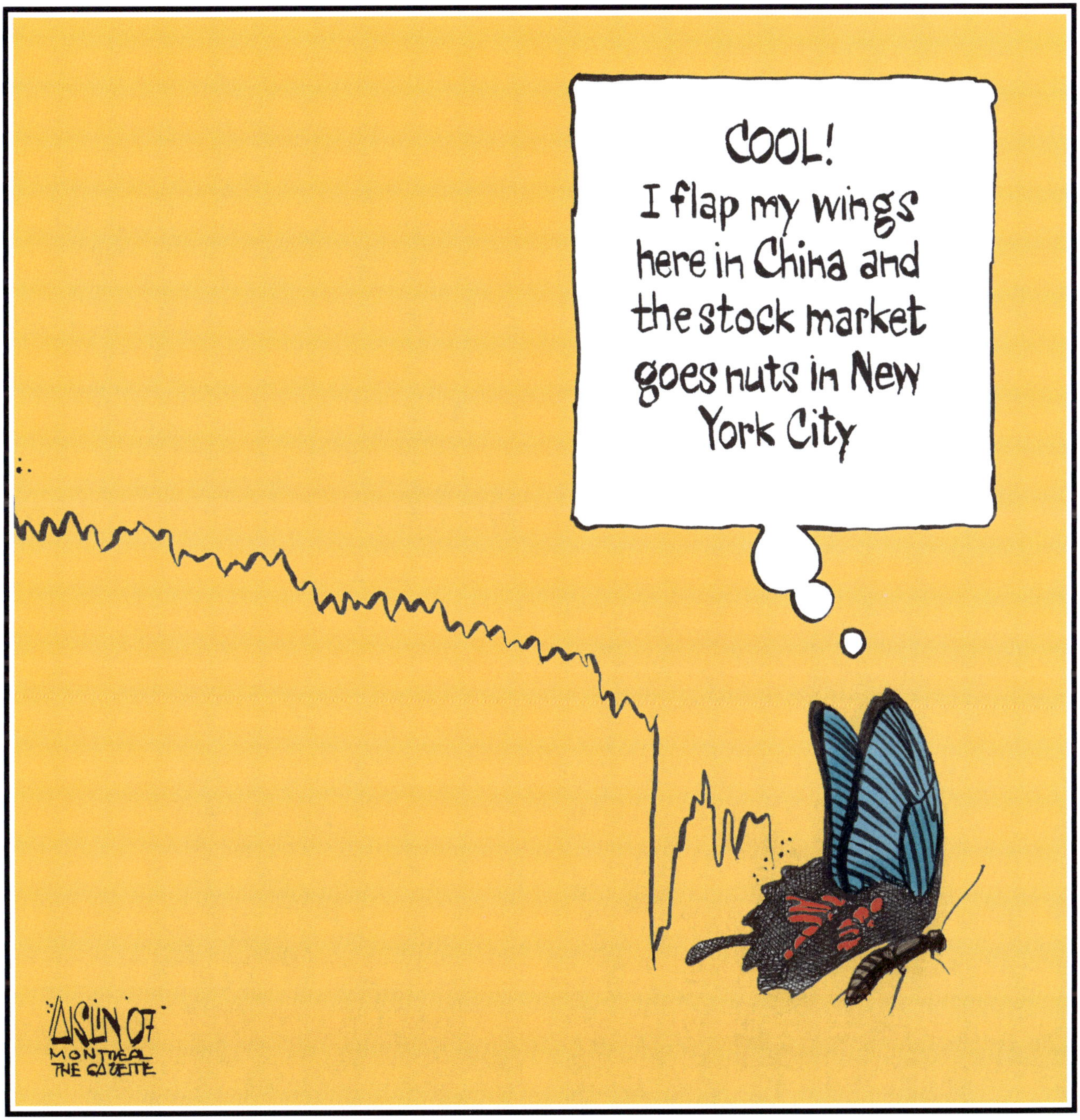
COOL!
I flap my wings here in China and the stock market goes nuts in New York City
AISLIN 07
MONTREAL THE GAZETTE

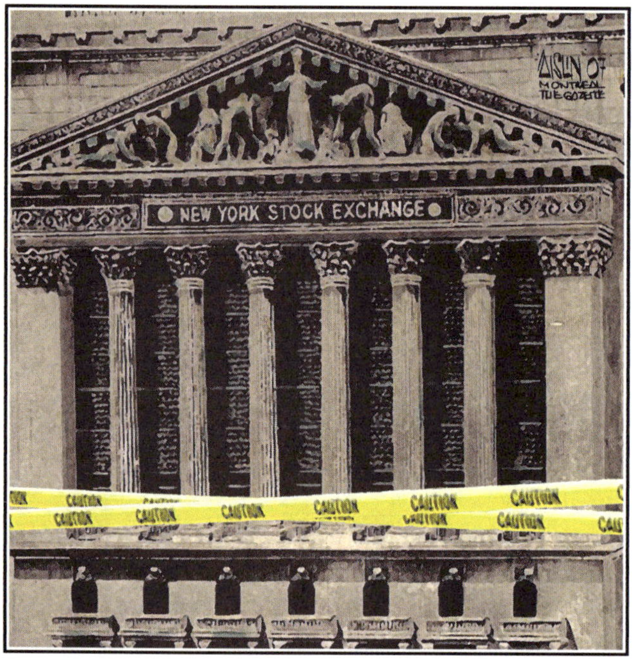
NEW YORK STOCK EXCHANGE
CAUTION

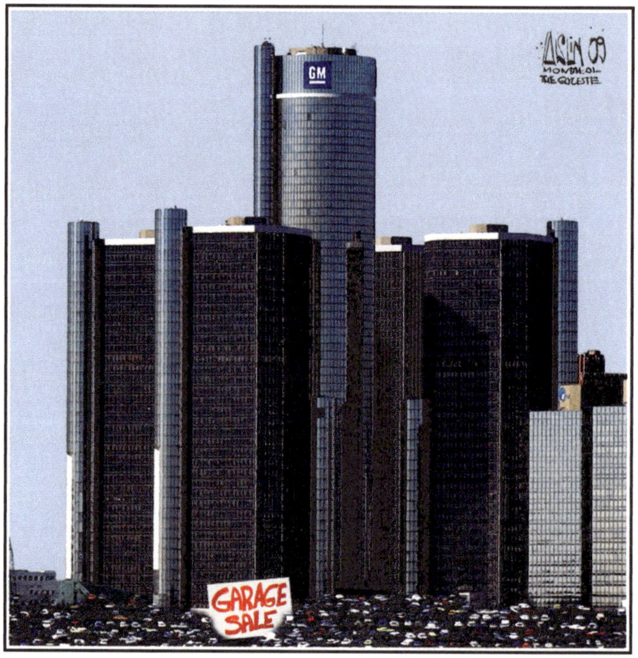
GM
GARAGE SALE

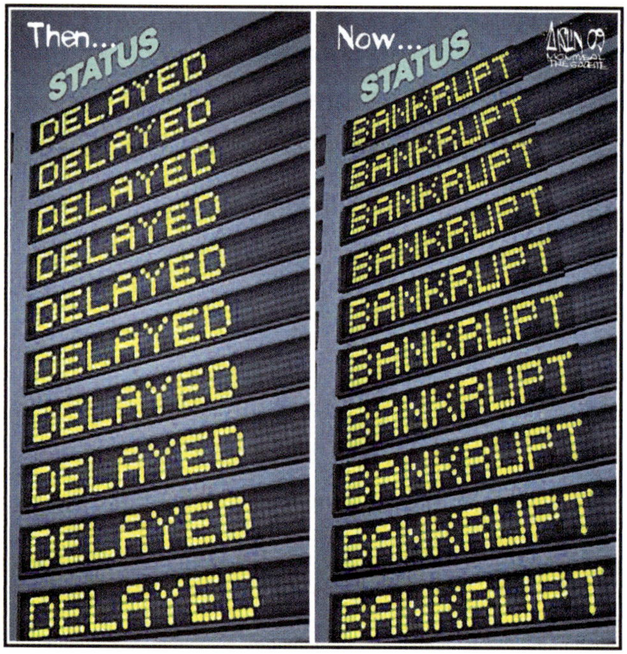
Then...
STATUS
DELAYED
DELAYED
DELAYED
DELAYED
DELAYED
DELAYED
DELAYED
DELAYED
DELAYED
DELAYED
DELAYED
Now...
STATUS
BANKRUPT
BANKRUPT
BANKRUPT
BANKRUPT
BANKRUPT
BANKRUPT
BANKRUPT
BANKRUPT
BANKRUPT
BANKRUPT
BANKRUPT

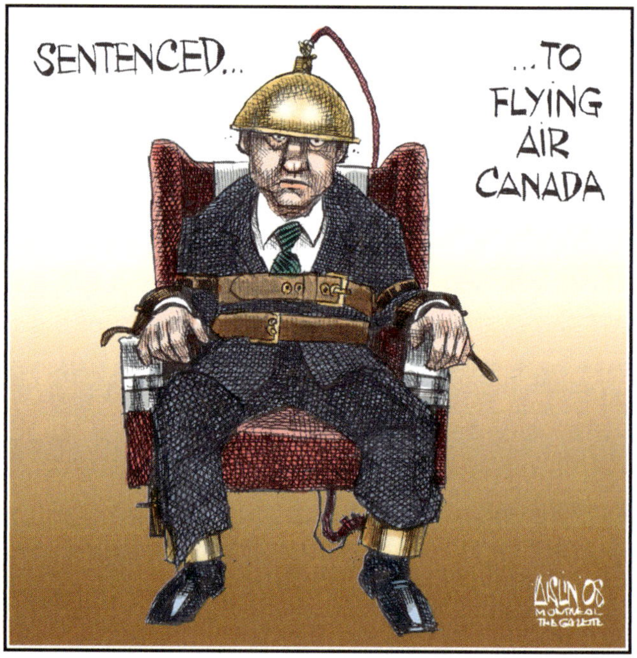
SENTENCED...
...TO FLYING AIR CANADA

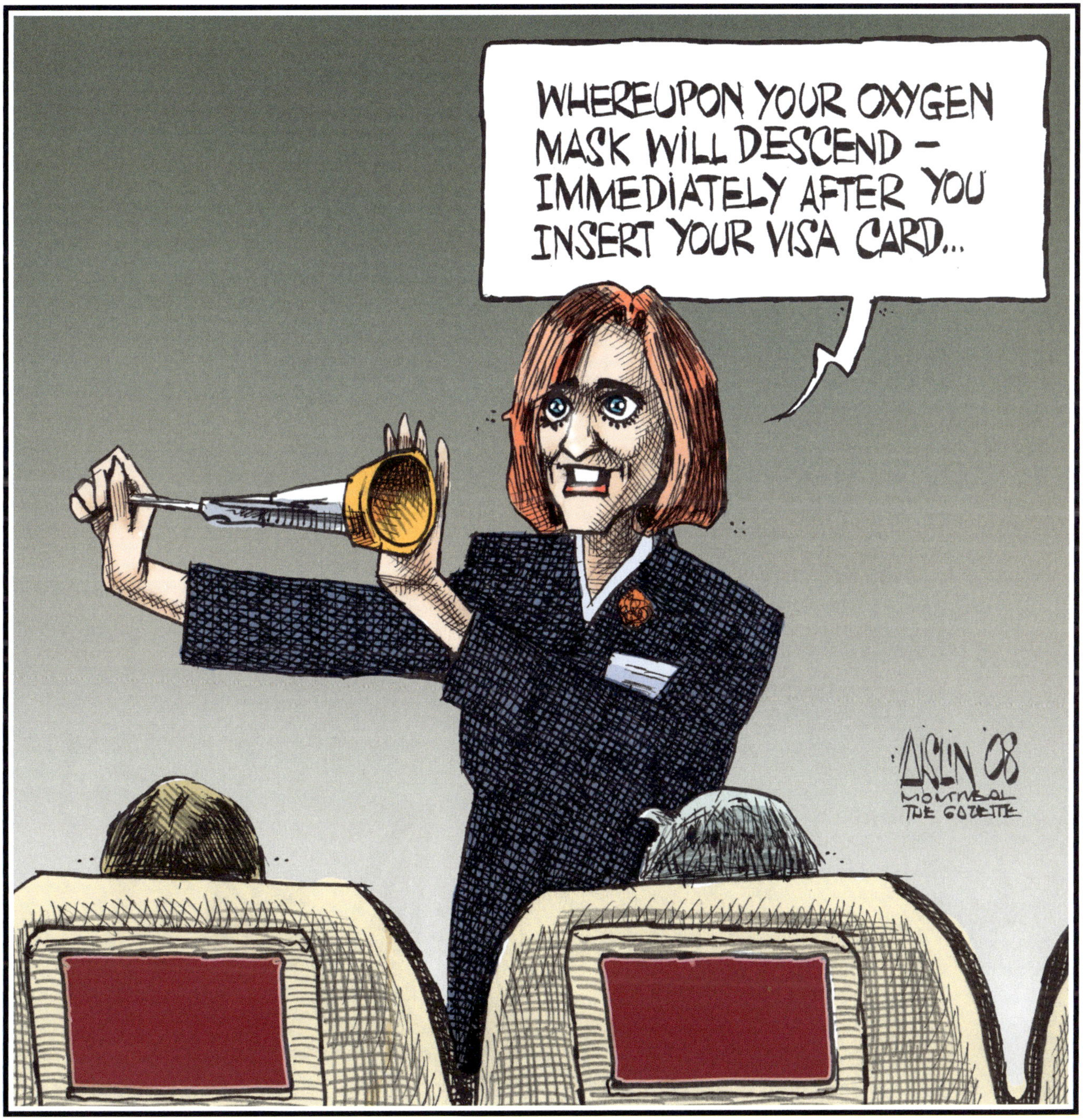
WHEREUPON YOUR OXYGEN MASK WILL DESCEND – IMMEDIATELY AFTER YOU INSERT YOUR VISA CARD...
AISLIN '08
MONTREAL THE GAZETTE

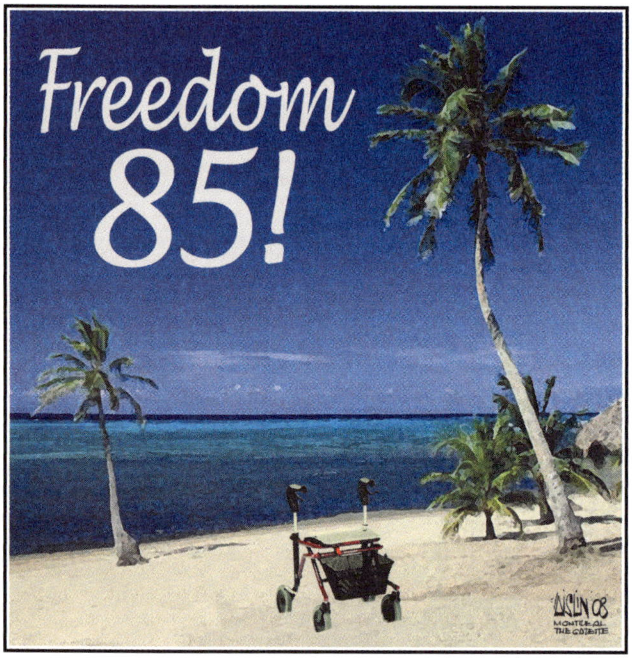
Freedom
85!

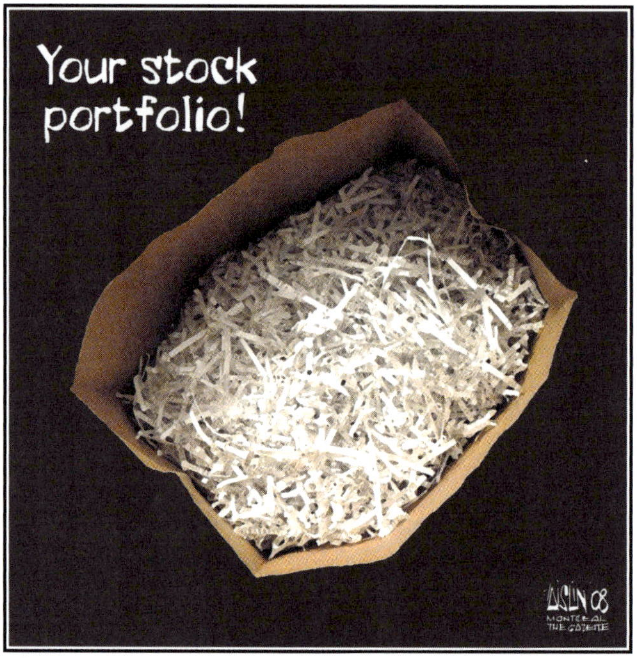
Your stock
portfolio!

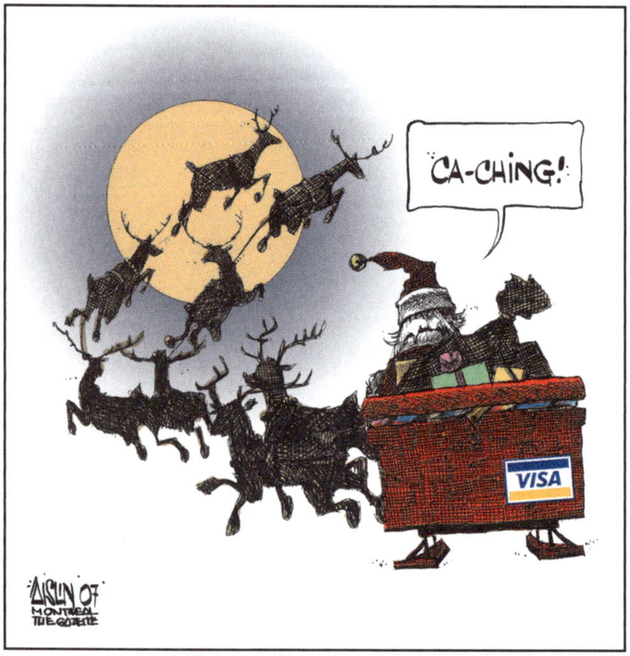
CA-CHING!
VISA

My Christmas card in 2007

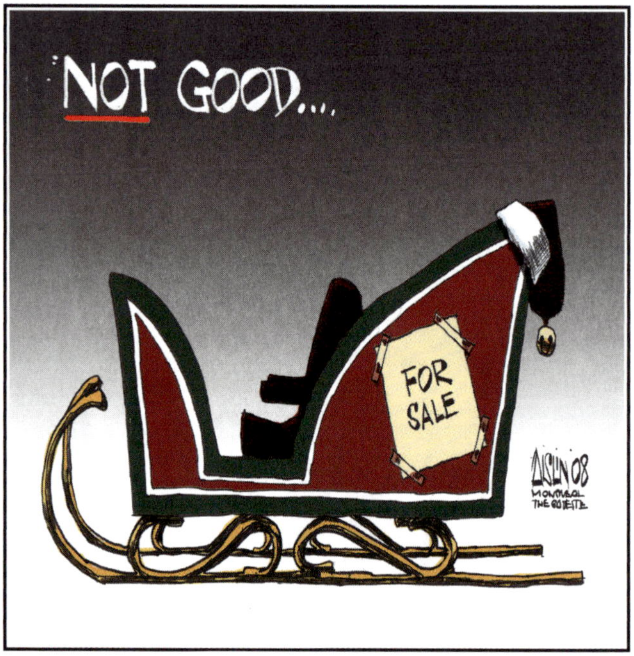
NOT GOOD....
FOR
SALE

My Christmas card in 2008

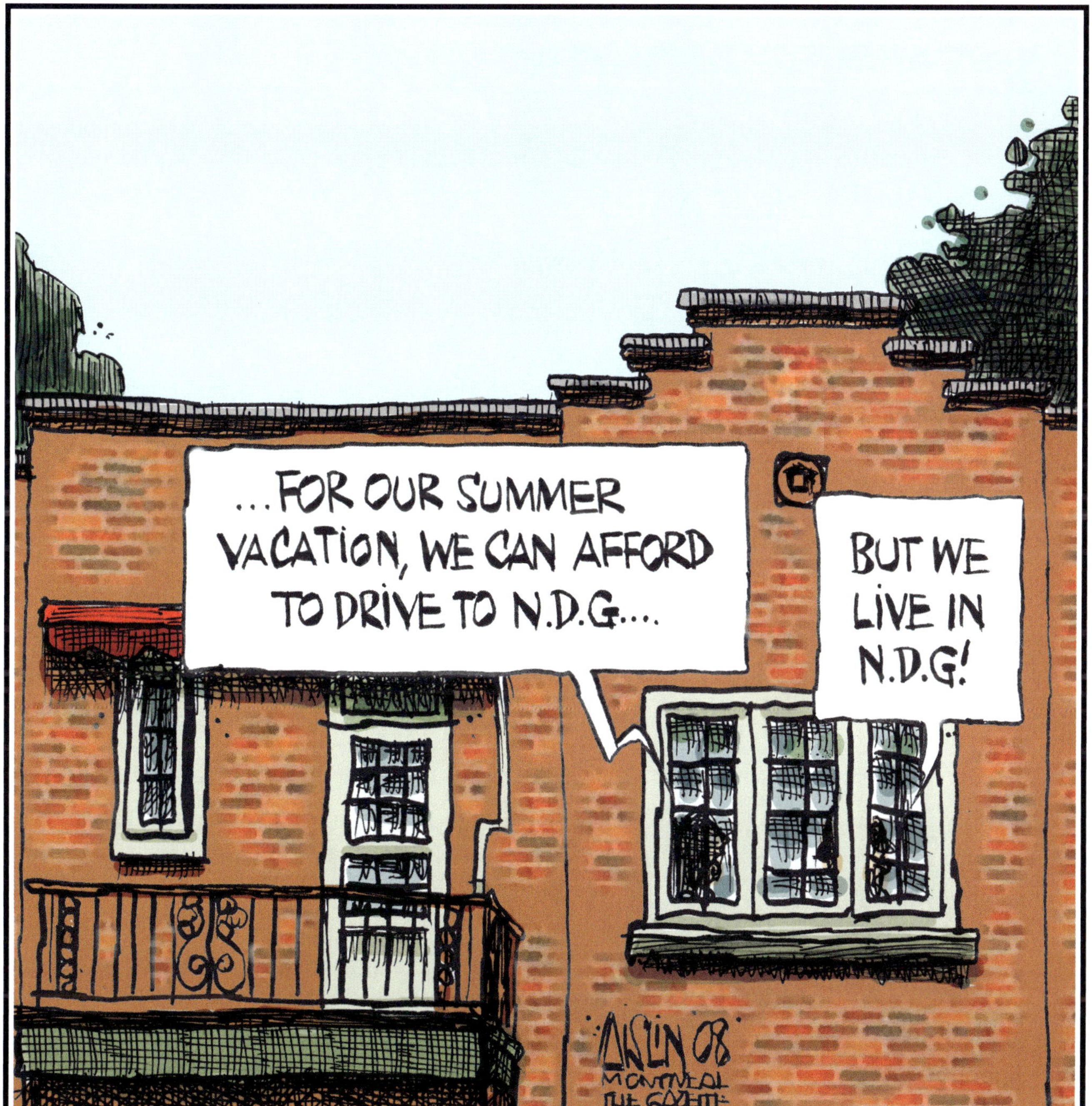
...FOR OUR SUMMER VACATION, WE CAN AFFORD TO DRIVE TO N.D.G....
BUT WE LIVE IN N.D.G!
AISLIN 08 MONTREAL THE GAZETTE

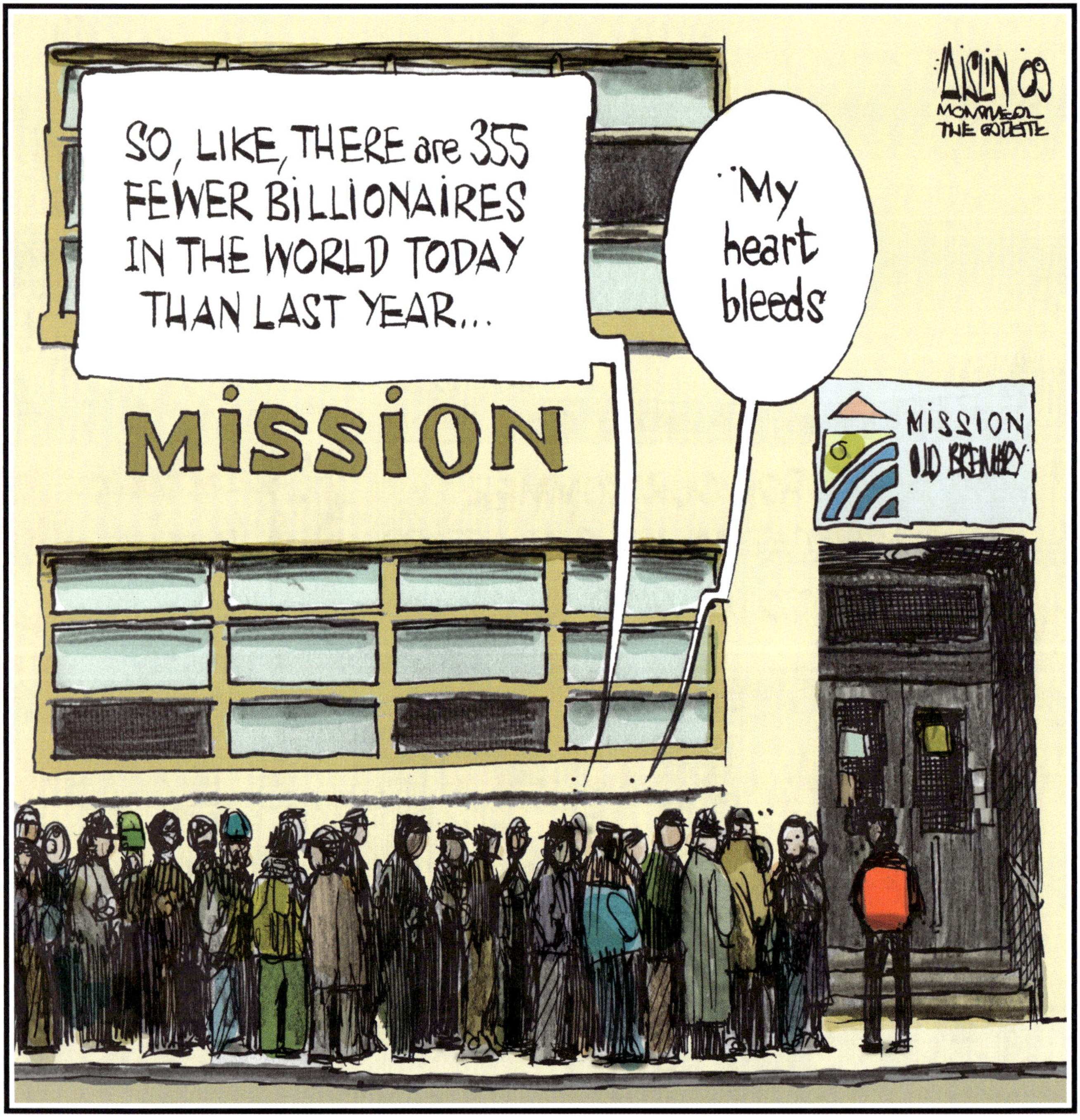

SO, LIKE, THERE are 355 FEWER BILLIONAIRES IN THE WORLD TODAY THAN LAST YEAR...
My heart bleeds
MISSION
MISSION OLD BREWERY
AISLIN 09 MONTREAL THE GAZETTE

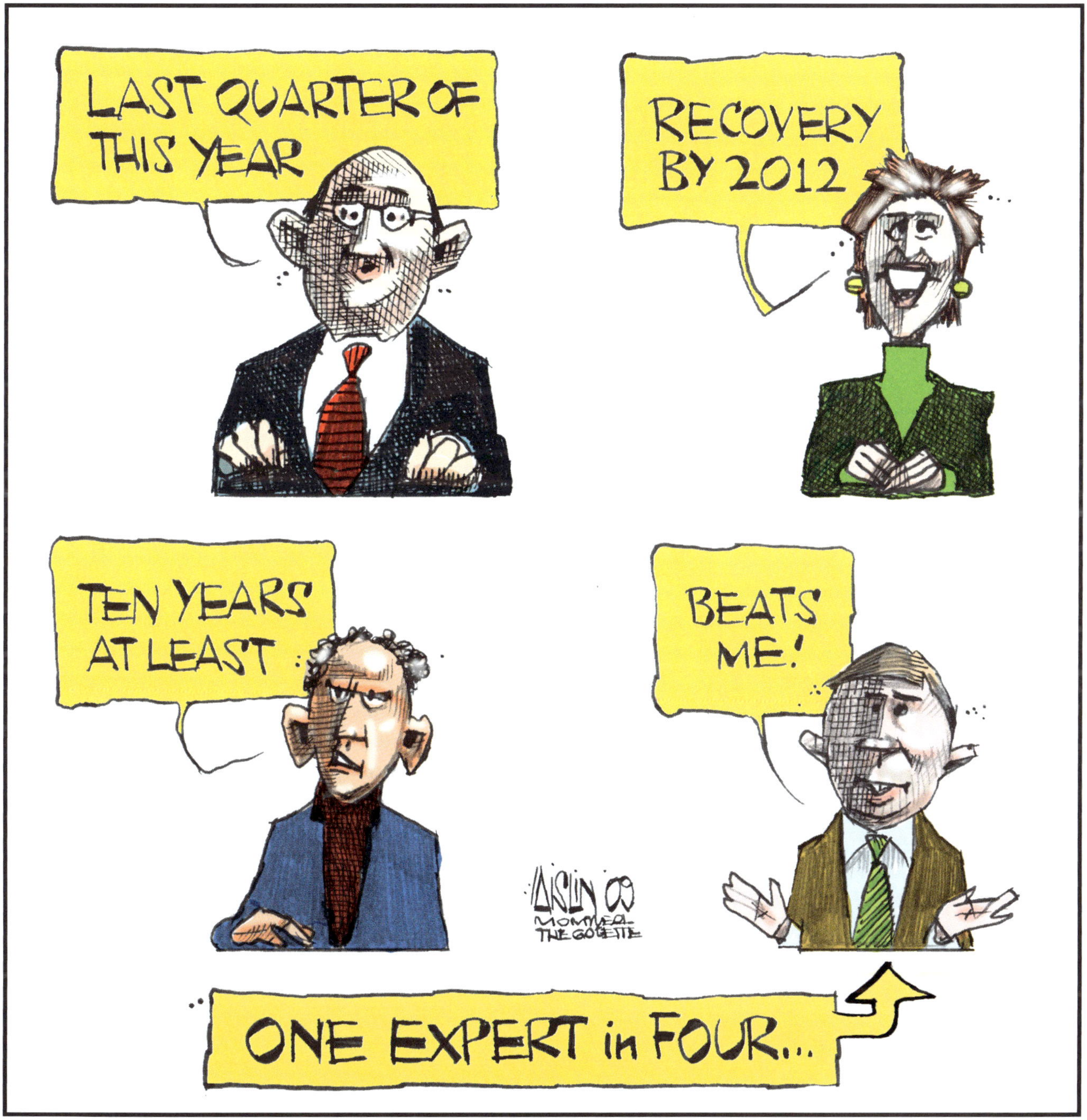
LAST QUARTER OF THIS YEAR
RECOVERY BY 2012
TEN YEARS AT LEAST
BEATS ME!
ONE EXPERT in FOUR...
AISLIN 09
MONTREAL THE GAZETTE
And the economy will be recovering by when?

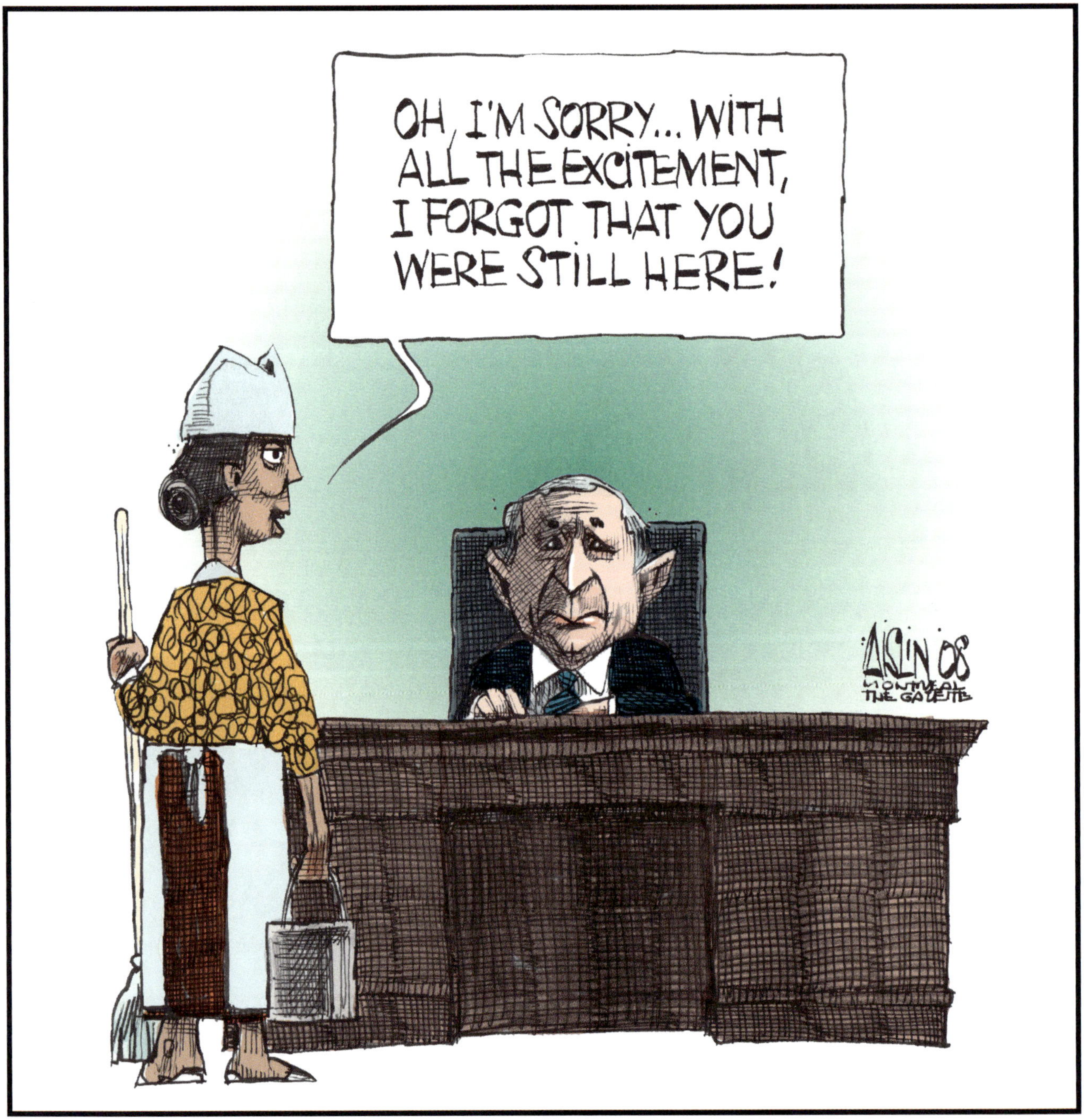
OH, I'M SORRY... WITH ALL THE EXCITEMENT, I FORGOT THAT YOU WERE STILL HERE!
AISLIN '08
MONTREAL THE GAZETTE

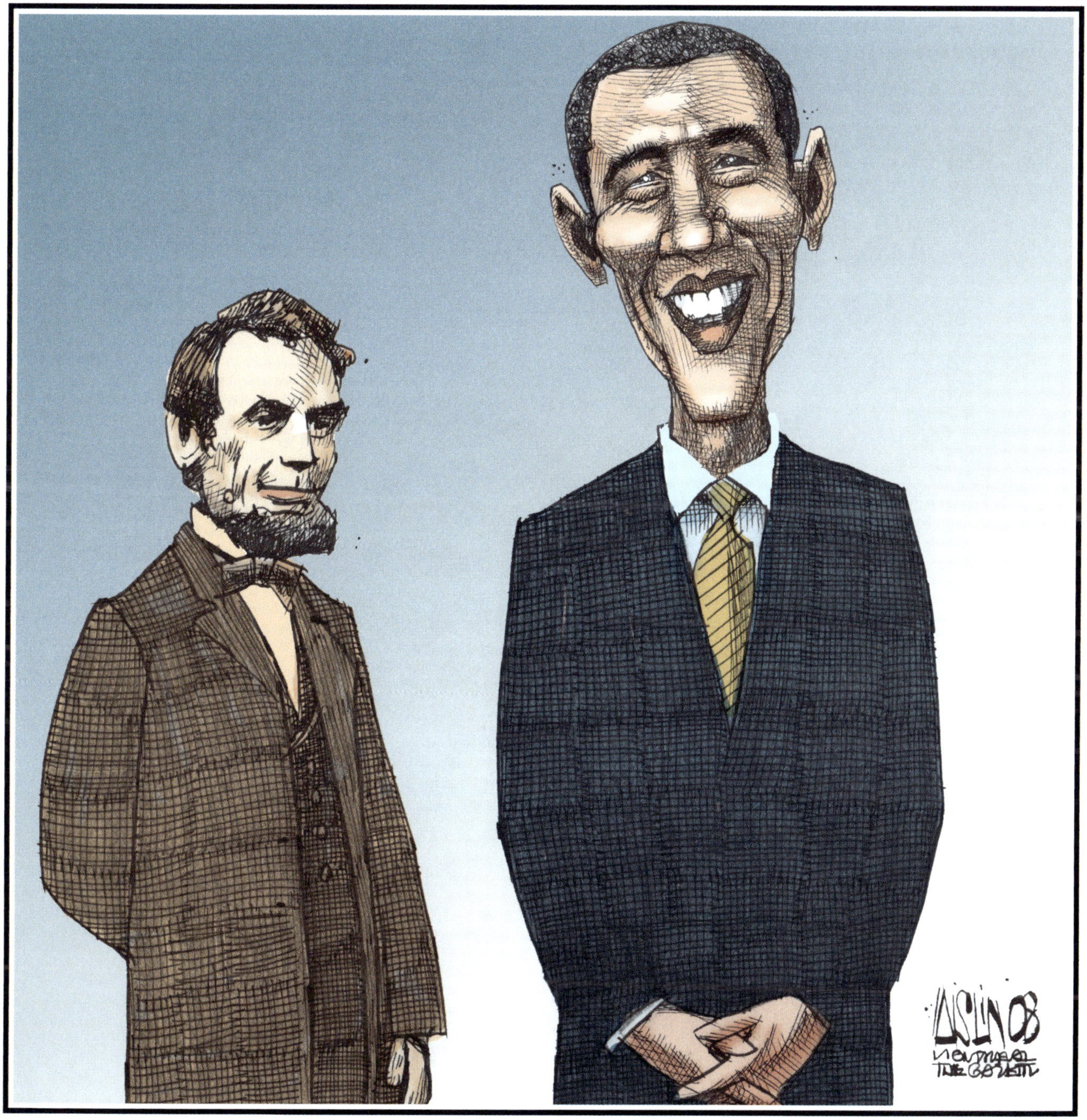

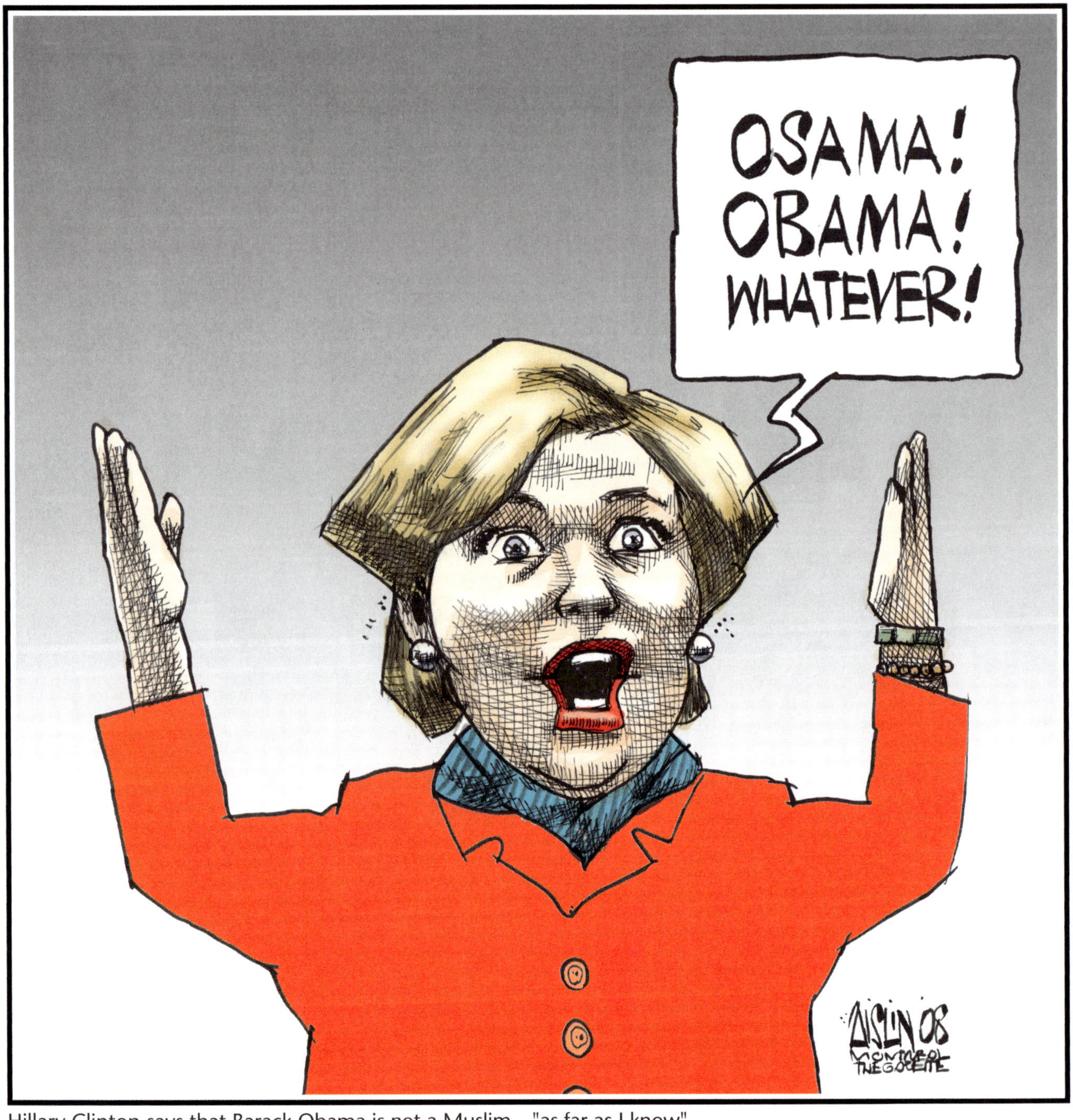
OSAMA! OBAMA! WHATEVER!
AISLIN 08
Hillary Clinton says that Barack Obama is not a Muslim…"as far as I know"

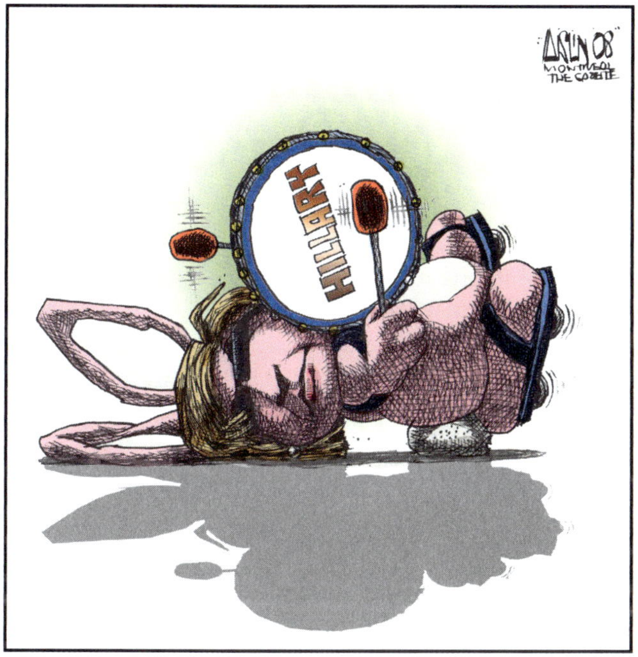
HILLARY
AISLIN 08 MONTREAL THE GAZETTE

Despite the numbers, Hillary just won't quit

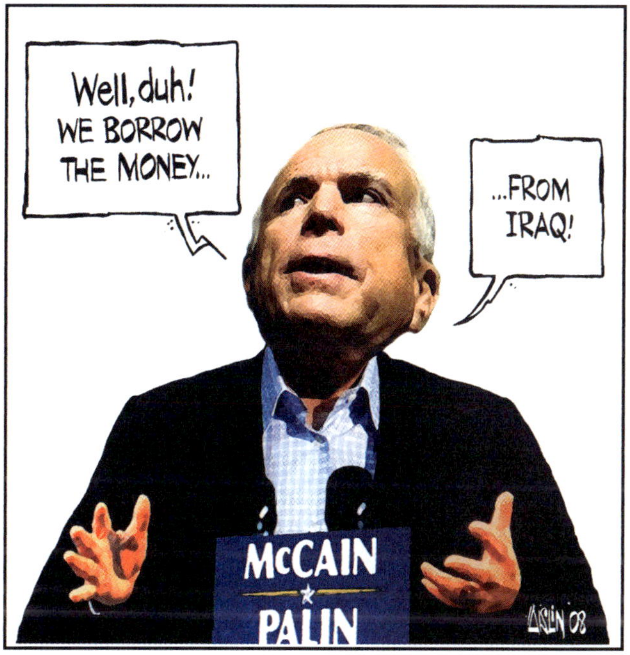
Well, duh! WE BORROW THE MONEY...
...FROM IRAQ!
McCAIN
PALIN
AISLIN 08

Iraq is reported to have an $80 billion surplus

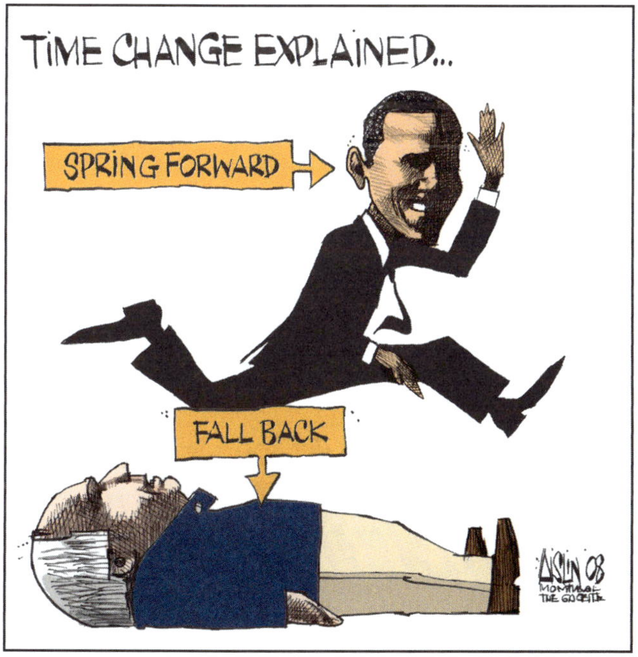
TIME CHANGE EXPLAINED...
SPRING FORWARD
FALL BACK
AISLIN 08 MONTREAL THE GAZETTE

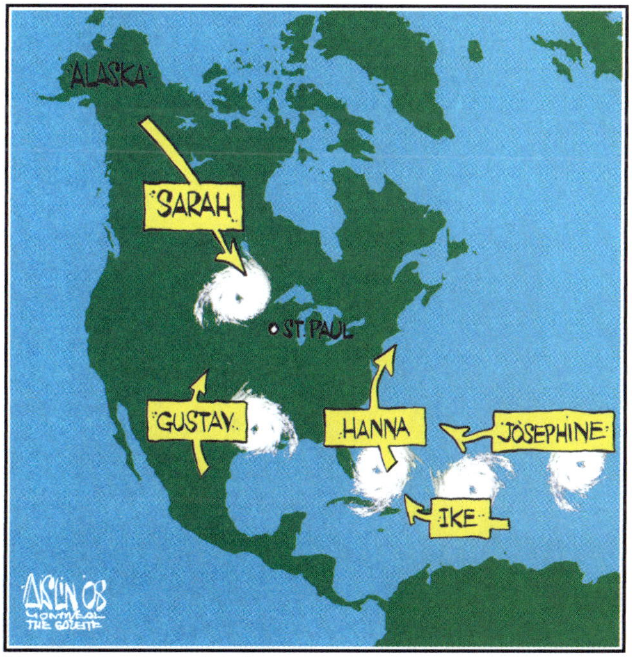
ALASKA
SARAH
ST. PAUL
GUSTAV
HANNA
JOSEPHINE
IKE
AISLIN 08 MONTREAL THE GAZETTE

Hurricane season begins

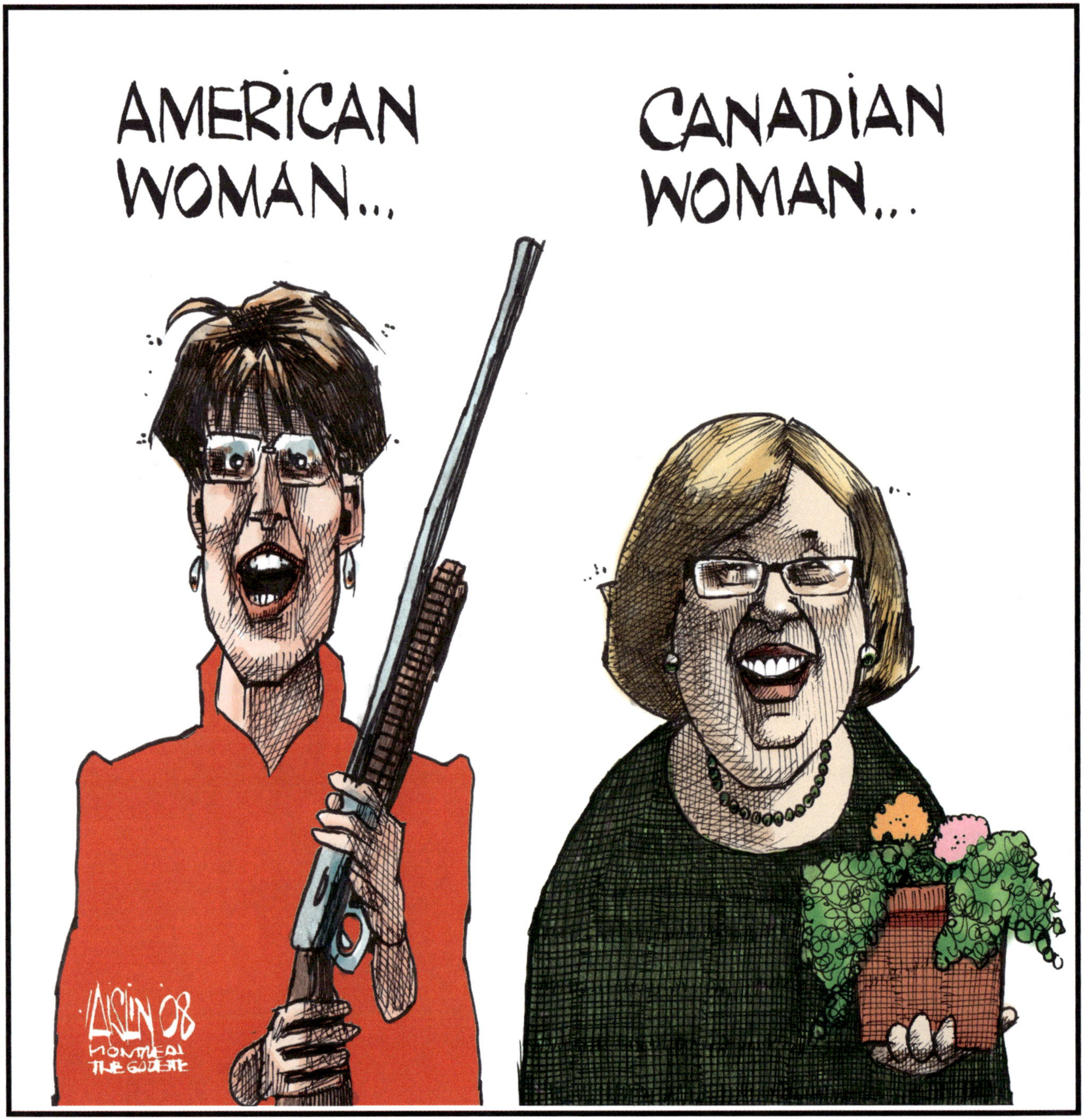
AMERICAN WOMAN...
CANADIAN WOMAN...
AISLIN 08
MONTREAL THE GAZETTE
Political women Sarah Palin and Elizabeth May

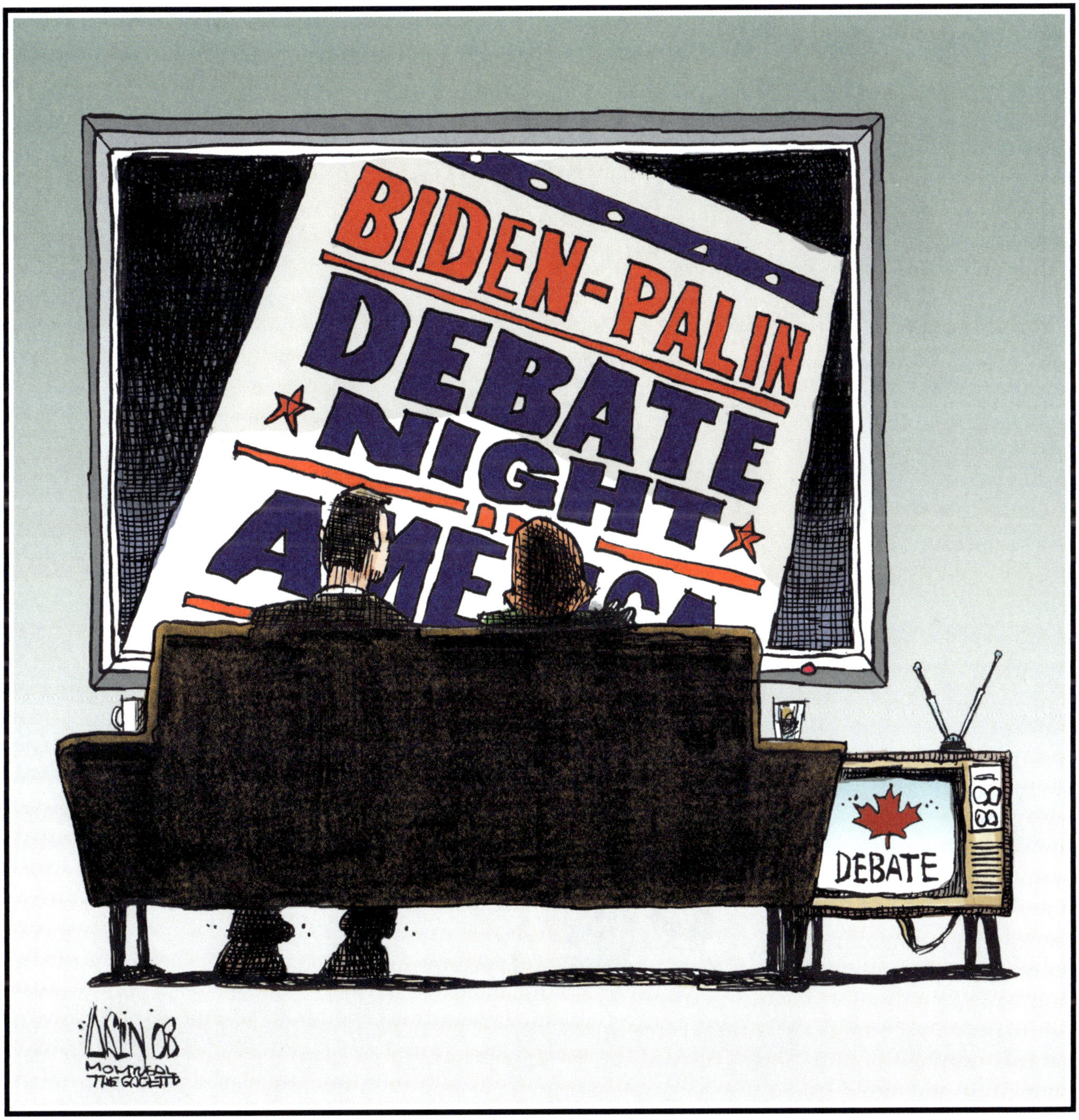
BIDEN-PALIN
DEBATE
NIGHT
DEBATE
1988

U.S. Vice-Presidential debate and Canadian federal election debate held on same evening

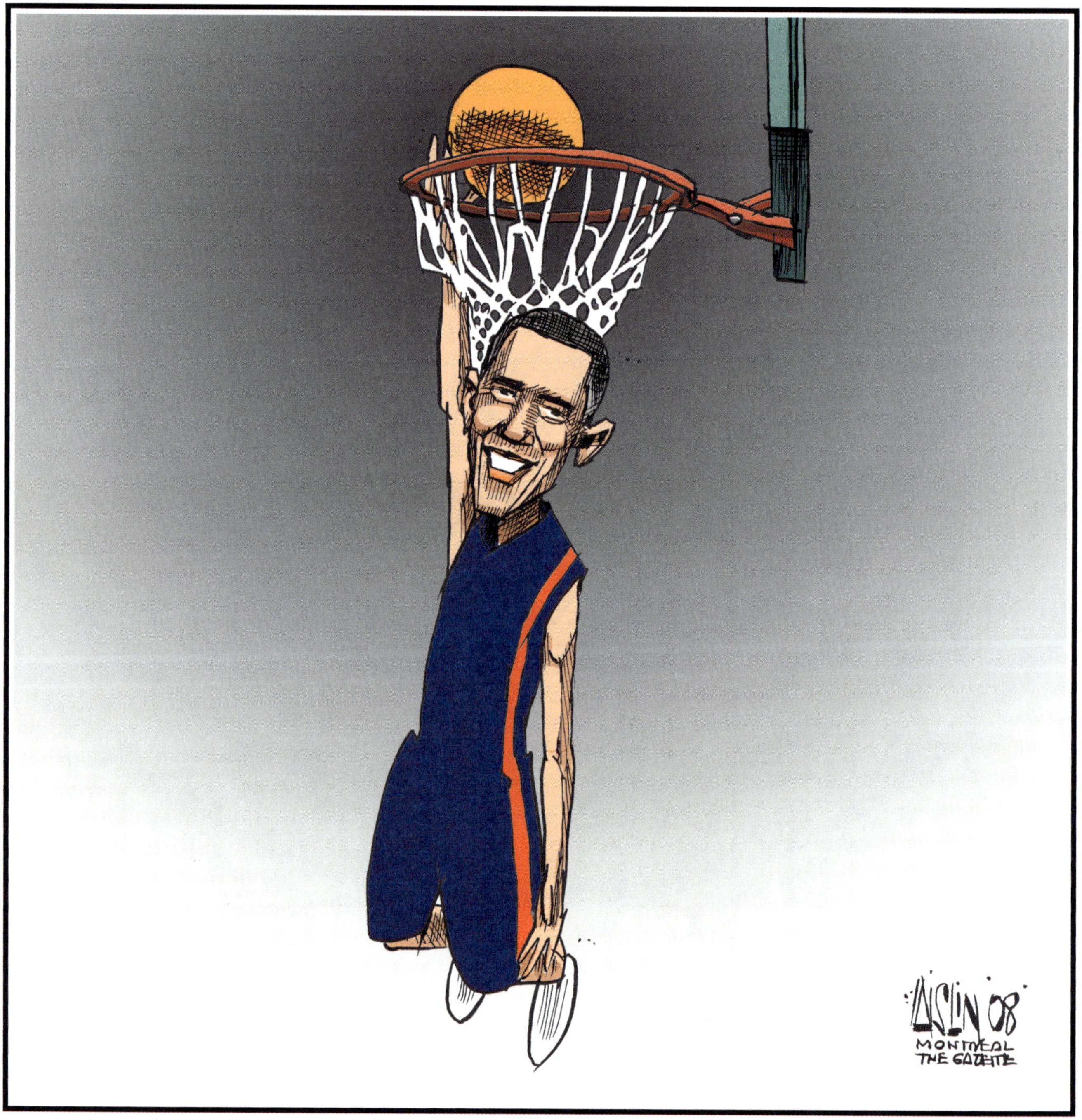
AISLIN '08
MONTREAL
THE GAZETTE

Barack Obama shoots a few hoops to relax on post-election morning

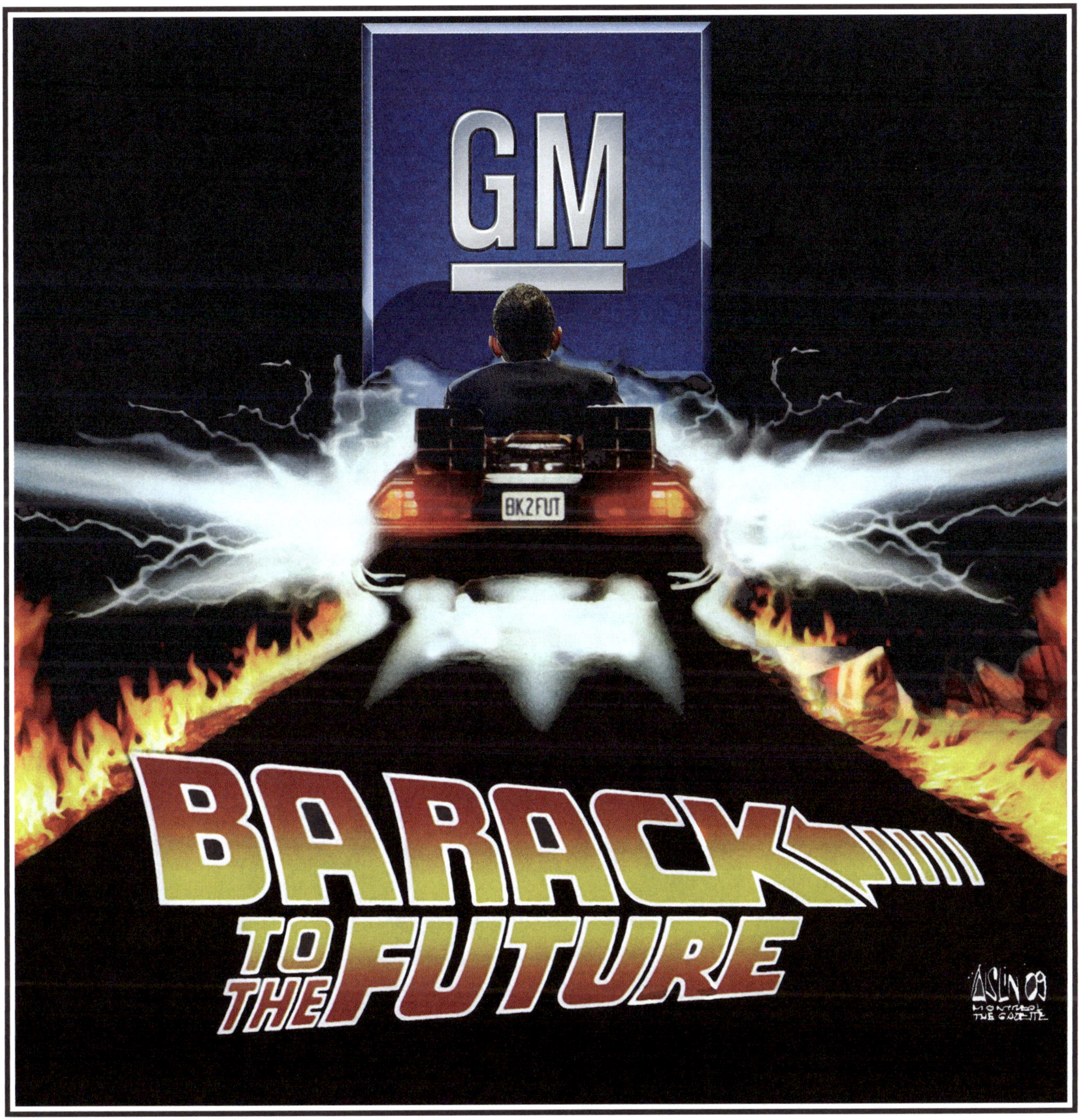
GM
BK2FUT
BARACK
TO THE FUTURE

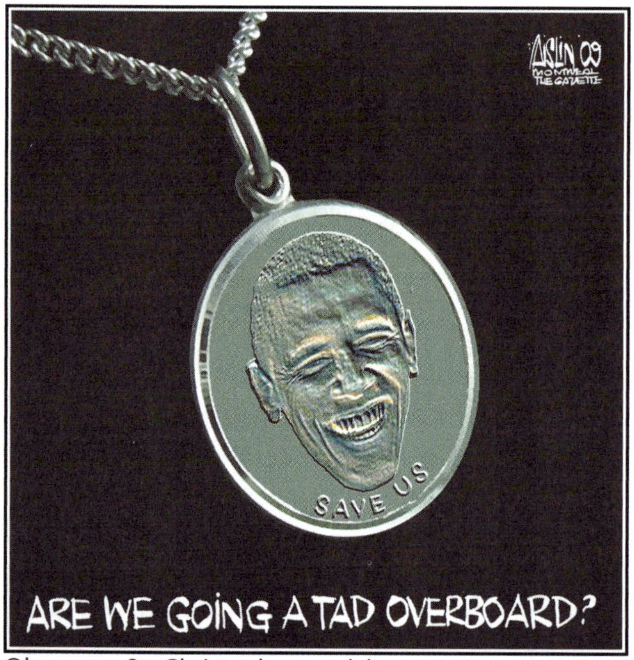
SAVE US
ARE WE GOING A TAD OVERBOARD?
Obama as St. Christopher medal

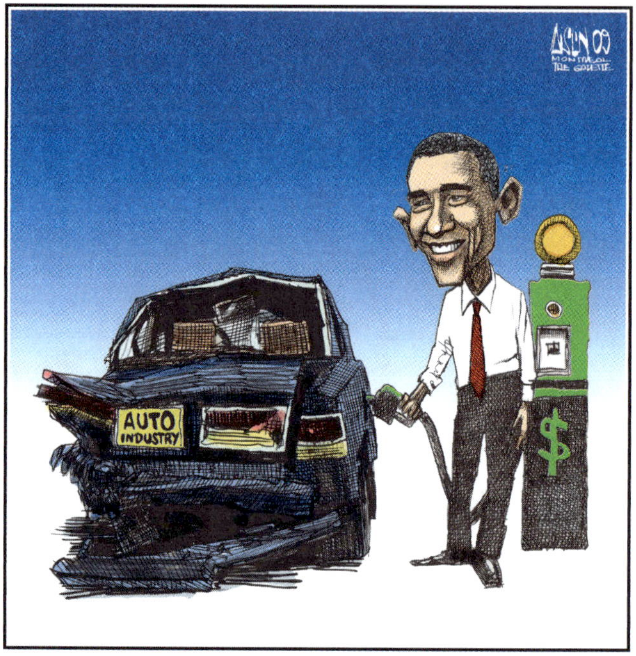
AUTO INDUSTRY

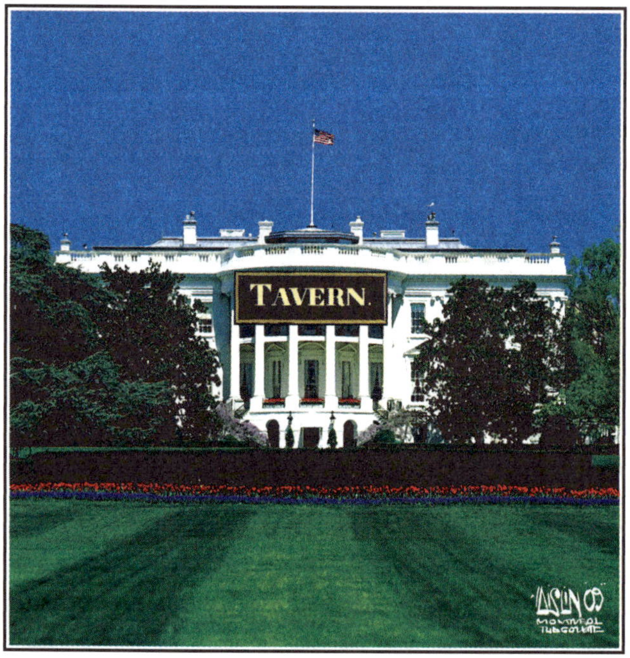
TAVERN
Beer summit held at White House to cool racial tensions

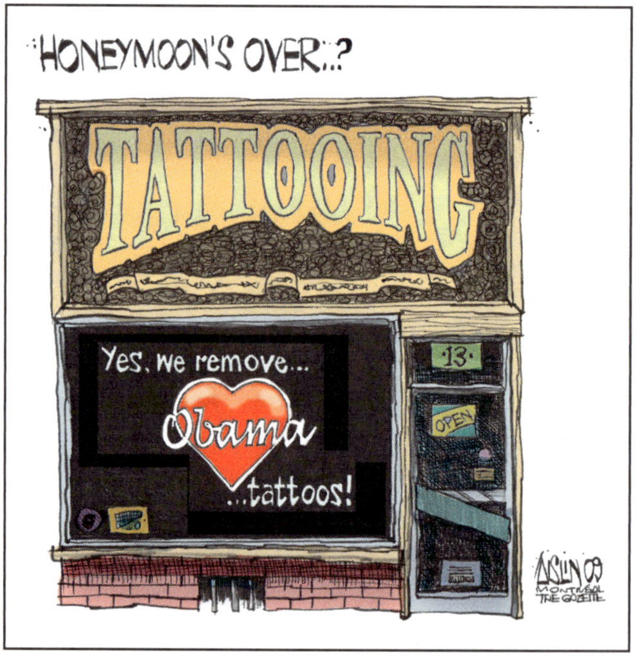
HONEYMOON'S OVER..?
TATTOOING
Yes, we remove...
Obama
...tattoos!
13
OPEN

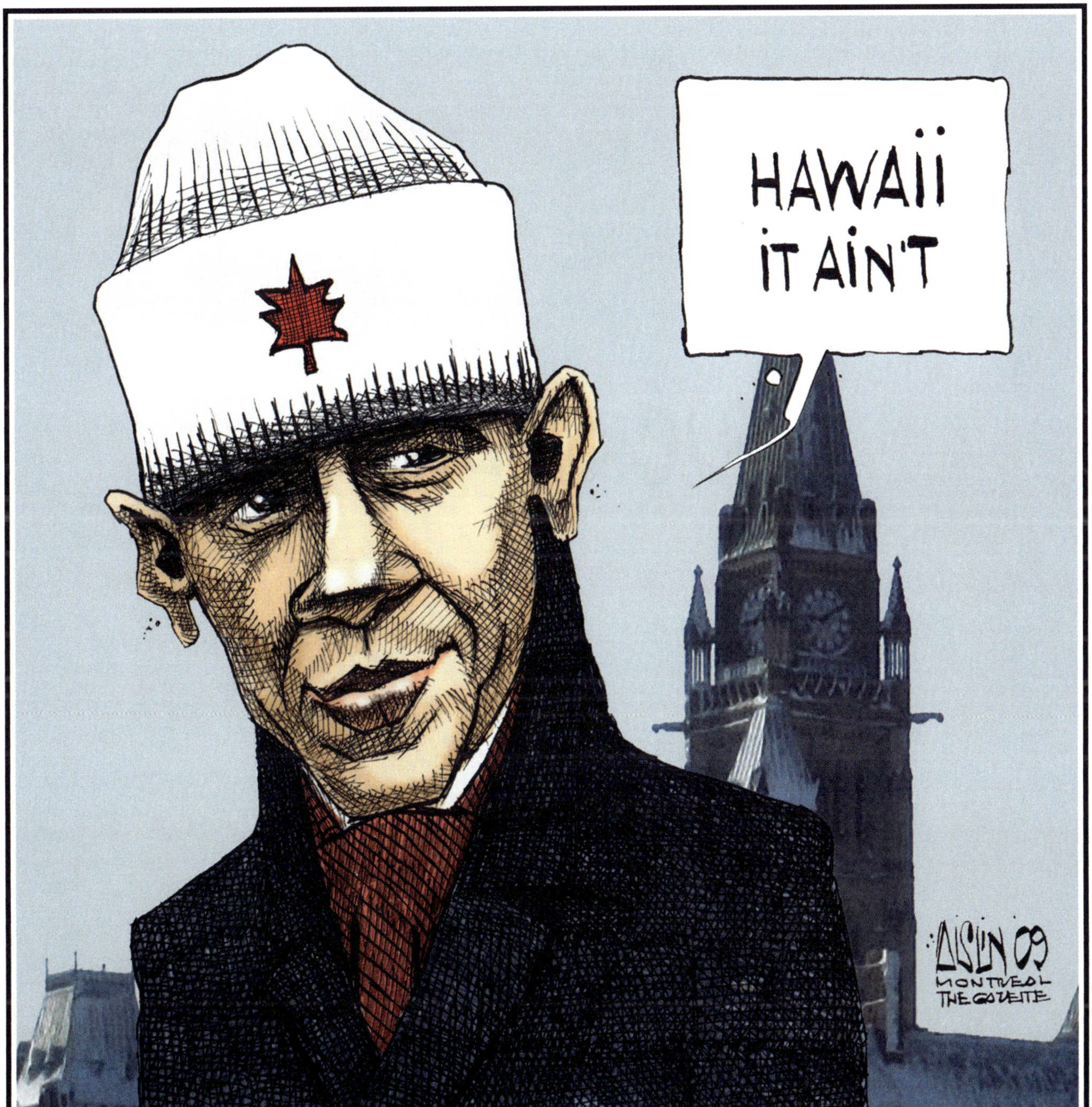
HAWAII IT AIN'T
AISLIN 09 MONTREAL THE GAZETTE
Barack Obama's first state visit is to Canada – in February

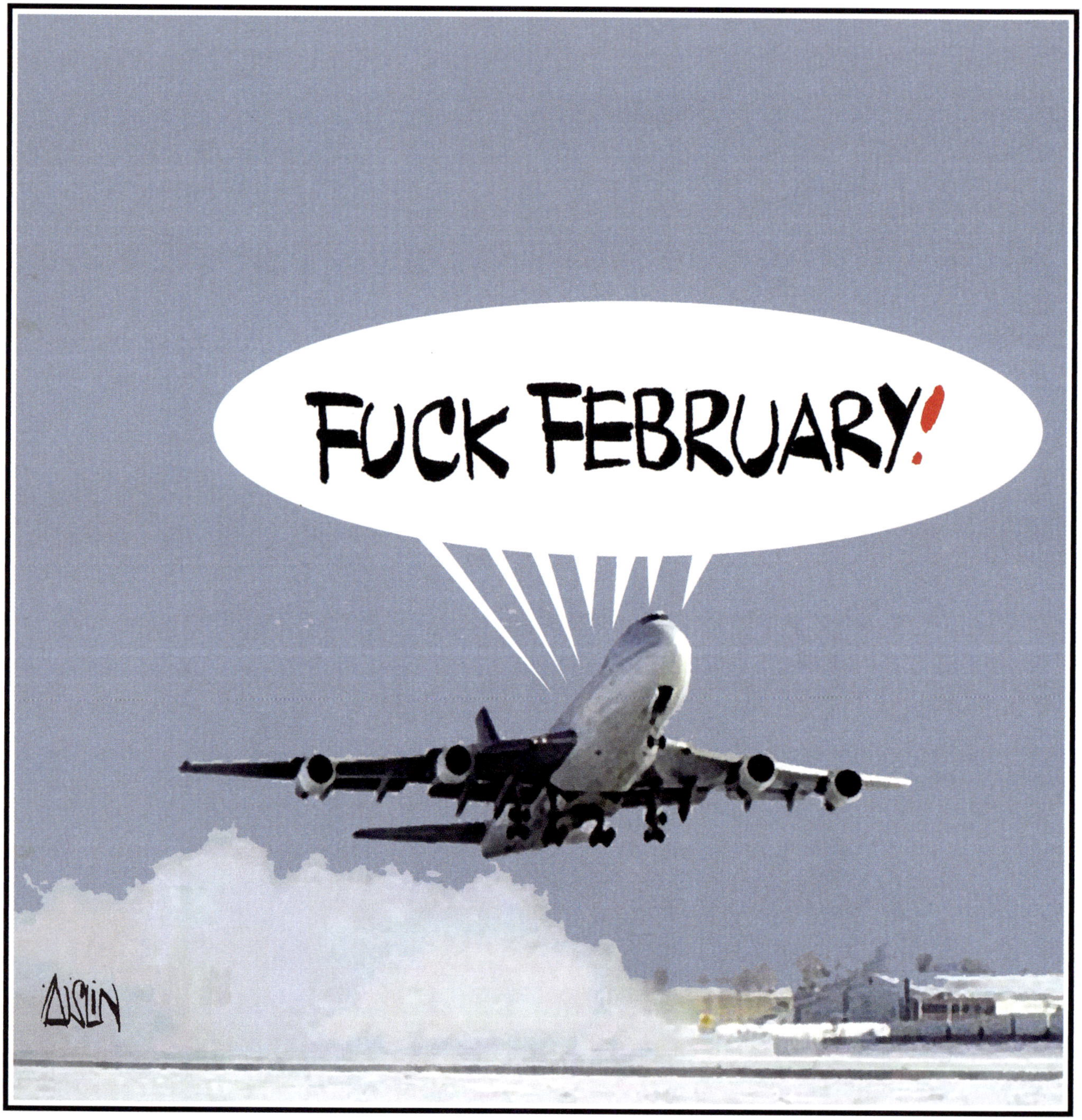
FUCK FEBRUARY!
AISLIN

CHAPTER 2

Oh, Canada!

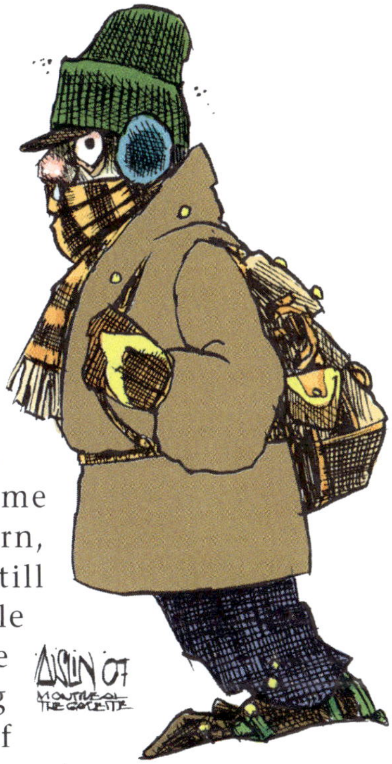
AISLIN 07
MONTREAL THE GAZETTE

Just who was responsible for having the new President of the United States visit Canada in February, that most dismal of months? Canadians who can afford it aren't even here in February – they're off vacationing in Florida, Hawaii or Arizona.

Canadians have learned that successfully surviving winter weather requires just a hint of conservatism in our character. We're thriftier than our American brethren, squirreling our loonies away in RRSPs for a snowy day. And hey! Who cares about being "fashion forward" when it's -35C outside. Long underwear, mitts and a balaclava look just fine. We're obsessed with winter weather and how to deal with it – from those icicle lights strung from every eave to a new law requiring the installation of snow tires. Is it any wonder we fortify ourselves with lots of alcohol and smoke more marijuana than any other industrialized nation? No one seems particularly worried about getting caught either – the RCMP has its own problems these days.

Like the mythic Canada of many foreigners' imaginations, the Arctic looms large in our self-image. Asserting sovereignty over Canada's vast northern region has suddenly become a public concern, but there is still little sustainable infrastructure in place. Flying the Maple Leaf in the face of growing U.S. and Russian claims that Canada's northern seaways are in fact international is urgent business. Whatever approach the Government takes will have to respect the rights and traditions of our northern peoples.

The Canadian electorate has a long memory and can be a harsh judge of a Prime Minister's character and achievements.

Paul Martin was ousted as Prime Minister because of Canadians' extreme disgust with the Liberal Party over the sponsorship scandal. Yet those events took place under the watch of Martin's predecessor, Jean Chrétien, who was later cleared of any responsibility for the fiasco. Furthermore,

Queen Elizabeth recently awarded Chrétien – Mr. Clean – the Order of Merit.

Brian Mulroney has fared the worst of all. As a result of the recent, $14-million public enquiry, he will now be remembered principally for having accepted envelopes of cash from lobbyist Karlheinz Schreiber – money initially not declared. The enquiry just confirmed what we all knew but didn't want to hear: Brian took the money. It's a real shame, because Mulroney was actually an innovative Prime Minister, certainly better at the job in his time than today's incumbent.

Called "the Ayatollah" behind his back by members of his own cabinet, Harper is a stern taskmaster in a role that demands a great deal of flexibility, particularly when dealing with Quebec. After the briefest of flirtations with the Tories, Quebec has once again turned its back on the Conservatives. Remember the embarrassing business of Minister Maxime Bernier leaving secret documents at the apartment of girlfriend Julie Couillard, former companion of bikers and mobsters? Much more damaging to Harper was his slashing of spending on the arts – a no-no in Quebec – and his proposal to severely increase penalties for juvenile offenders.

The Conservatives under Harper have so far failed to win a majority government and without support from Quebec's electors, the likelihood of ever doing so seems remote. Harper's arrogance in tabling an economic recovery plan without consulting the opposition parties nearly got him a third chance to try his luck.

Outraged by the Prime Minister's unilateral action, the three opposition parties formed a coalition of convenience and announced their willingness to force an election or form a government at the Governor General's request. In response, Harper prorogued Parliament to let things cool off and give his government a chance to regroup. The Governor General later sanctioned Harper's move, understanding that an election was the last thing irritated Canadians wanted.

Stephen Harper has enjoyed the upper hand over the last few years, thanks largely to disarray in the opposition parties.

After losing the 2006 election to Harper, Paul Martin stepped aside as Liberal leader. Everyone expected that either Bob Rae or Michael Ignatieff would emerge as Martin's successor at the leadership convention. Imagine their surprise when Stéphane Dion snuck up the middle to take the prize. It was an unintended result and an unwise choice in the end. While very capable, the cerebral and awkward Dion was unable to win Canadians' hearts and had trouble rallying his own troops. In the election of 2008, Dion led the Liberals to their worst showing in recent memory: just 78 seats. Dion resigned, clearing the way for the virtual coronation of Michael Ignatieff – no bothersome convention this time.

The other opposition parties simply

tread water. In election after election, the NDP fails to garner even 20% of the popular vote. The Bloc Québécois remains entrenched in Ottawa, a one-trick pony only interested in protecting its definition of Quebec's interests. Leader Gilles Duceppe briefly flirted with the idea of returning to Quebec to run for the leadership of the Parti Québécois. However, when the popular Pauline Marois declared her intention to run, Duceppe scurried back to the safe confines of Ottawa.

Where are the Rhinos when you really need them?

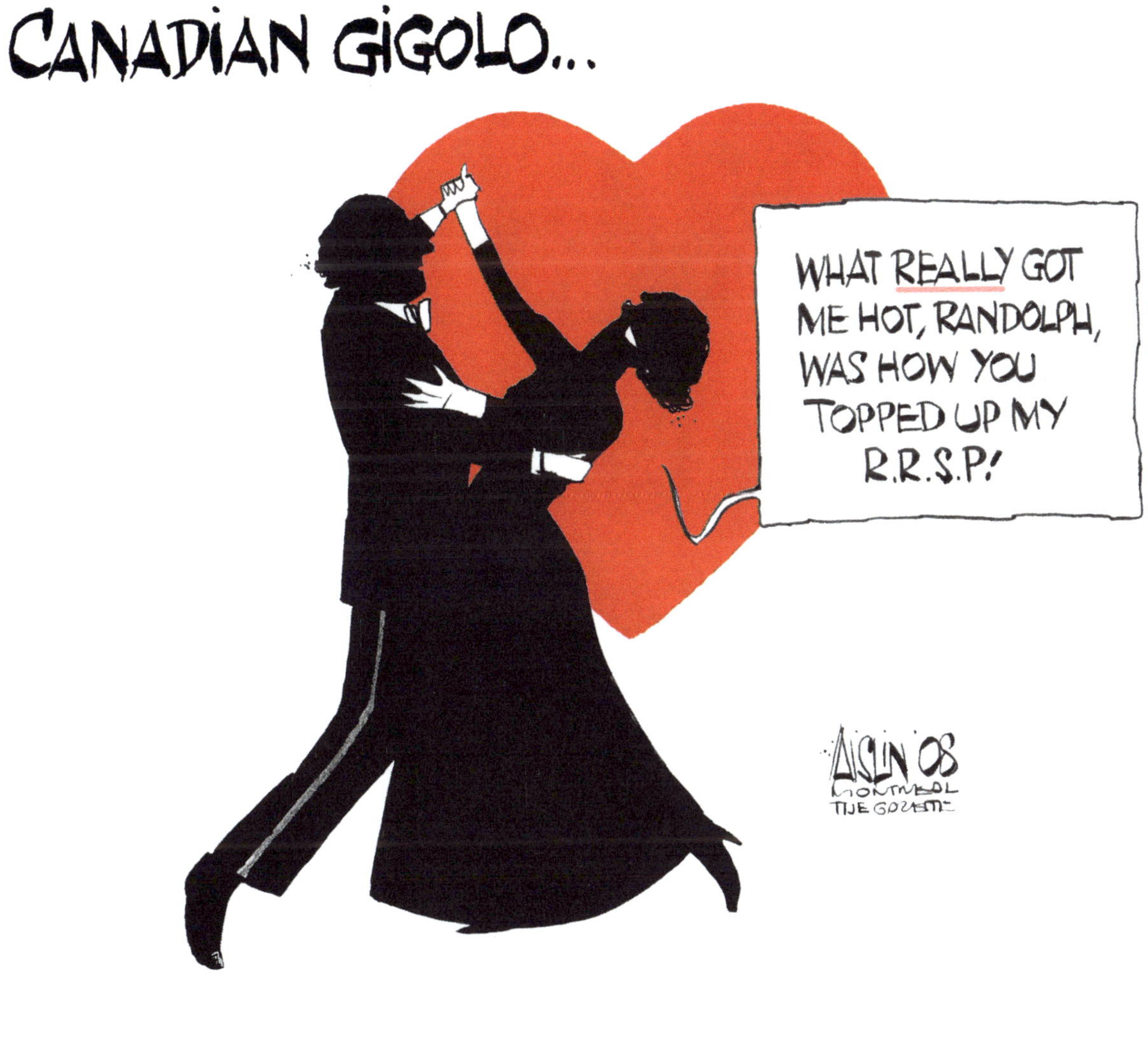
CANADIAN GIGOLO...
WHAT REALLY GOT ME HOT, RANDOLPH, WAS HOW YOU TOPPED UP MY R.R.S.P.!
AISLIN '08

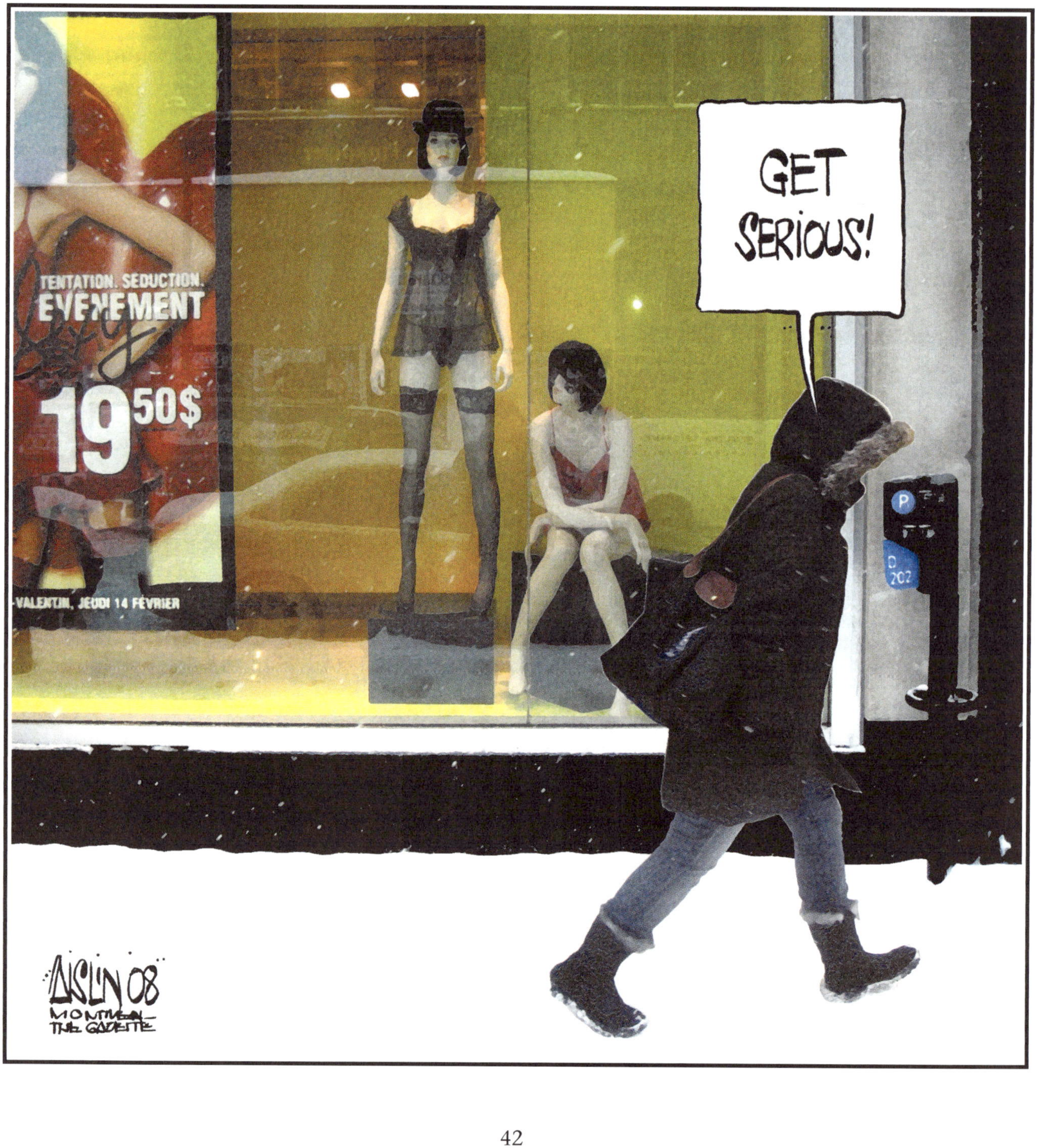
GET SERIOUS!
TENTATION. SEDUCTION.
EVENEMENT
19 50$
-VALENTIN, JEUDI 14 FÉVRIER
AISLIN 08
MONTREAL THE GAZETTE

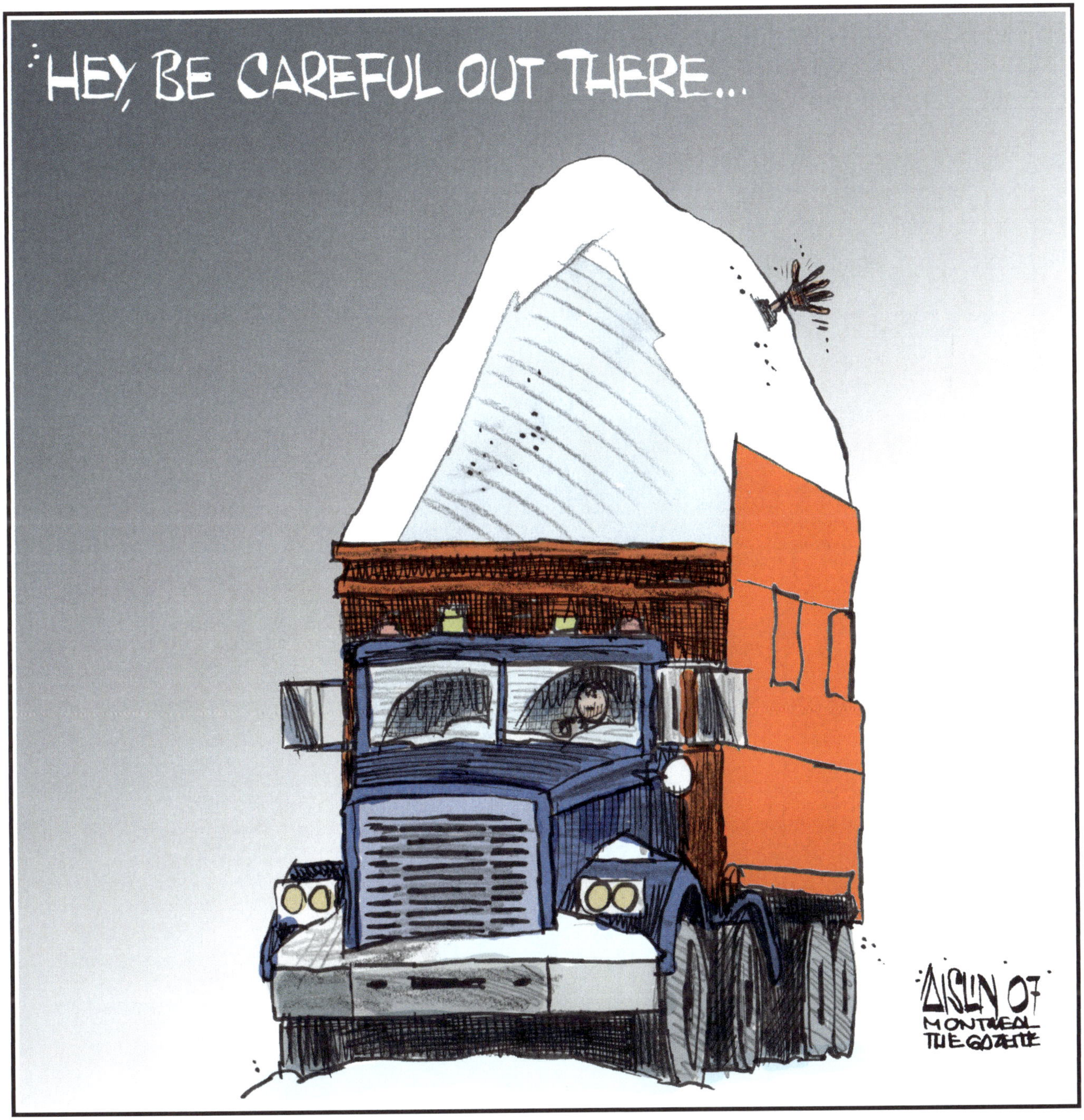
HEY, BE CAREFUL OUT THERE...
AISLIN 07
MONTREAL
THE GAZETTE

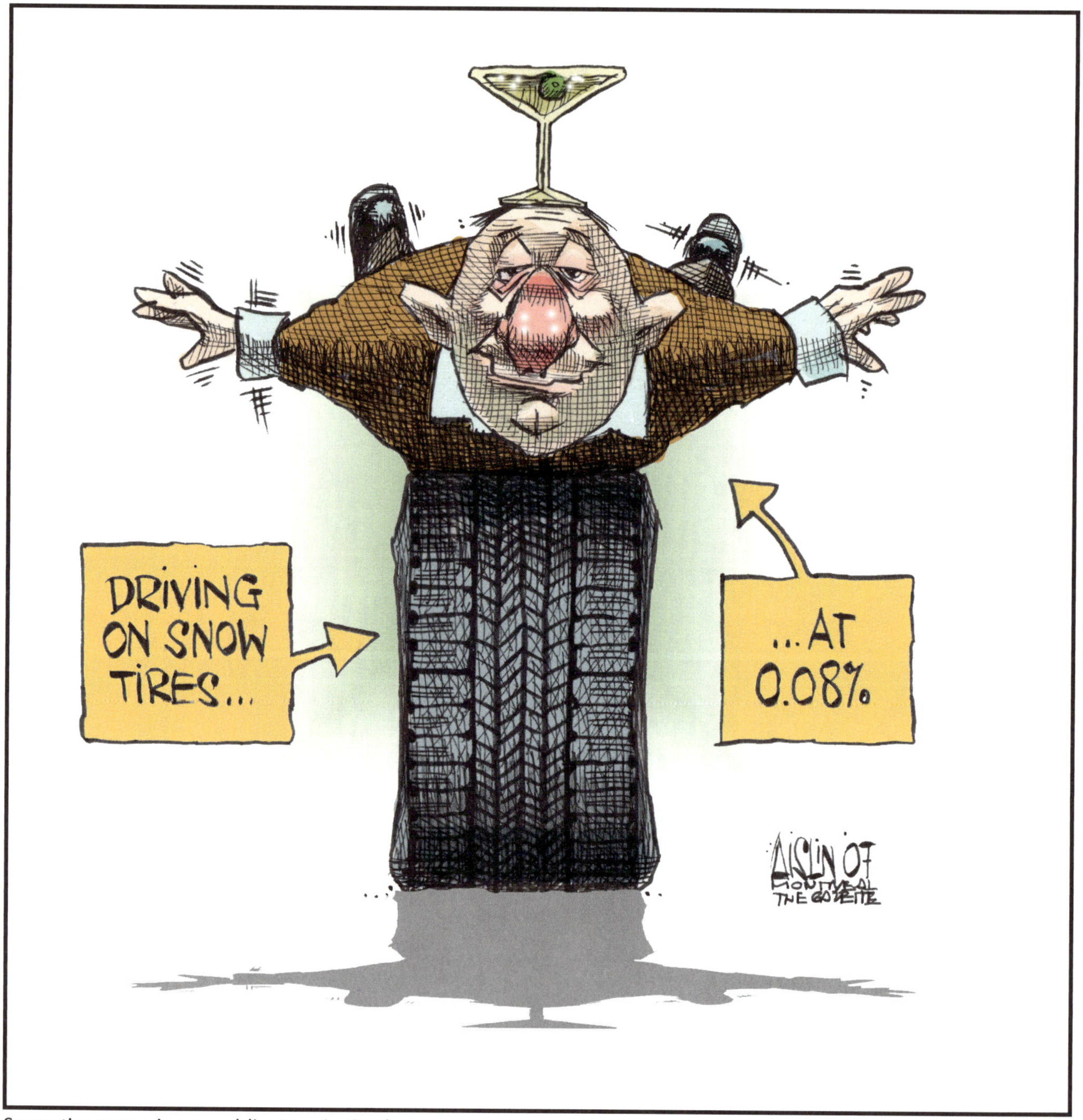
DRIVING ON SNOW TIRES...
...AT 0.08%
AISLIN 07
MONTREAL THE GAZETTE
Snow tire usage is now obligatory in Quebec…

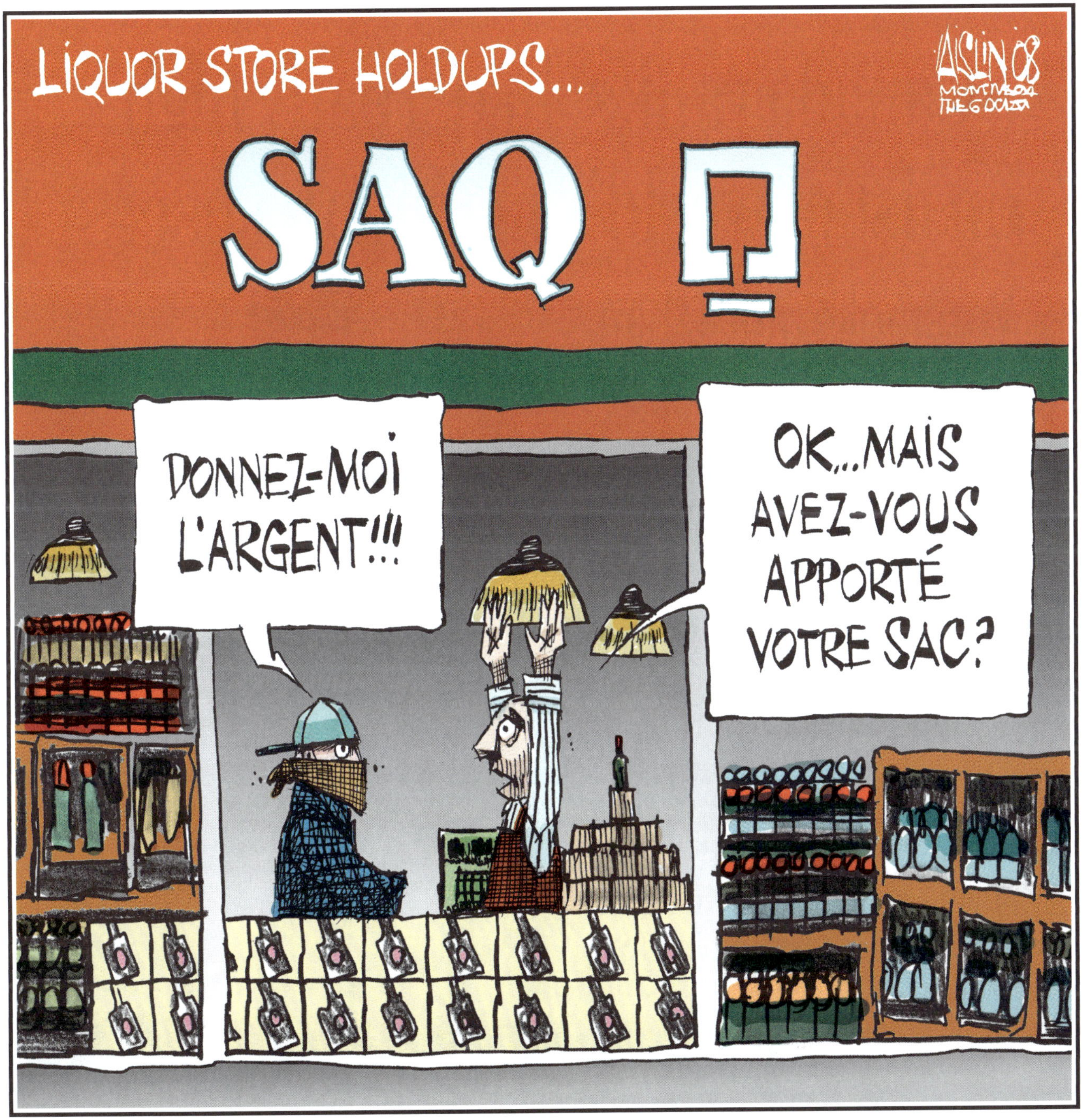
LIQUOR STORE HOLDUPS...
SAQ
DONNEZ-MOI L'ARGENT!!!
OK...MAIS AVEZ-VOUS APPORTÉ VOTRE SAC?

…as is bringing your own shopping bag to many stores

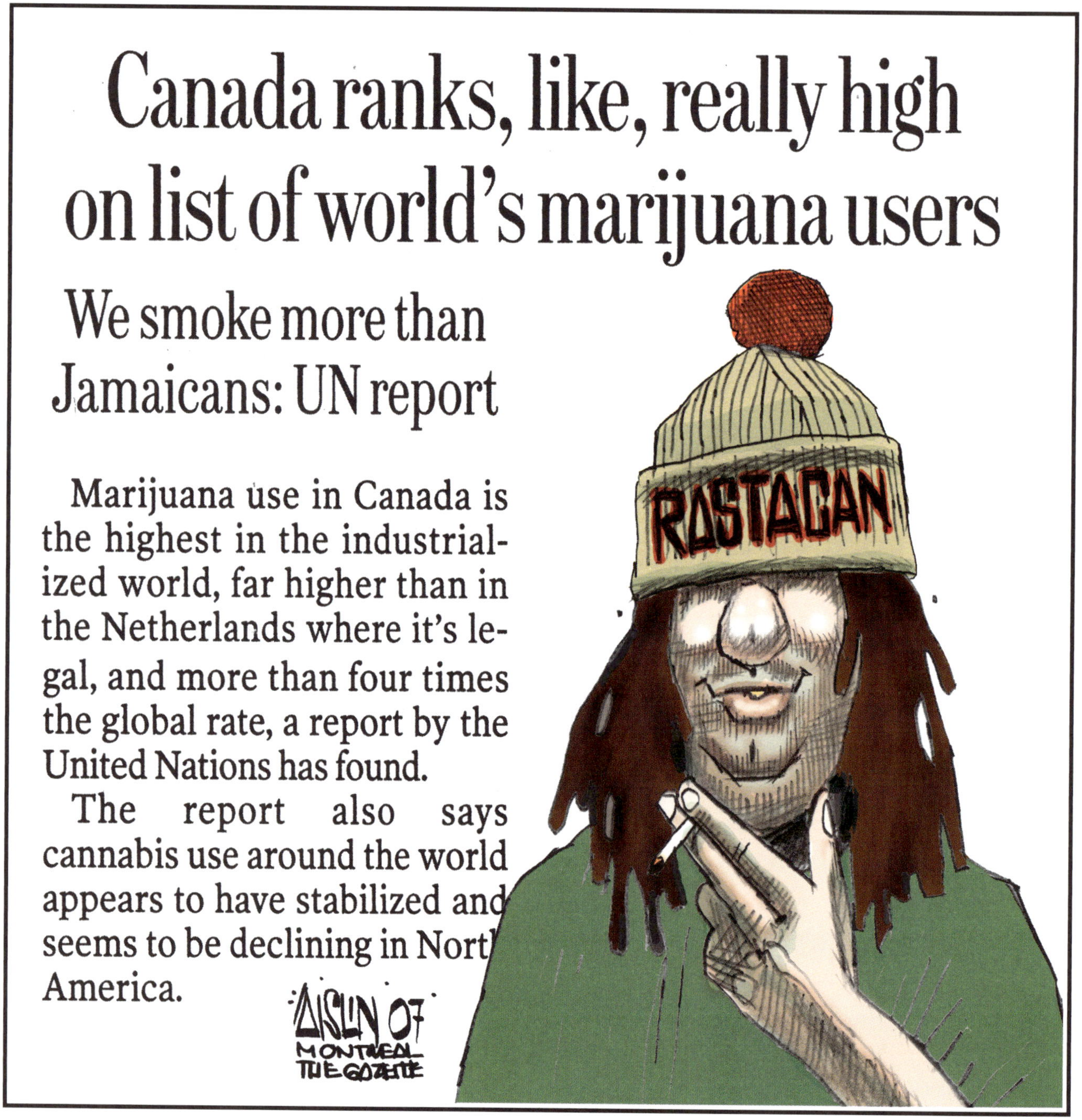
Canada ranks, like, really high on list of world's marijuana users
We smoke more than Jamaicans: UN report
Marijuana use in Canada is the highest in the industrialized world, far higher than in the Netherlands where it's legal, and more than four times the global rate, a report by the United Nations has found.
The report also says cannabis use around the world appears to have stabilized and seems to be declining in North America.
RASTAGAN
AISLIN 07
MONTREAL THE GAZETTE

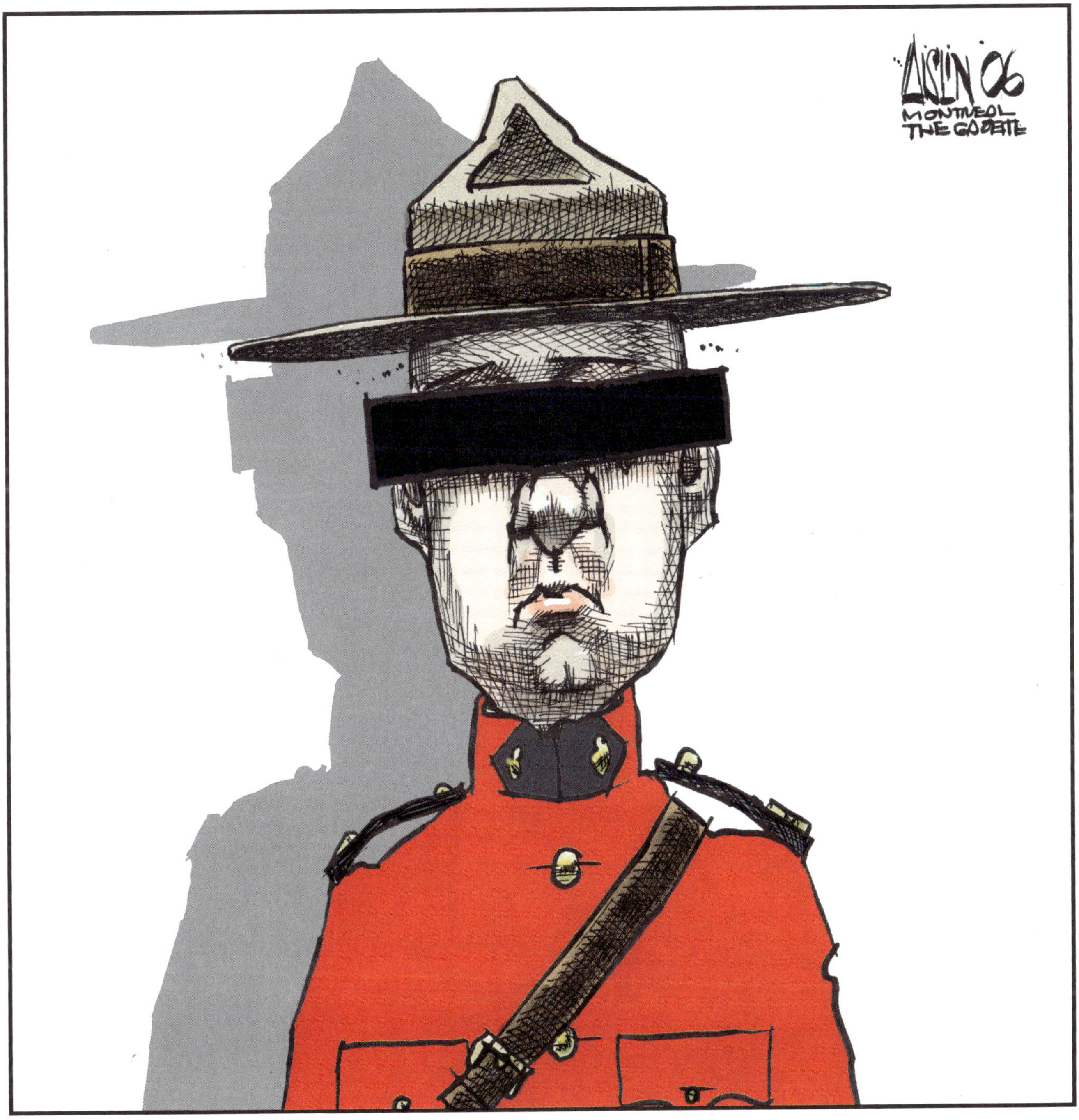
AISLIN '06
MONTREAL
THE GAZETTE
Inquiry into RCMP's usage of taser guns

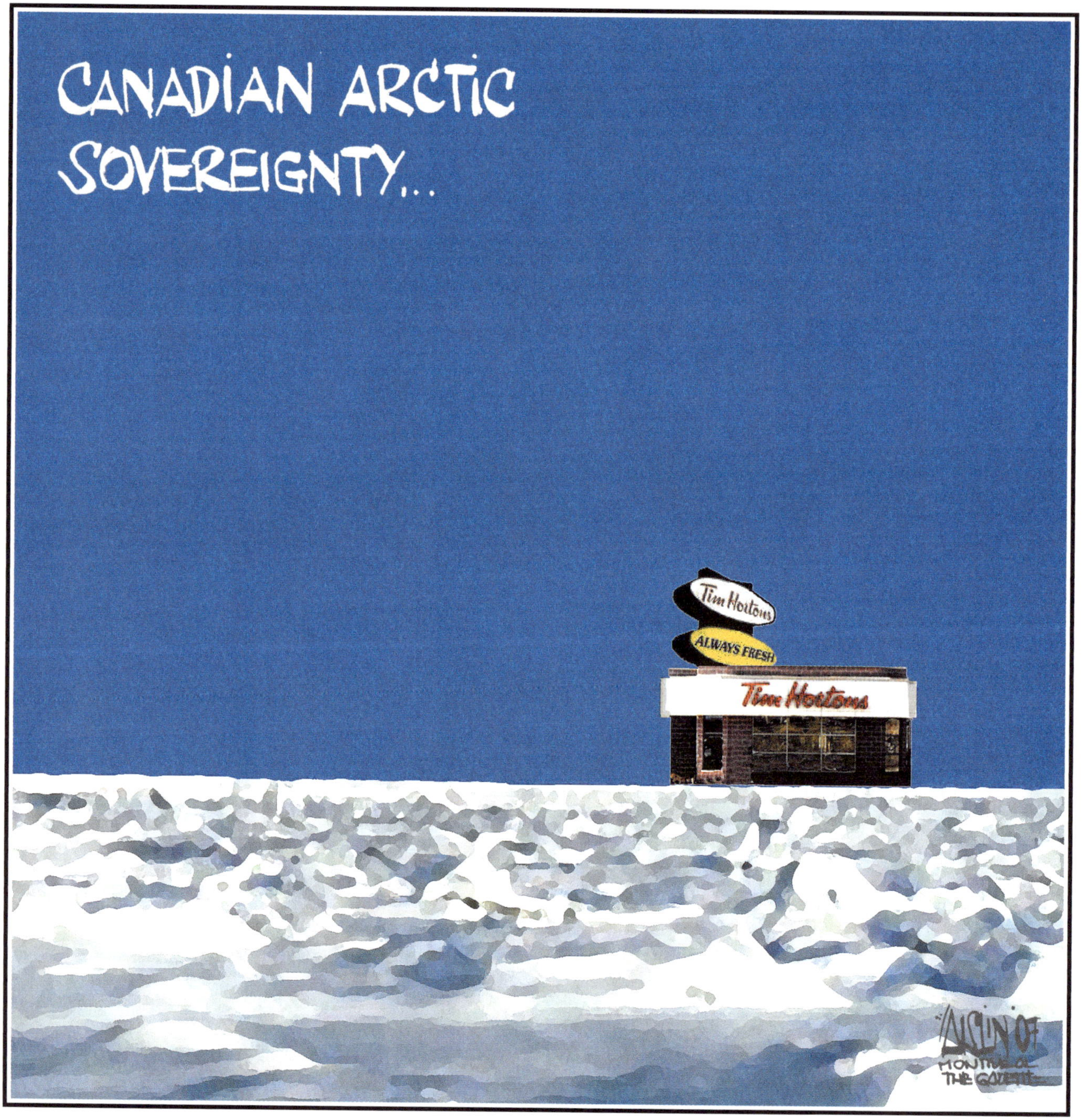
CANADIAN ARCTIC
SOVEREIGNTY...
Tim Hortons
ALWAYS FRESH
Tim Hortons
AISLIN 07
MONTREAL
THE GAZETTE

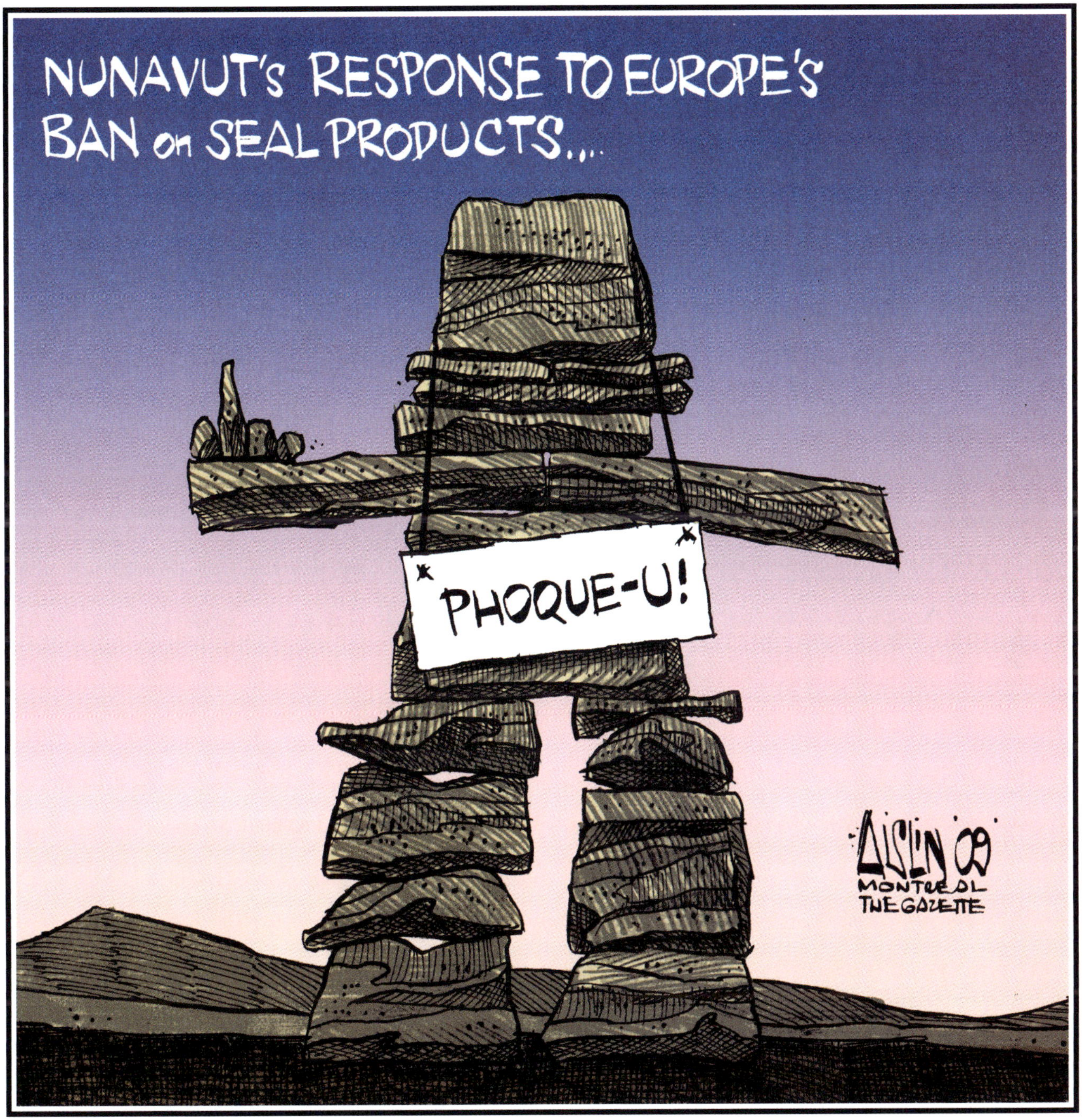
NUNAVUT'S RESPONSE TO EUROPE'S BAN on SEAL PRODUCTS....
PHOQUE-U!
AISLIN '09
MONTREAL THE GAZETTE

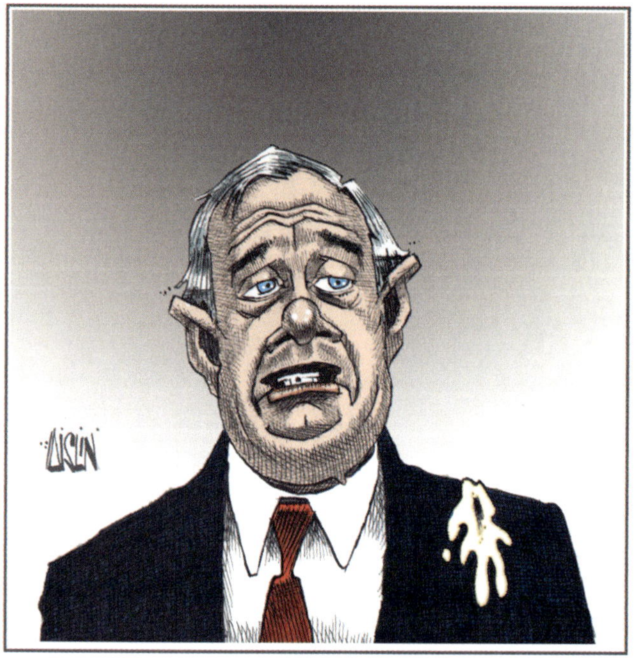
AISLIN

Martin pays the price for sponsorship scandal…

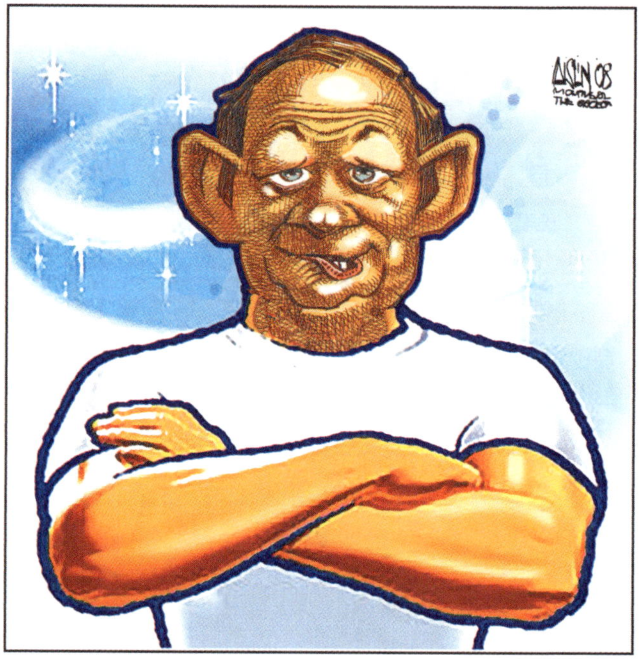
AISLIN 08

…while Chrétien found innocent in sponsorship scandal

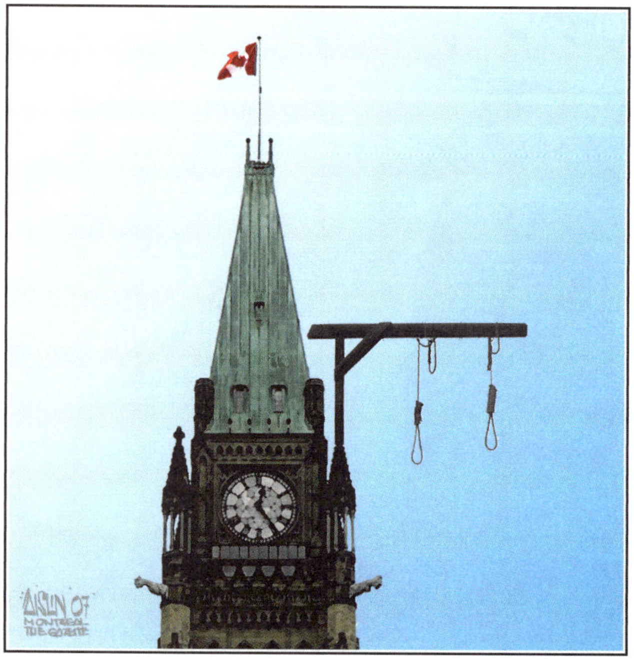
AISLIN 07
MONTREAL
THE GAZETTE

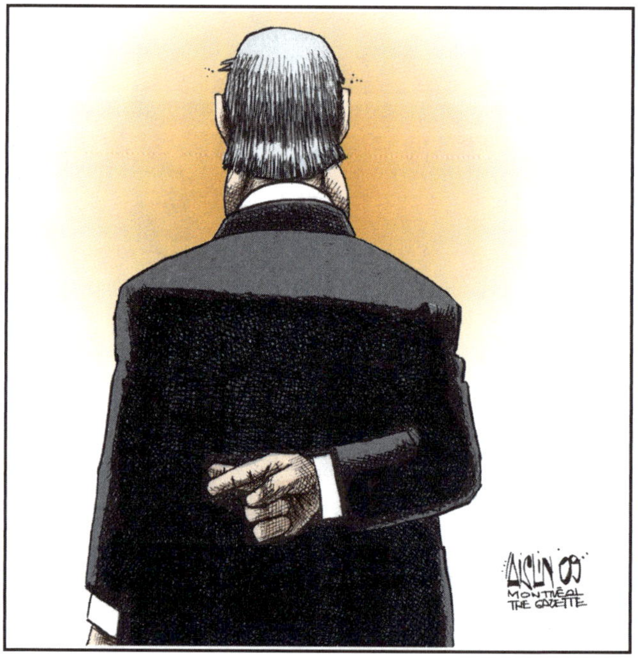
AISLIN 08
MONTRÉAL
THE GAZETTE

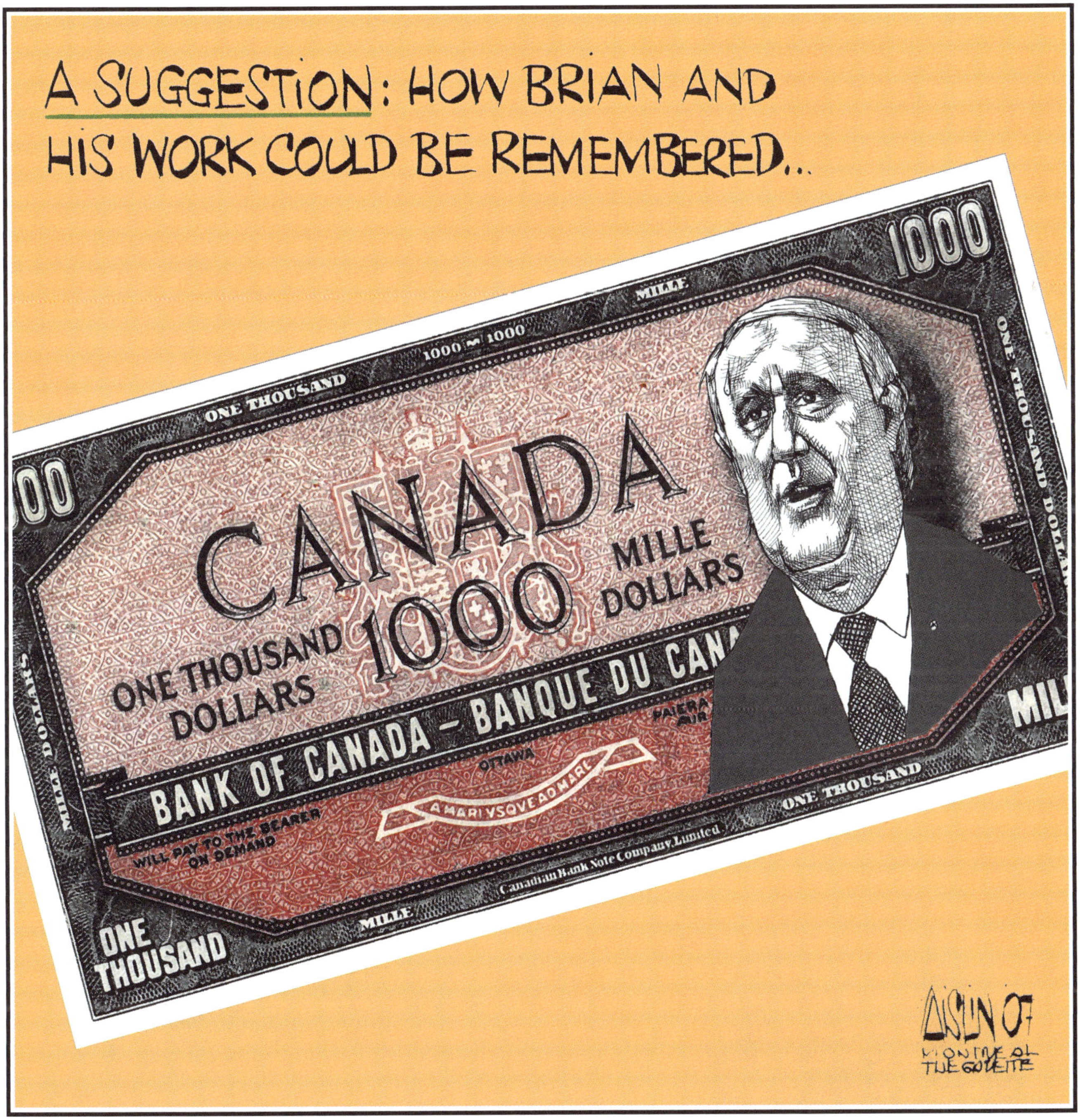
A SUGGESTION: HOW BRIAN AND HIS WORK COULD BE REMEMBERED...
1000
MILLE
ONE THOUSAND
1000 ~ 1000
CANADA
MILLE DOLLARS
ONE THOUSAND DOLLARS
1000
BANK OF CANADA - BANQUE DU CAN
BANK OF CANADA - BANQUE DU CANADA
OTTAWA
A MARI VSQVE AD MARE
WILL PAY TO THE BEARER ON DEMAND
Canadian Bank Note Company, Limited
ONE THOUSAND
MILLE
AISLIN 07
MONTREAL THE GAZETTE

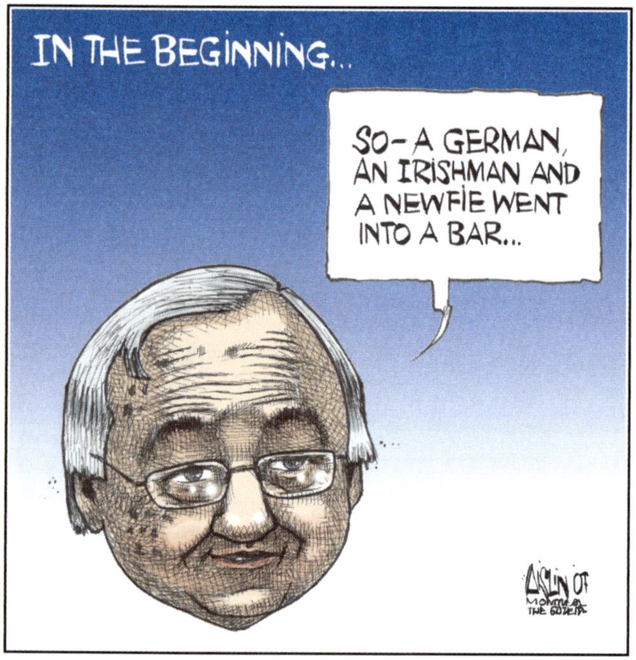
IN THE BEGINNING...
SO- A GERMAN, AN IRISHMAN AND A NEWFIE WENT INTO A BAR...
AISLIN 07 MONTREAL THE GAZETTE

Karleinz Schreiber, Brian Mulroney and Frank Moores

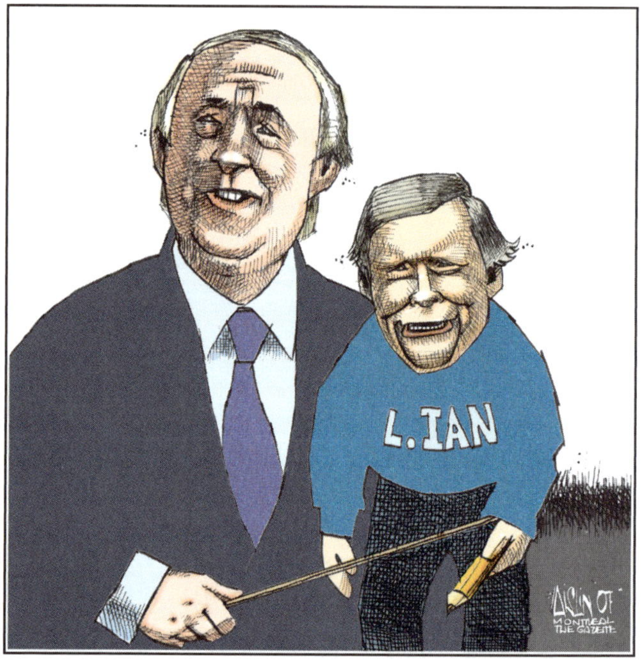
L.IAN
AISLIN 07 MONTREAL THE GAZETTE

Gazette columnist, L. Ian MacDonald (unpublished)

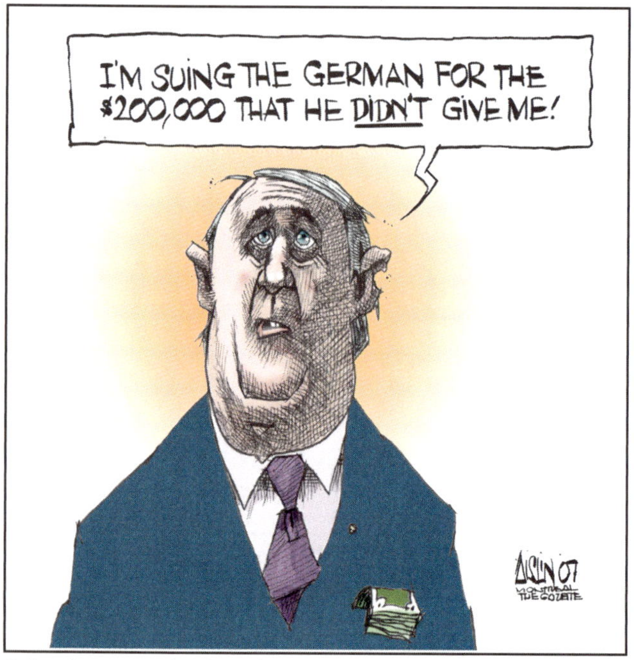
I'M SUING THE GERMAN FOR THE $200,000 THAT HE DIDN'T GIVE ME!
AISLIN 07 MONTREAL THE GAZETTE

Schreiber says he had $500,000 set aside for Mulroney

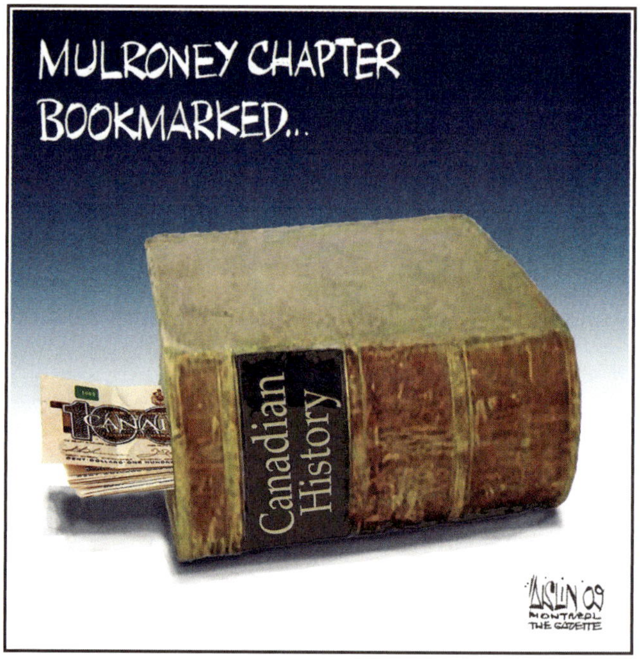
MULRONEY CHAPTER BOOKMARKED...
Canadian History
AISLIN 09 MONTREAL THE GAZETTE

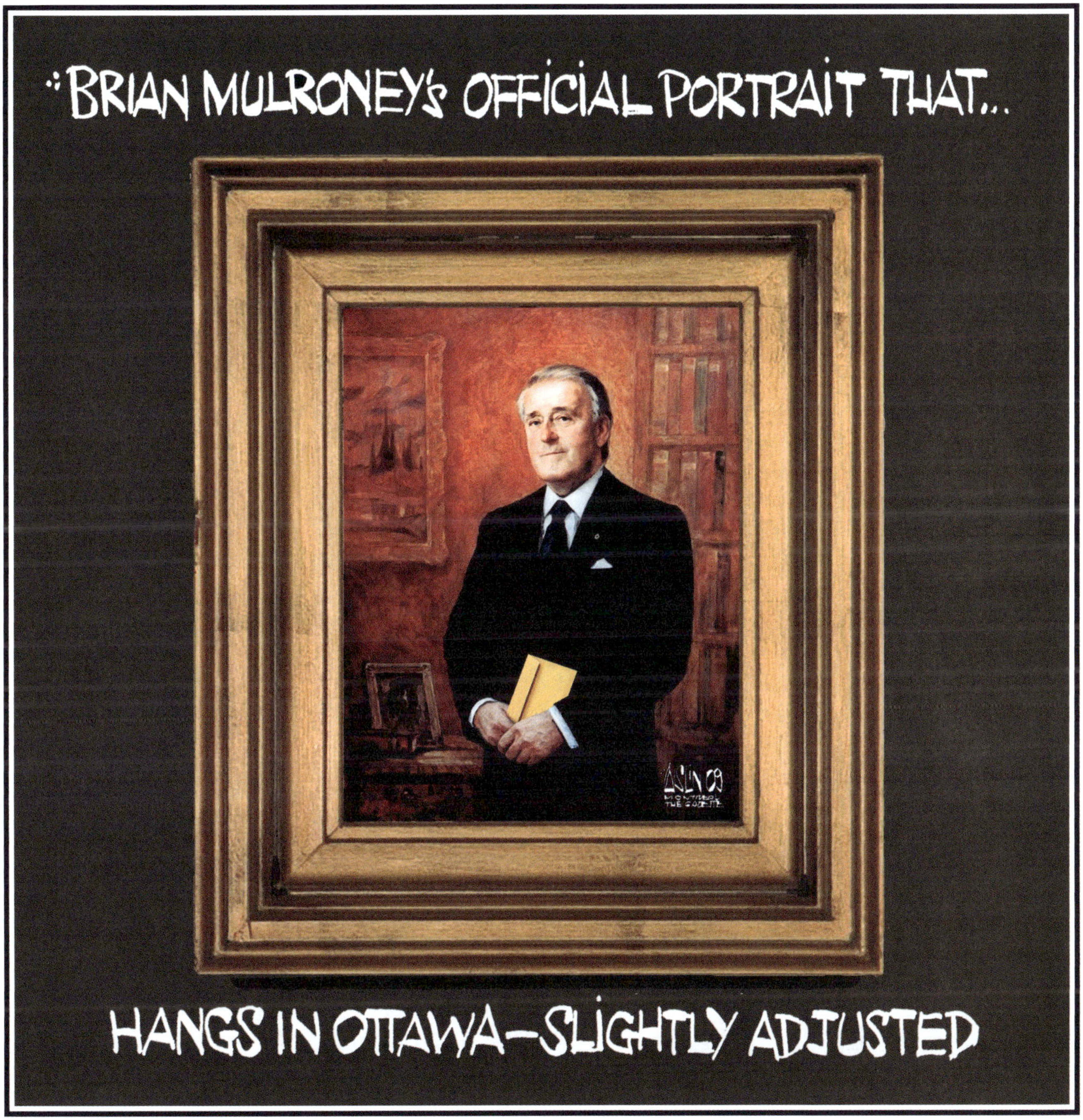

∴BRIAN MULRONEY'S OFFICIAL PORTRAIT THAT...
HANGS IN OTTAWA–SLIGHTLY ADJUSTED

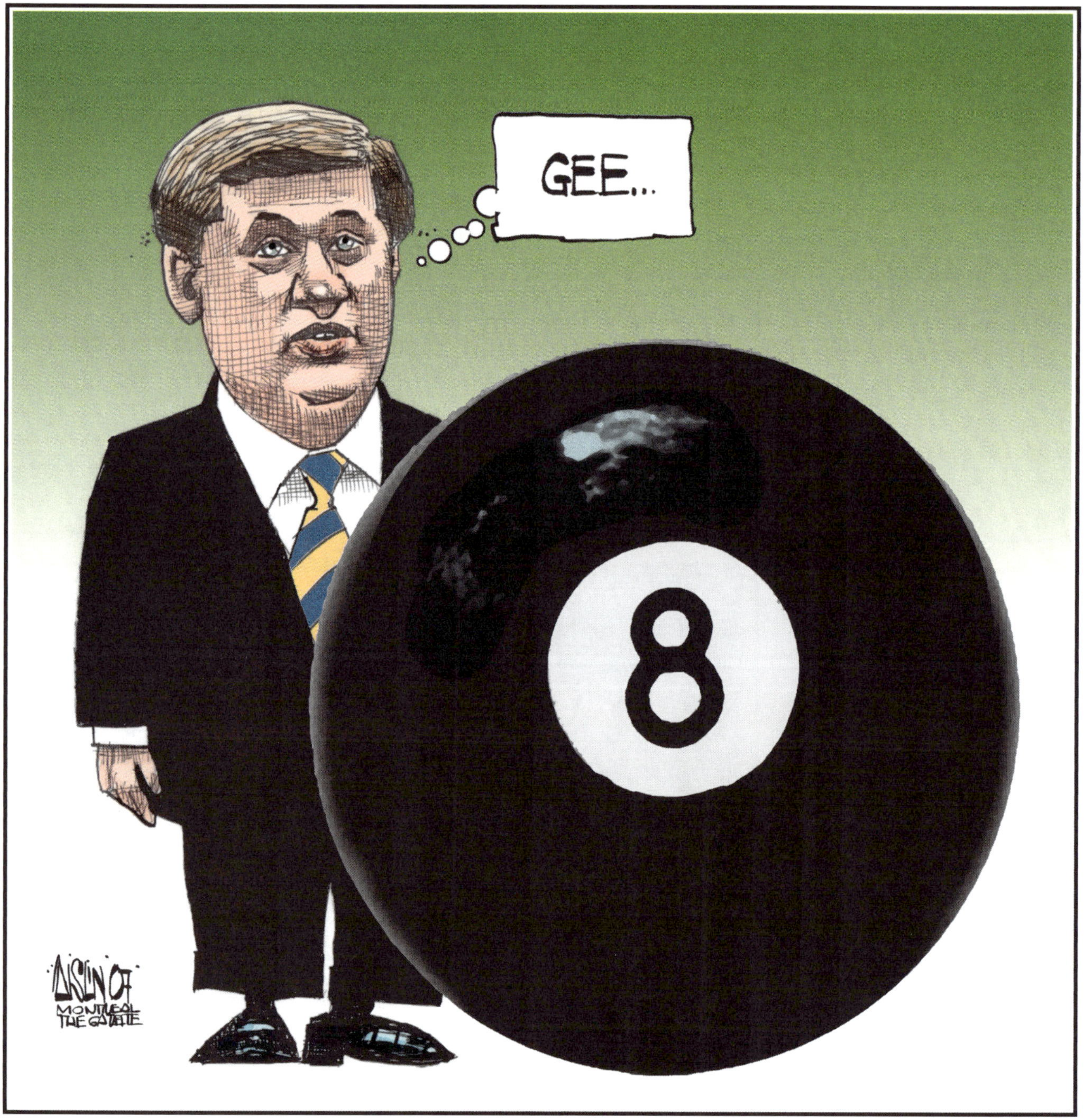
GEE...
8

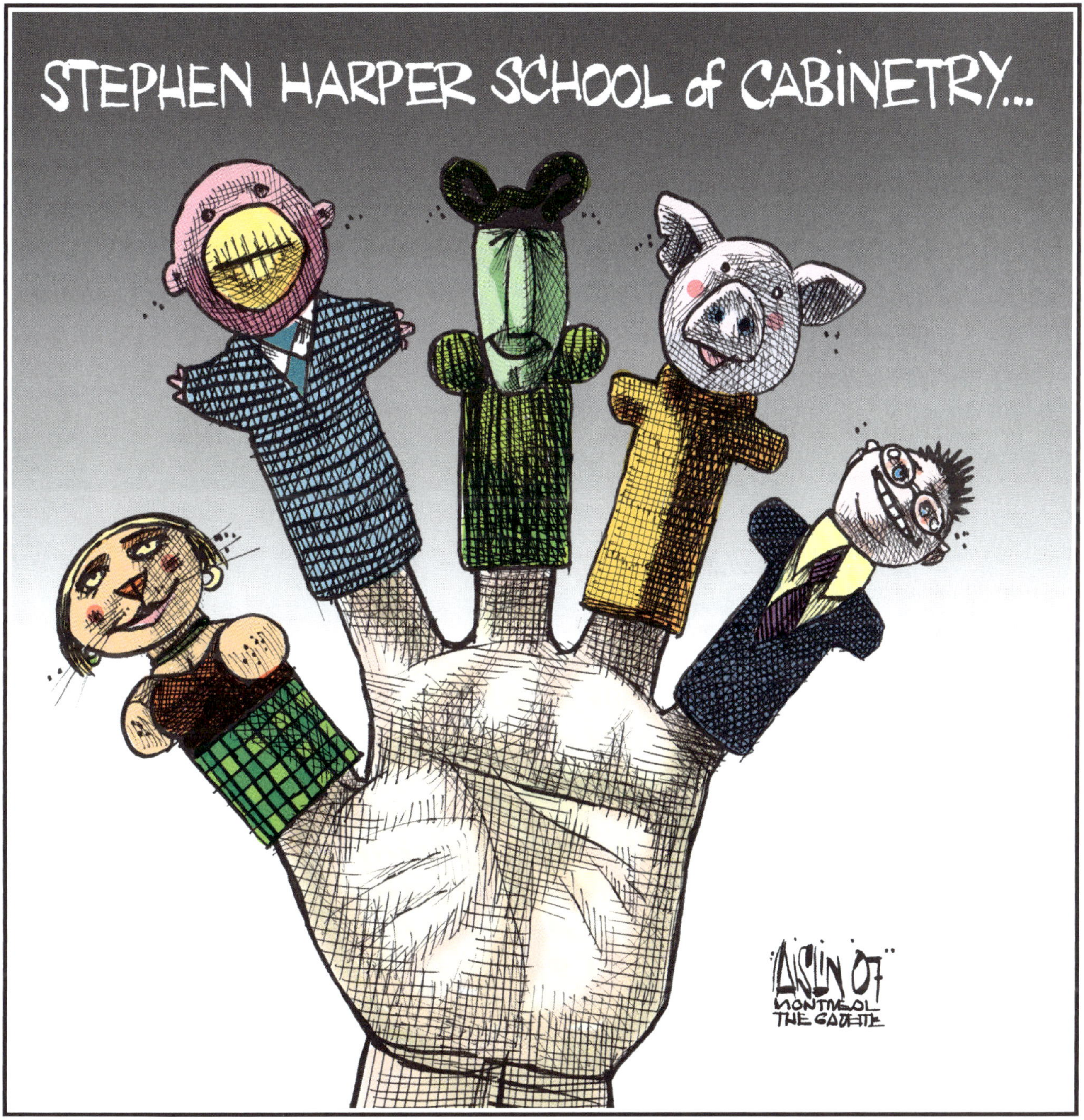
STEPHEN HARPER SCHOOL of CABINETRY...
AISLIN 07
MONTREAL THE GAZETTE

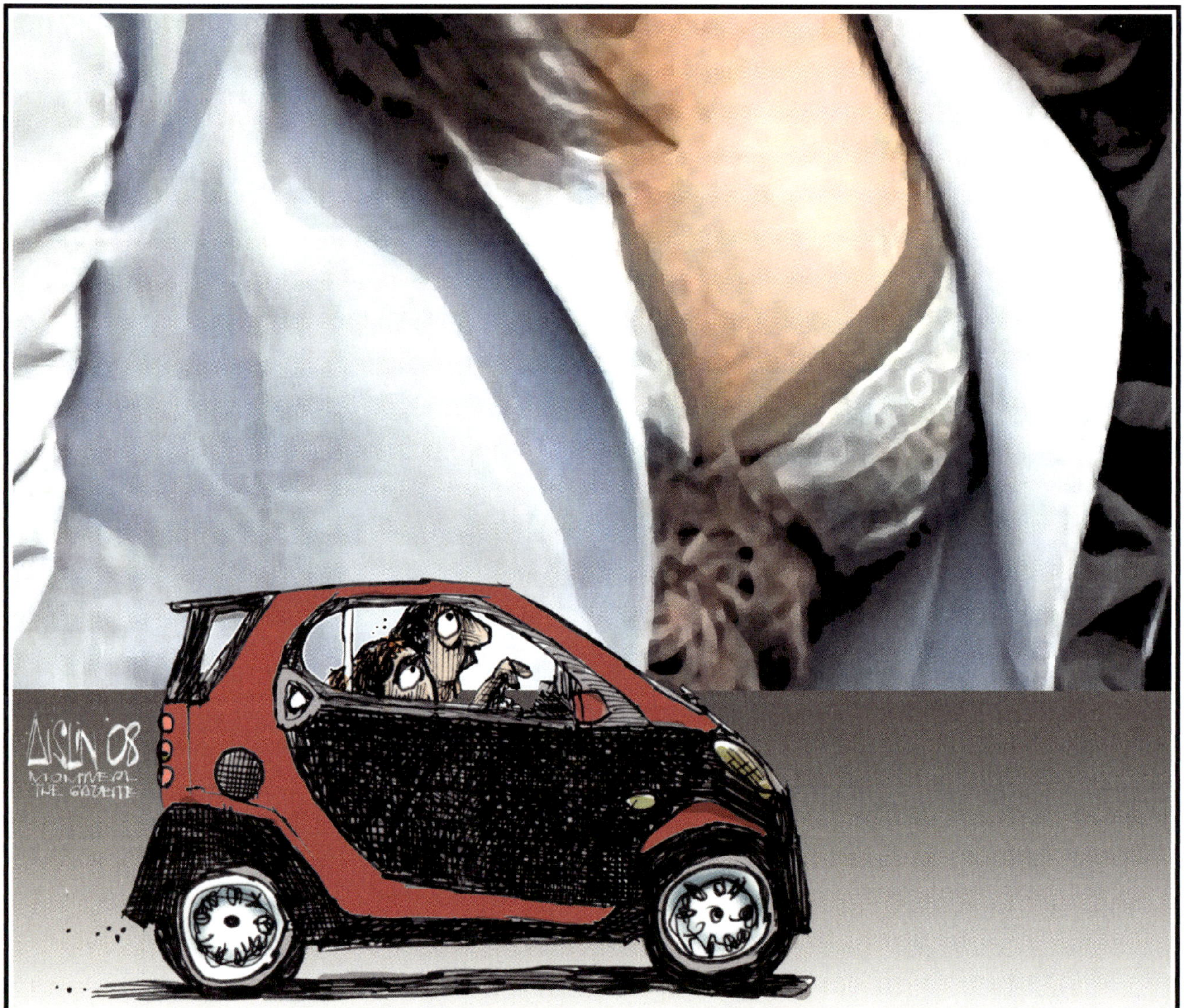
AISLIN '08
MONTREAL THE GAZETTE

"YOU'RE RIGHT. THERE'S ABSOLUTELY NO ESCAPE. WE'VE BEEN PURSUED EVERYWHERE, ALL WEEK, BY JULIE'S BOOB!"

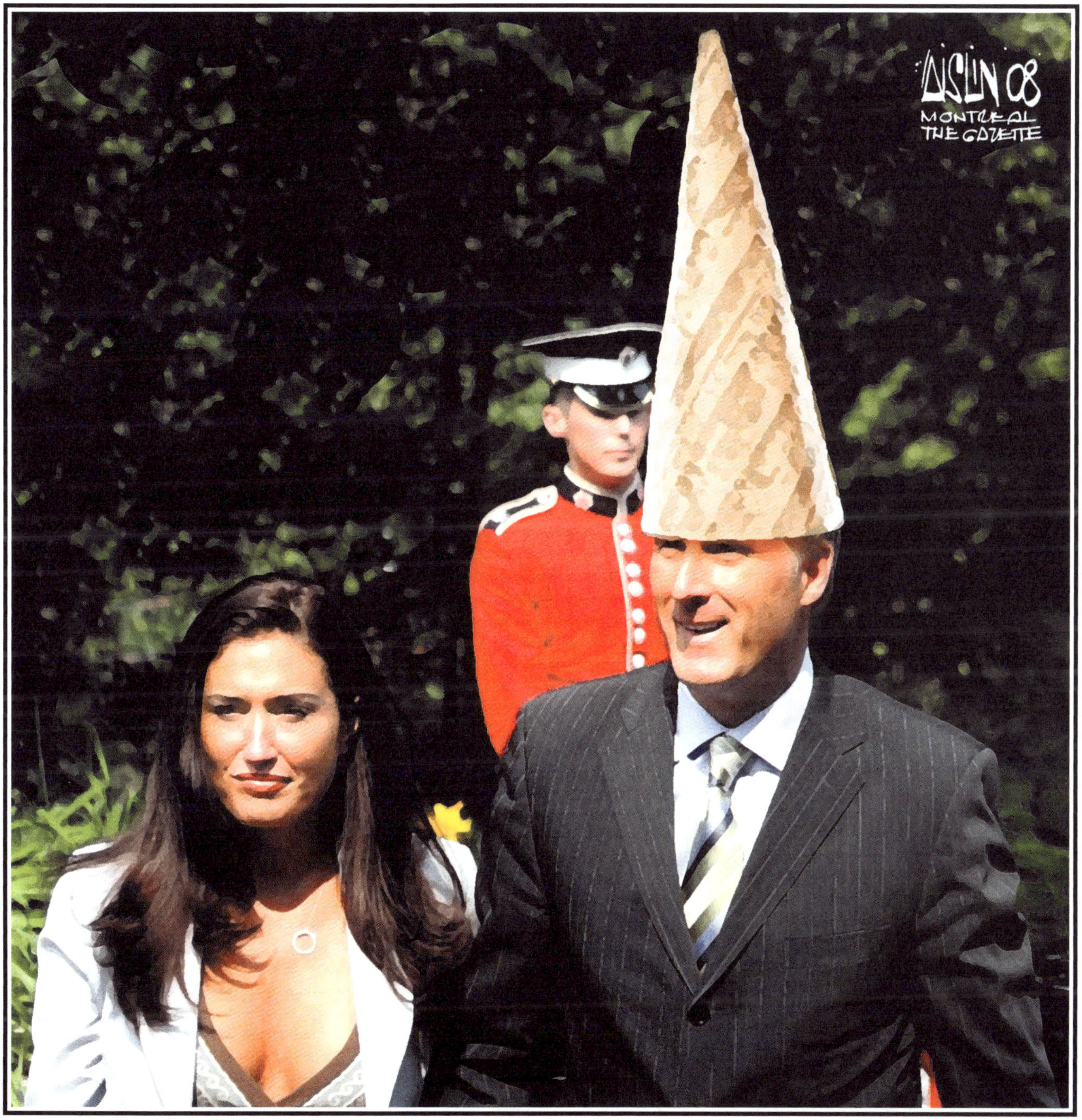
AISLIN 08
MONTREAL
THE GAZETTE

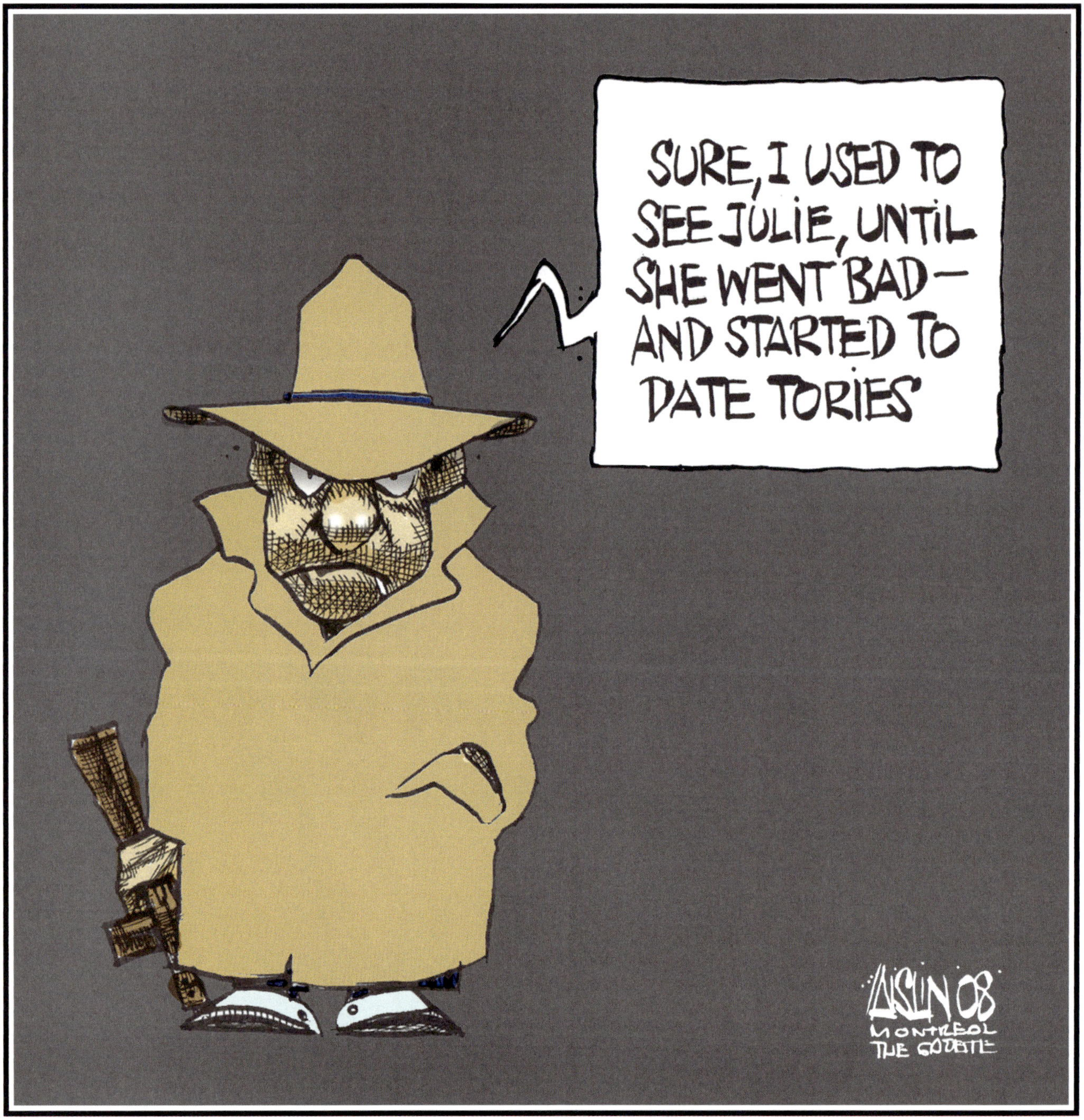
SURE, I USED TO SEE JULIE, UNTIL SHE WENT BAD— AND STARTED TO DATE TORIES
AISLIN 08
MONTREAL THE GAZETTE
Julie Couillard dated mobsters before she started going out with cabinet minister Maxime Bernier

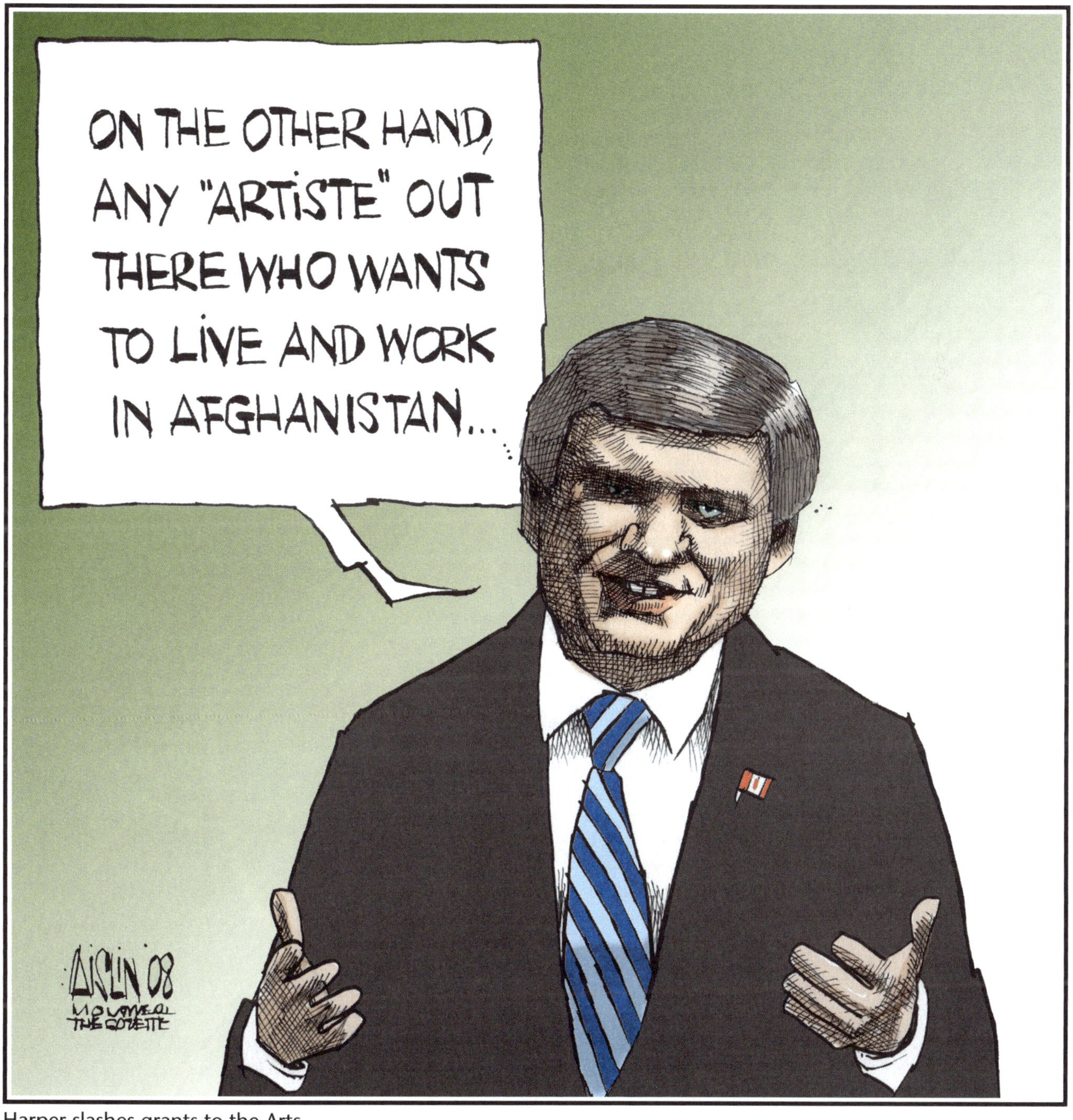
ON THE OTHER HAND, ANY "ARTISTE" OUT THERE WHO WANTS TO LIVE AND WORK IN AFGHANISTAN...
AISLIN 08

Harper slashes grants to the Arts

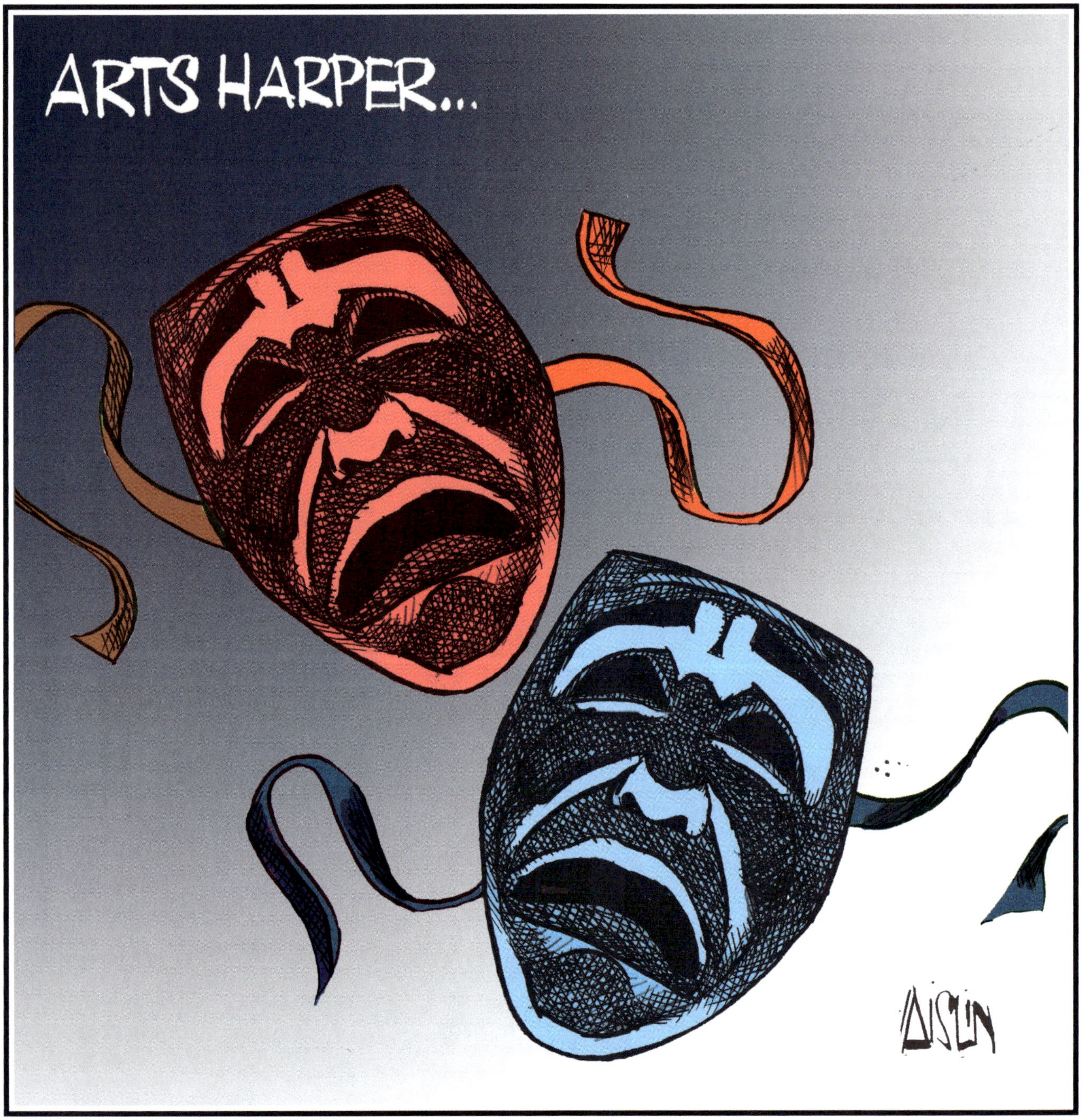
ARTS HARPER...
AISLIN

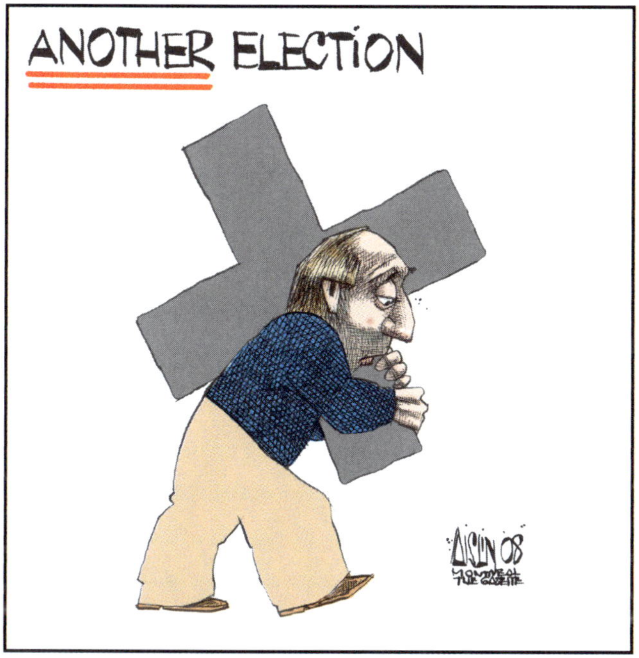
ANOTHER ELECTION
AISLIN 08
MONTREAL THE GAZETTE

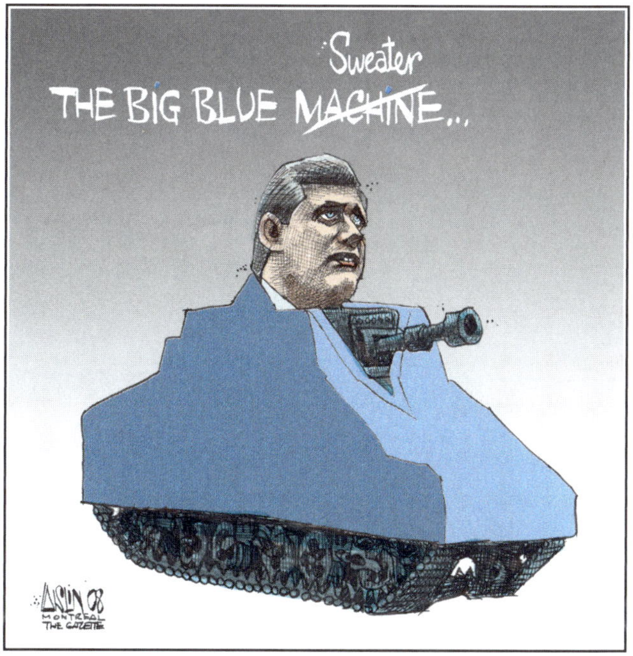
THE BIG BLUE MACHINE... Sweater
AISLIN 08
MONTREAL THE GAZETTE

Harper sports a blue sweater to soften his image

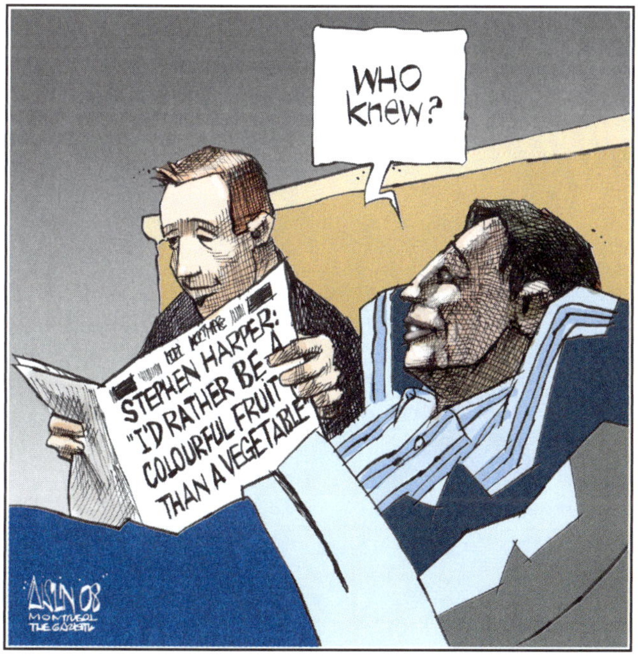
WHO knew?
STEPHEN HARPER: "I'D RATHER BE A COLOURFUL FRUIT THAN A VEGETABLE"
AISLIN 08
MONTREAL THE GAZETTE

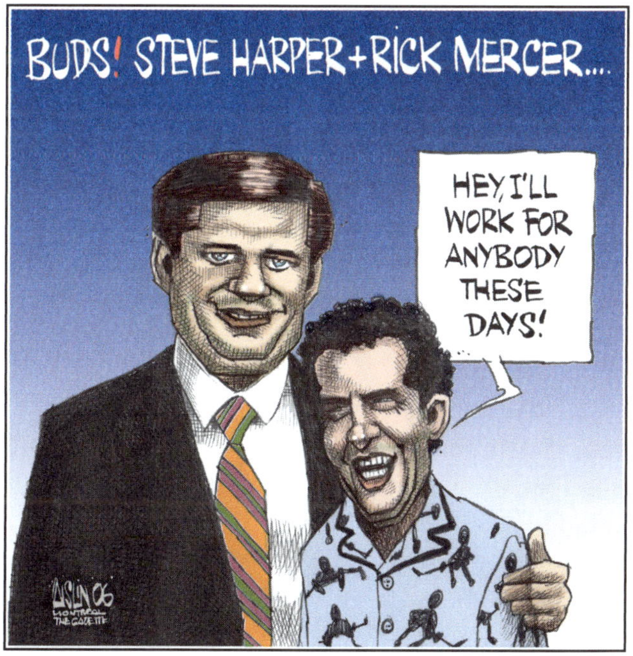
BUDS! STEVE HARPER + RICK MERCER...
HEY, I'LL WORK FOR ANYBODY THESE DAYS!
AISLIN 06
MONTREAL THE GAZETTE

Rick Mercer spends a night at 24 Sussex Drive

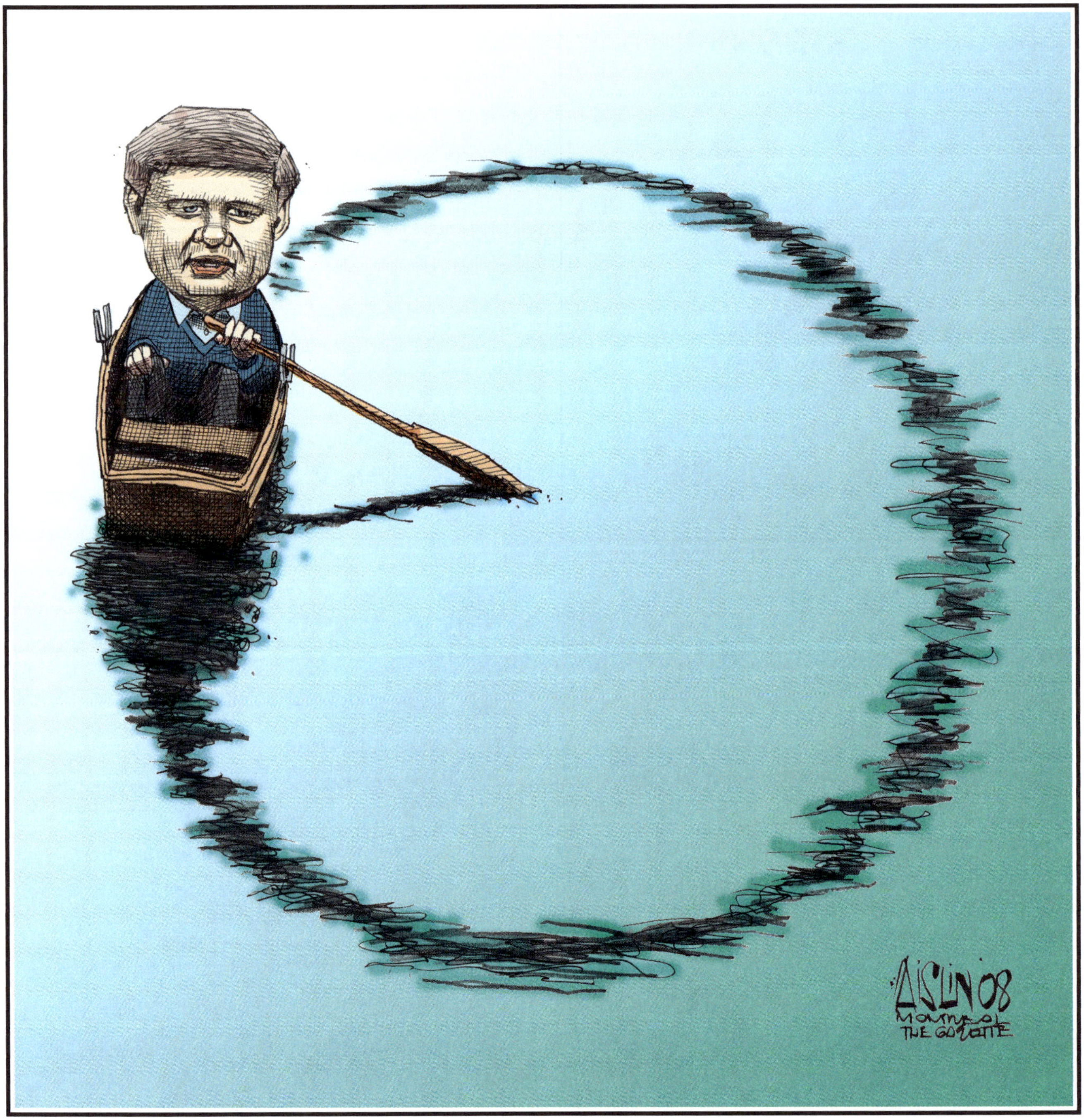
AISLIN 08
MONTREAL
THE GAZETTE

Stephen Harper wins another minority government

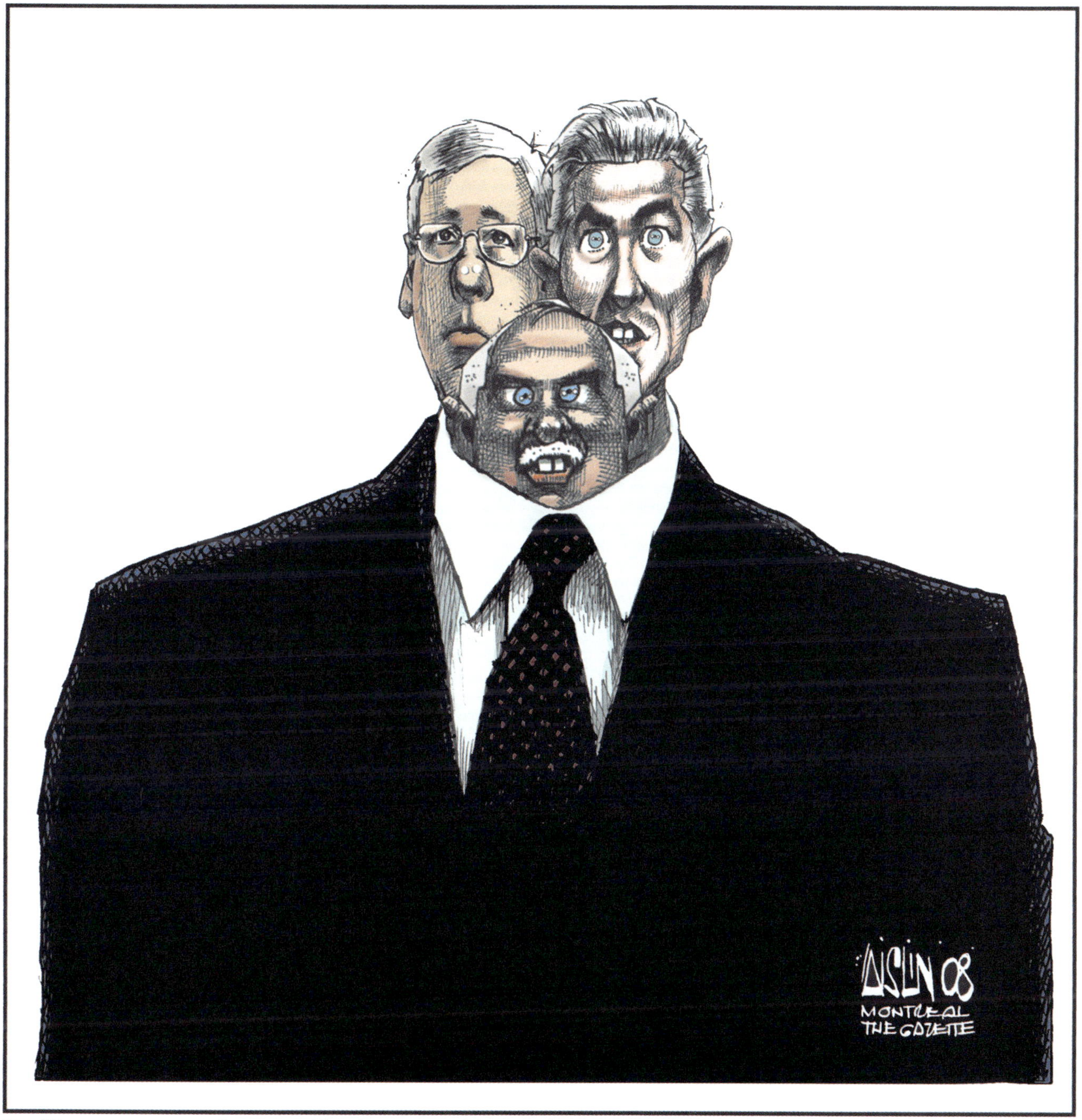
AISLIN 08
MONTREAL
THE GAZETTE
Coalition government threatened by three opposition parties

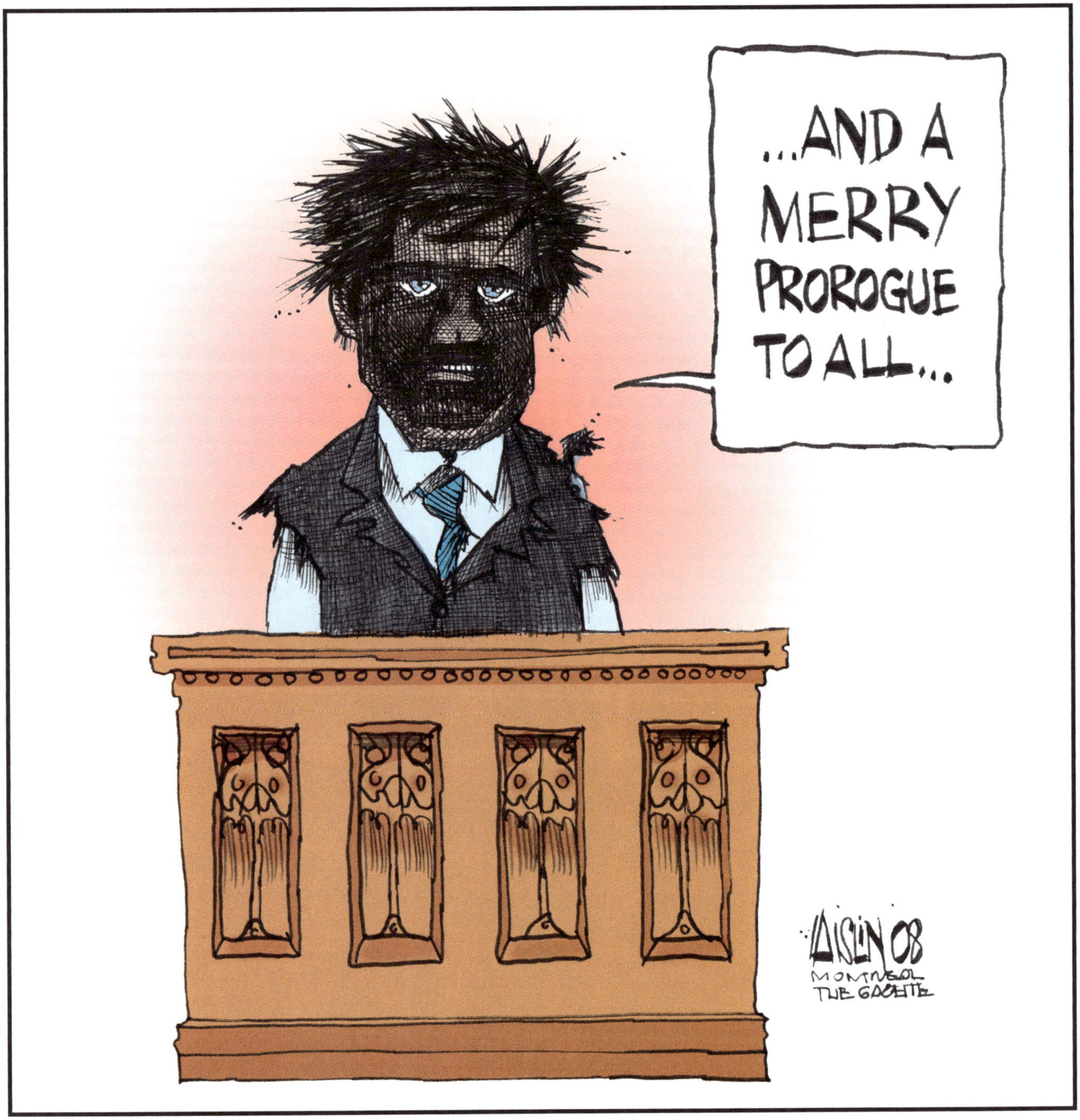
...AND A MERRY PROROGUE TO ALL...
AISLIN 08
MONTREAL THE GAZETTE

Stephen Harper prorogues Parliament in December

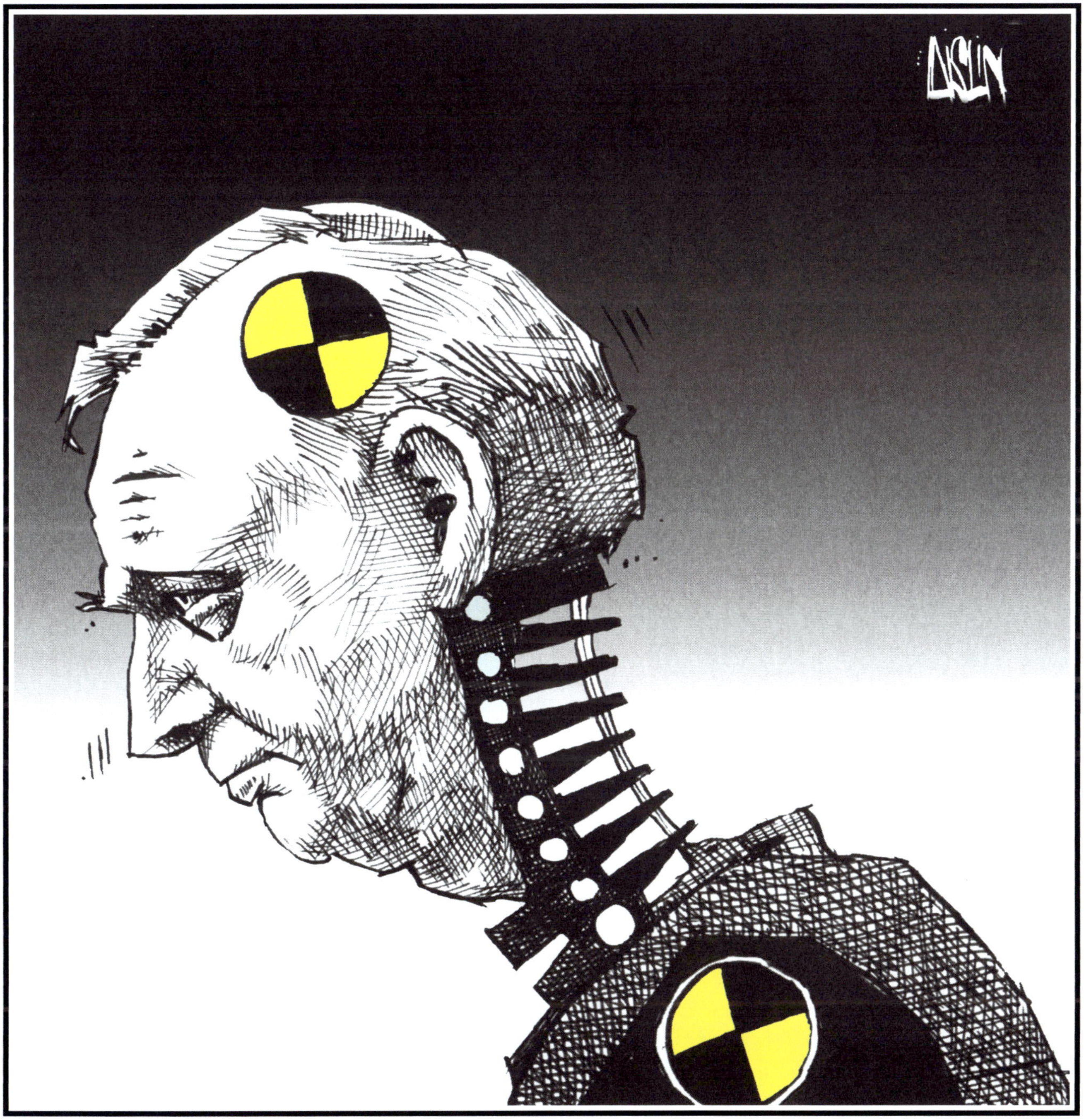
AISLIN

Paul Martin steps down as Liberal Party leader

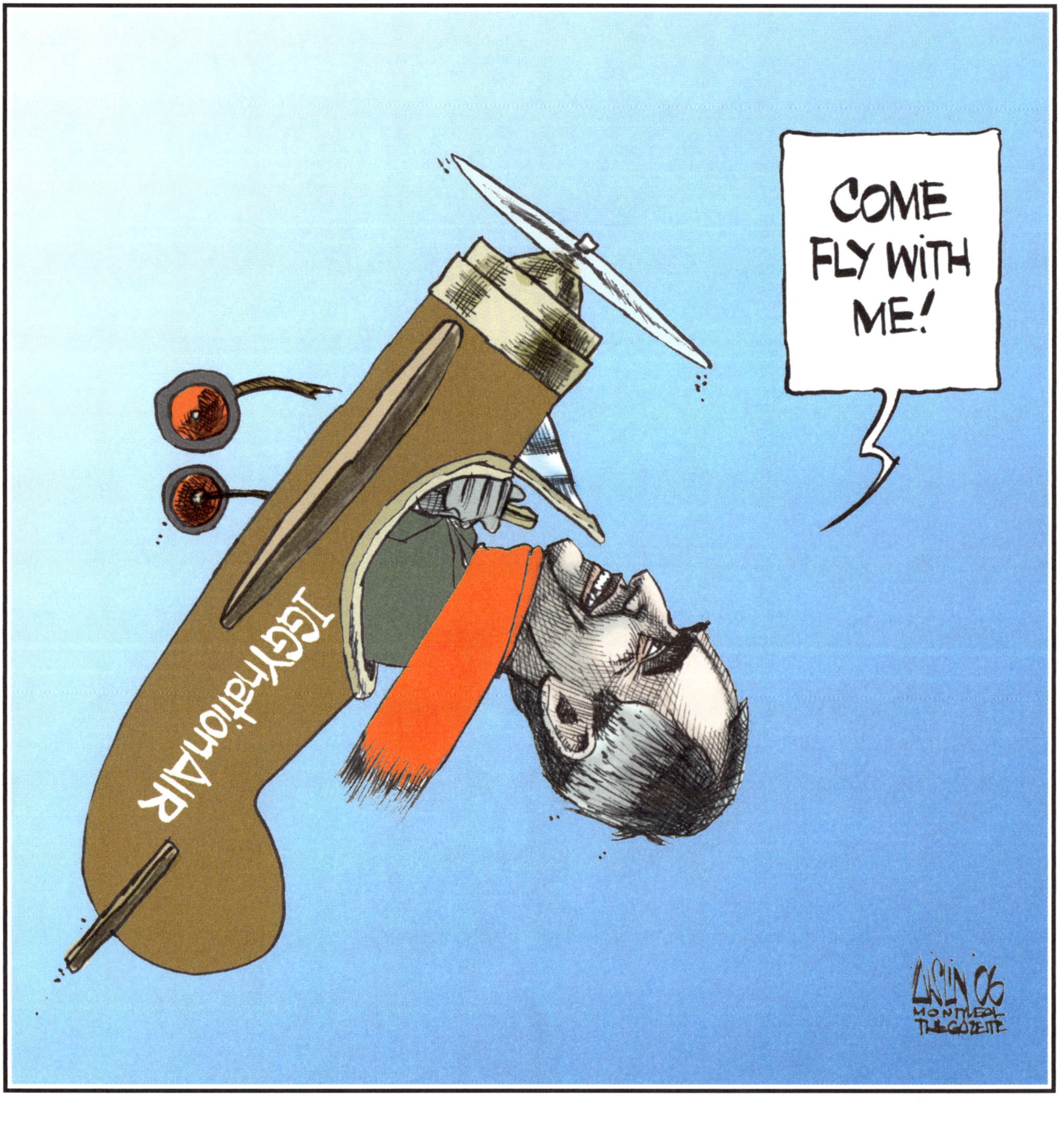
COME FLY WITH ME!
IGGYnationAIR

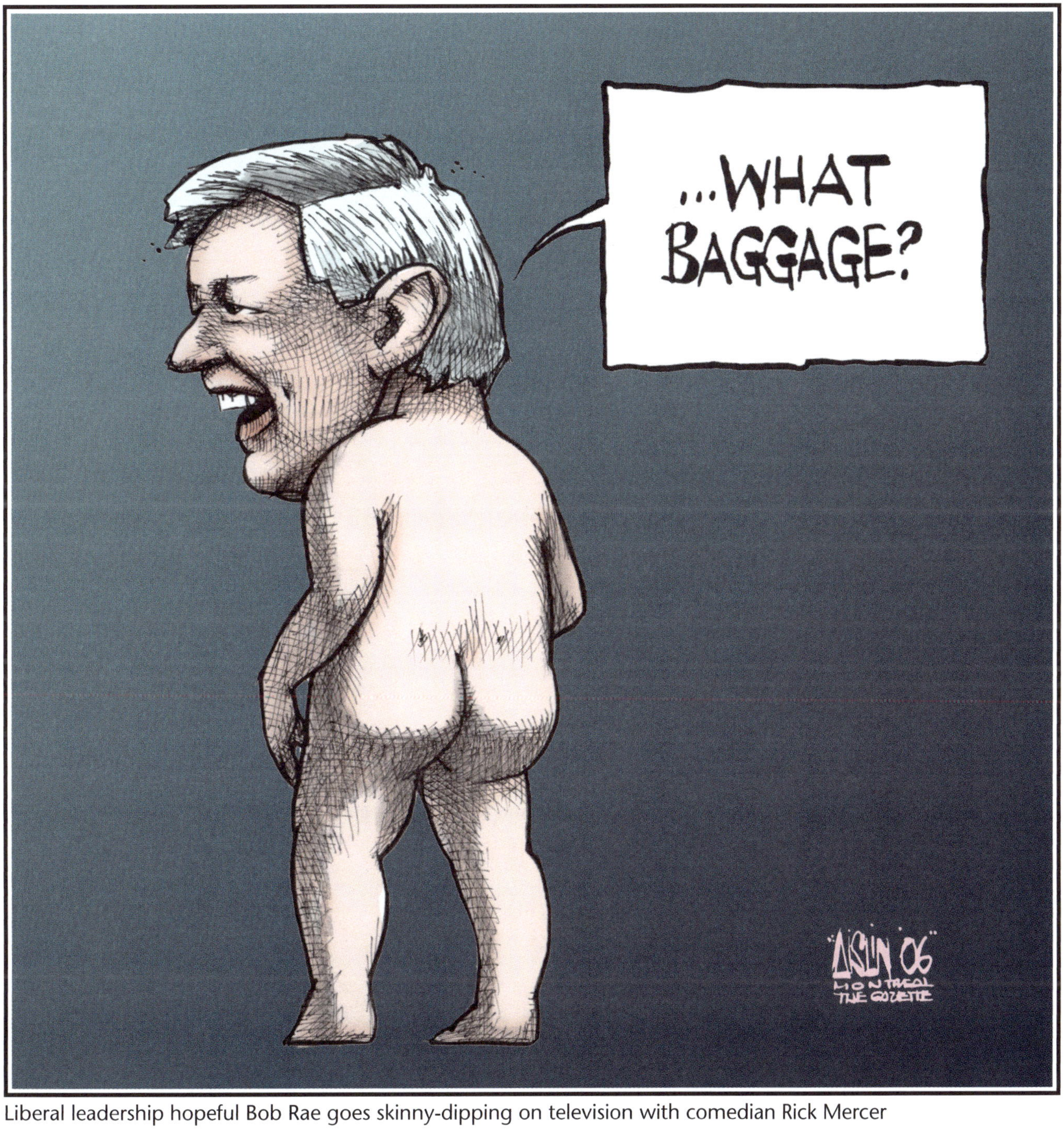

...WHAT BAGGAGE?
AISLIN 06
MONTREAL THE GAZETTE

Liberal leadership hopeful Bob Rae goes skinny-dipping on television with comedian Rick Mercer

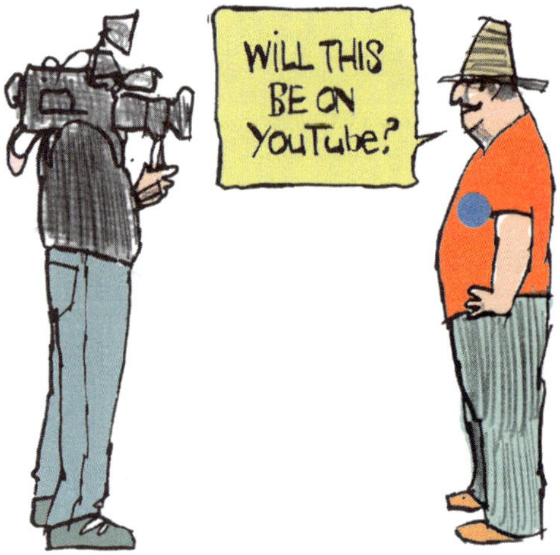
WILL THIS BE ON YouTube?

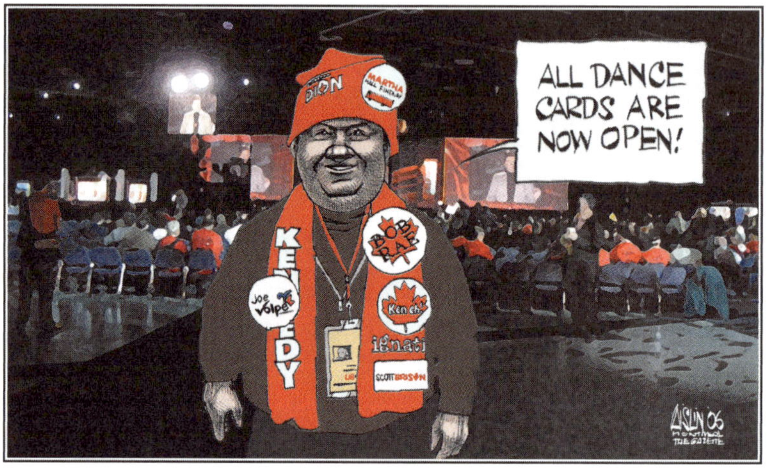
ALL DANCE CARDS ARE NOW OPEN!
DION
MARTHA
KENNEDY
BOB RAE
AISLIN 06

The Liberal Party gathers at a leadership convention in Montreal and surprise everyone…

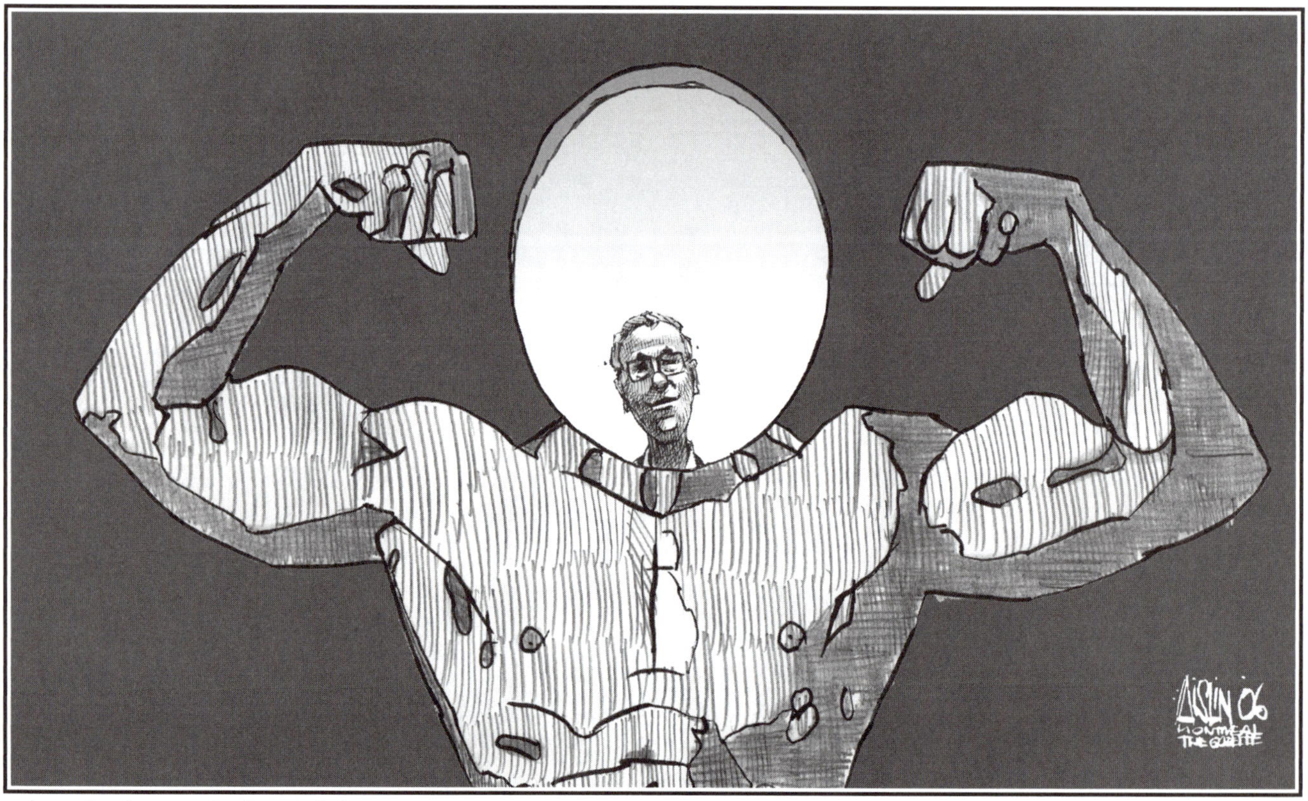
AISLIN 06
MONTREAL
THE GAZETTE

…by selecting underdog Stéphane Dion…

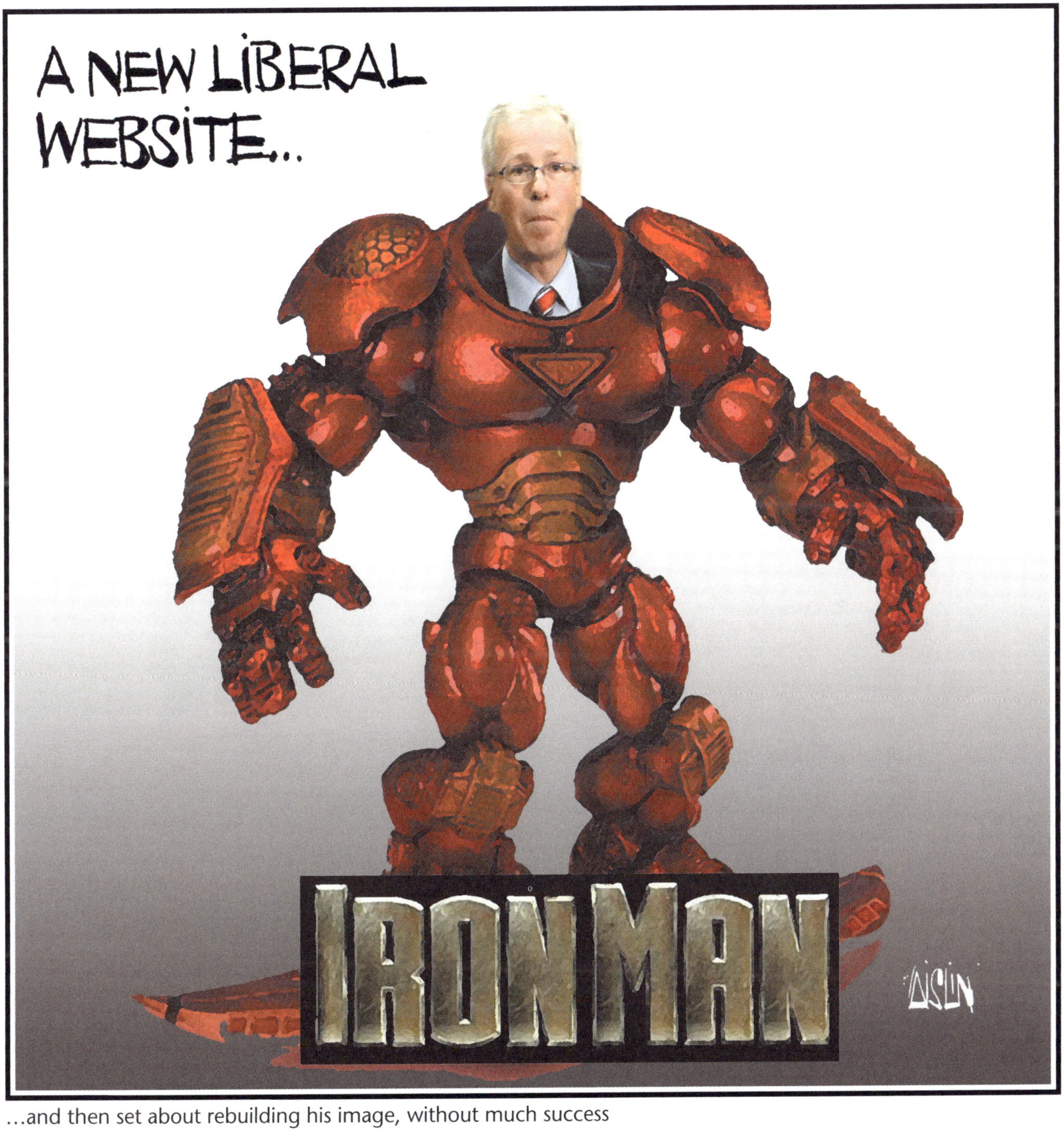
A NEW LIBERAL WEBSITE...
IRONMAN
AISLIN
…and then set about rebuilding his image, without much success

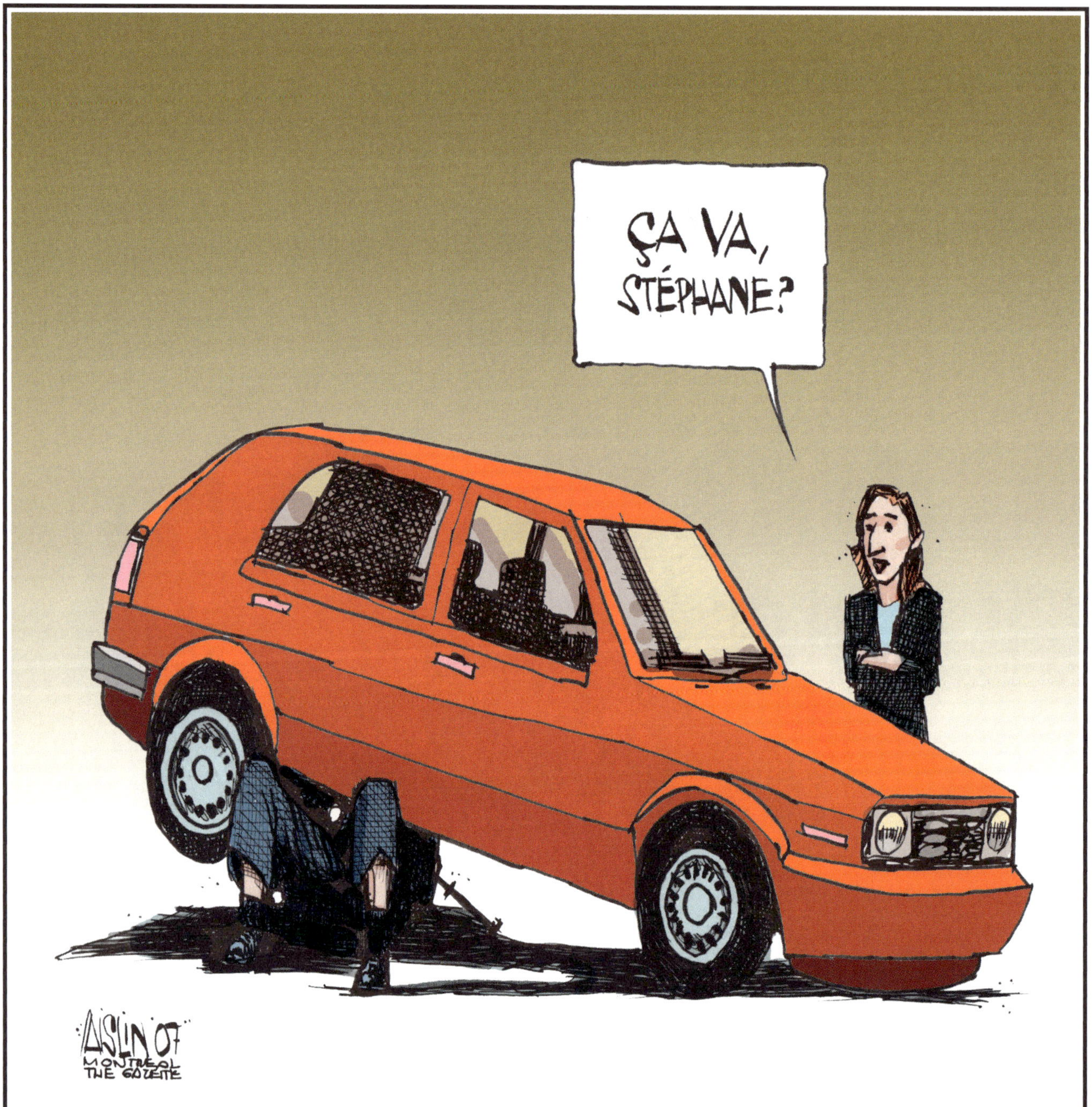
ÇA VA, STÉPHANE?
AISLIN 07 MONTREAL THE GAZETTE

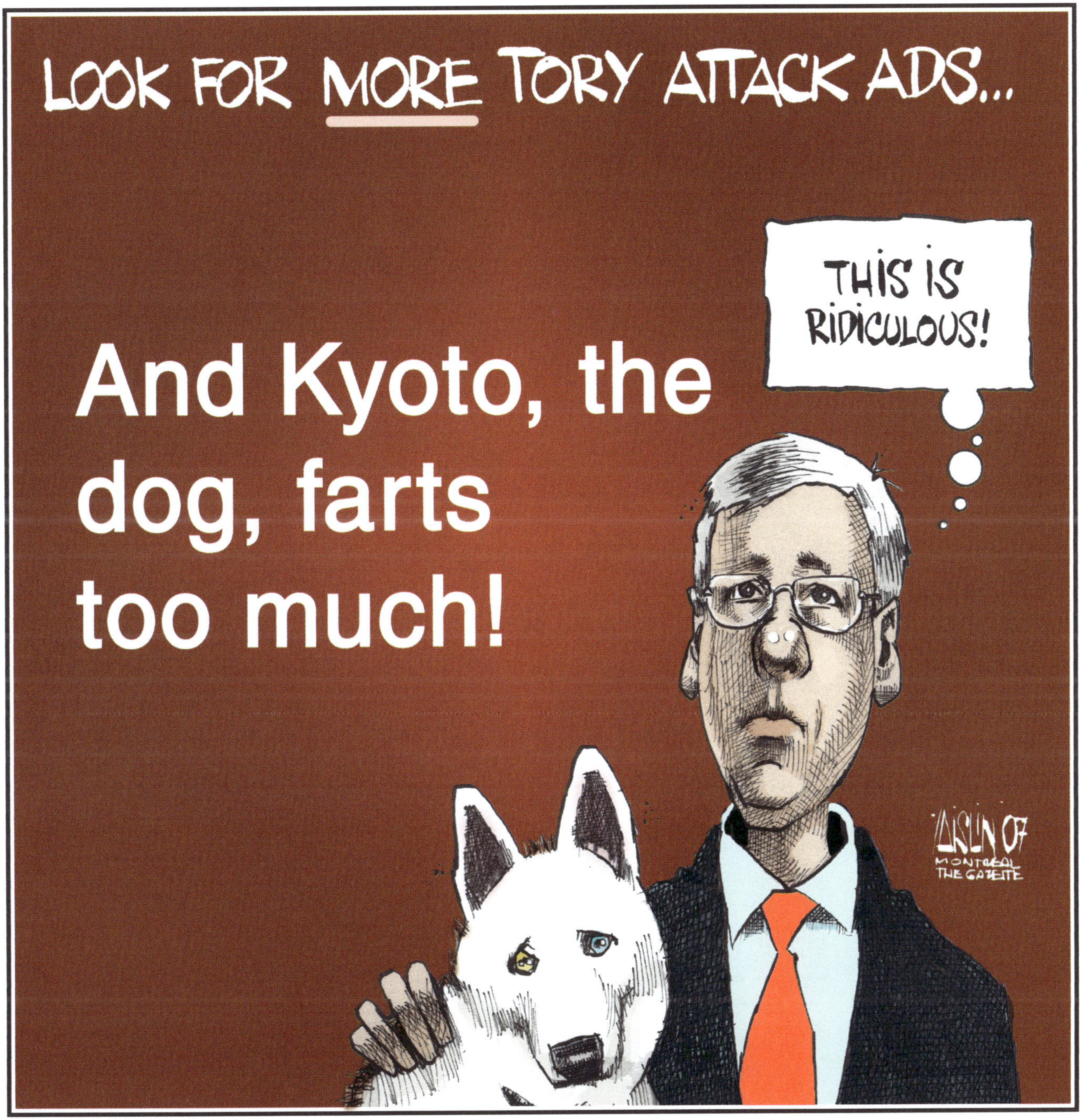
LOOK FOR MORE TORY ATTACK ADS...
THIS IS RIDICULOUS!
And Kyoto, the dog, farts too much!
AISLIN 07
MONTREAL THE GAZETTE

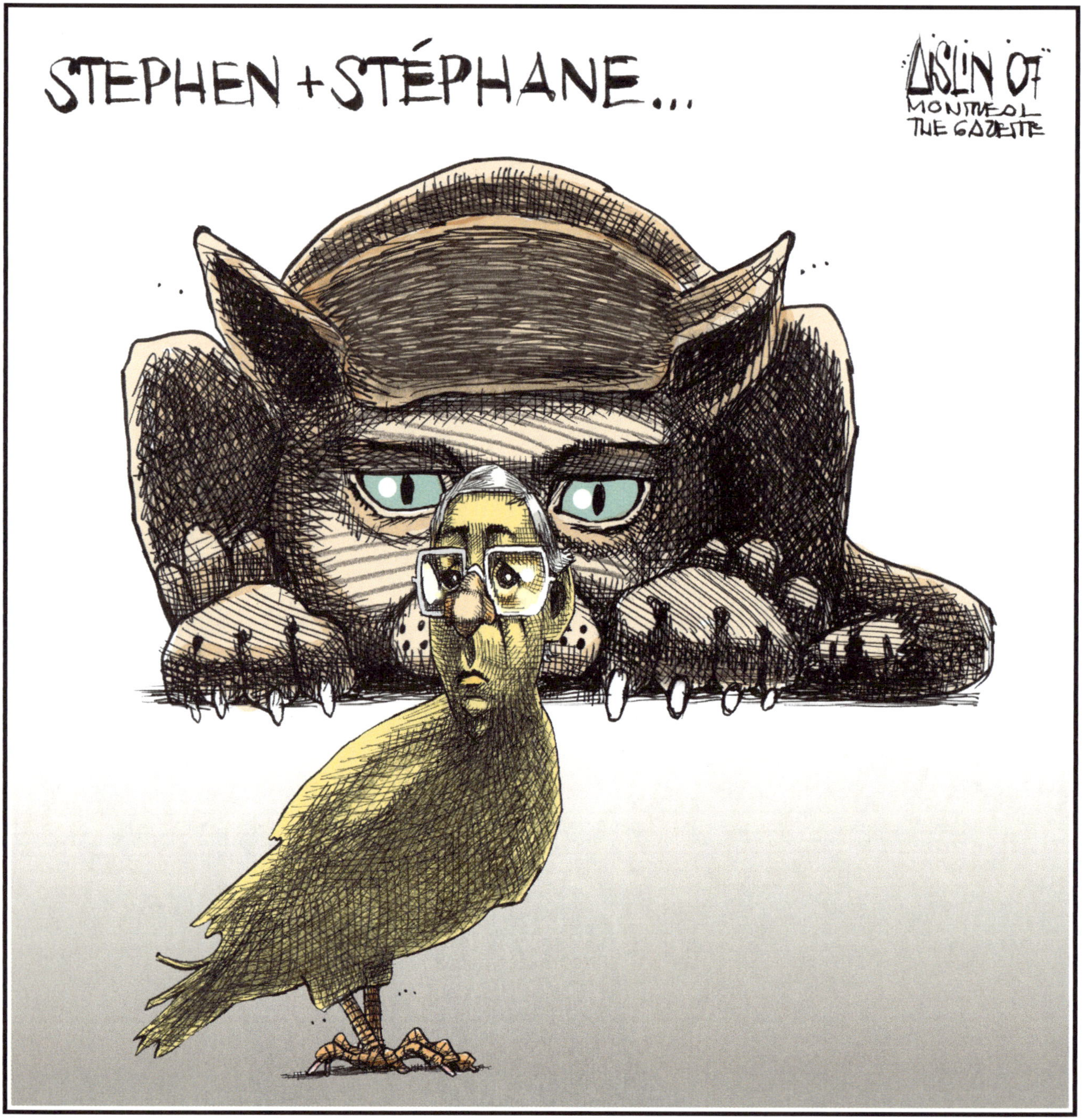
STEPHEN + STÉPHANE...
AISLIN 07
MONTREAL THE GAZETTE

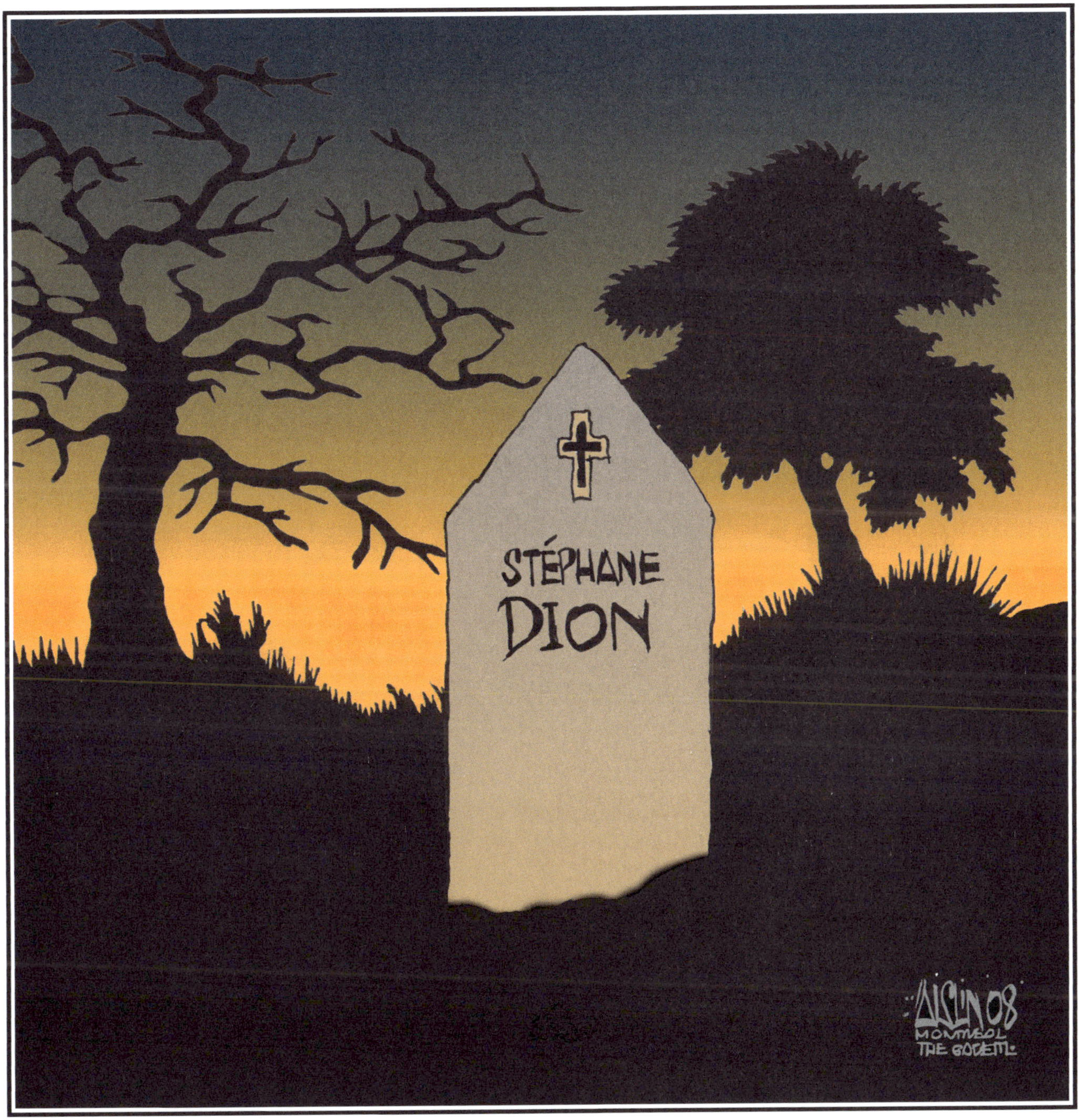
STÉPHANE
DION

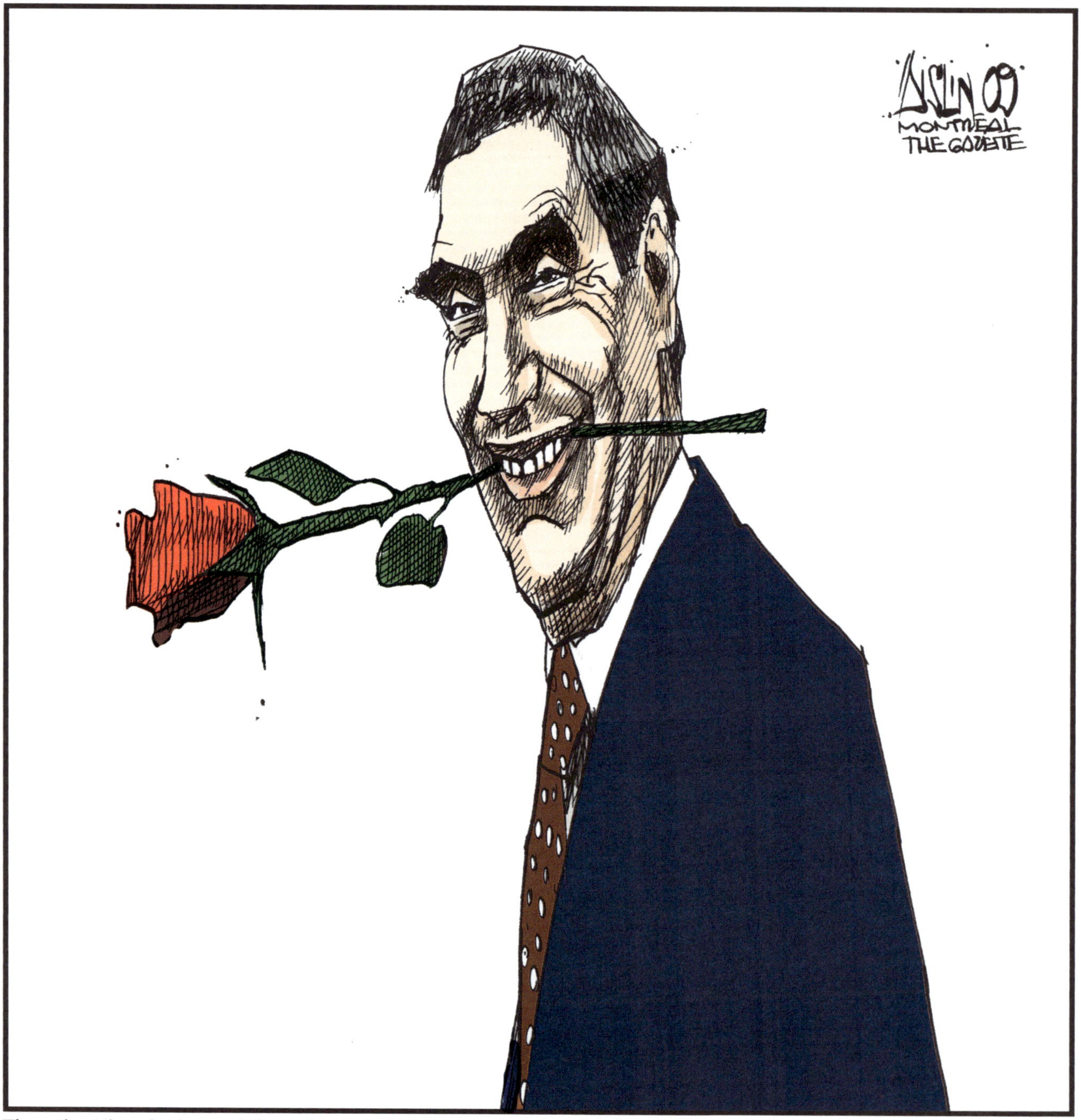
AISLIN 09
MONTREAL
THE GAZETTE

Then the Liberals choose Michael Ignatieff as yet another new leader…

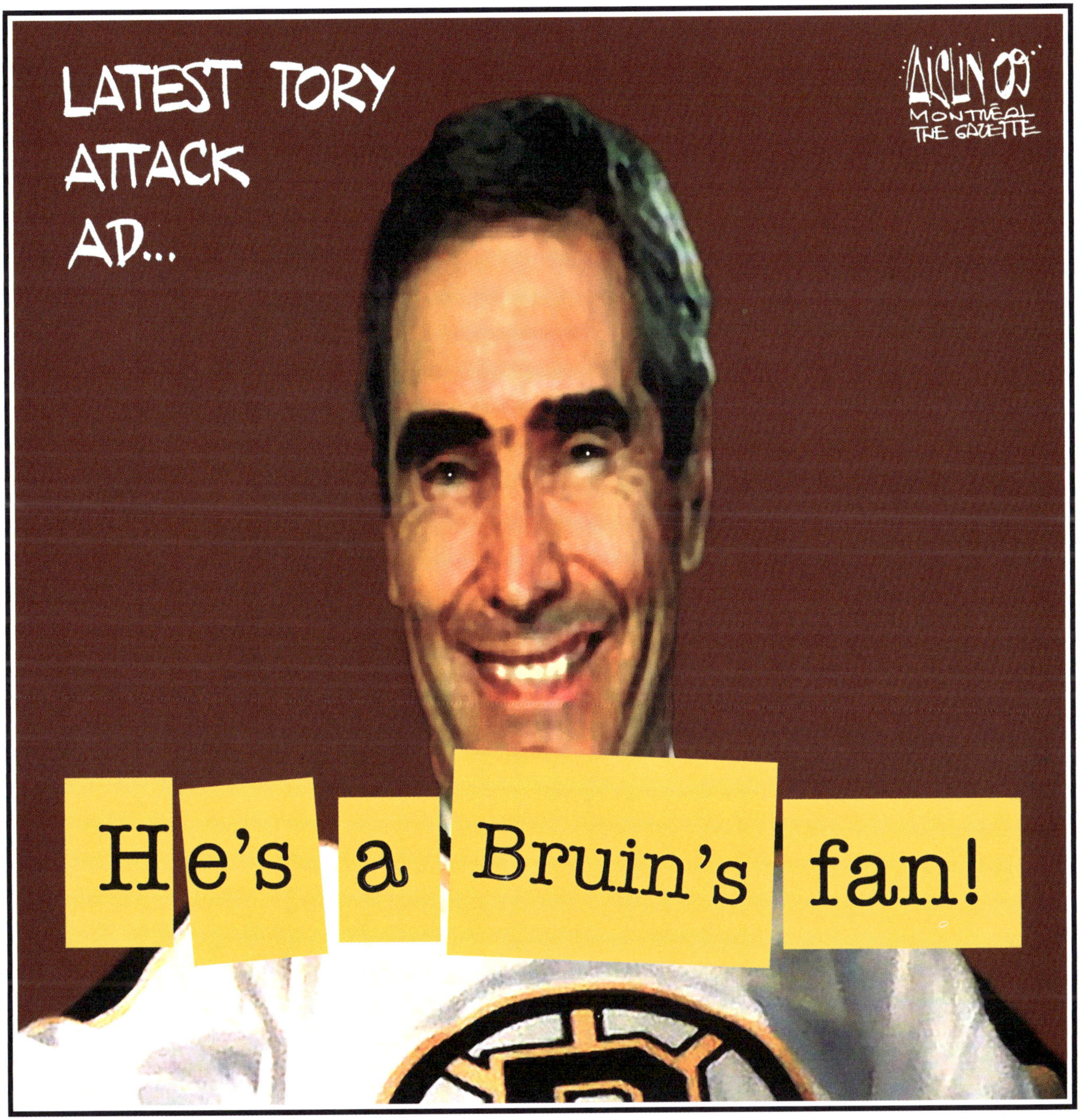
LATEST TORY ATTACK AD...
AISLIN 09 MONTRÉAL THE GAZETTE
He's a Bruin's fan!

…and the attack ads begin again

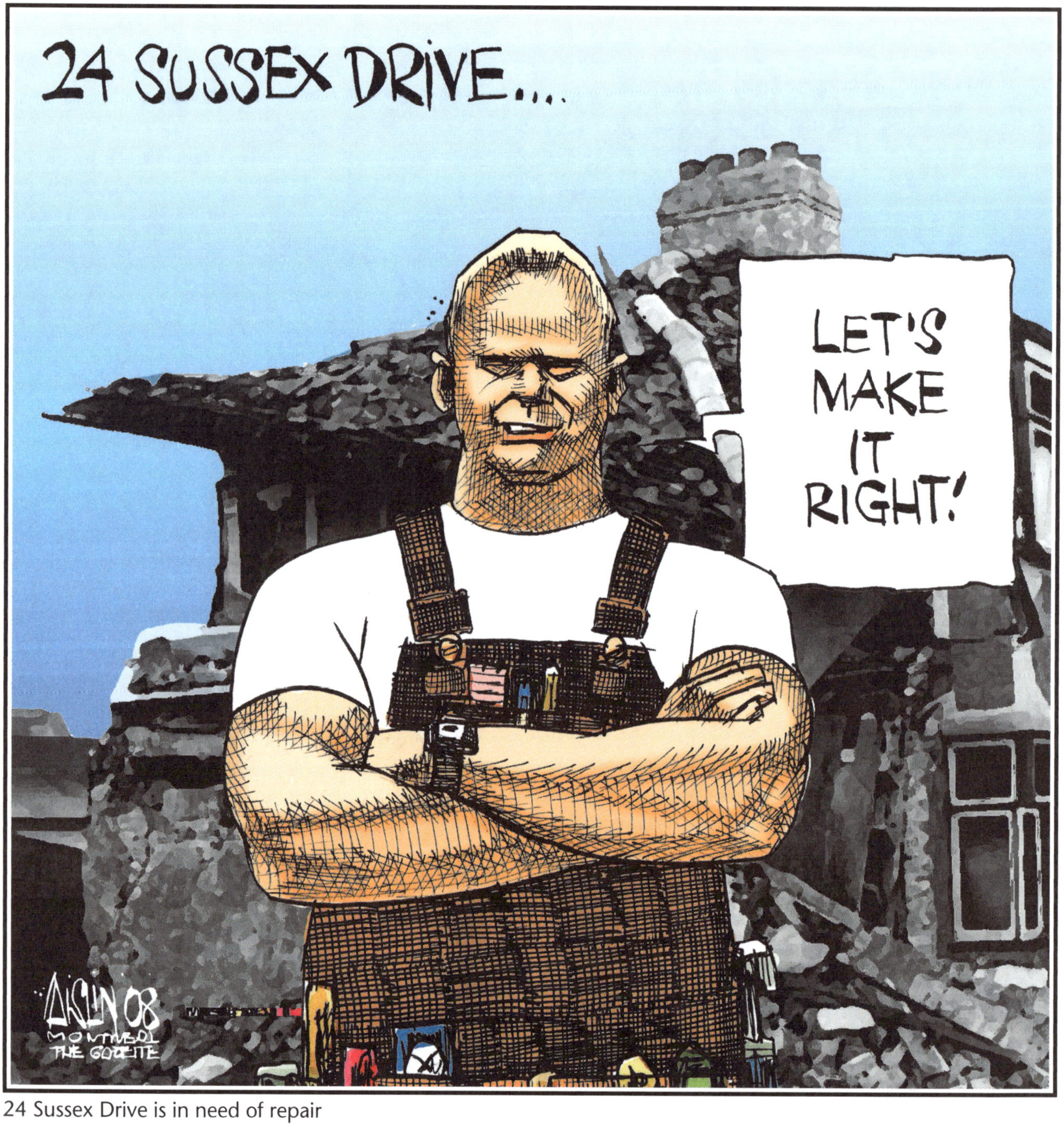
24 SUSSEX DRIVE....
LET'S MAKE IT RIGHT!
AISLIN 08 MONTREAL THE GAZETTE
24 Sussex Drive is in need of repair

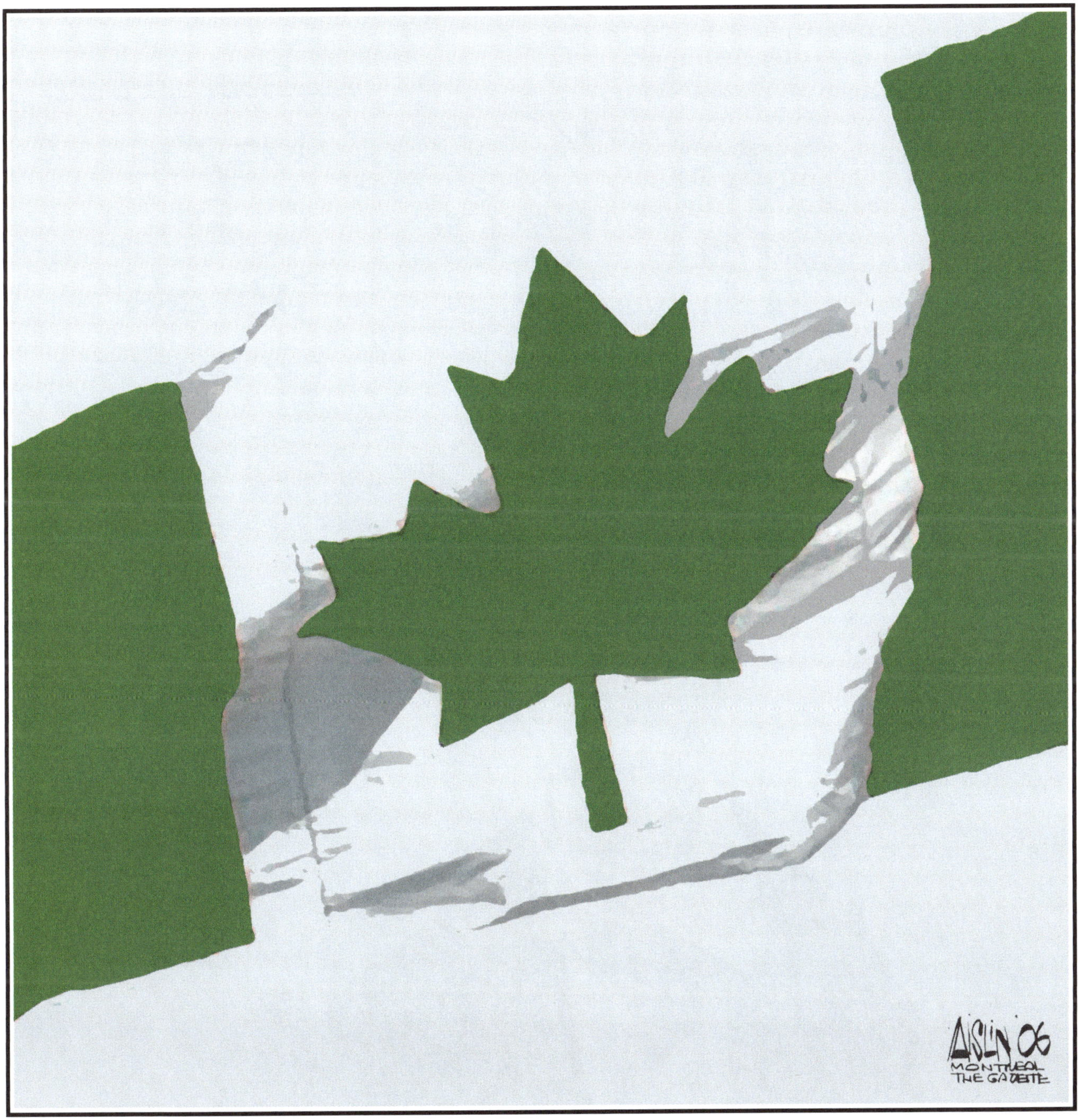
AISLIN '06
MONTREAL
THE GAZETTE
The Green Party of Canada

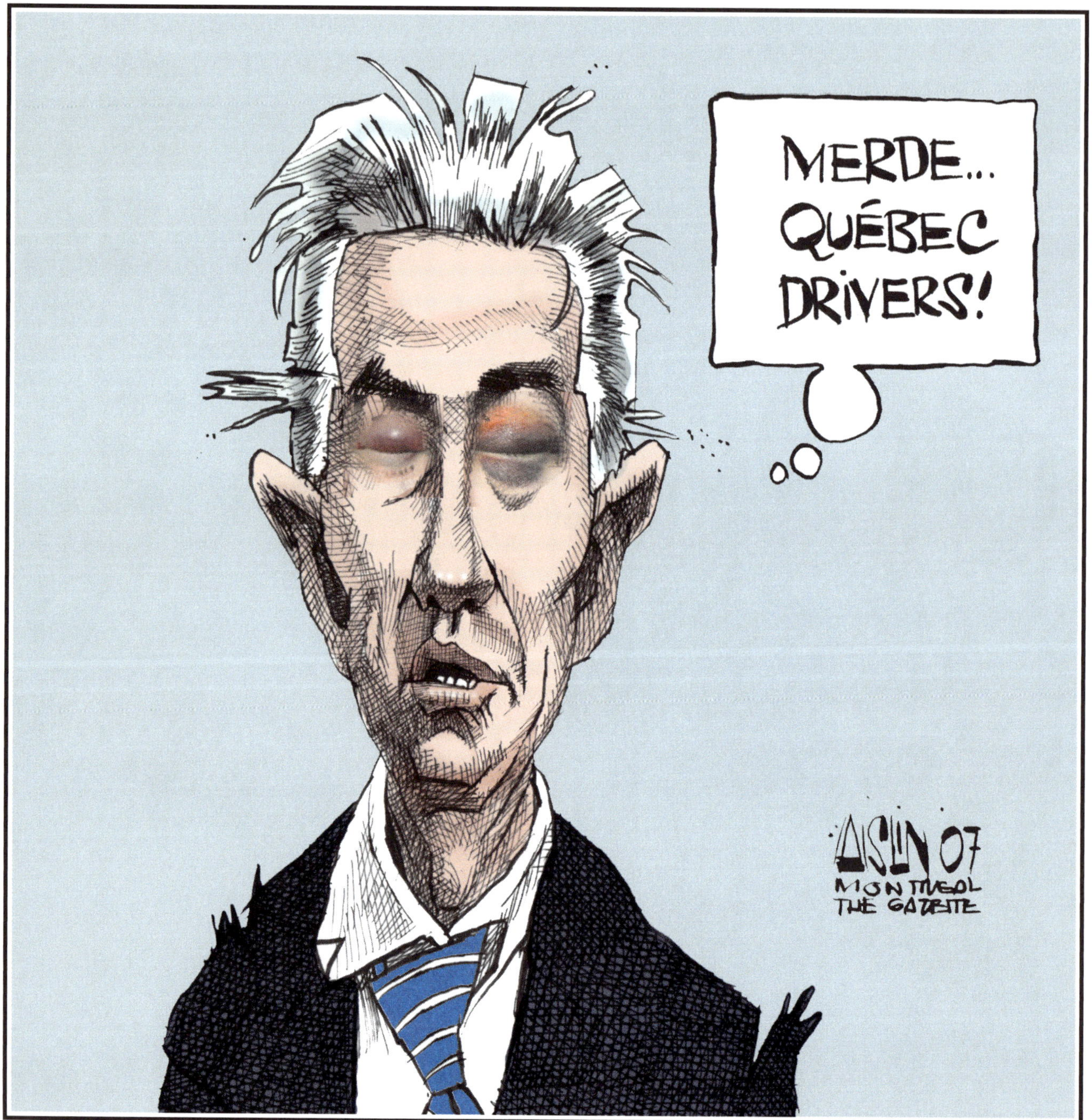
MERDE...
QUÉBEC
DRIVERS!
AISLIN 07
MONTREAL
THE GAZETTE

Gilles Duceppe thinks briefly of returning to Quebec to become leader of the Parti Québécois…

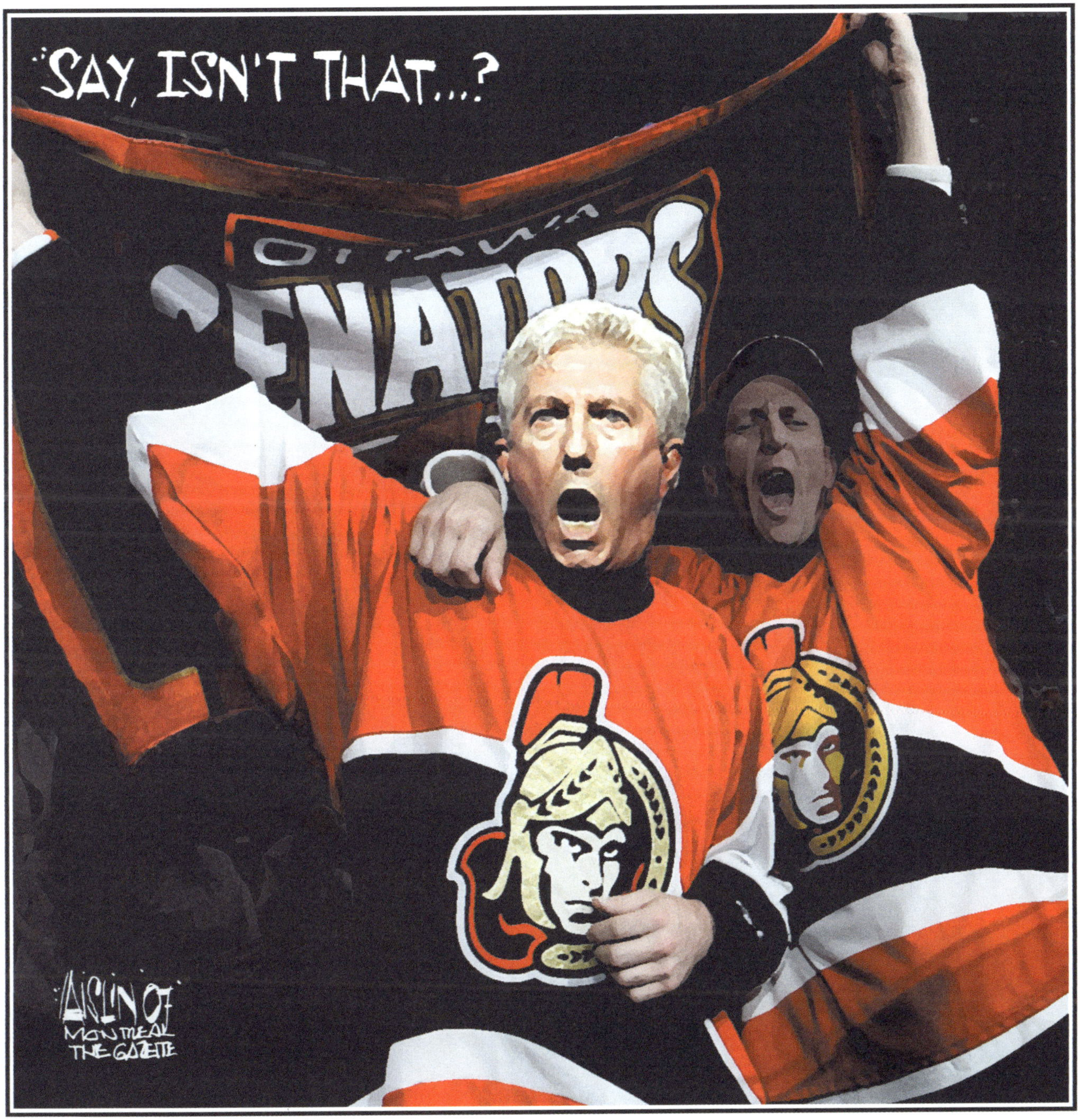
"SAY, ISN'T THAT...?
AISLIN 07
MONTREAL
THE GAZETTE

...but the scurries back to safe old Ottawa

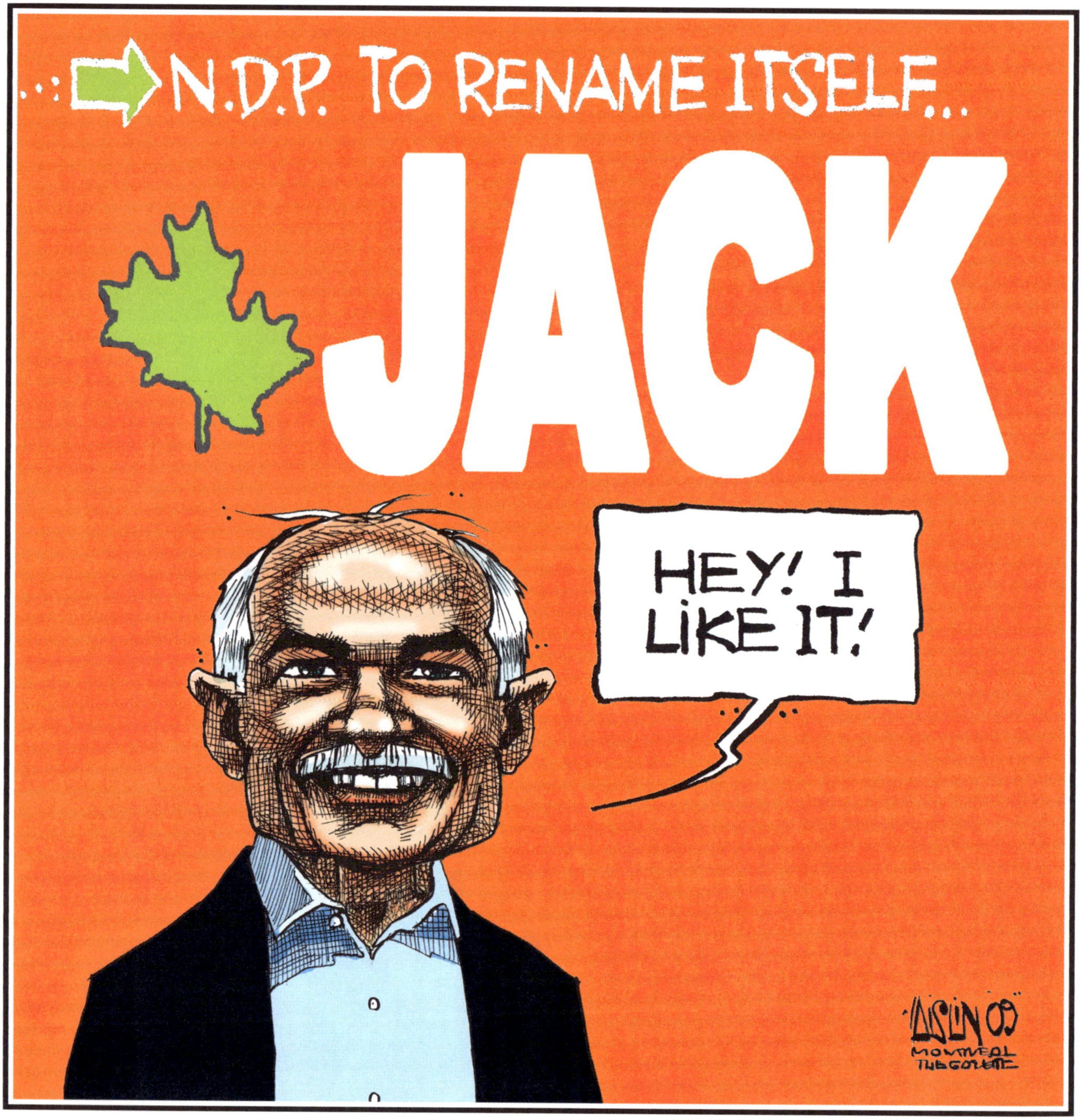
N.D.P. TO RENAME ITSELF...
JACK
HEY! I LIKE IT!
AISLIN 09
MONTREAL THE GAZETTE

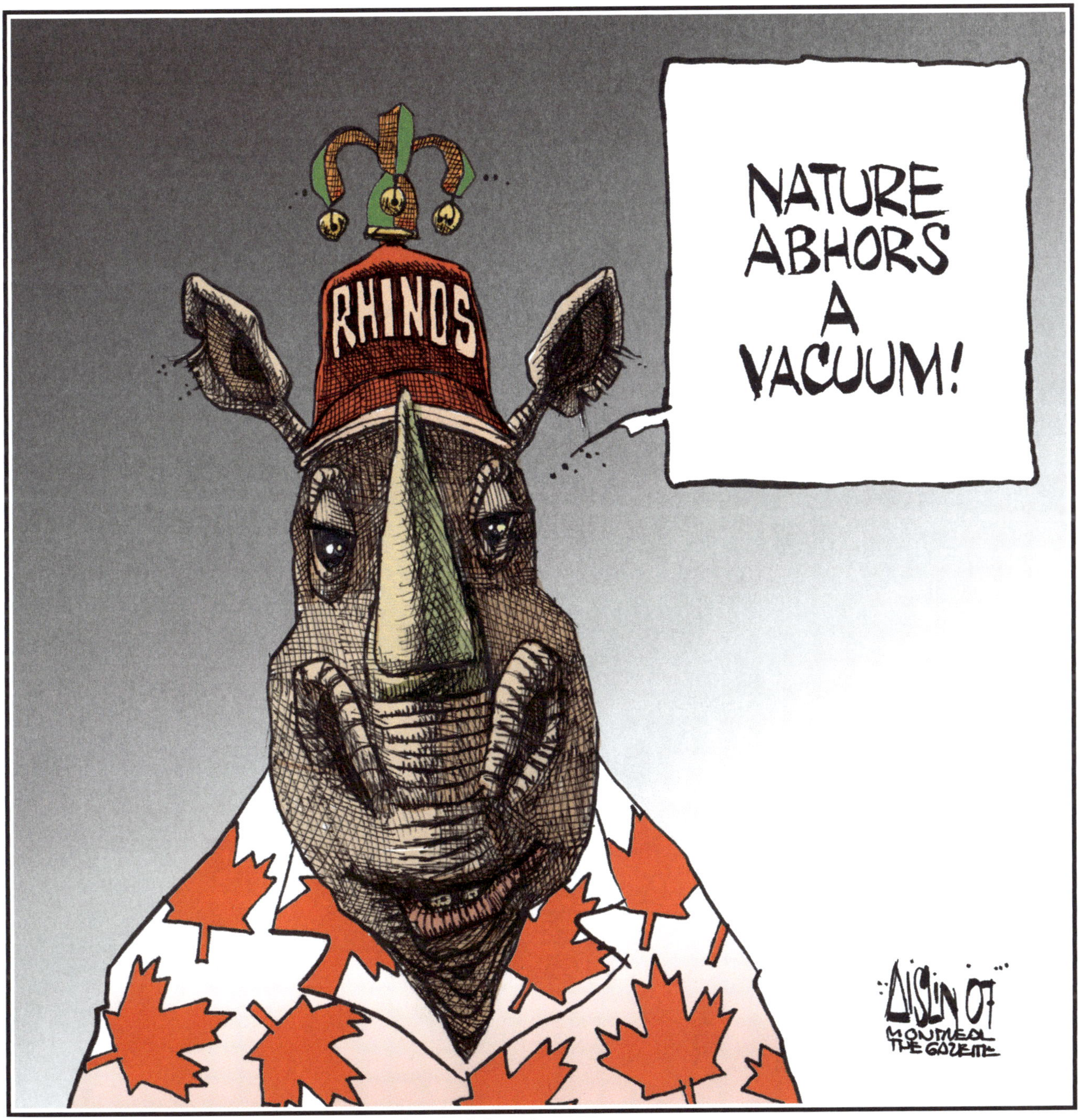
NATURE ABHORS A VACUUM!
RHINOS
AISLIN 07
MONTREAL THE GAZETTE
Where are the Rhinos when you really, really need them?

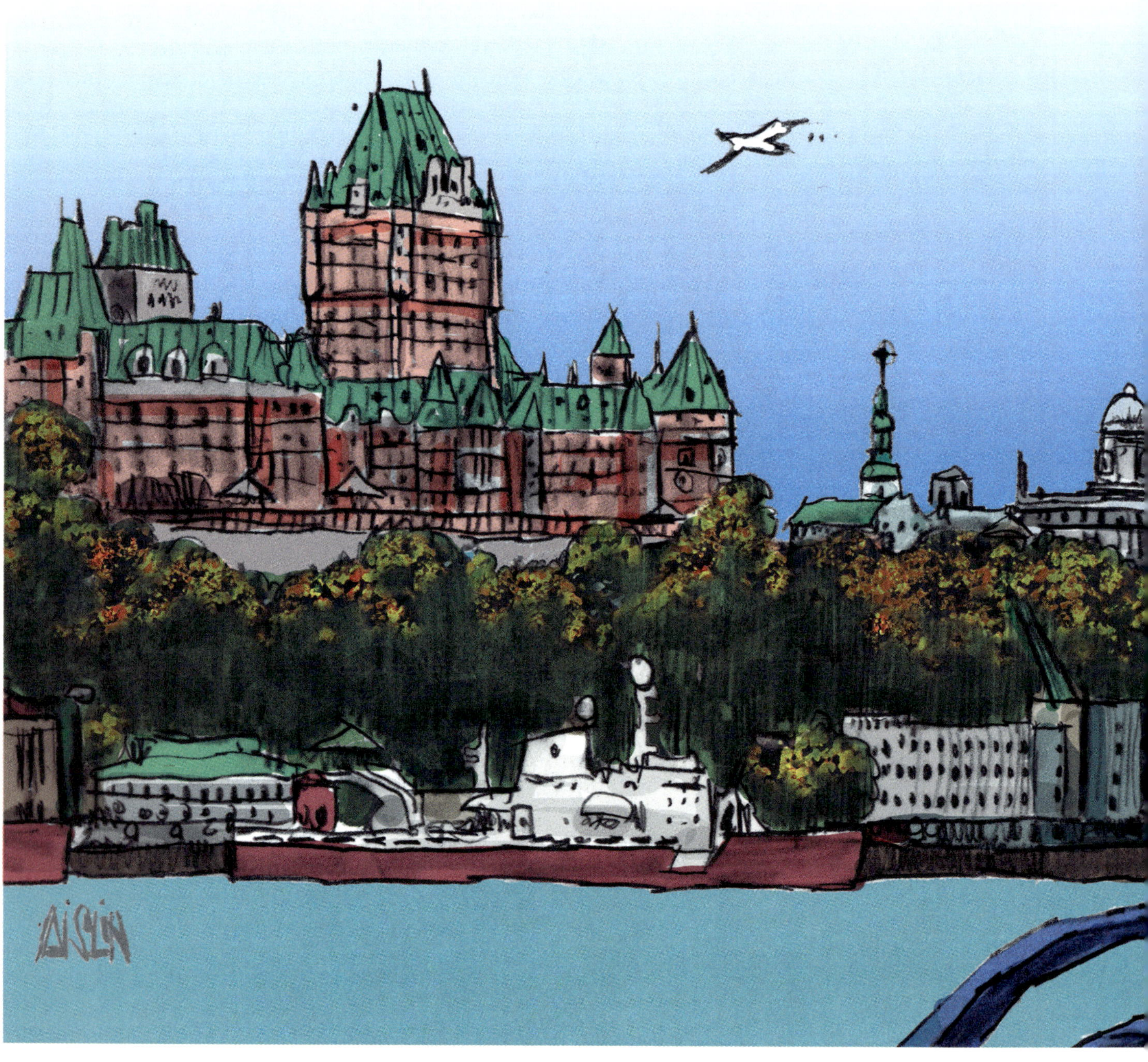
AISLIN

CHAPTER 3

I am a Quebecaholic

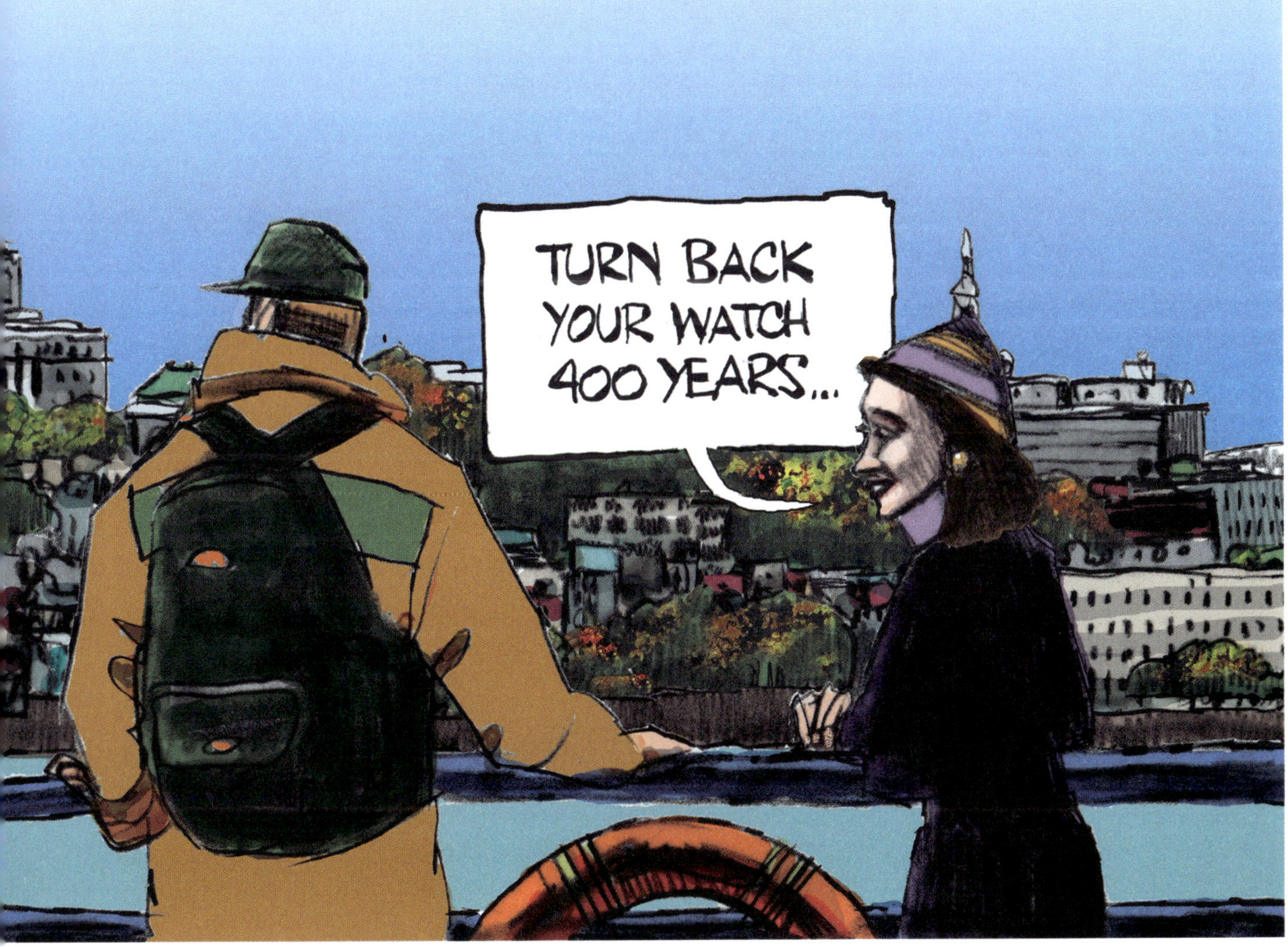
TURN BACK YOUR WATCH 400 YEARS...

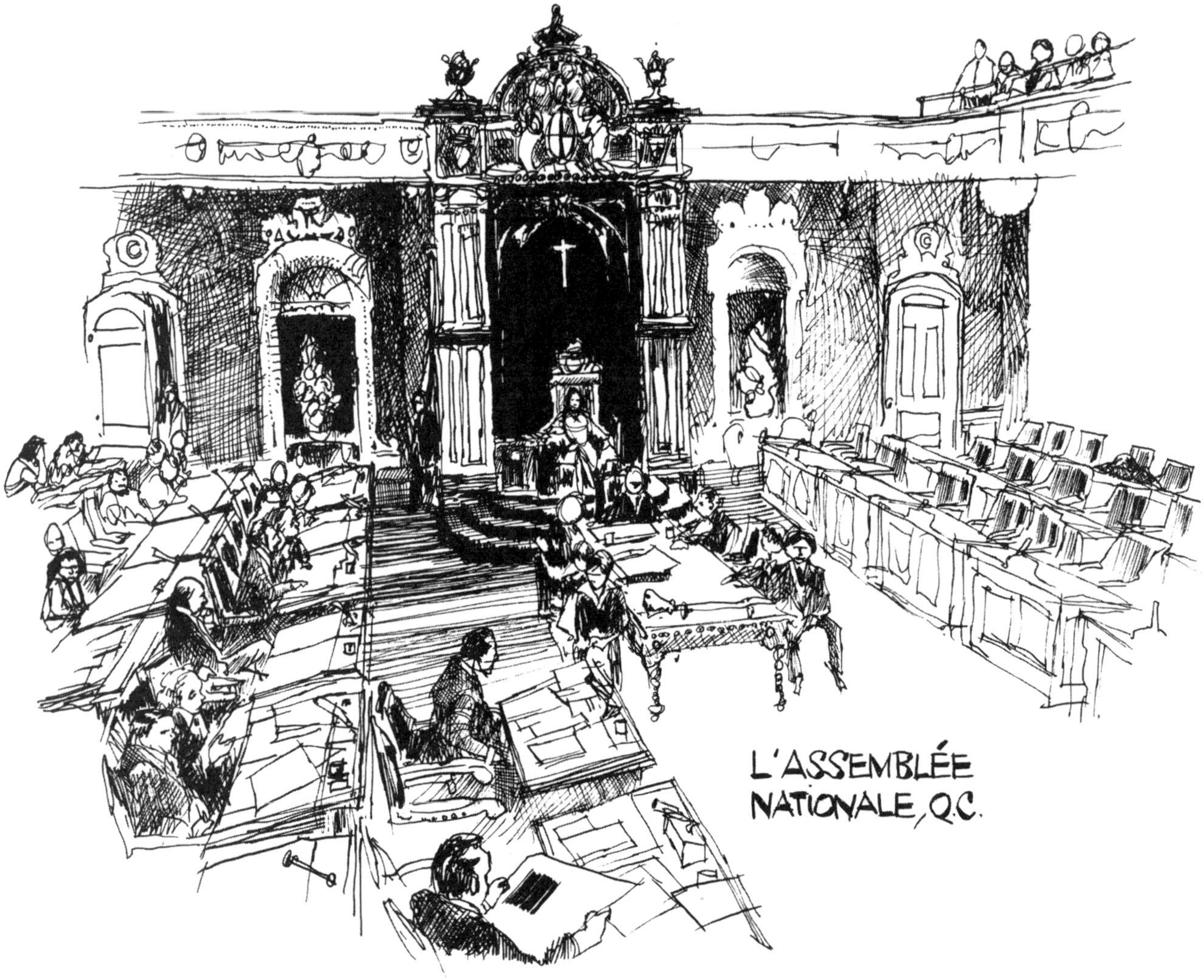
L'ASSEMBLÉE
NATIONALE, Q.C.

My entire professional career as a cartoonist has been spent in Quebec. I am addicted to this place – it's the most innately political environment in all of Canada.

My newspaper – The Gazette – has sent me to Quebec City on a number of occasions over the years to prepare sketchbooks. I've enjoyed the opportunity because Quebec City is where I got started: I studied at l'École des beaux-arts and during the summers, plied my trade in the local artist's alley, la rue du Trésor, before moving up the river to Montreal to work as a cartoonist.

In 2008, Quebec City threw a glorious

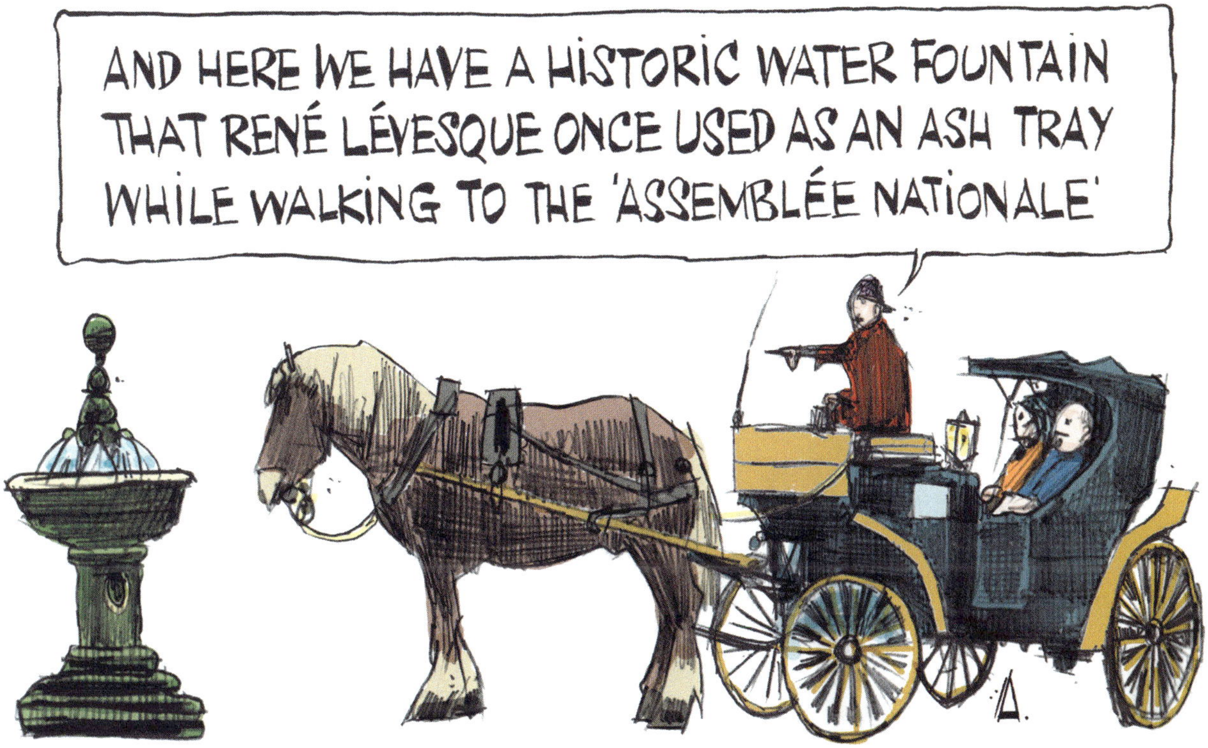
AND HERE WE HAVE A HISTORIC WATER FOUNTAIN THAT RENÉ LÉVESQUE ONCE USED AS AN ASH TRAY WHILE WALKING TO THE 'ASSEMBLÉE NATIONALE'

birthday party to celebrate the 400th anniversary of its founding by Samuel de Champlain. However, many nationalists balked at the idea of re-enacting the defeat of French forces on the Plains of Abraham 250 years earlier, so the event was cancelled. A local radio station saved the day, dreaming up its own comedic re-enactment scenario – complete with water guns!

The Parti Québéois no longer seems the powerhouse it once was. It has jettisoned six different leaders since its founding and the process has always been nasty. In 2005, the PQ elected André Boisclair – young, hip and openly gay. However, he proved to be too cosmopolitan for the populace beyond the cities. Boisclair was forced to step down after losing the election of 2007, which toppled the PQ from its status as official opposition to third place. The ever-popular Pauline Marois returned from retirement to become the current leader.

Mario Dumont, the new leader of the opposition and head of the Action Démocratique du Québec, took advantage of the PQ's waning popularity and rode a

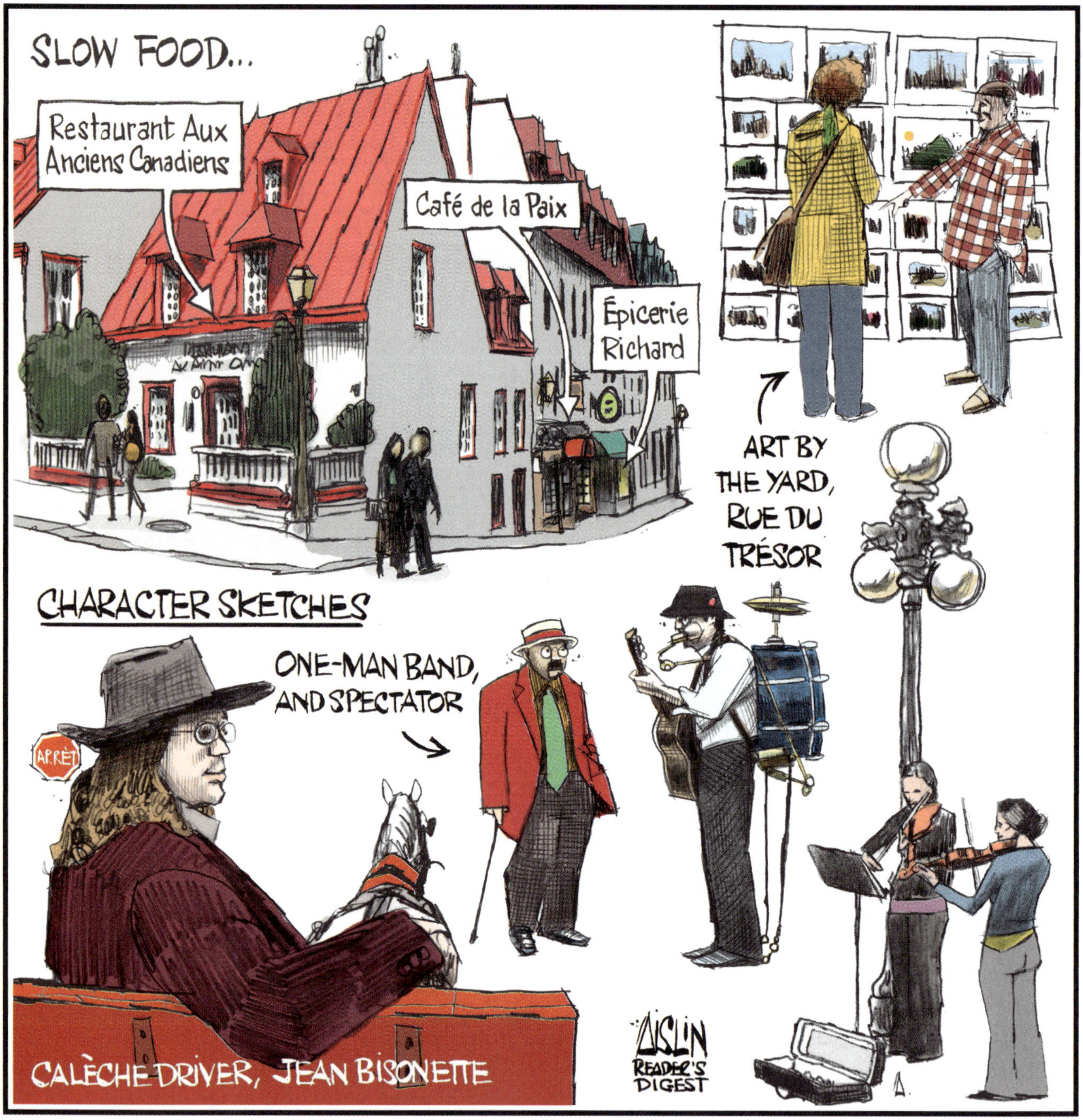
SLOW FOOD...
Restaurant Aux Anciens Canadiens
Café de la Paix
Épicerie Richard
ART BY THE YARD, RUE DU TRÉSOR
CHARACTER SKETCHES
ONE-MAN BAND, AND SPECTATOR
ARRÊT
CALÈCHE DRIVER, JEAN BISONETTE
AISLIN
READER'S DIGEST

groundswell of support into the 2007 election, winning an astonishing 41 seats, with 31% of the popular vote. Unfortunately, the new members proved to be very short on actual talent. In the following year's snap election, the ADQ was virtually eliminated.

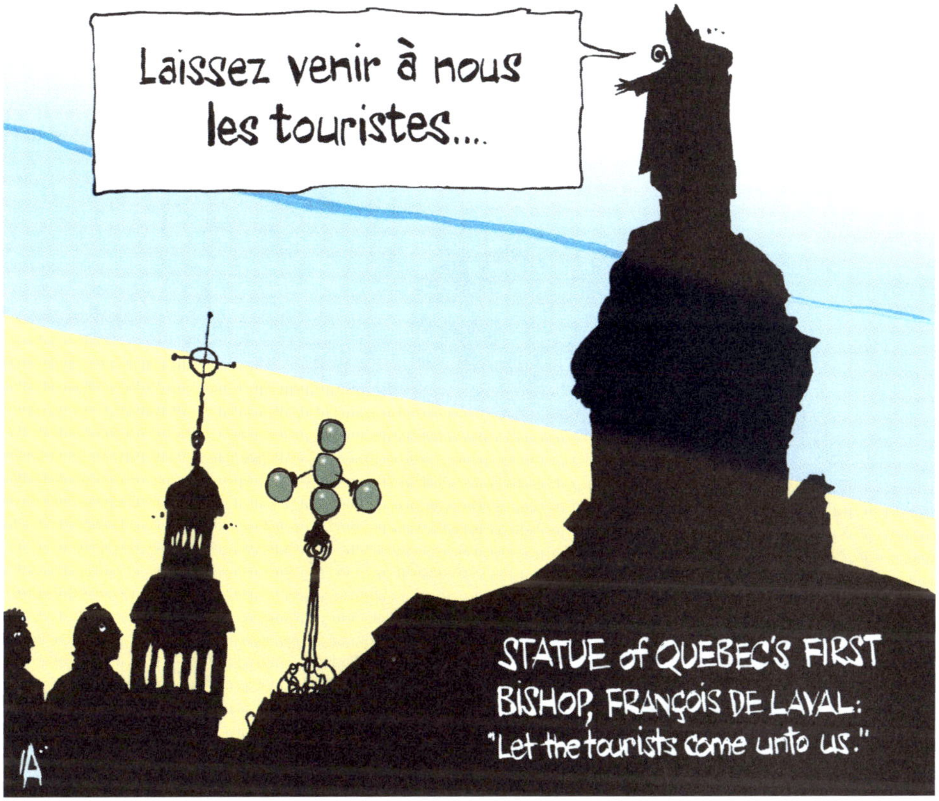
Laissez venir à nous les touristes....
STATUE of QUEBEC'S FIRST BISHOP, FRANÇOIS DE LAVAL: "Let the tourists come unto us."
IA

Jean Charest has ridden out all these storms to remain Quebec's Premier. He seems to have learned something from Robert Bourassa: his popularity increases the longer he remains in power.

Charest has weathered a number of controversial debates, including the especially delicate issue of the reasonable accommodation of minorities. The small Quebec town of Hérouxville had passed some controversial measures regarding the cultural practices of potential new immigrants. The uproar attracted international attention. In response, the Premier appointed the Taylor-Bouchard Royal Commission to investigate how the province was accommodating its minority populations. Much was said and written about intolerance, but Québec, like most places, tends to be far more open to minorities in its larger cities.

In the meantime, Quebec's Anglophone population seems to have accepted its role as a minority within a minority within a minority, only grumbling occasionally about some language dispute or other. Of late, Montreal's West Island Anglos have been more worried about the trains running on time to downtown – and the disappearance of their life savings under the stewardship of disgraced financial advisor Earl Jones.

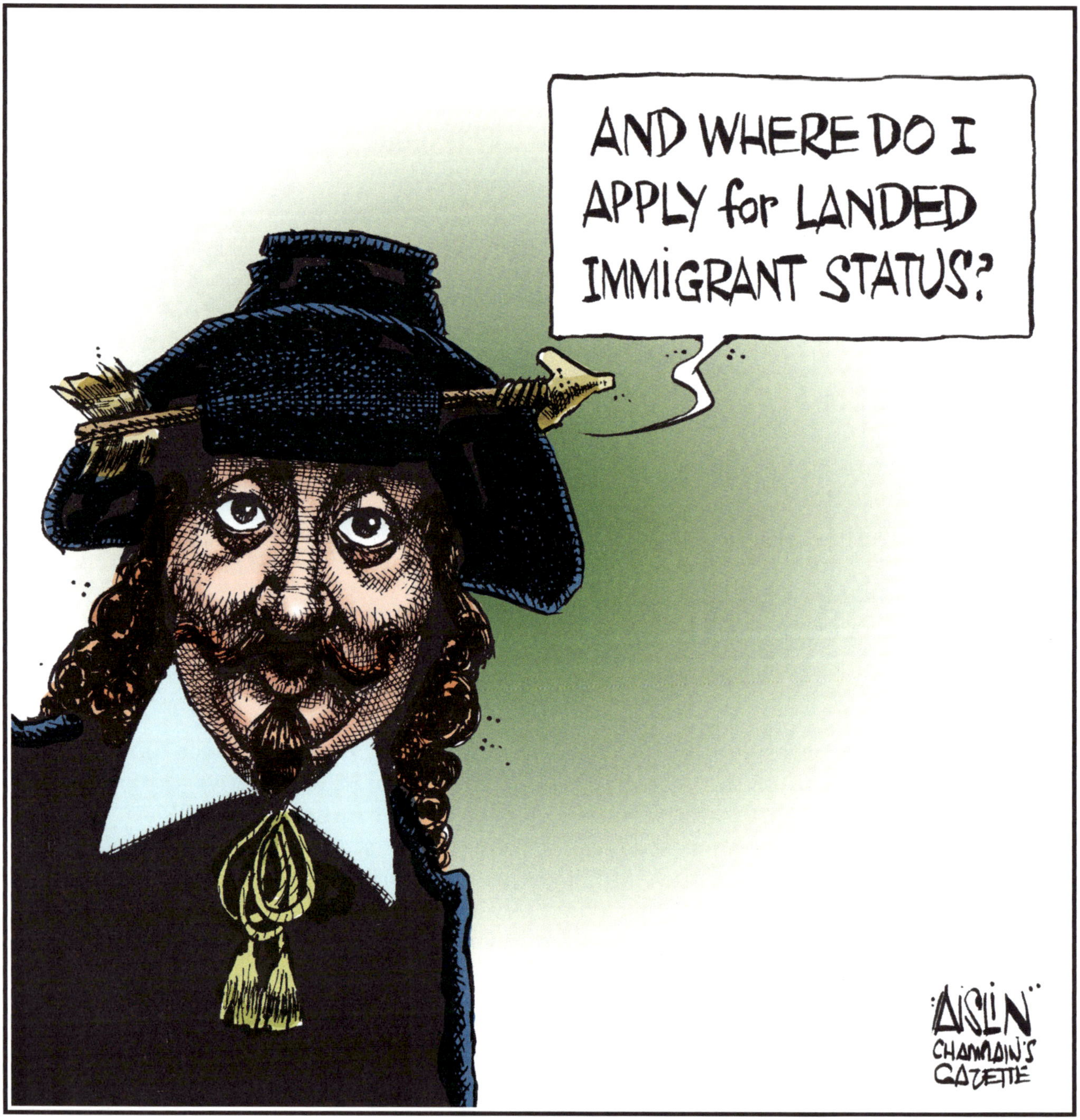
AND WHERE DO I APPLY for LANDED IMMIGRANT STATUS?
AISLIN
CHAMPLAIN'S GAZETTE

4ooth anniversary of Samuel de Champlain's arrival in Quebec

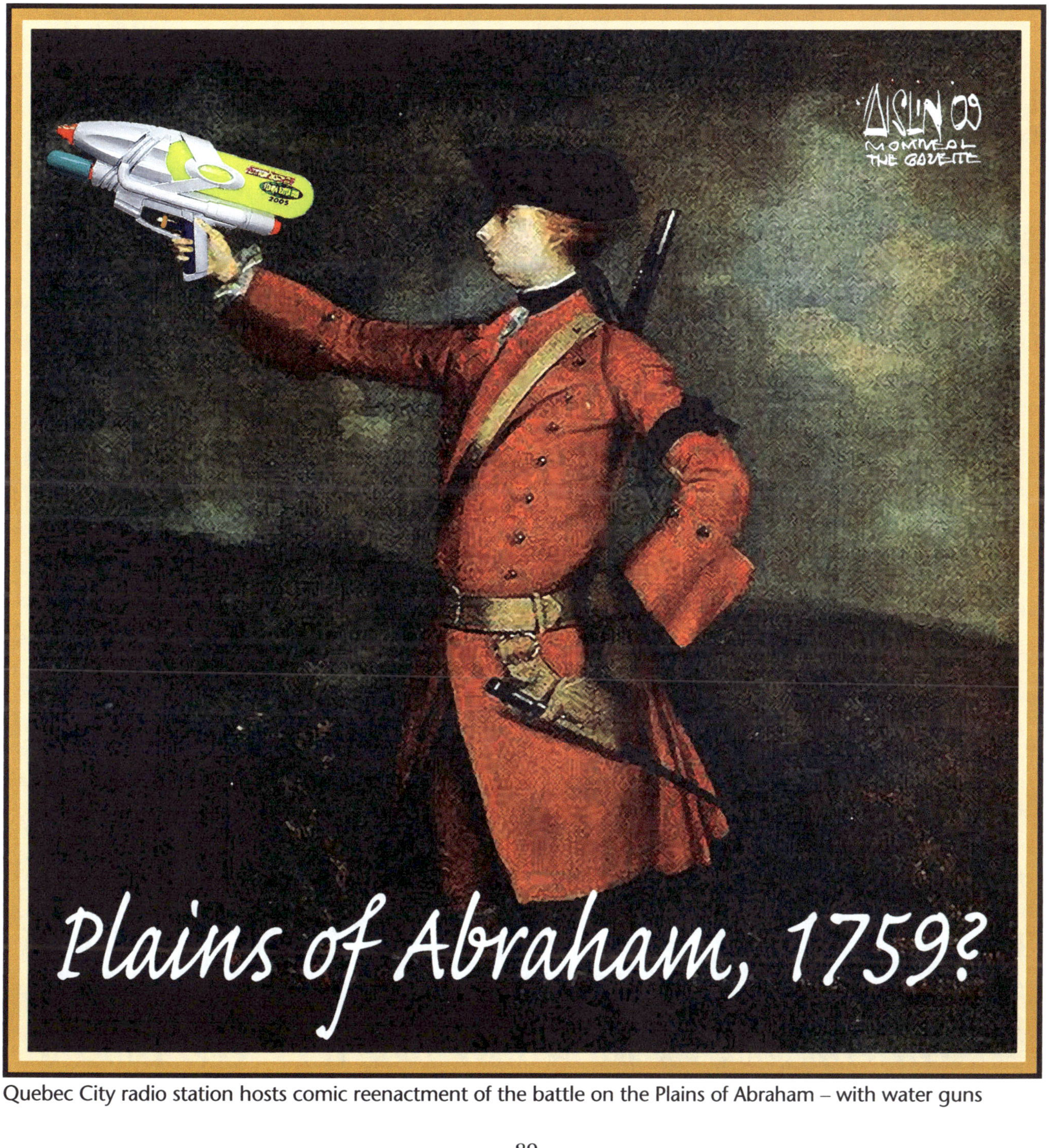
Plains of Abraham, 1759?

Quebec City radio station hosts comic reenactment of the battle on the Plains of Abraham – with water guns

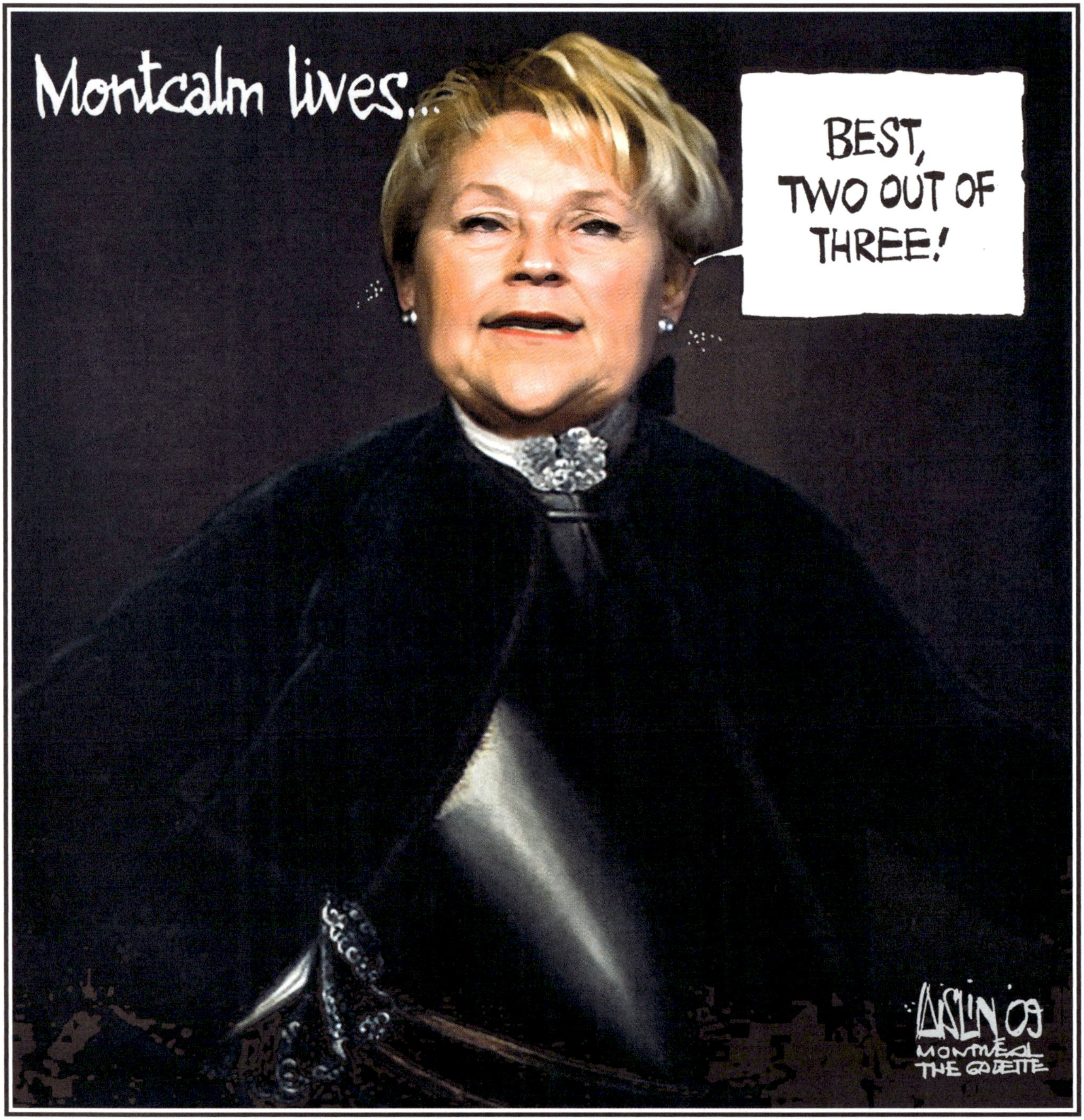
Montcalm lives...
BEST, TWO OUT OF THREE!
AISLIN 09
MONTREAL THE GAZETTE

And if Quebec nationalists were to host a legitimate reenactment of the battle of the Plains of Abraham?

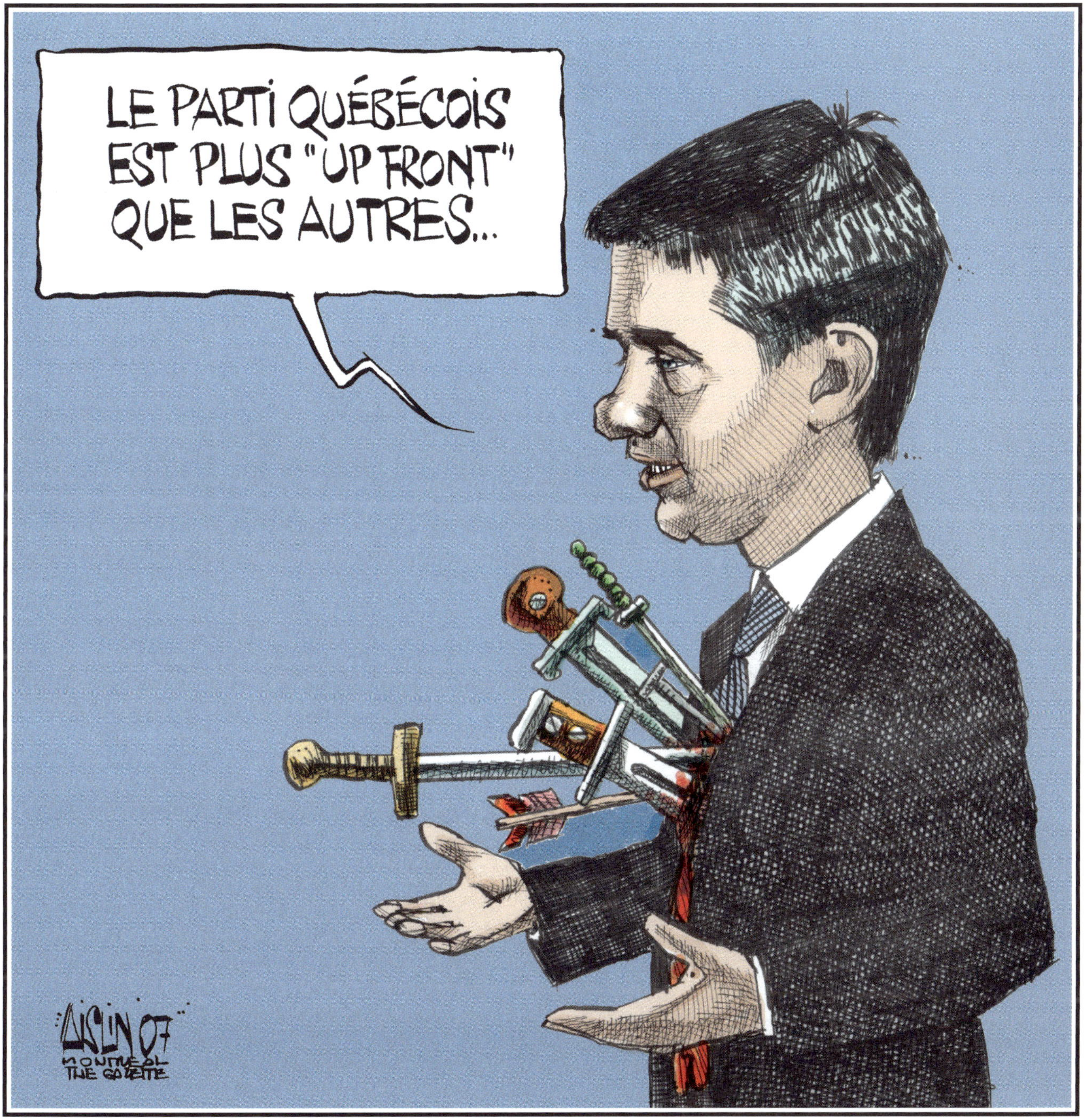
LE PARTI QUÉBÉCOIS EST PLUS "UP FRONT" QUE LES AUTRES...
AISLIN 07
MONTREAL THE GAZETTE
André Boisclair, the ever-so-brief leader of the Parti Québécois

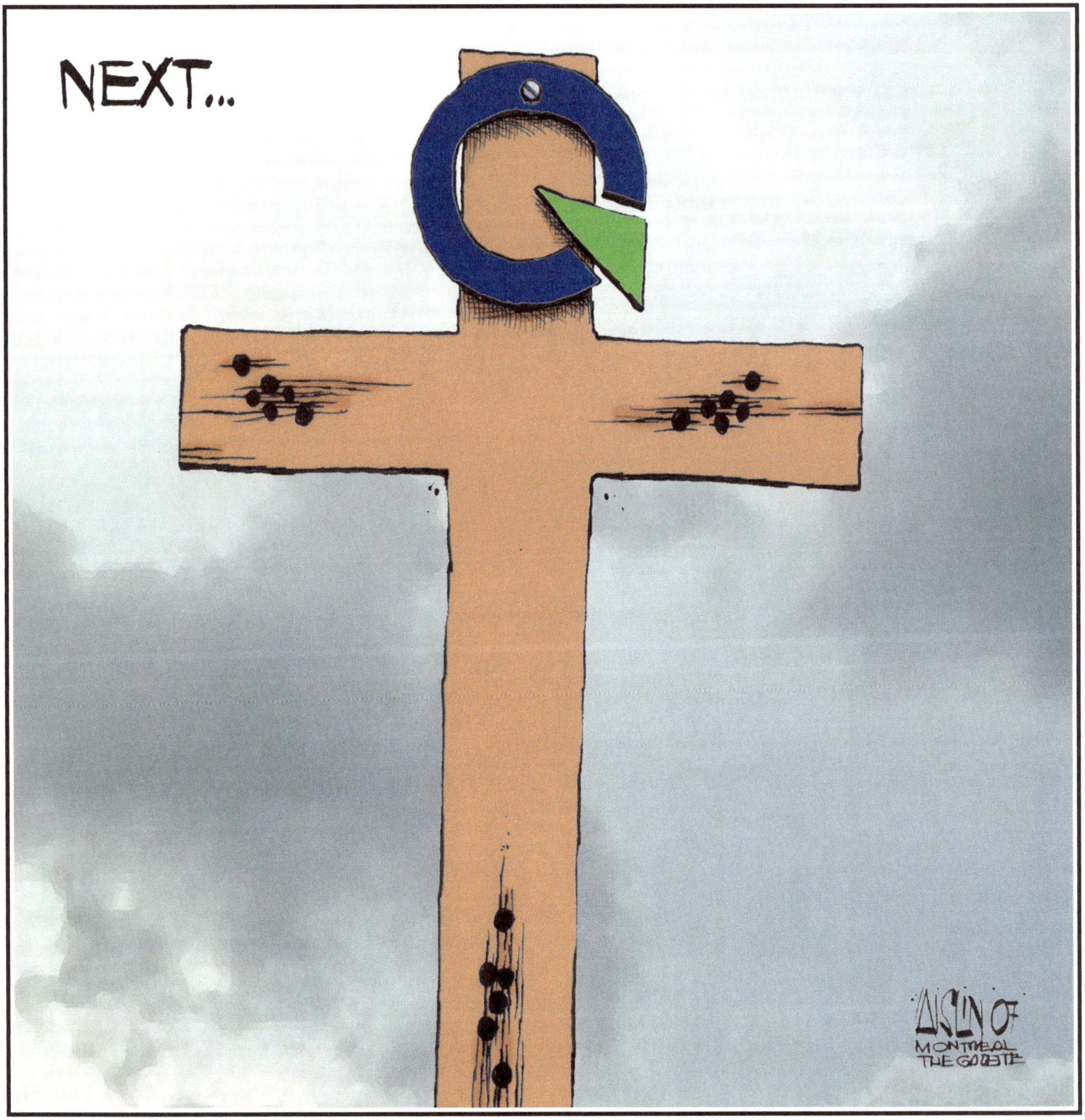
NEXT...
AISLIN OF MONTREAL THE GAZETTE

Le Parti Québécois: Six leaders, six sets of nail holes

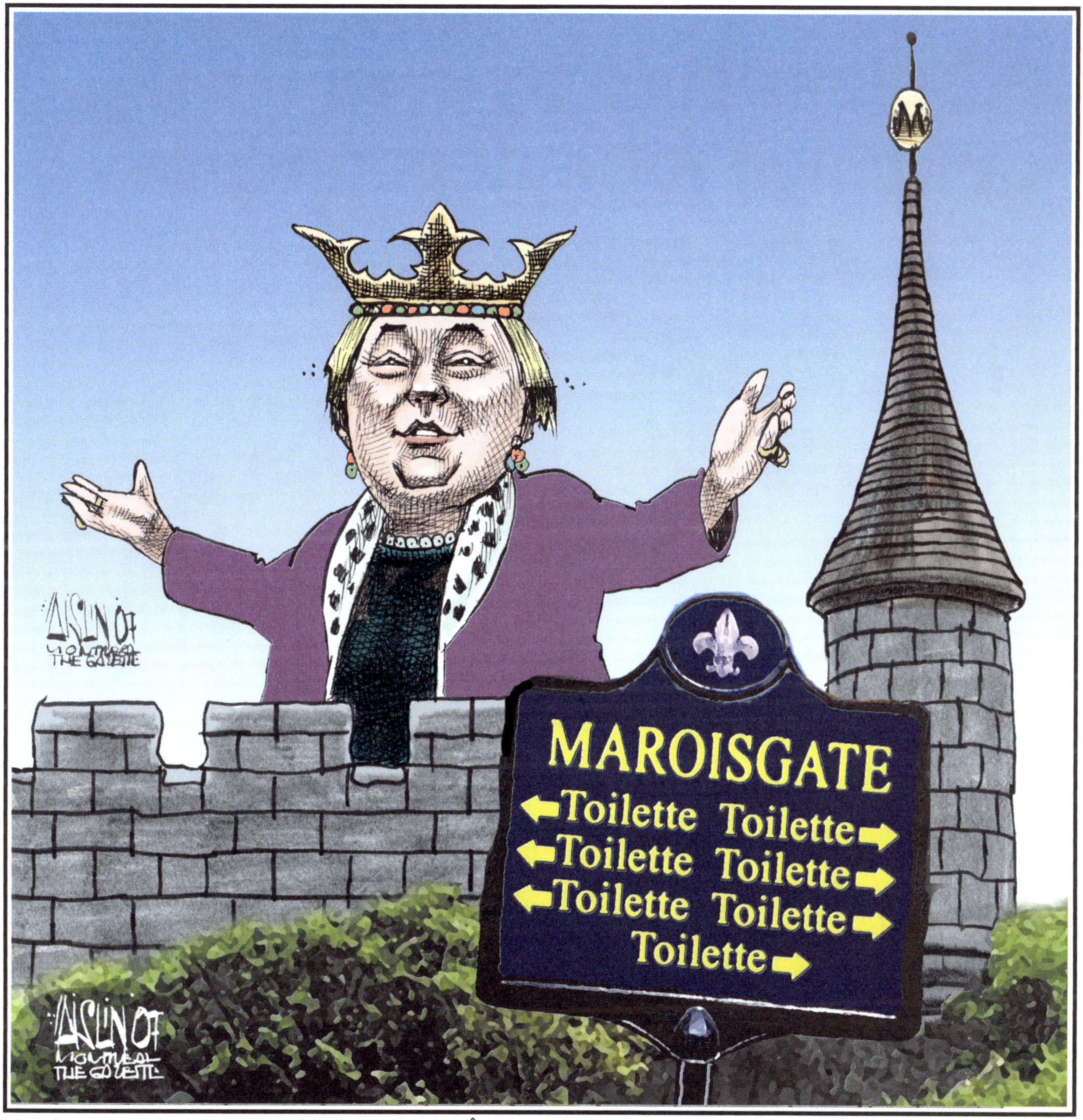
MAROISGATE
Toilette Toilette
Toilette Toilette
Toilette Toilette
Toilette
New Parti Québécois leader Pauline Marois in her Île Bizard mansion

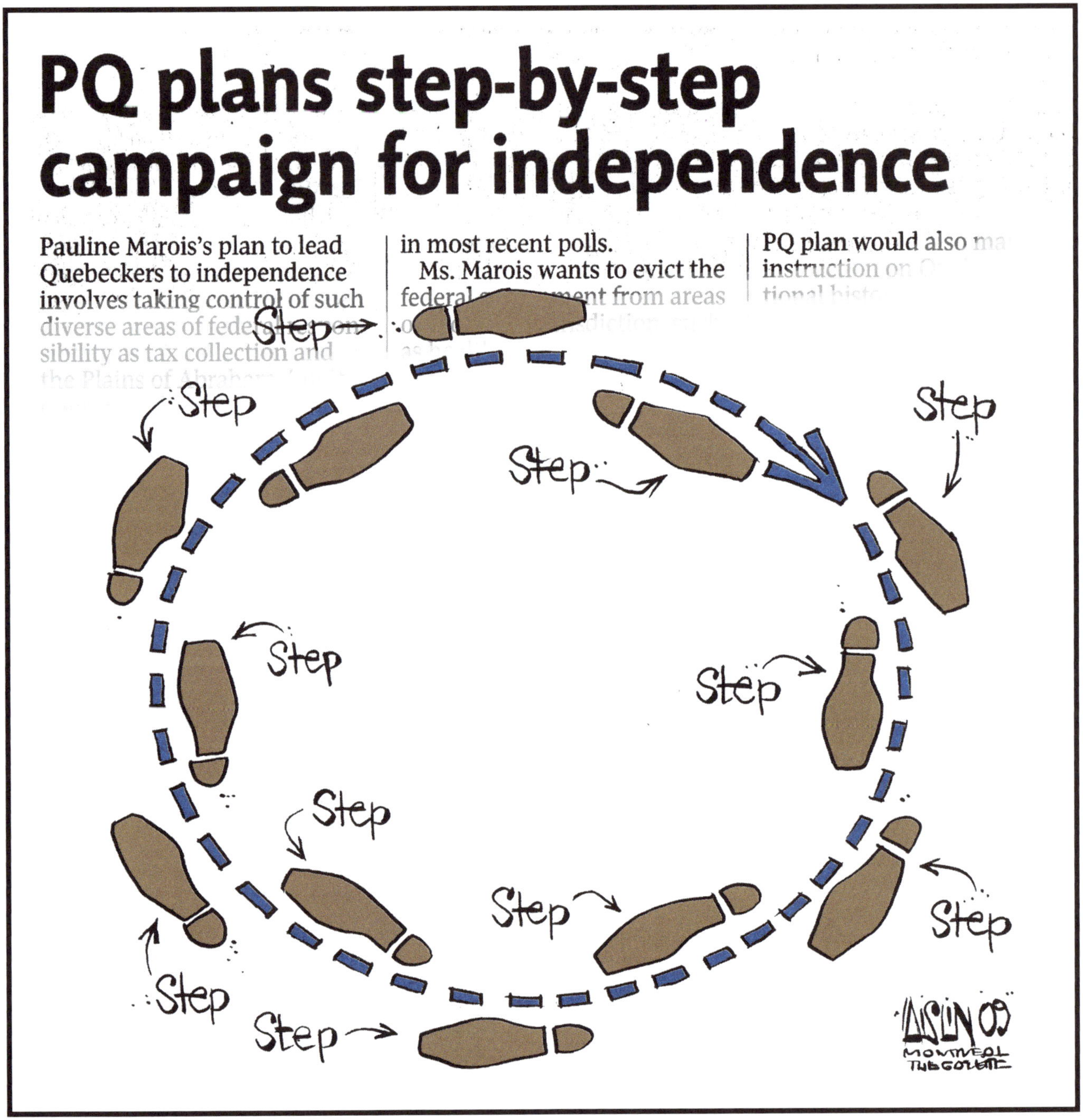
PQ plans step-by-step campaign for independence
Pauline Marois's plan to lead Quebeckers to independence involves taking control of such diverse areas of federal responsibility as tax collection and
in most recent polls.
Ms. Marois wants to evict the federal government from areas
PQ plan would also
instruction on
Step
Step
Step
Step
Step
Step
Step
Step
Step
Step
Step
Step
AISLIN 09
MONTREAL THE GAZETTE

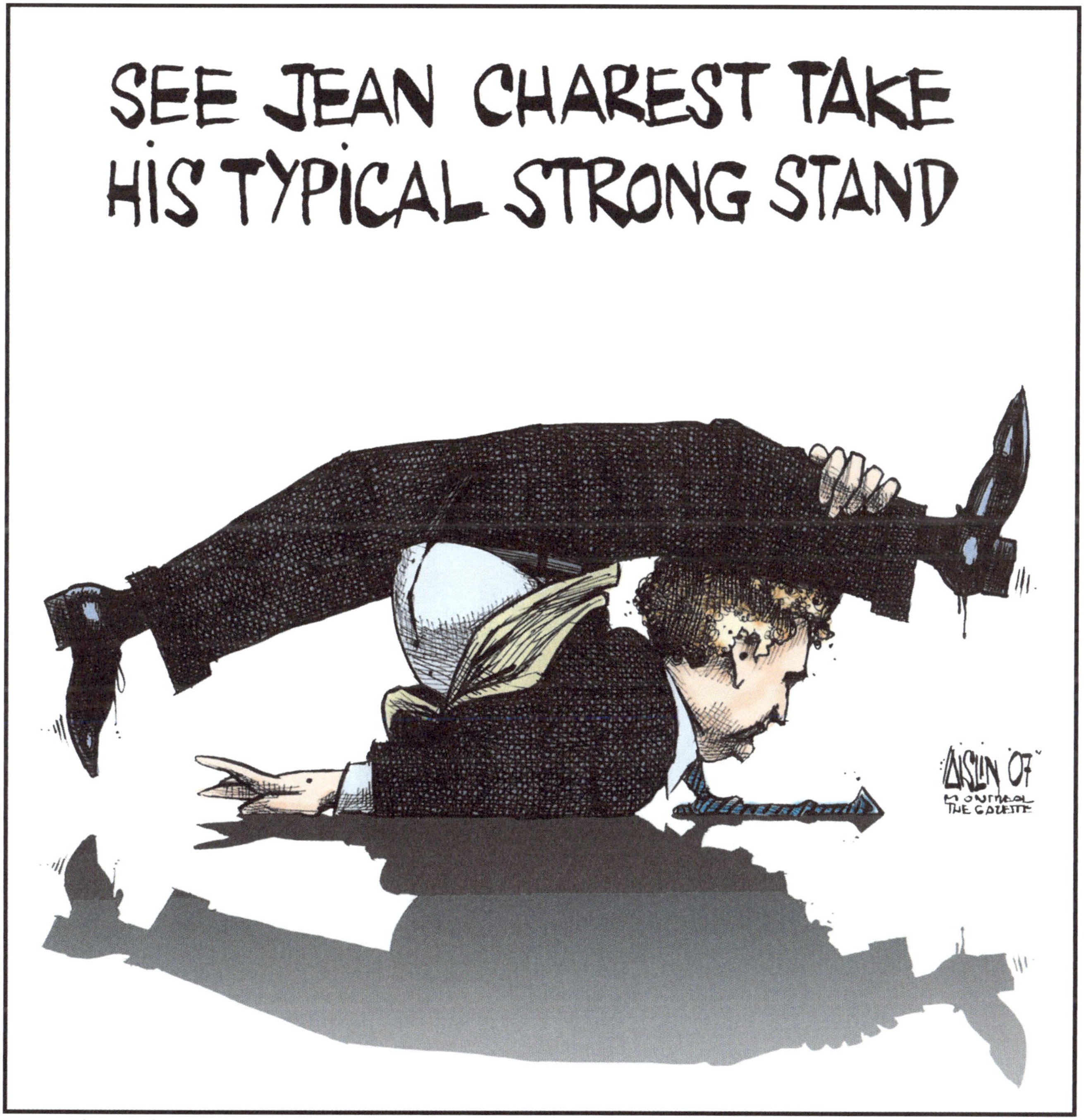
SEE JEAN CHAREST TAKE HIS TYPICAL STRONG STAND
AISLIN '07
MONTREAL THE GAZETTE

Is Jean Charest the new Robert Bourassa?

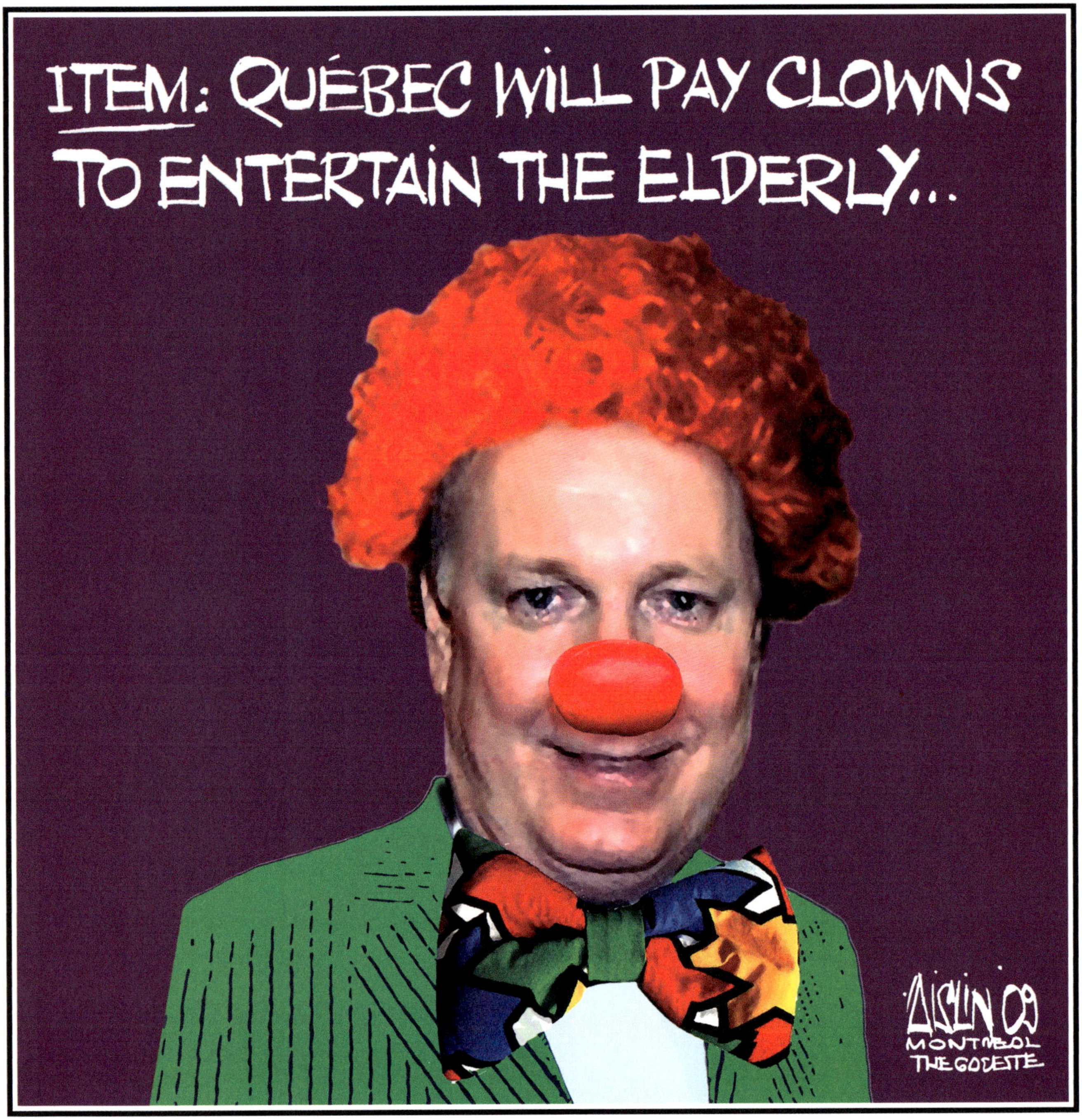
ITEM: QUÉBEC WILL PAY CLOWNS TO ENTERTAIN THE ELDERLY...
AISLIN 09
MONTREAL THE GAZETTE

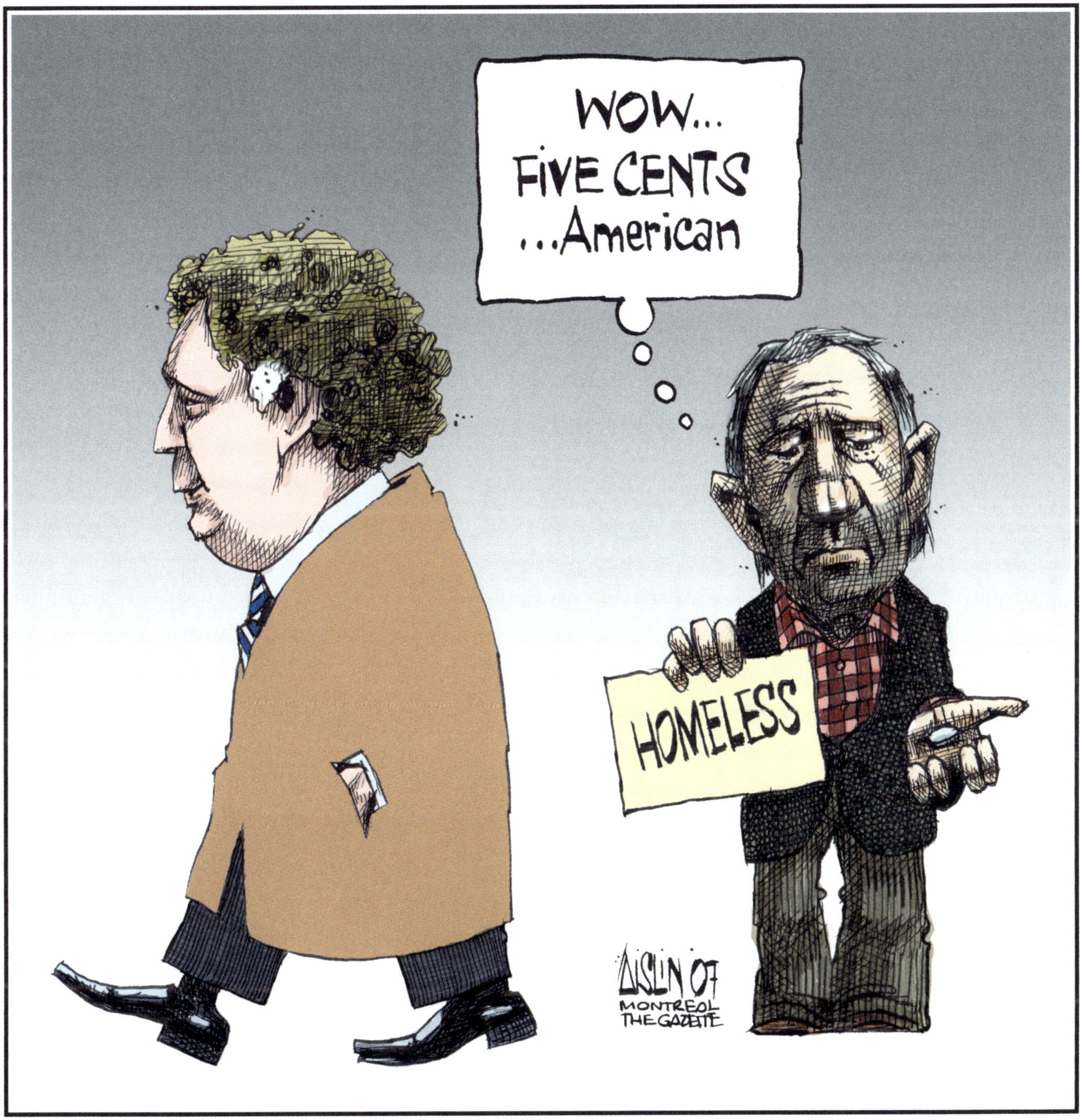
WOW...
FIVE CENTS
...American
HOMELESS
AISLIN '07
MONTREAL
THE GAZETTE

Quebec's record on funding for homeless is very poor

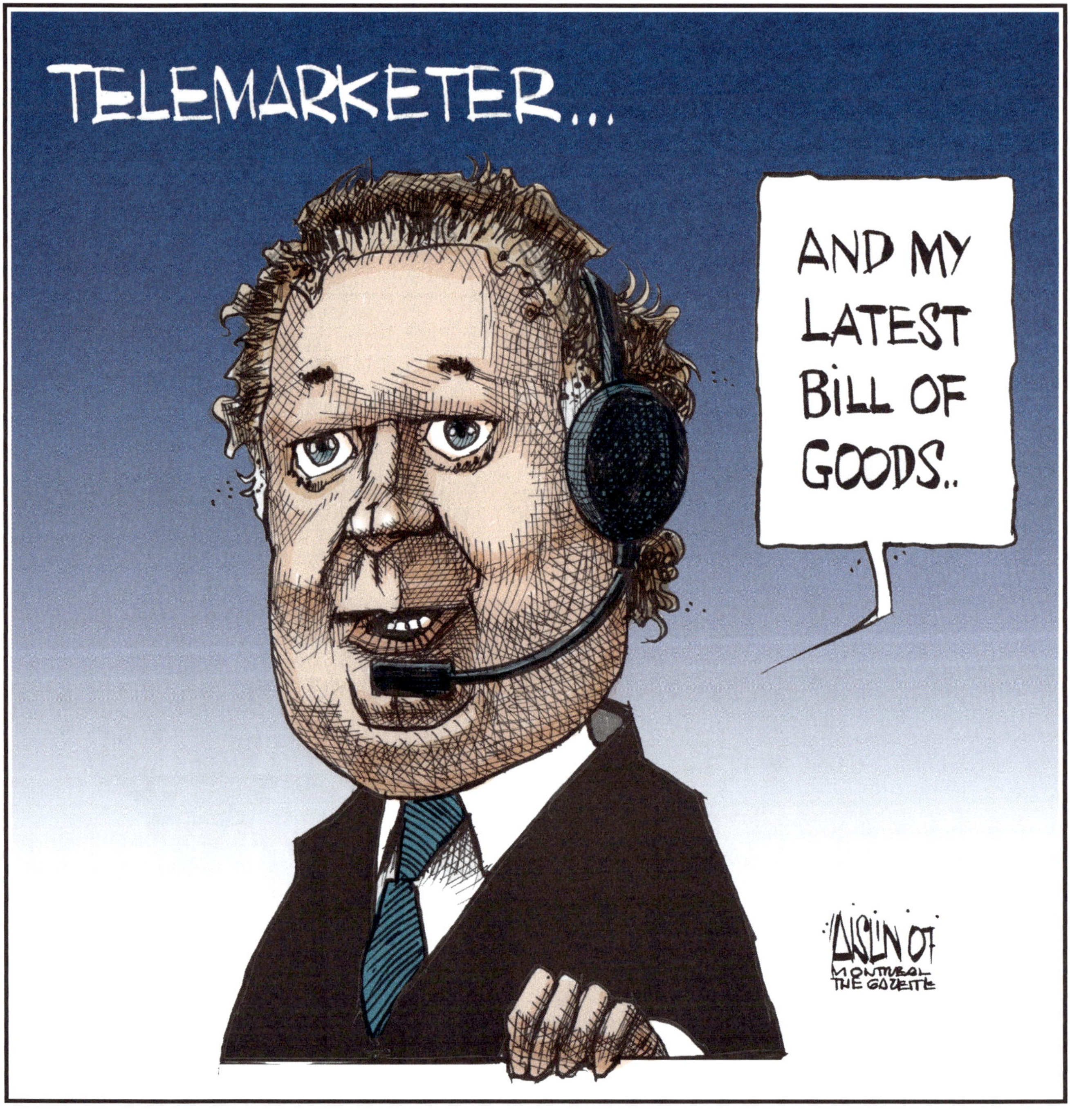
TELEMARKETER...
AND MY LATEST BILL OF GOODS..
AISLIN 07
MONTREAL THE GAZETTE

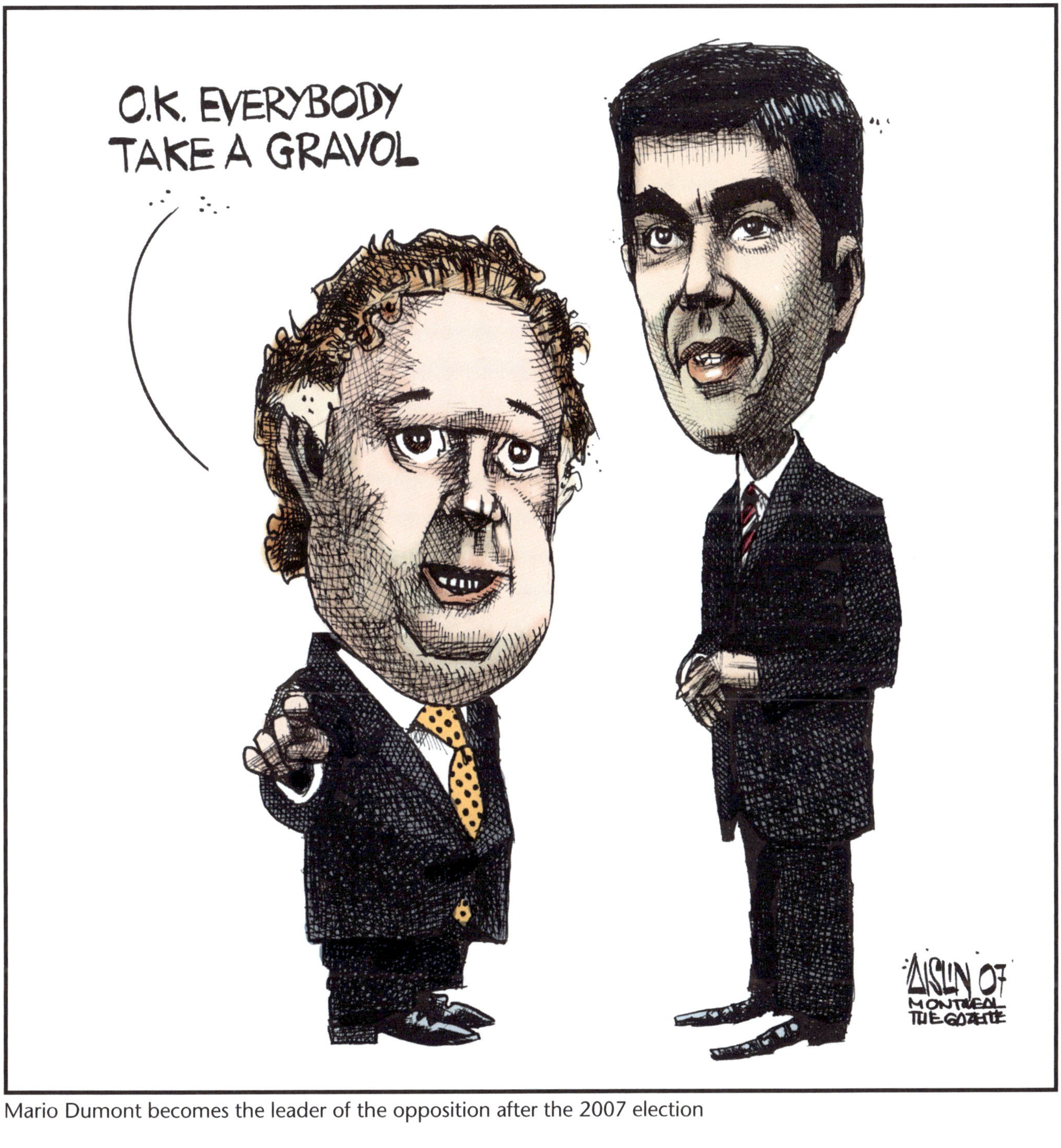
O.K. EVERYBODY
TAKE A GRAVOL

Mario Dumont becomes the leader of the opposition after the 2007 election

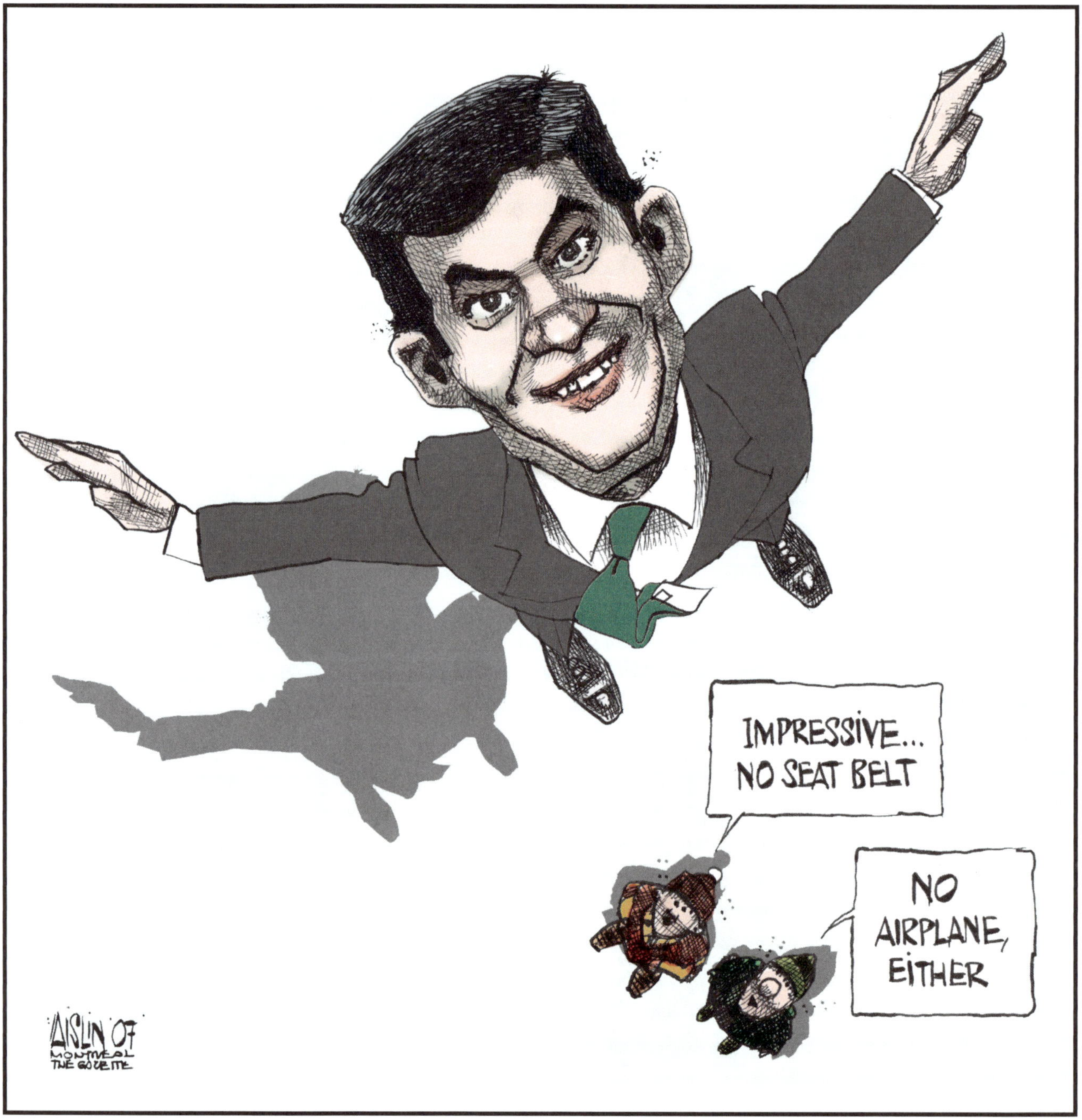
IMPRESSIVE...
NO SEAT BELT
NO AIRPLANE, EITHER
AISLIN 07
MONTREAL THE GAZETTE

After flying high for a brief period of time…

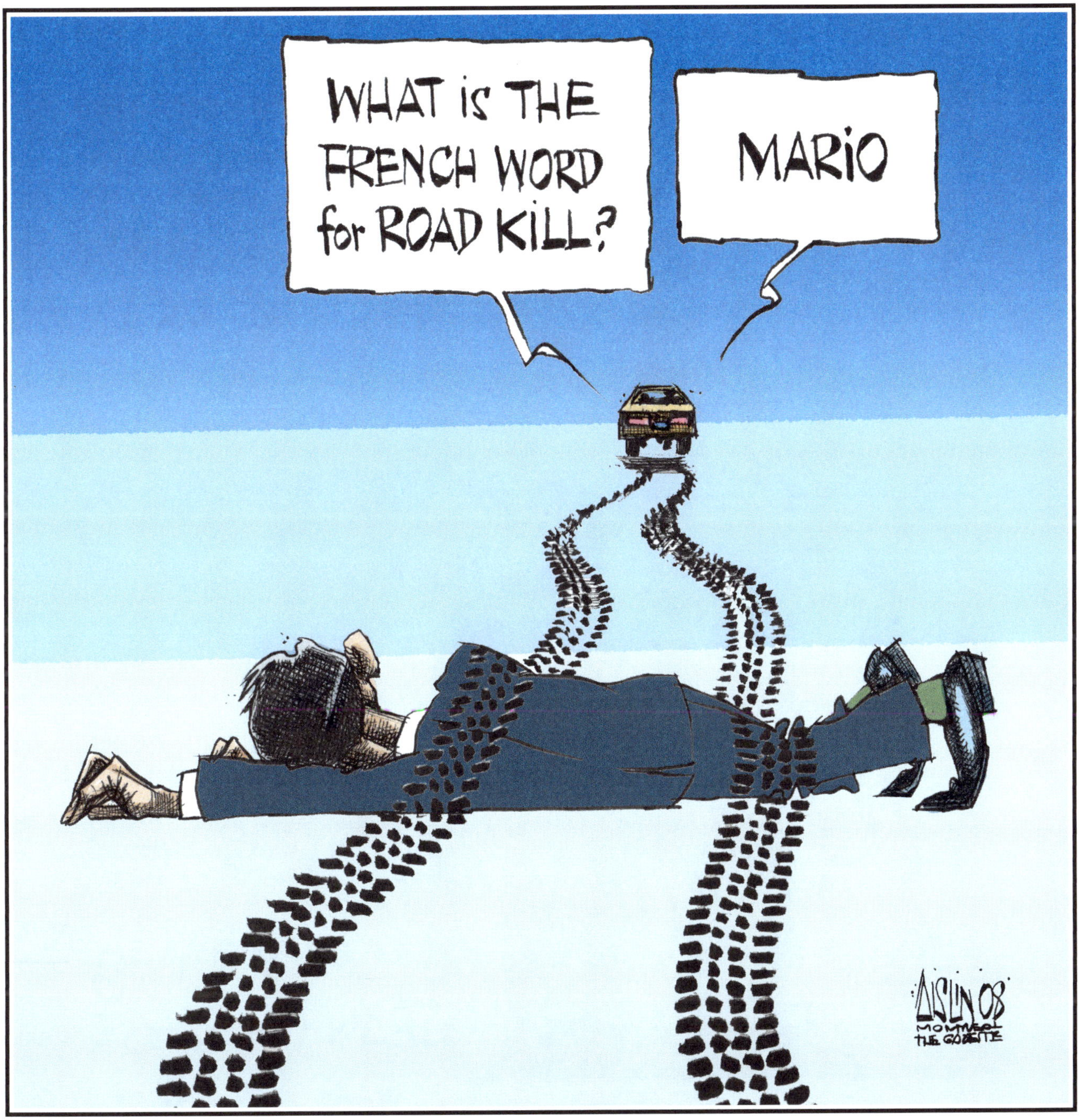

WHAT is THE FRENCH WORD for ROAD KILL?
MARIO
AISLIN 08
MONTREAL THE GAZETTE

…Mario Dumot crashes back to earth after the snap election of 2008

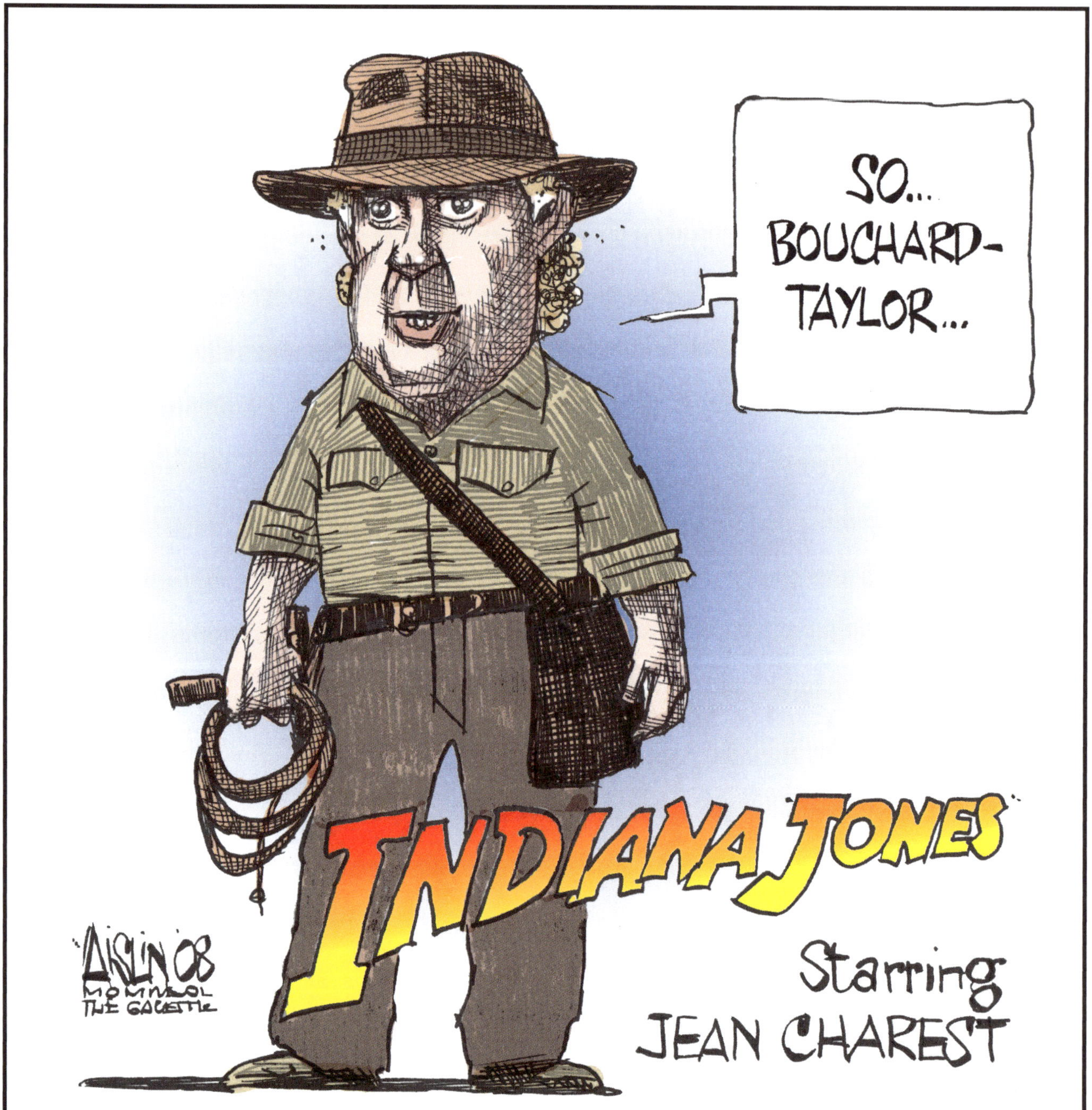
SO...
BOUCHARD-
TAYLOR...
INDIANA JONES
Starring
JEAN CHAREST
AISLIN '08
Charest calls for an inquiry to measure reasonable accommodation towards newcomers in Quebec

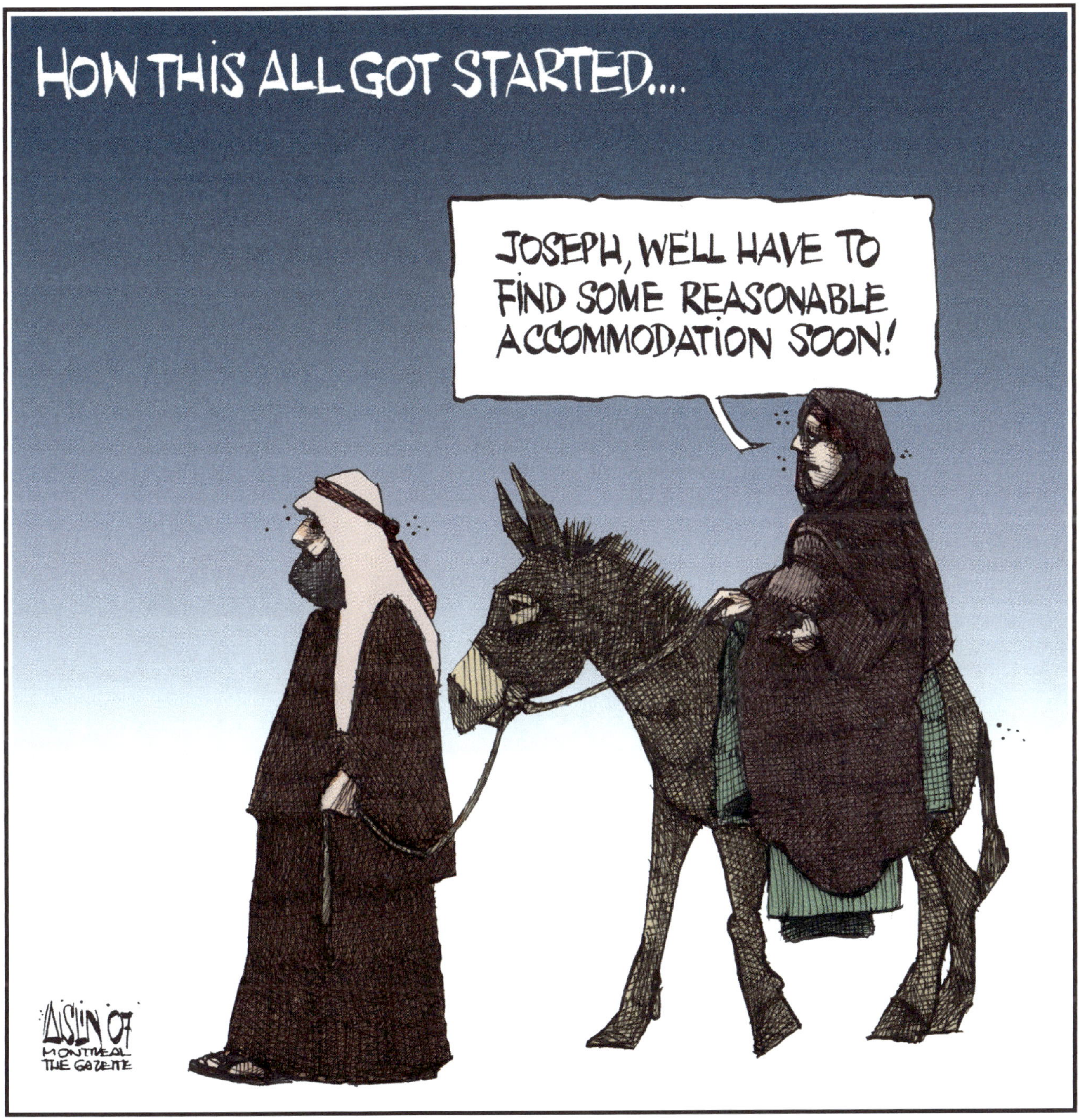
HOW THIS ALL GOT STARTED....
JOSEPH, WE'LL HAVE TO FIND SOME REASONABLE ACCOMMODATION SOON!
AISLIN 07
MONTREAL THE GAZETTE

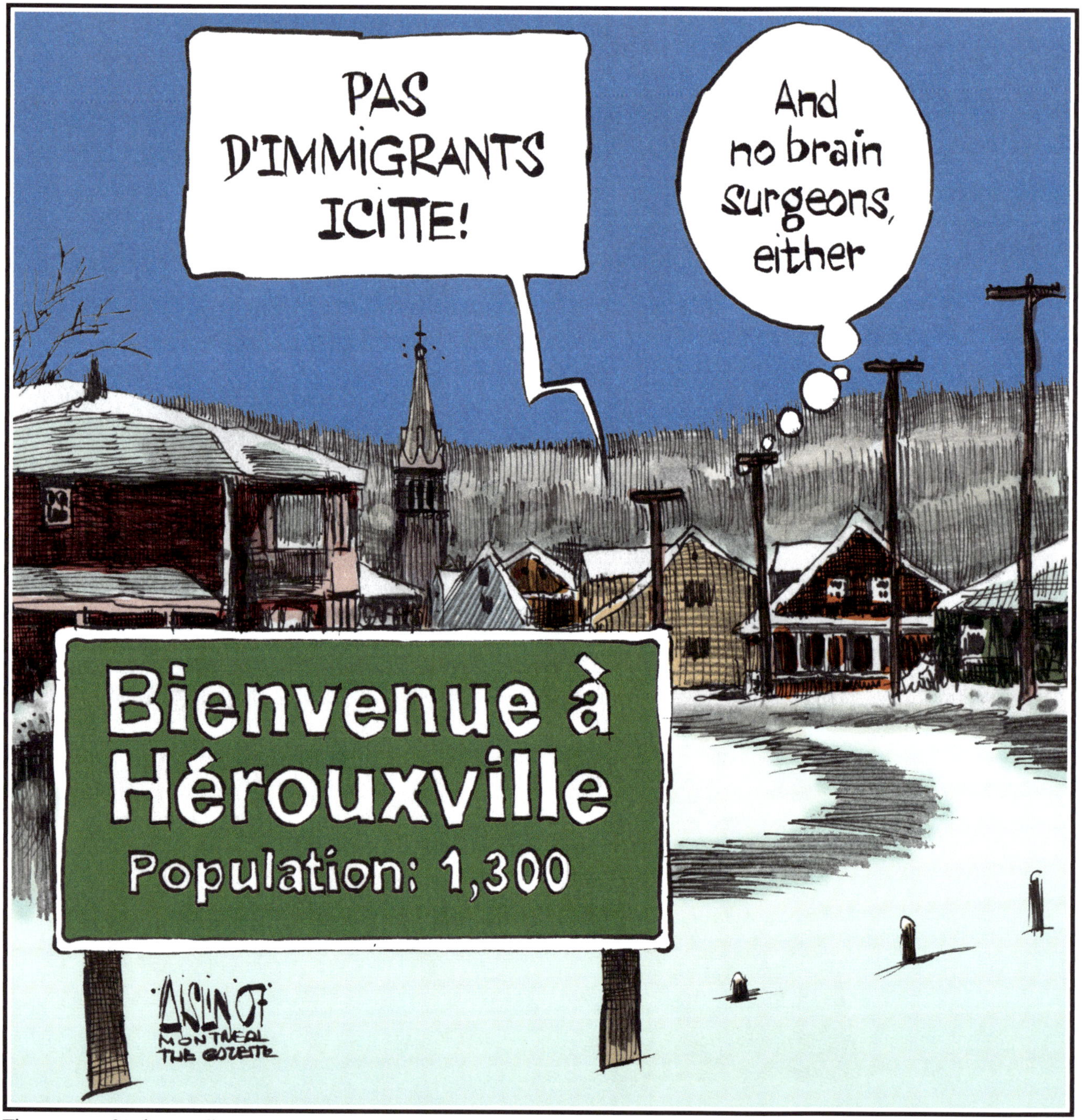
PAS D'IMMIGRANTS ICITTE!
And no brain surgeons, either
Bienvenue à Hérouxville
Population: 1,300
AISLIN 07
MONTREAL THE GAZETTE
The town of Hérouxville establishes a code of conduct for any possible immigrants that might arrive there

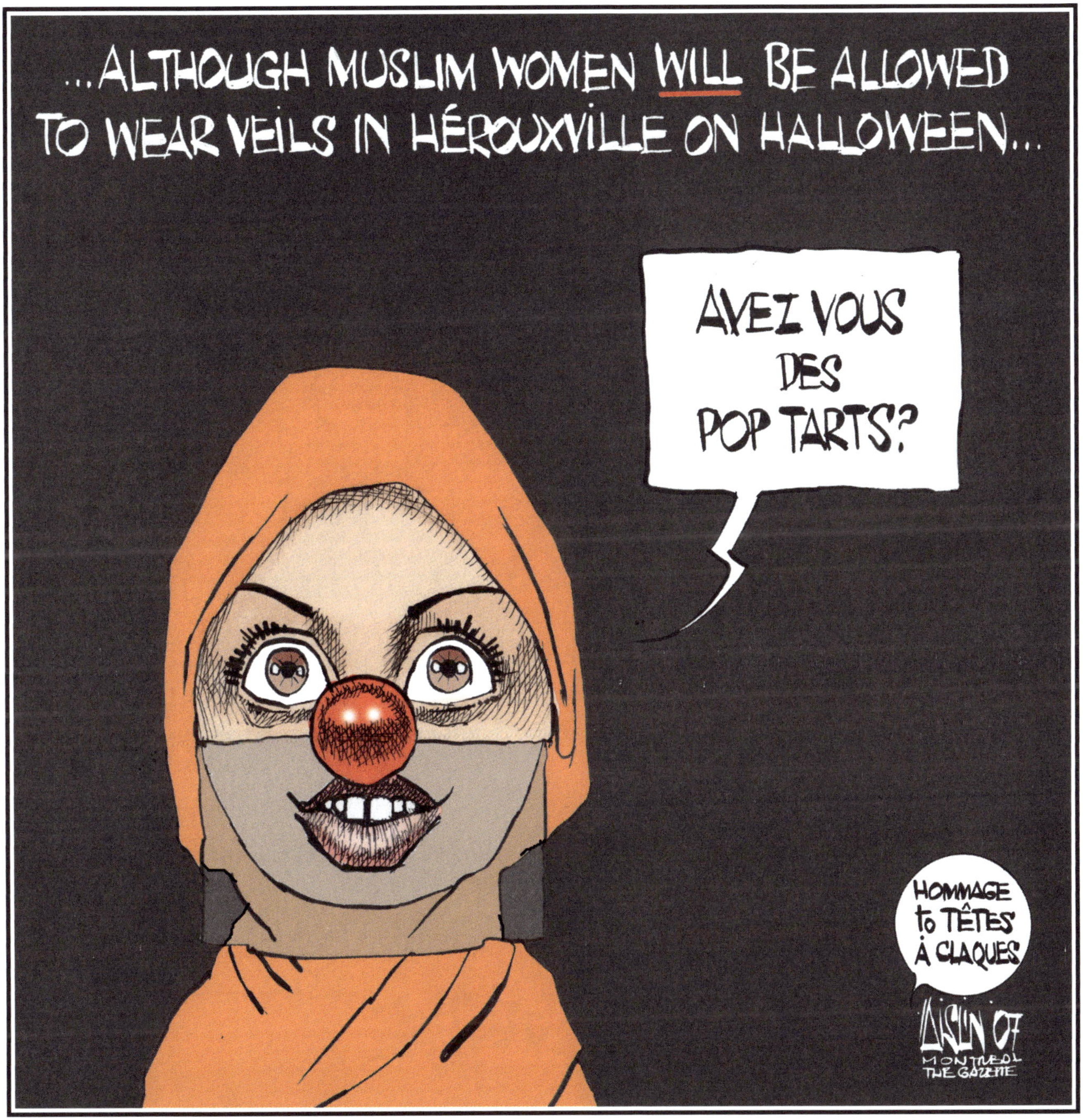
...ALTHOUGH MUSLIM WOMEN WILL BE ALLOWED TO WEAR VEILS IN HÉROUXVILLE ON HALLOWEEN...
AVEZ VOUS DES POP TARTS?
HOMMAGE TO TÊTES À CLAQUES
AISLIN 07
MONTREAL THE GAZETTE

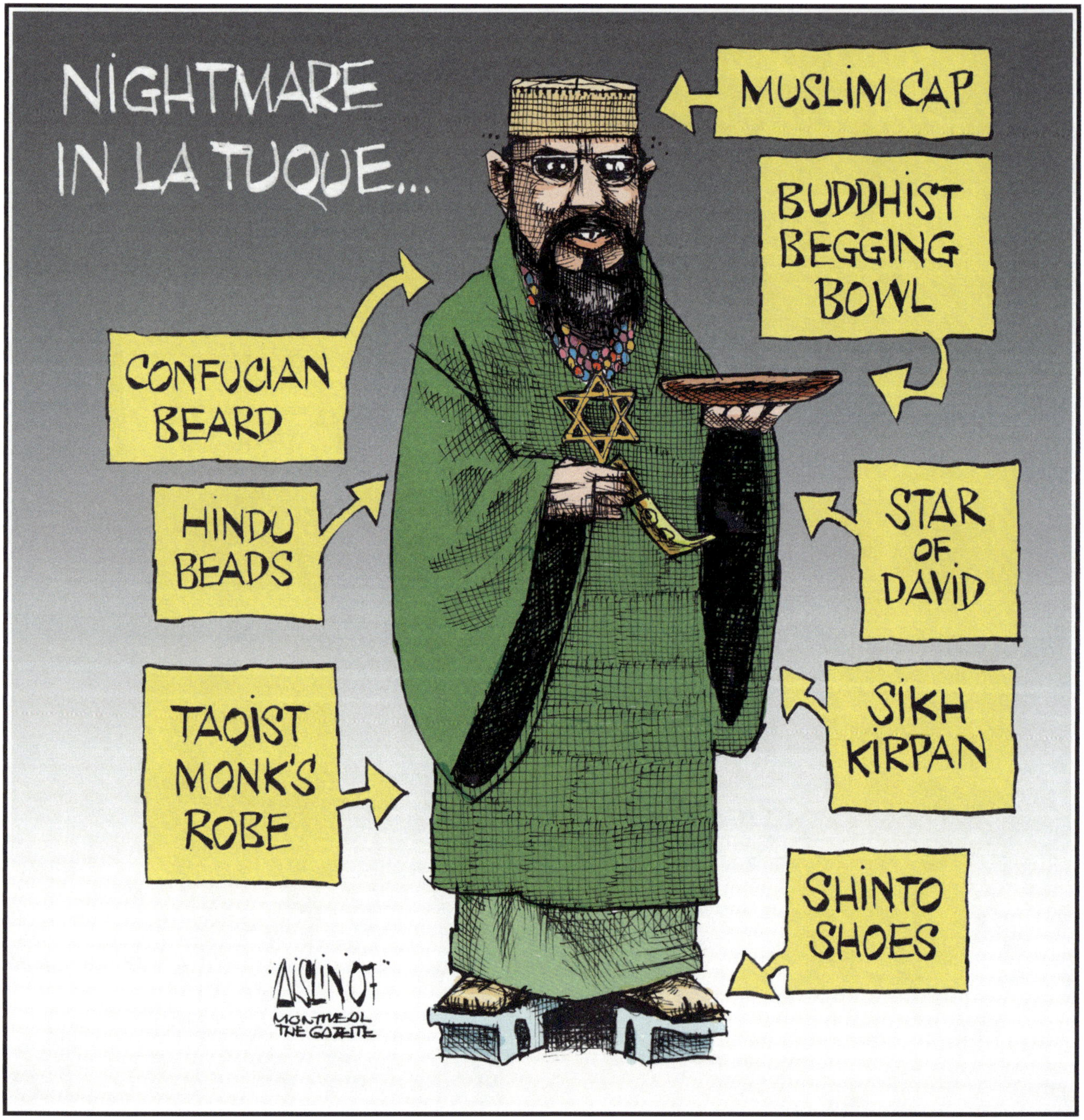
NIGHTMARE IN LA TUQUE...
MUSLIM CAP
BUDDHIST BEGGING BOWL
CONFUCIAN BEARD
HINDU BEADS
STAR OF DAVID
TAOIST MONK'S ROBE
SIKH KIRPAN
SHINTO SHOES
AISLIN 07
MONTREAL THE GAZETTE
Nightmare in La Tuque

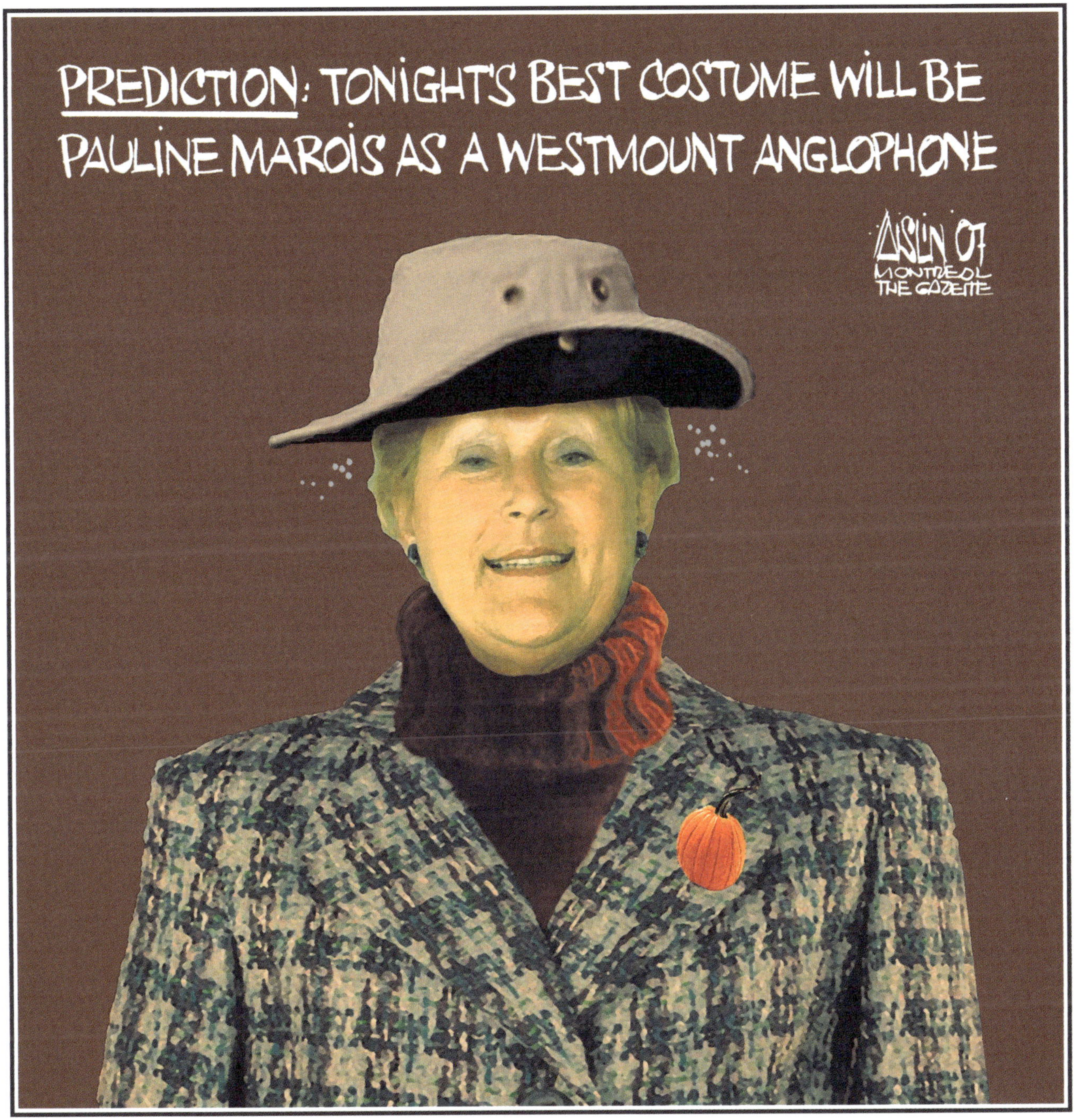
PREDICTION: TONIGHT'S BEST COSTUME WILL BE
PAULINE MAROIS AS A WESTMOUNT ANGLOPHONE
AISLIN 07
MONTREAL
THE GAZETTE

Nightmare in Westmount

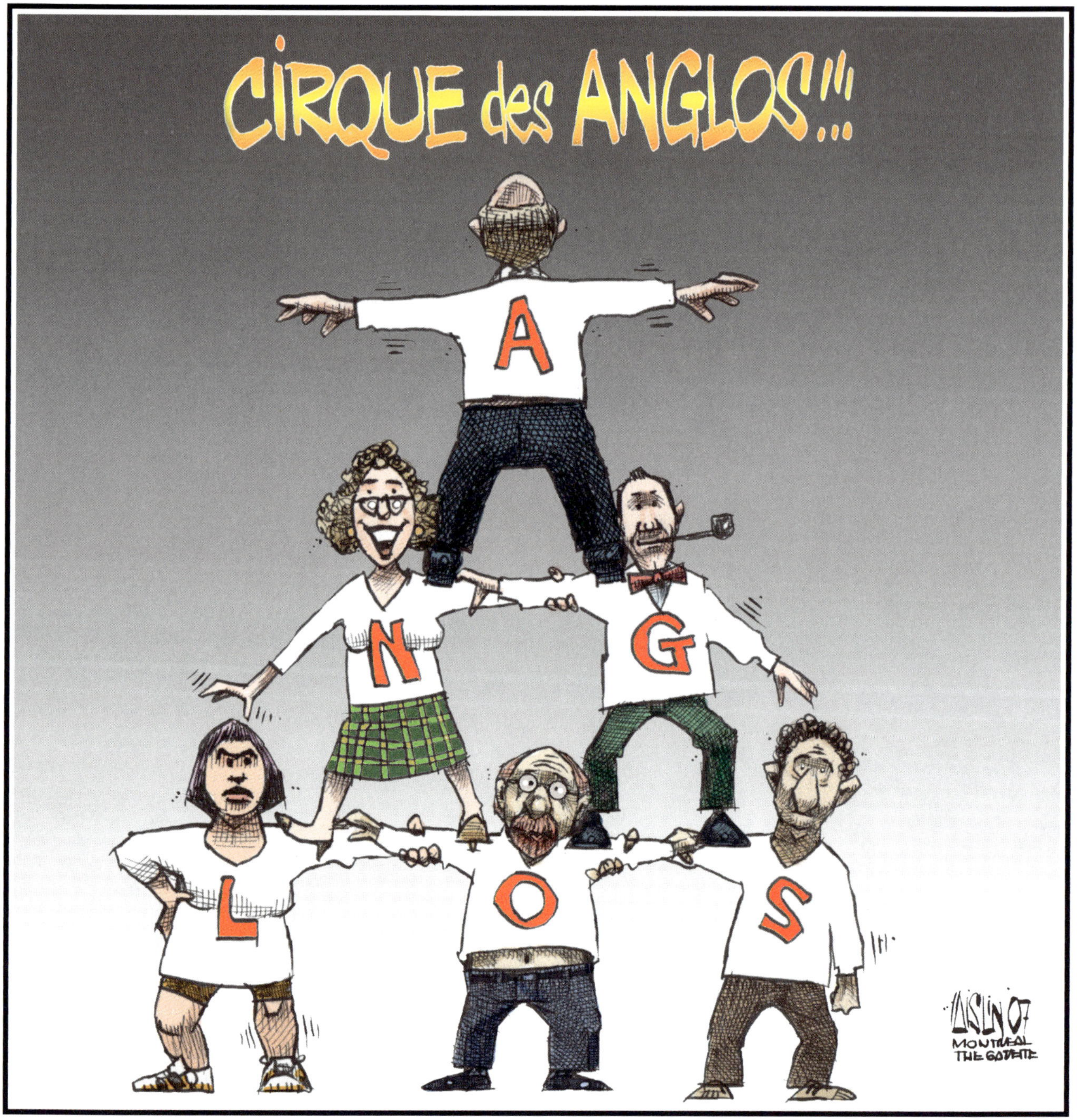
CIRQUE des ANGLOS!!!
A
N
G
L
O
S
AISLIN 07
MONTREAL THE GAZETTE

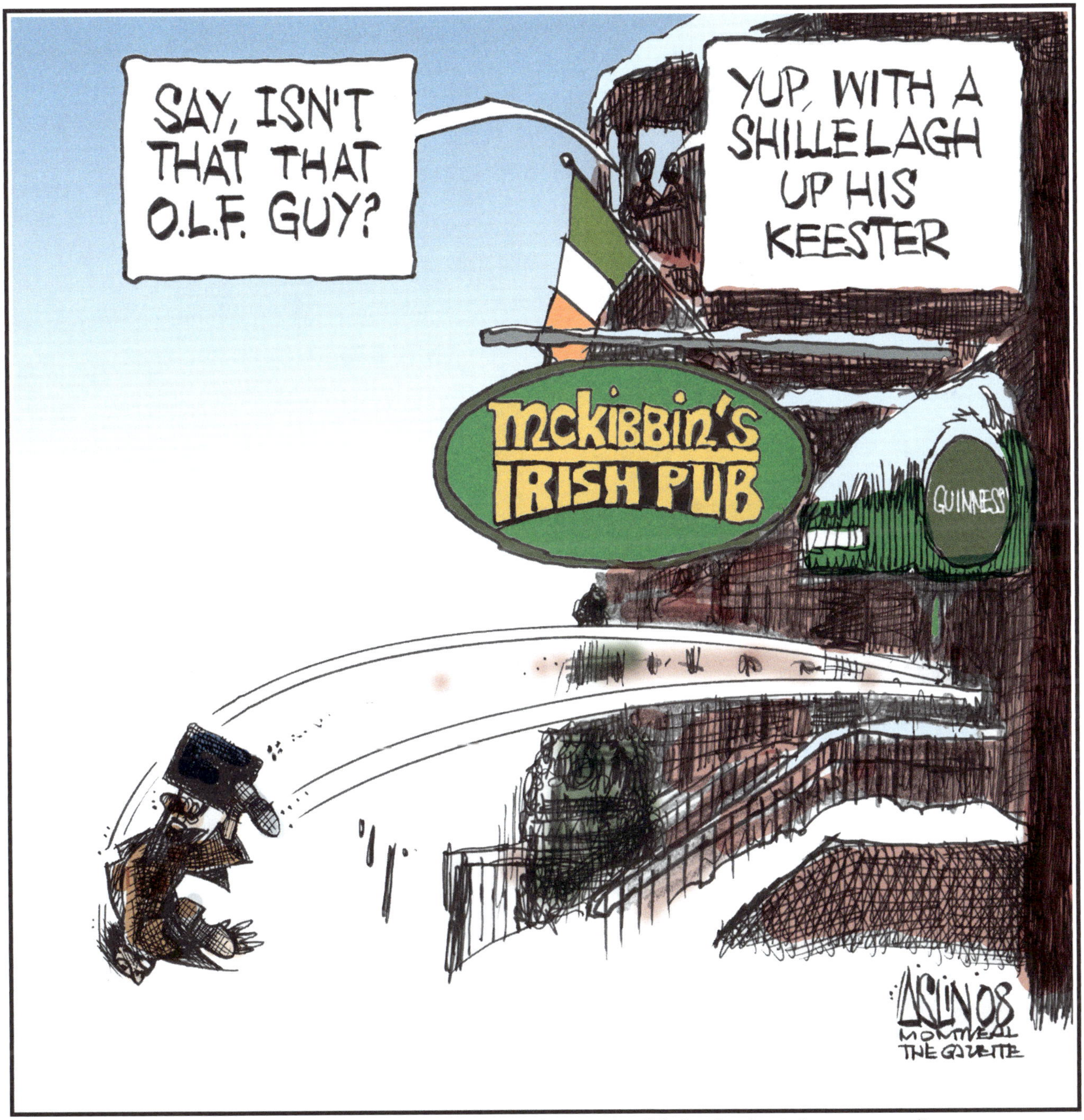
SAY, ISN'T THAT THAT O.L.F. GUY?
YUP, WITH A SHILLELAGH UP HIS KEESTER
McKIBBIN'S IRISH PUB
GUINNESS
ASLIN 08 MONTREAL THE GAZETTE

The decor in McKibbin's Irish Pub in downtown Montreal is too English for Quebec's language police

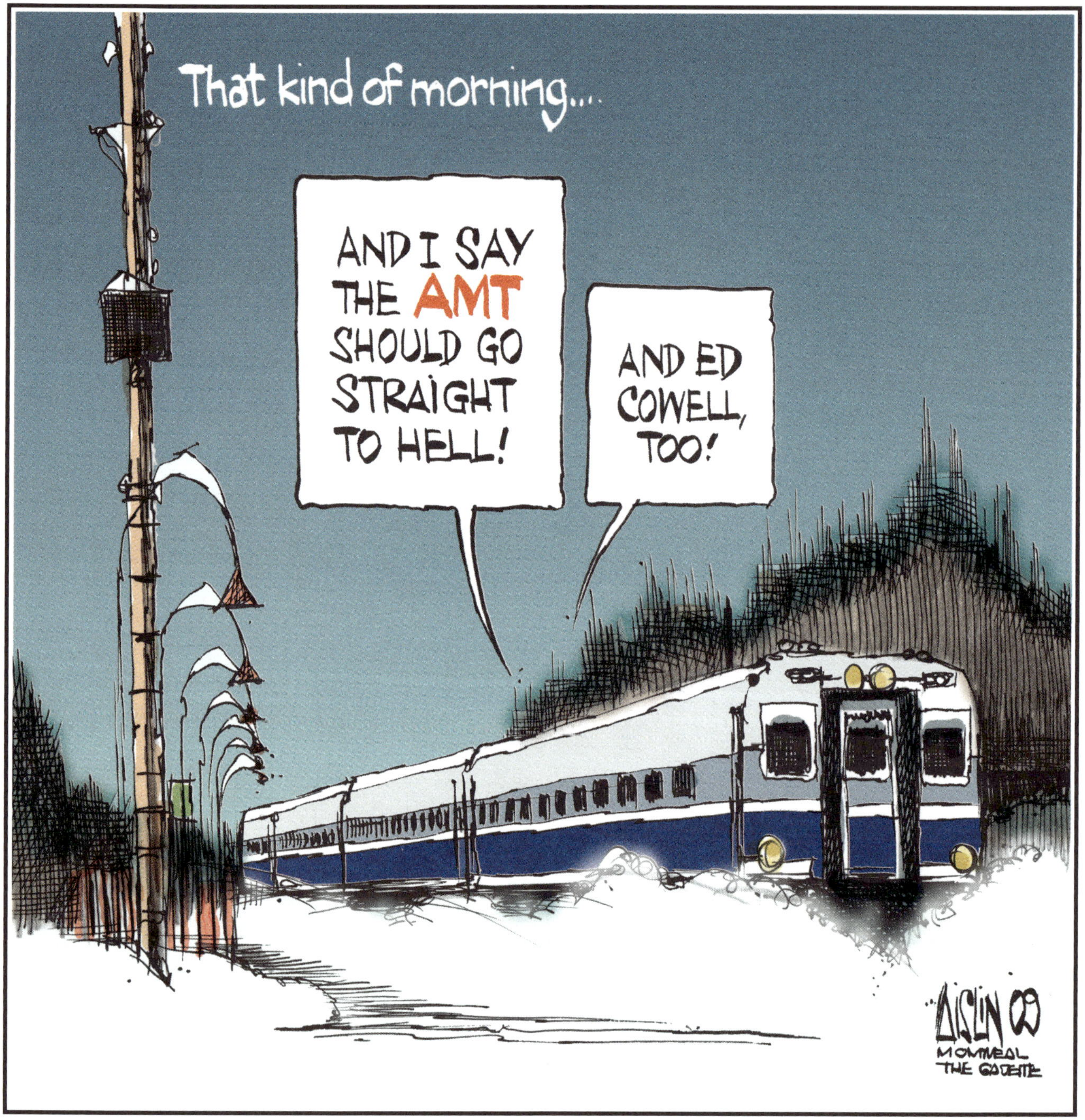
That kind of morning...
AND I SAY THE AMT SHOULD GO STRAIGHT TO HELL!
AND ED COWELL, TOO!
AISLIN
MONTREAL THE GAZETTE

West Island angst over poor train service to downtown

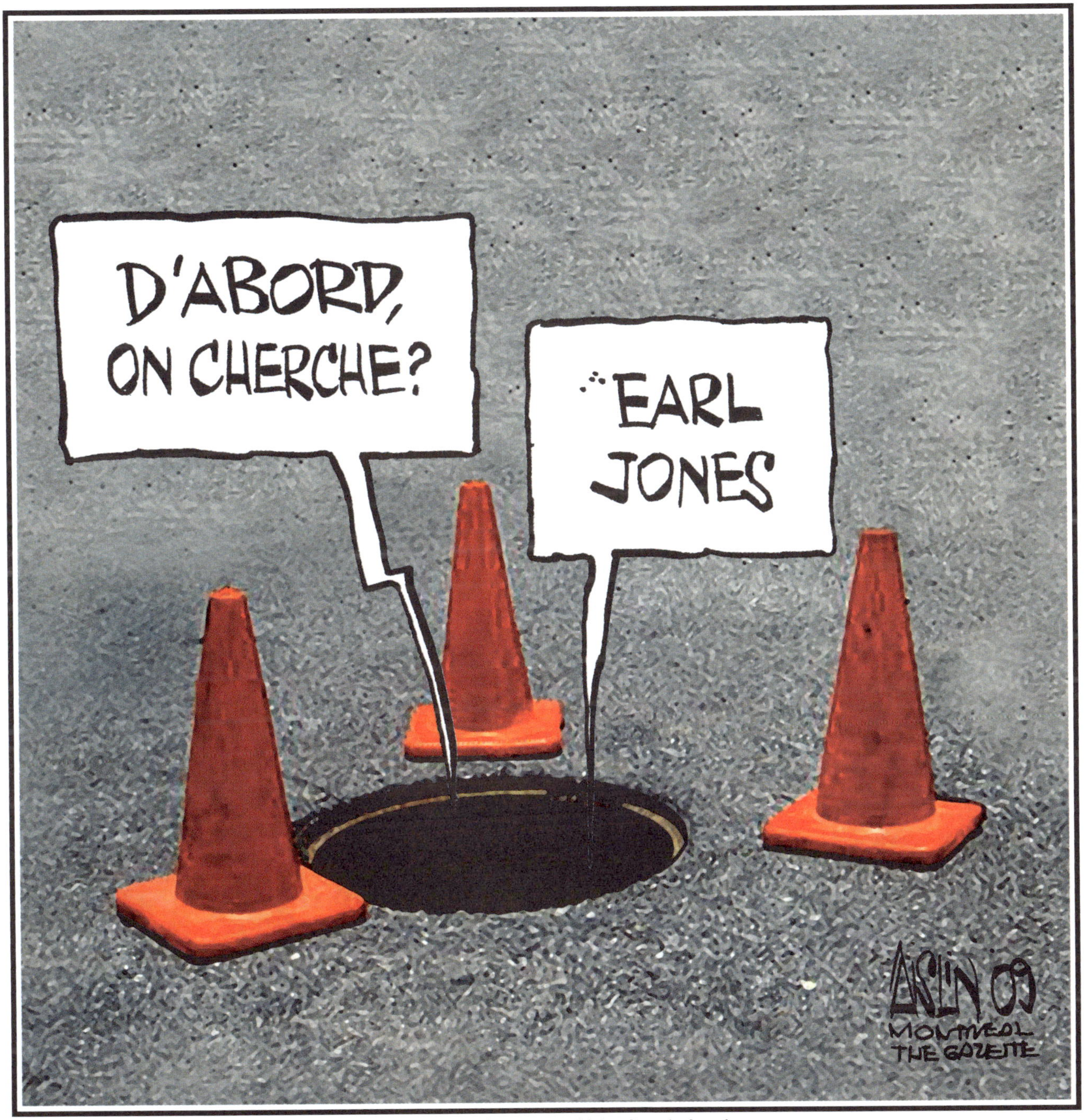
D'ABORD, ON CHERCHE?
EARL JONES
ASLIN 09
MONTREAL THE GAZETTE

Montreal financial advisor Earl Jones disappears with many of his client's funds

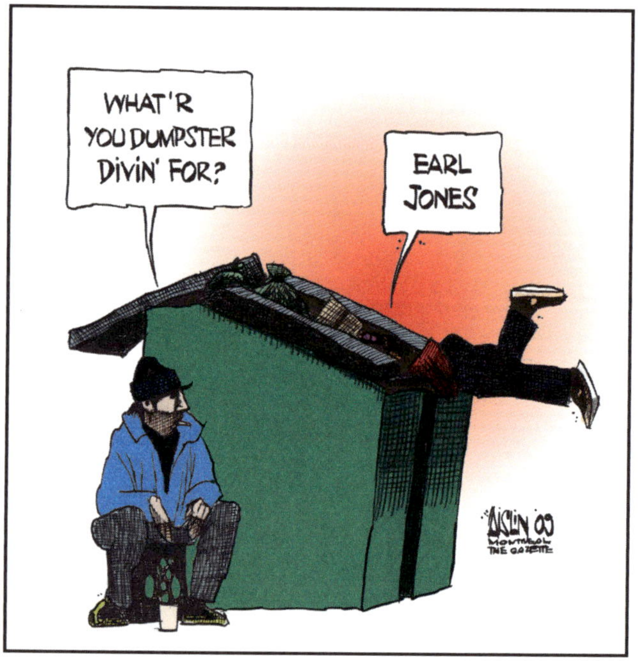
WHAT'R YOU DUMPSTER DIVIN' FOR?
EARL JONES

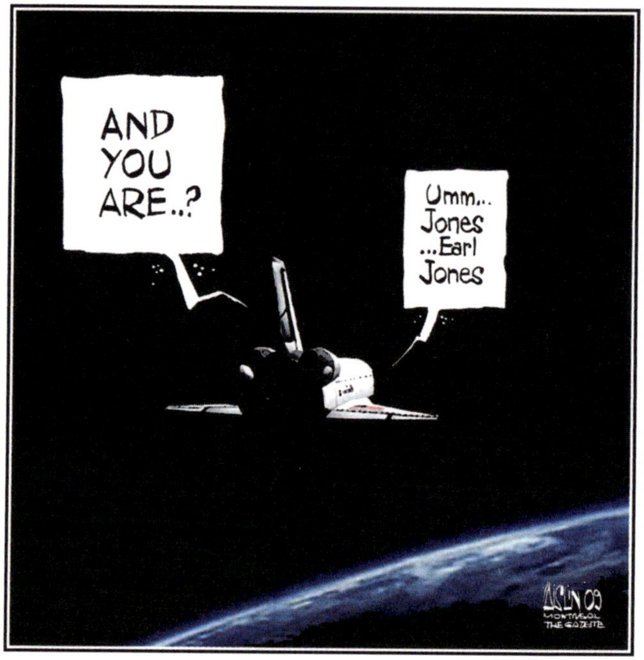
AND YOU ARE..?
Umm... Jones ...Earl Jones

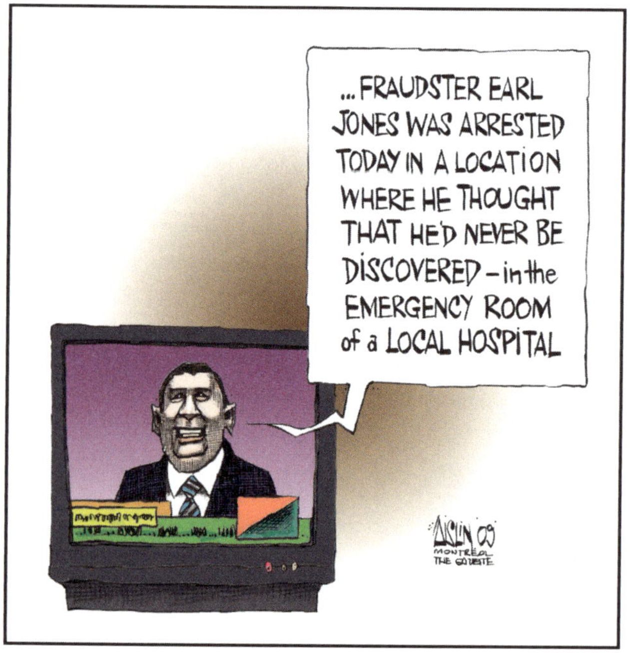
...FRAUDSTER EARL JONES WAS ARRESTED TODAY IN A LOCATION WHERE HE THOUGHT THAT HE'D NEVER BE DISCOVERED – in the EMERGENCY ROOM of a LOCAL HOSPITAL

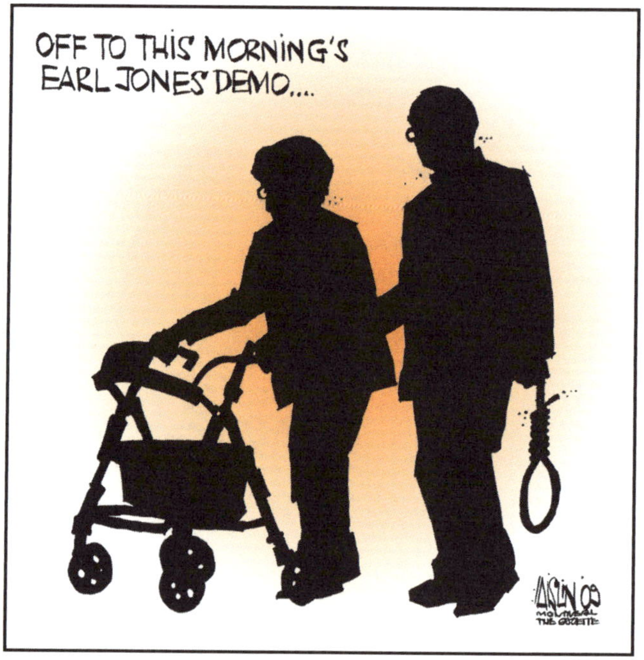
OFF TO THIS MORNING'S EARL JONES' DEMO...

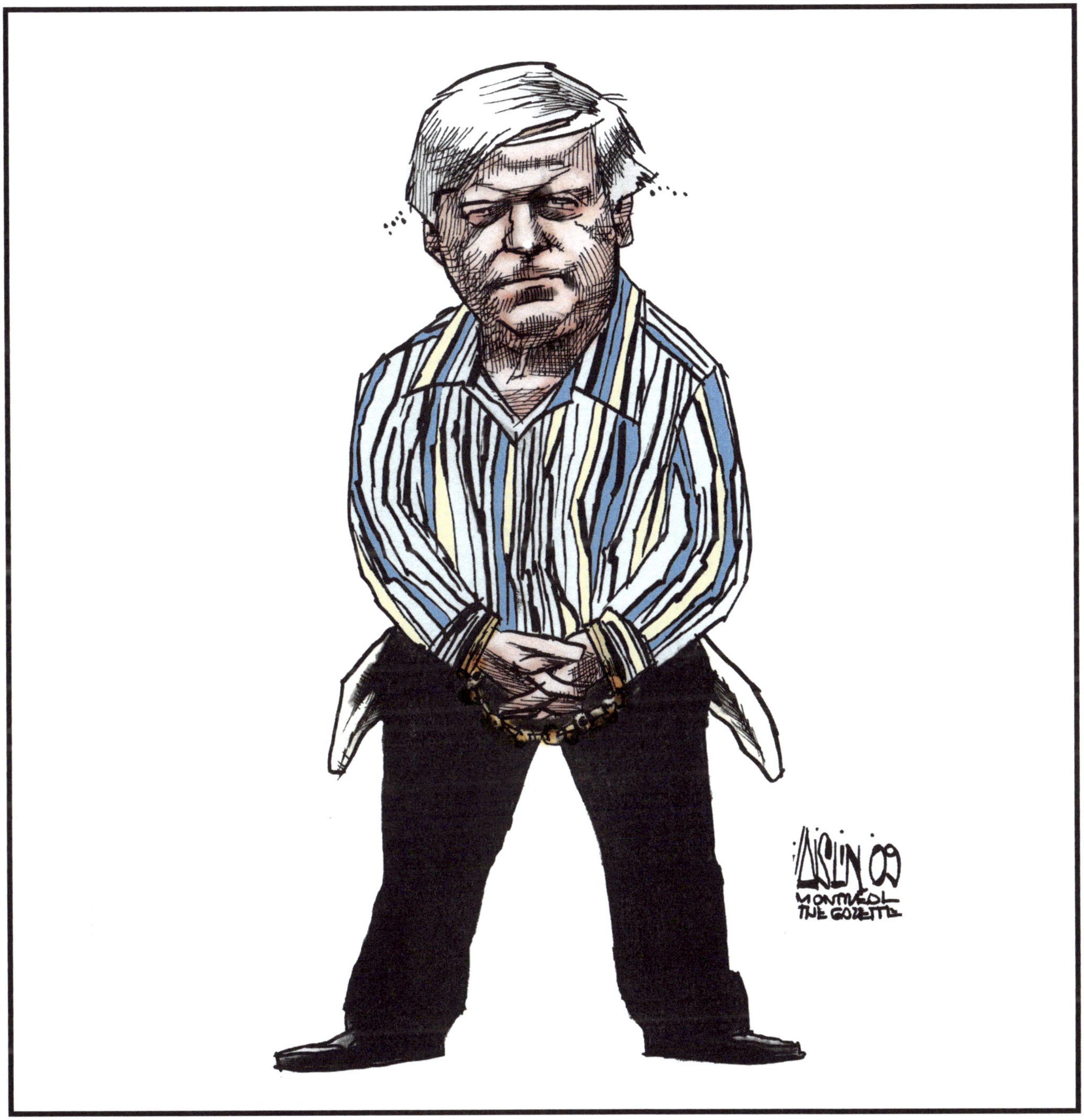
AISLIN 09
MONTREAL
THE GAZETTE

Earl Jones arrested

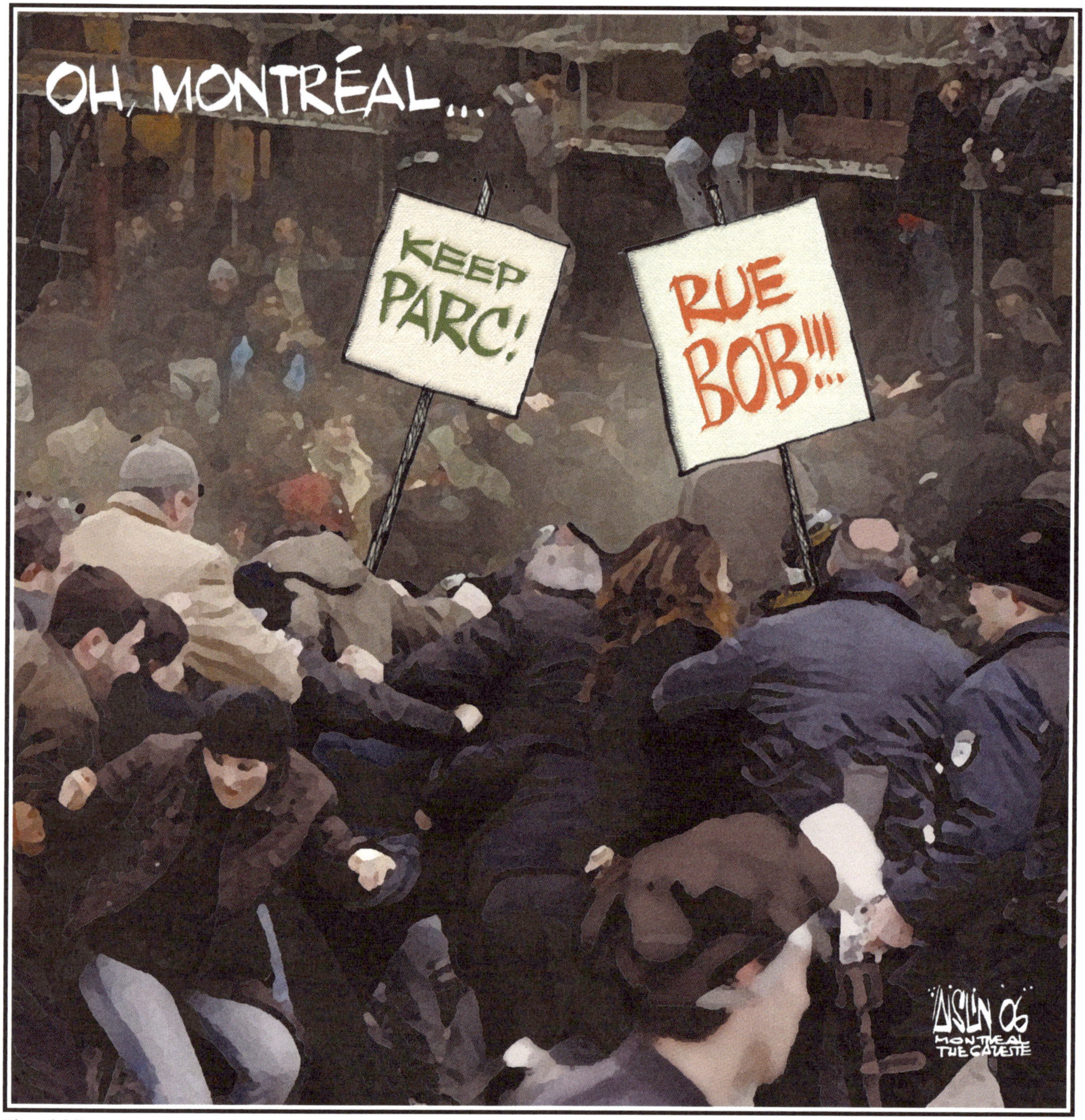
OH, MONTRÉAL...
KEEP PARC!
RUE BOB!!!...
AISLIN 06
MONTREAL THE GAZETTE

Should l'Avenue du Parc be renamed Rue Robert-Bourassa?

CHAPTER 4

Festival Montréal!

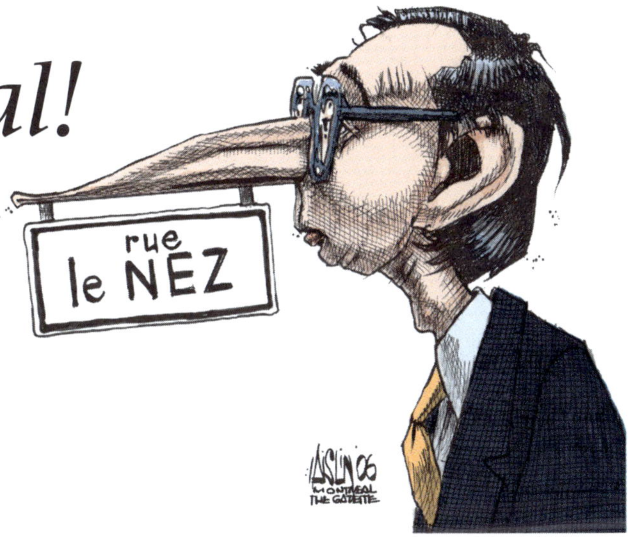
rue
le NEZ

Montreal is famously a city of street festivals: the Rename-Your-Street Festival, the Repave-Your-Street Festival, the Crumbling-Overpass Festival, the Pay-Off-Your-Politician Festival, the Too-Poor-to-Piss-in-a-Pothole Festival – and of course there are the better known Jazz and Comedy Festivals.

Montrealers love their sports, too. We have always been enthusiastic about football and support our Alouettes. Even though the Expos have left town, we still follow baseball, occasionally glancing at the box scores to see how poorly the Washington Nationals are doing. Schadenfreude. Soccer has certainly caught on, with interest peaking at World Cup time. When the Olympic Games are on, we are glued to our TVs, rooting for our Canadian and Quebec athletes.

But all that enthusiasm pales in comparison with the passion that unites all Montrealers.

Hockey.

It's the new religion, complete with its own prayers and rituals. Every October, as the season opens, we just know that the Habs are headed for a Stanley Cup victory. Then, mid-winter reality sets in and we wonder if we are actually going to make the playoffs. Some years we do, some years we don't. But if we do, we only last for the first round or two. Then we go into collective mourning. The current GM shuffles the deck. Perhaps a new owner for the team comes forward, as happened this year. October rolls around again. For sure we're headed for a Stanley Cup this time...

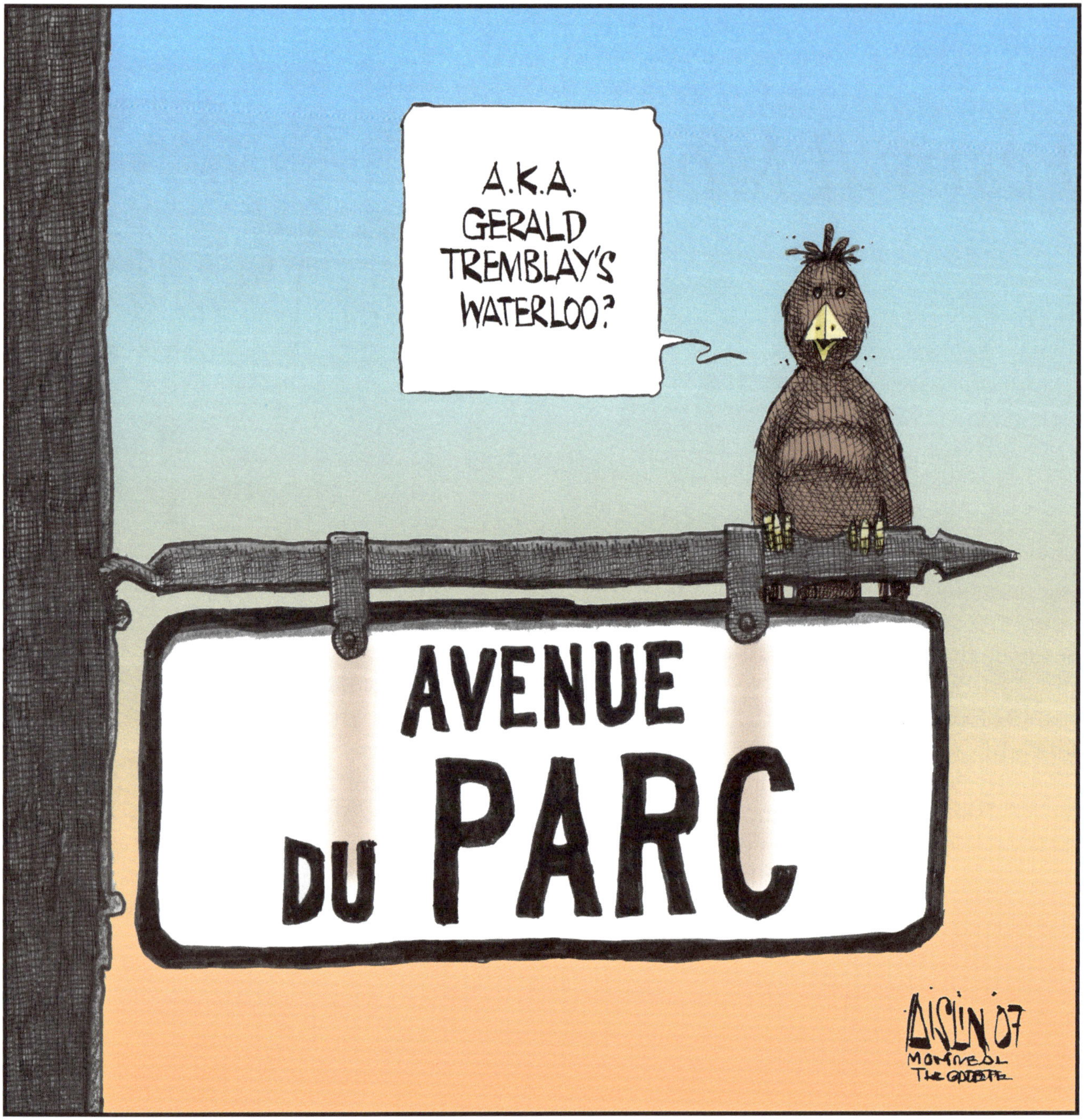
A.K.A. GERALD TREMBLAY'S WATERLOO?
AVENUE DU PARC
AISLIN '07

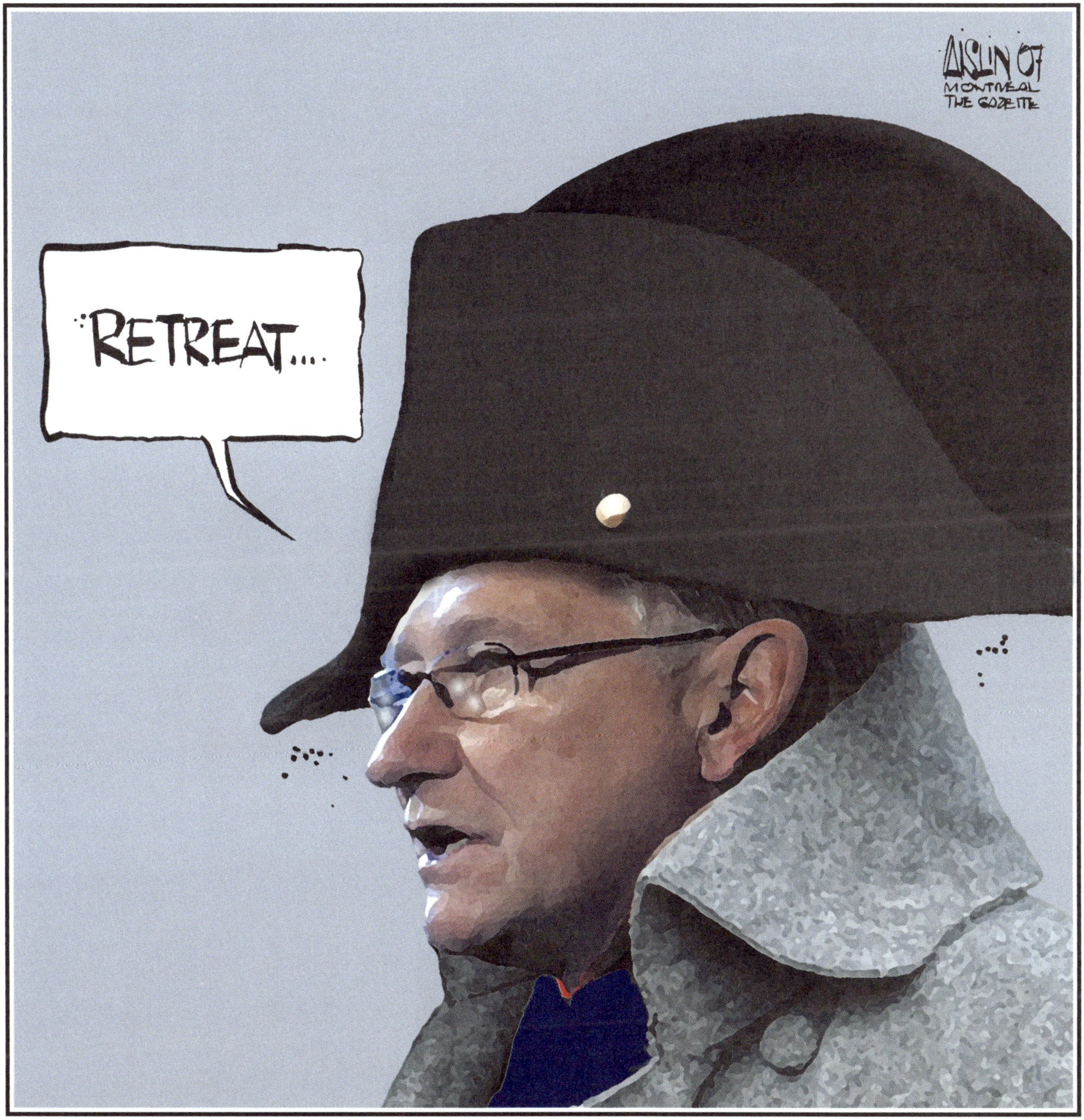
RETREAT....
AISLIN 07
MONTREAL
THE GAZETTE
Mayor Gerald Tremblay abandons plans for l'Avenue du Parc name change

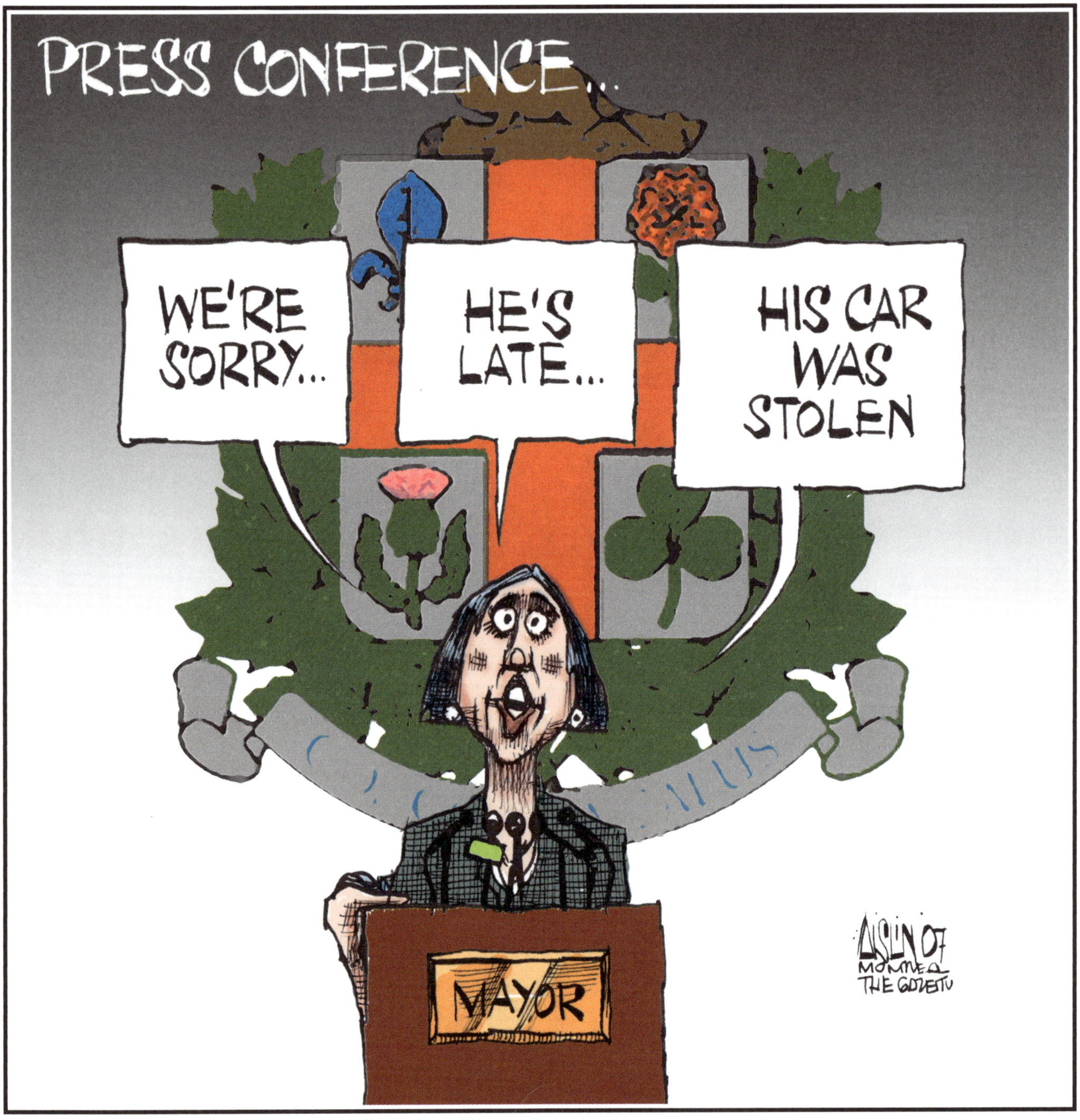
PRESS CONFERENCE...
WE'RE SORRY...
HE'S LATE...
HIS CAR WAS STOLEN
MAYOR

Montreal has the lowest return rate in Canada on stolen cars

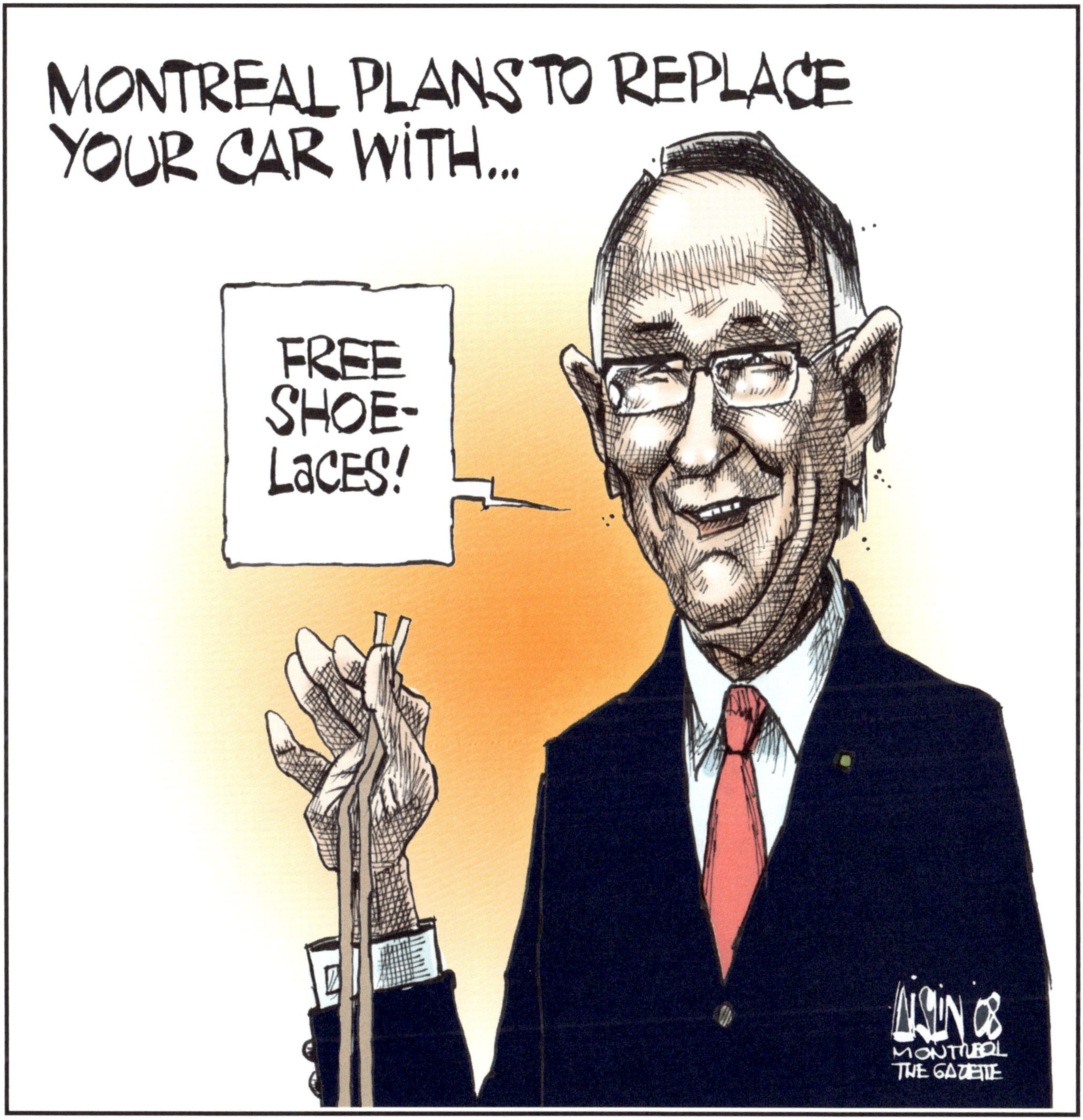
MONTREAL PLANS TO REPLACE YOUR CAR WITH...
FREE SHOE-LACES!
AISLIN 08
MONTREAL THE GAZETTE

Traffic chaos in downtown Montreal

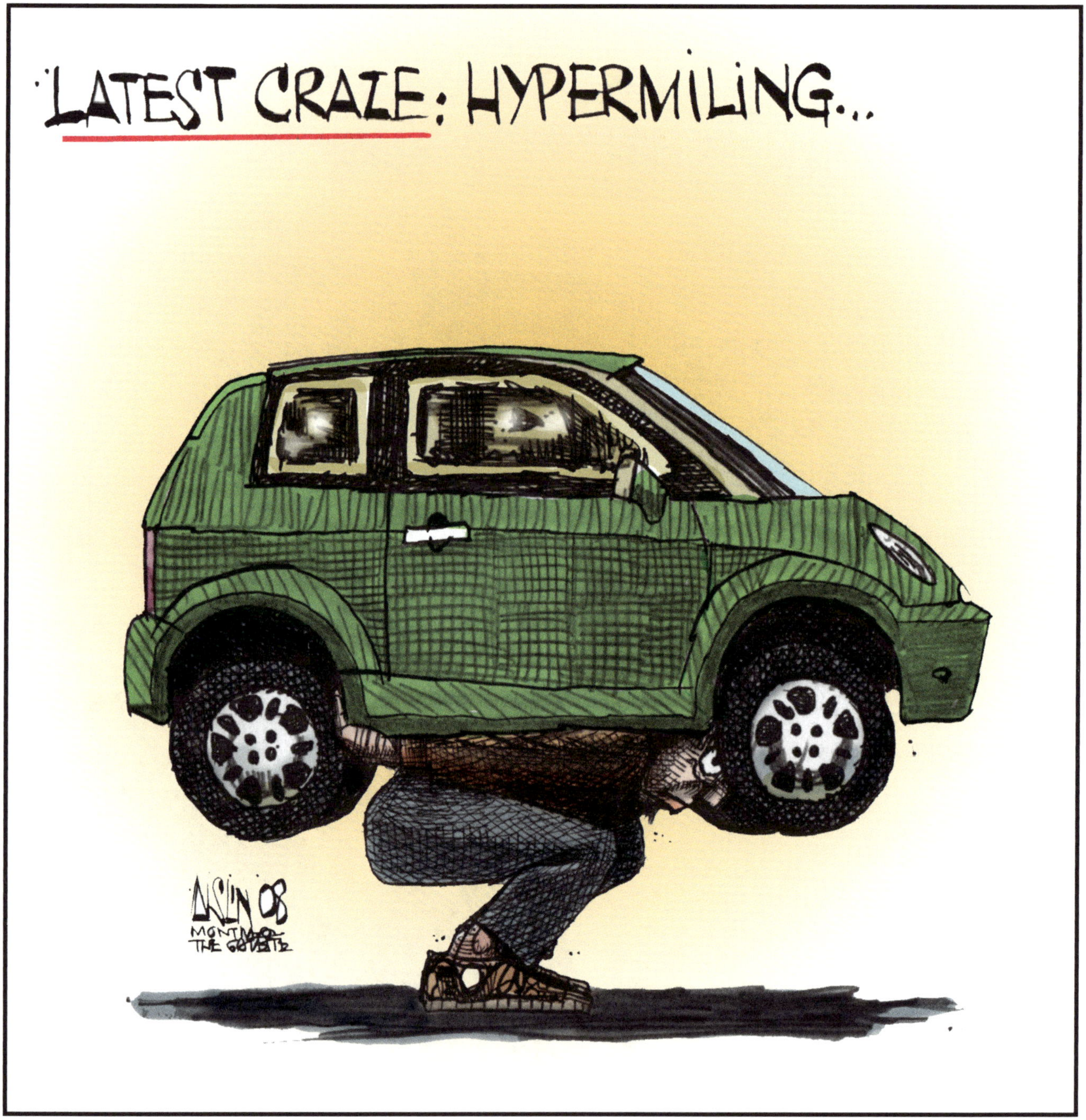
LATEST CRAZE: HYPERMILING...

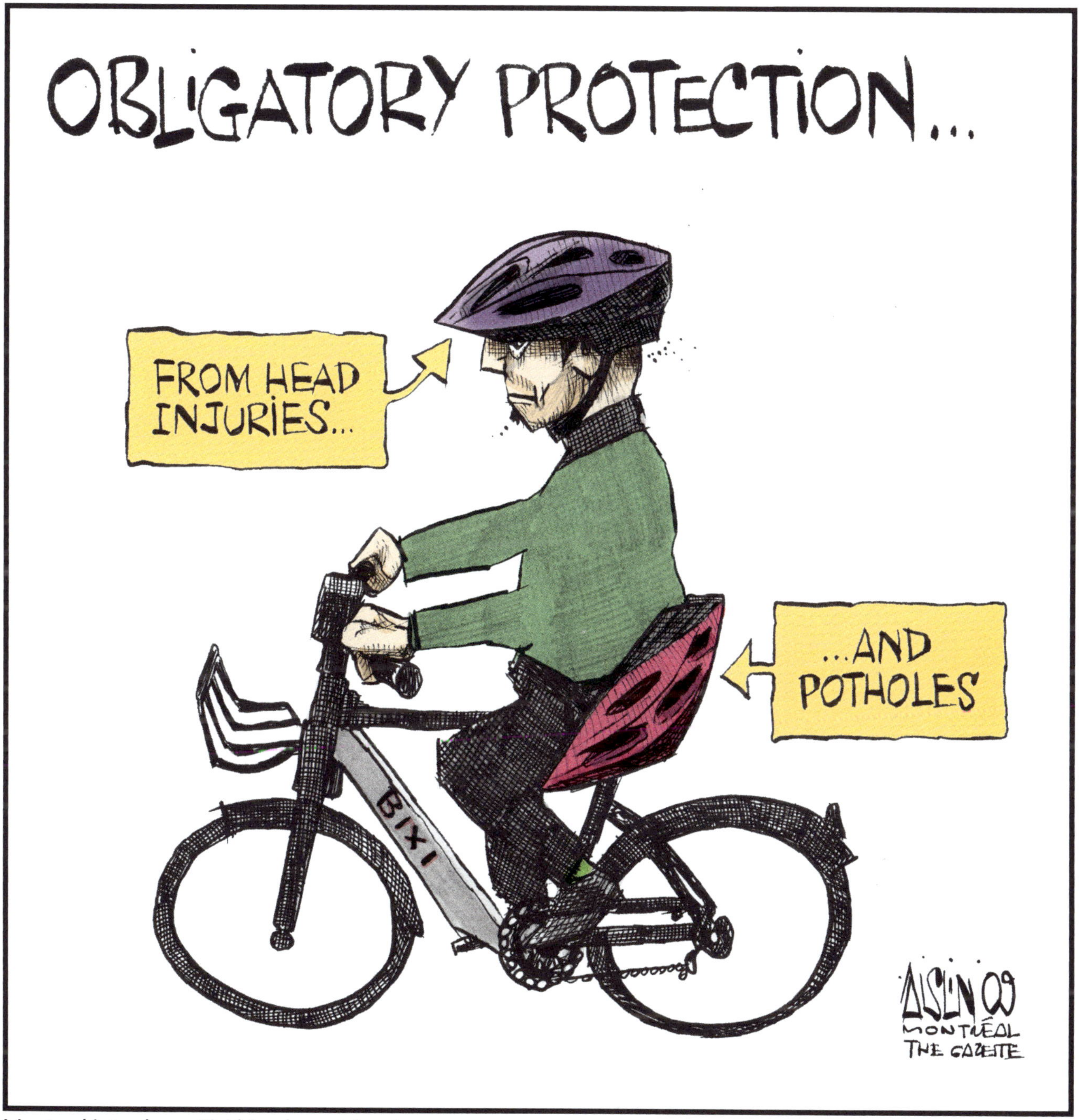
OBLIGATORY PROTECTION...
FROM HEAD INJURIES...
...AND POTHOLES
BIXI
AISLIN 09
MONTRÉAL
THE GAZETTE
Montreal introduces Bixi bicycle rental system

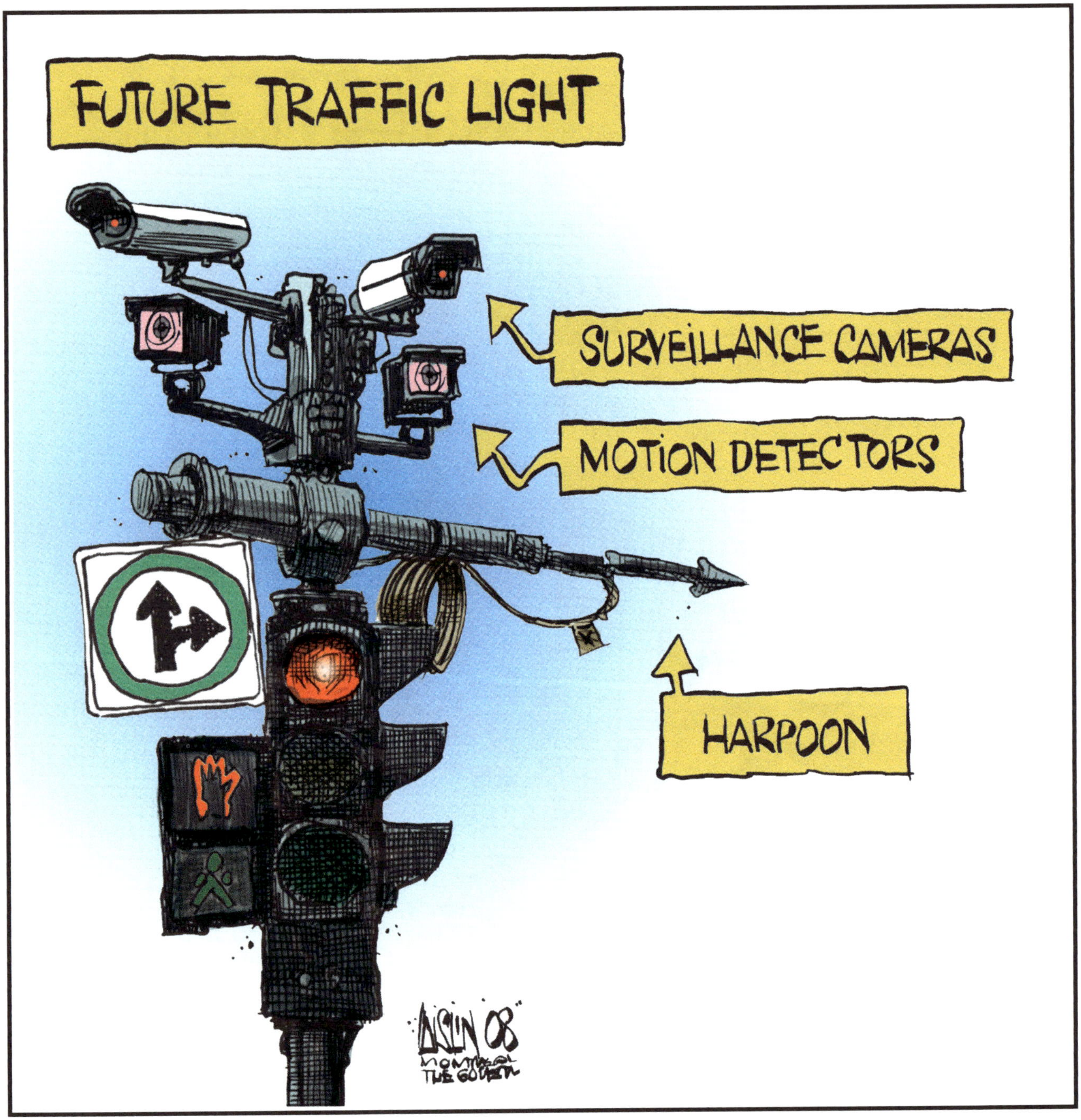
FUTURE TRAFFIC LIGHT
SURVEILLANCE CAMERAS
MOTION DETECTORS
HARPOON

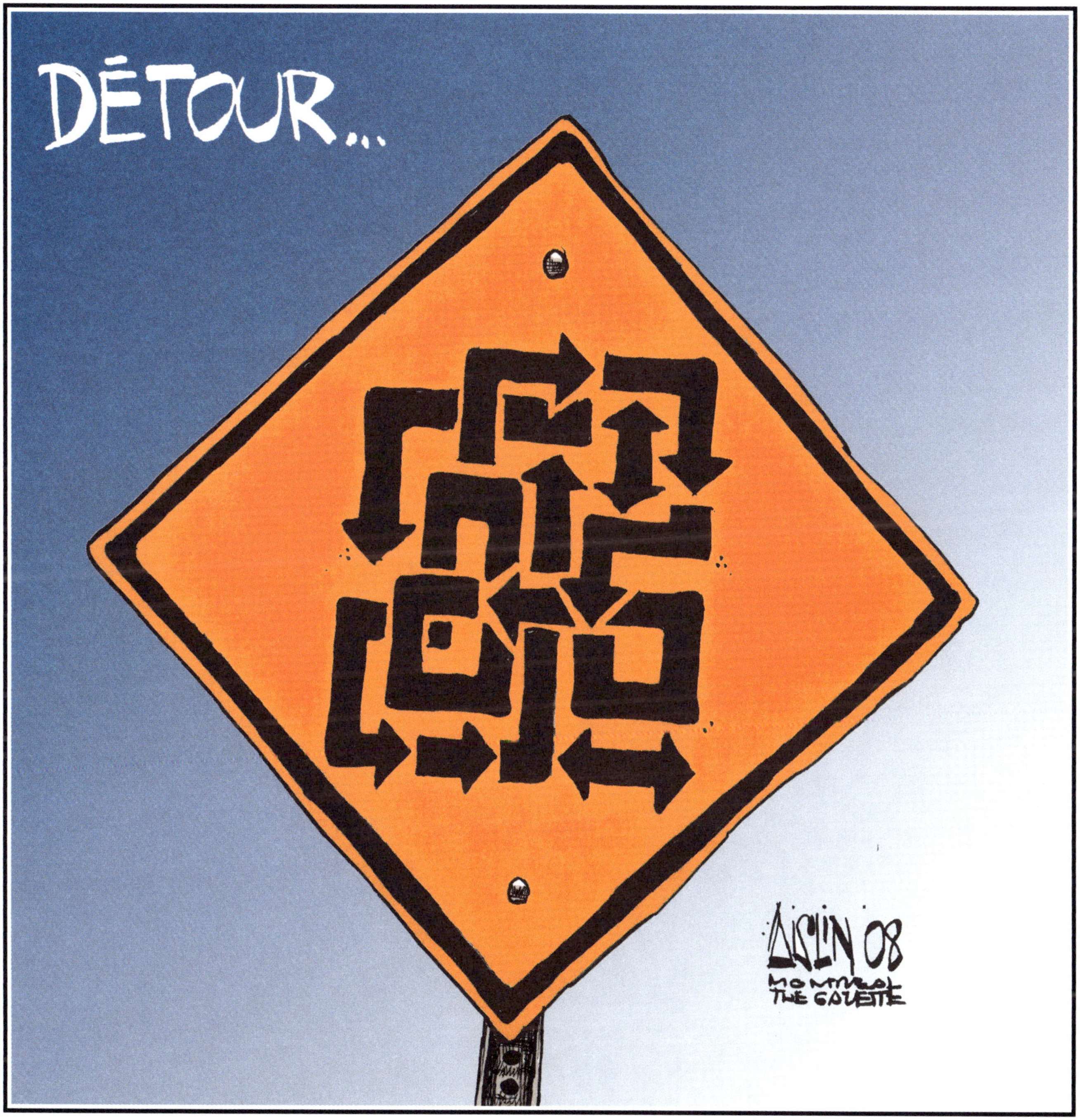
DÉTOUR...
AISLIN 08
MONTREAL THE GAZETTE

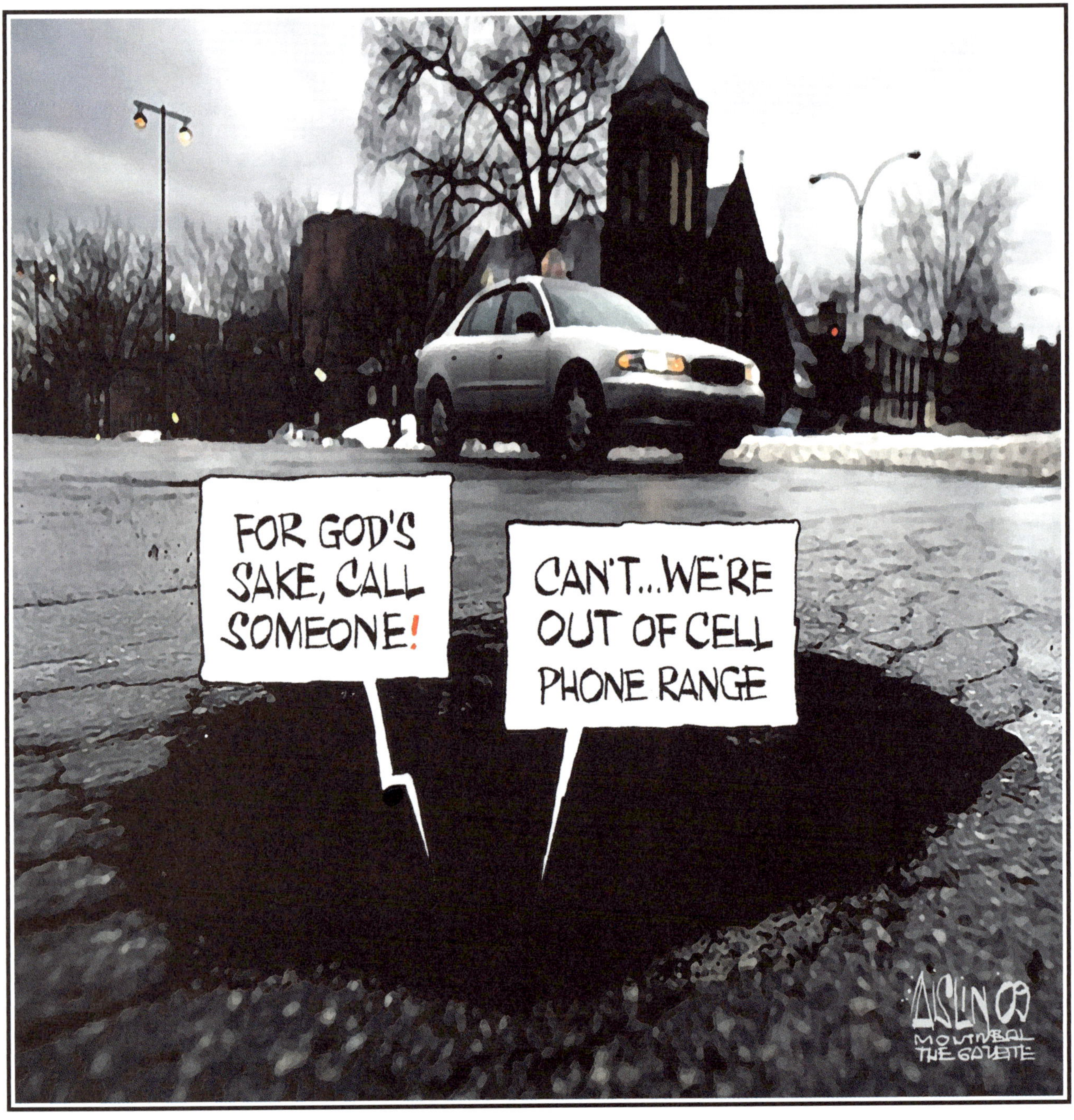
FOR GOD'S SAKE, CALL SOMEONE!
CAN'T...WE'RE OUT OF CELL PHONE RANGE
AISLIN 09
MONTREAL THE GAZETTE

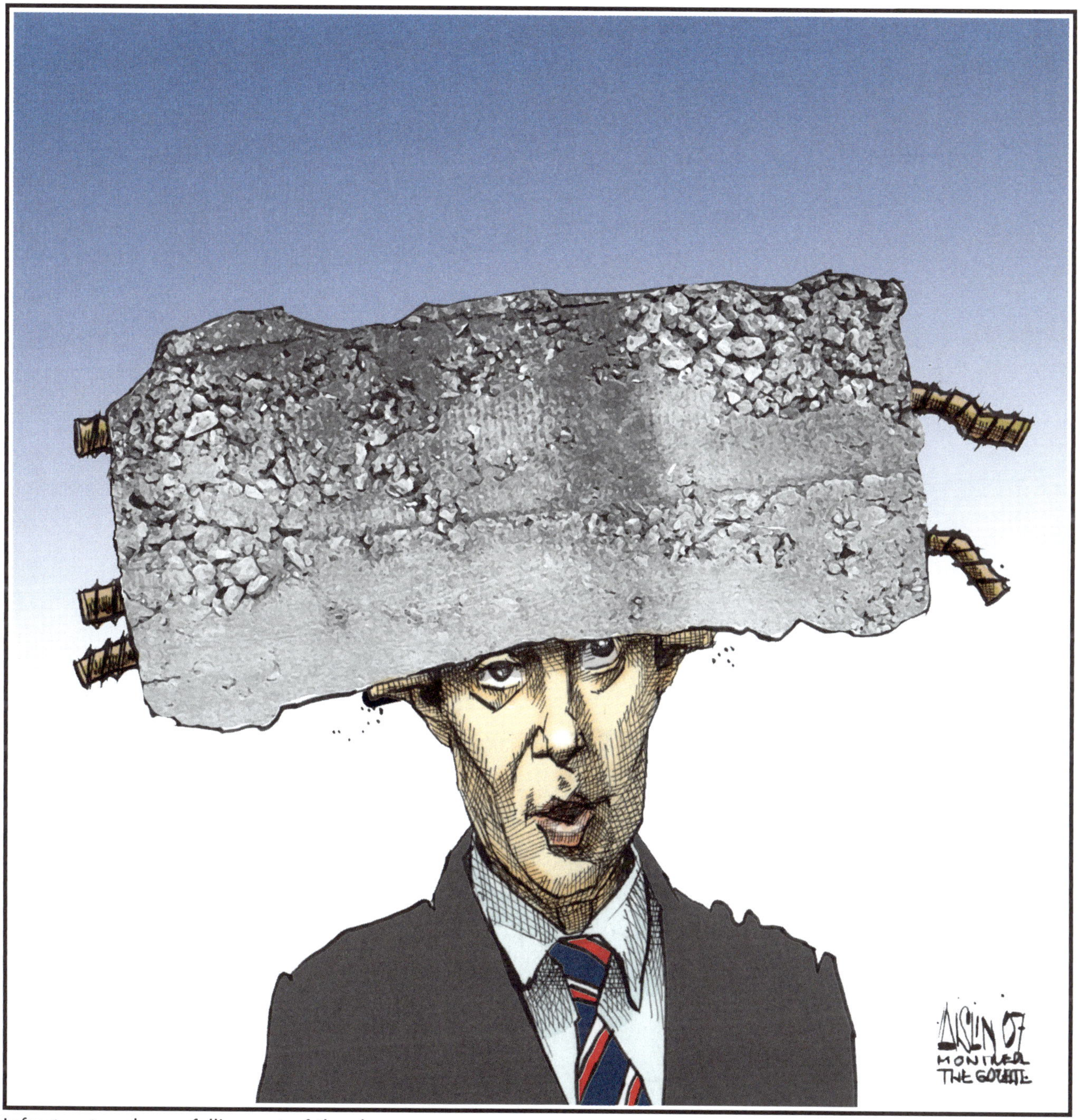
AISLIN 07
MONTREAL
THE GAZETTE

Infrastructure keeps falling out of the sky

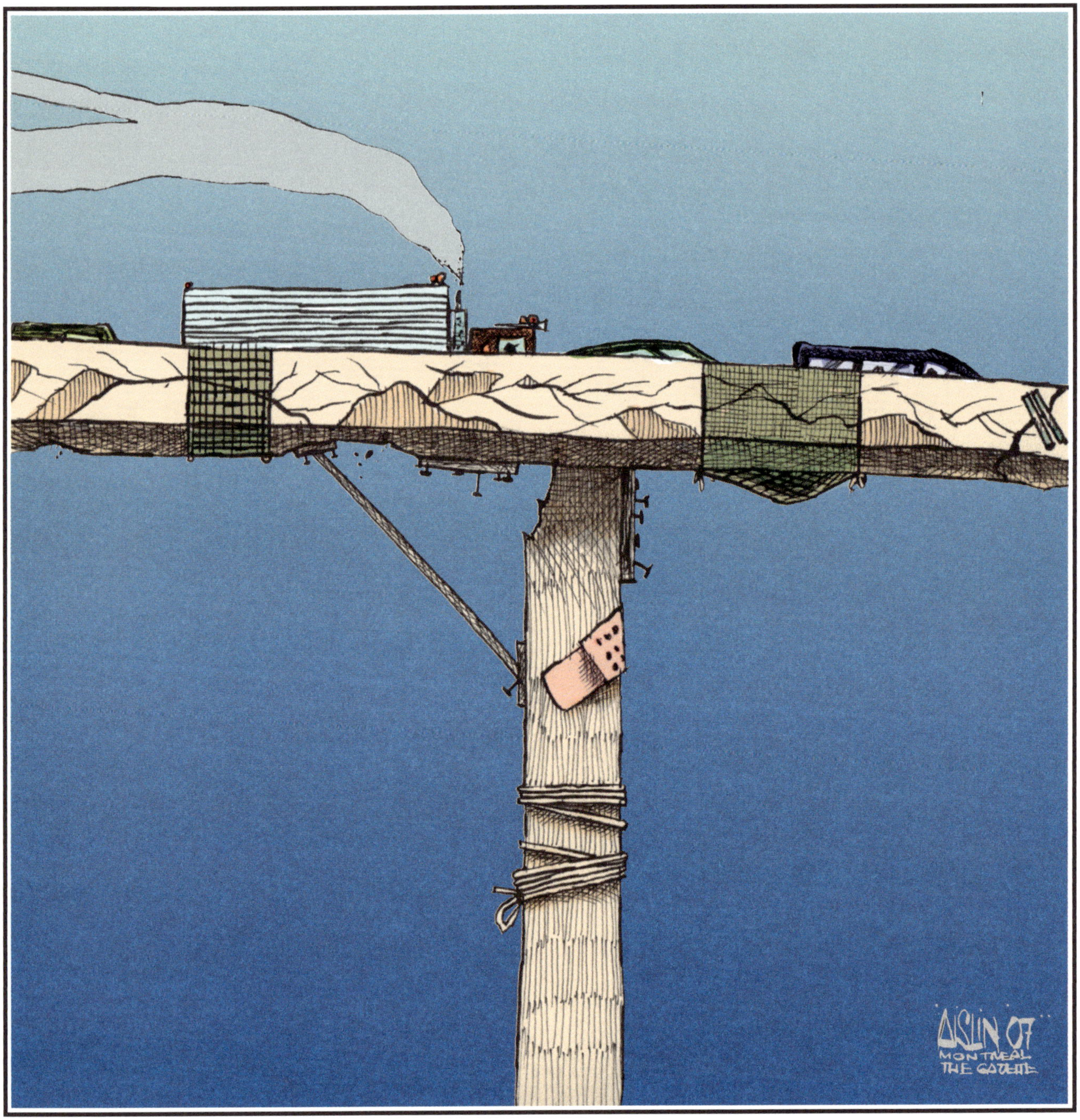
AISLIN 07
MONTREAL
THE GAZETTE

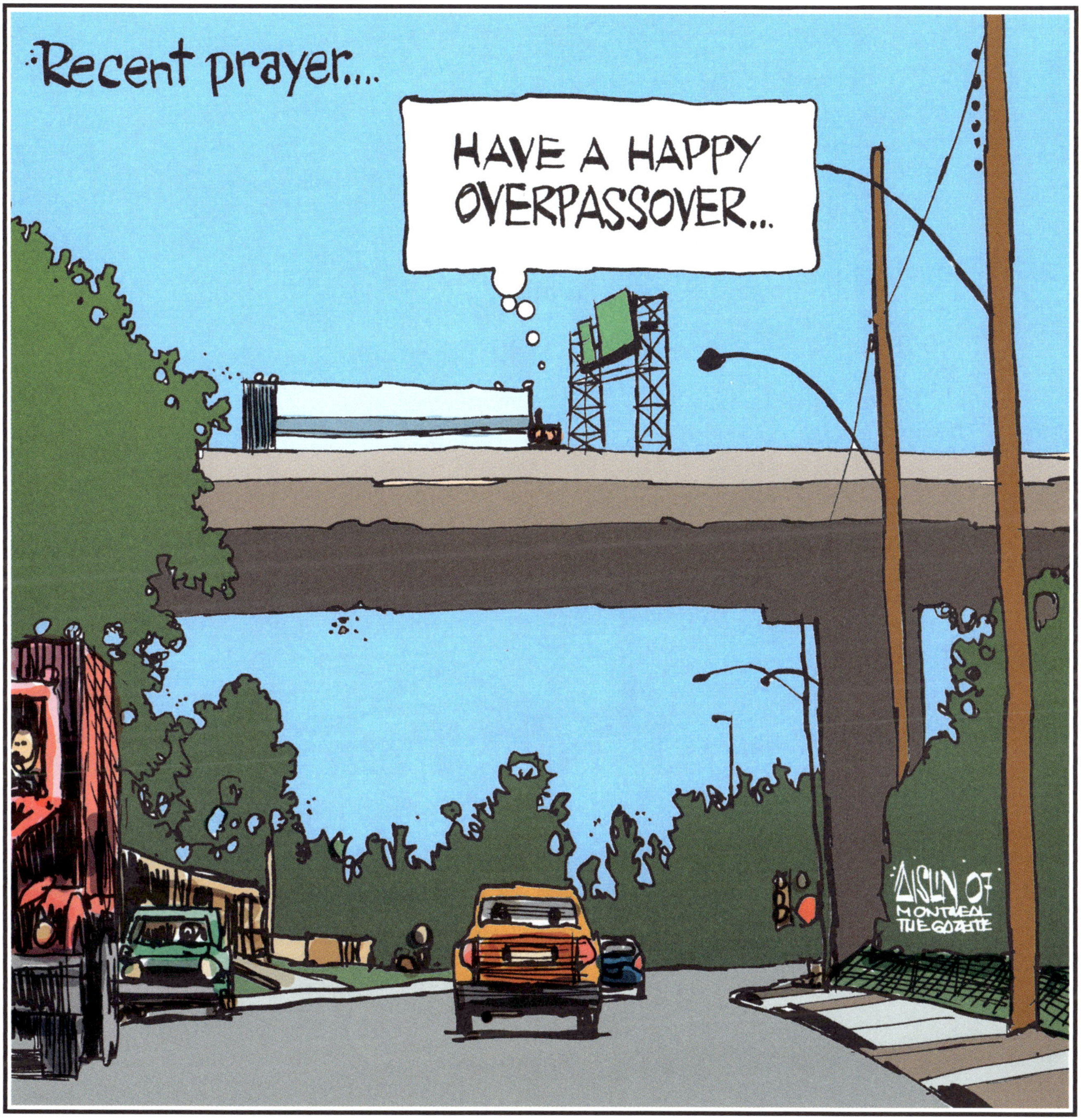
Recent prayer....
HAVE A HAPPY OVERPASSOVER...
AISLIN 07
MONTREAL THE GAZETTE

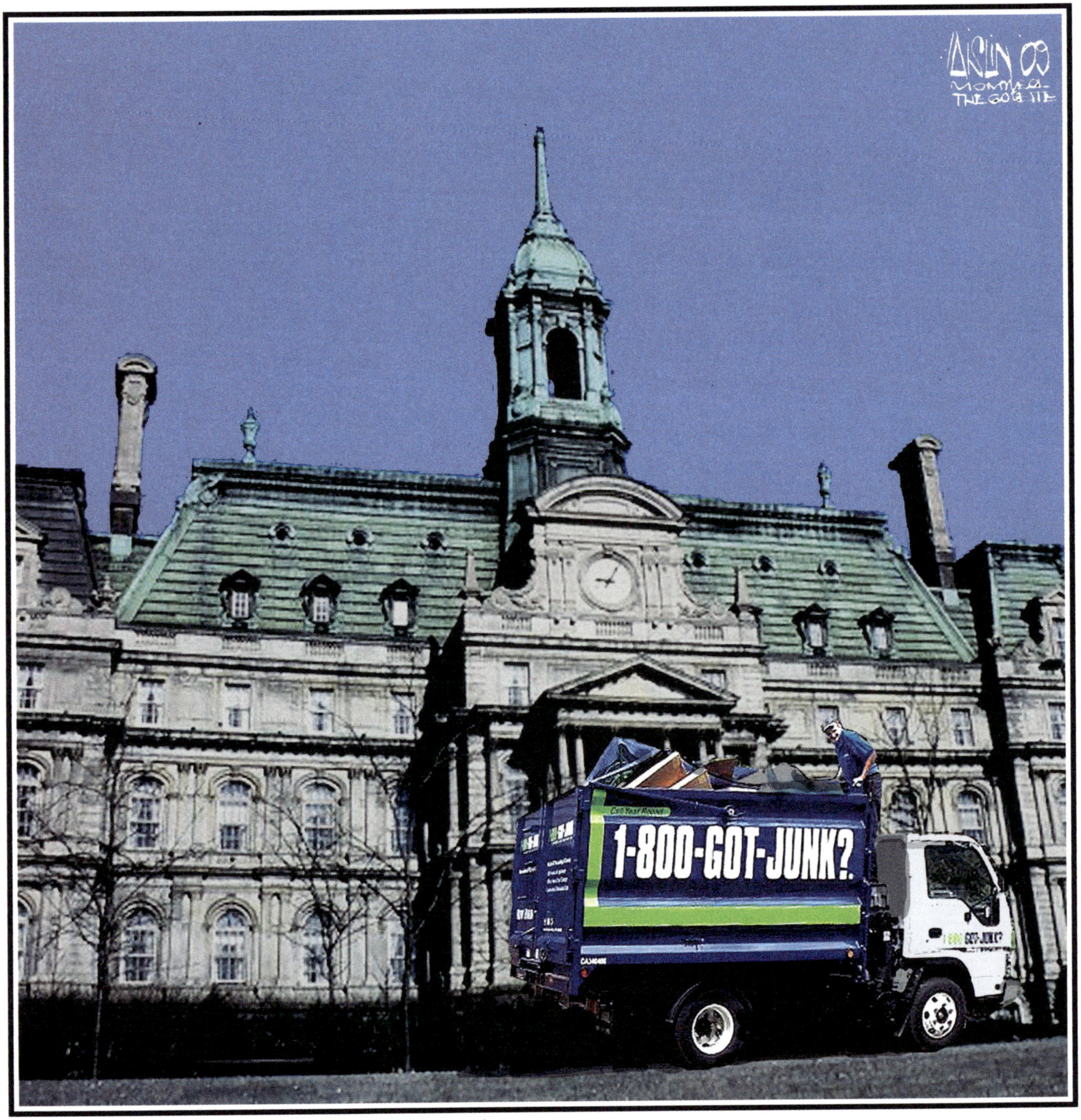
1-800-GOT-JUNK?

Montreal's city hall mired in an ethics scandal over finances

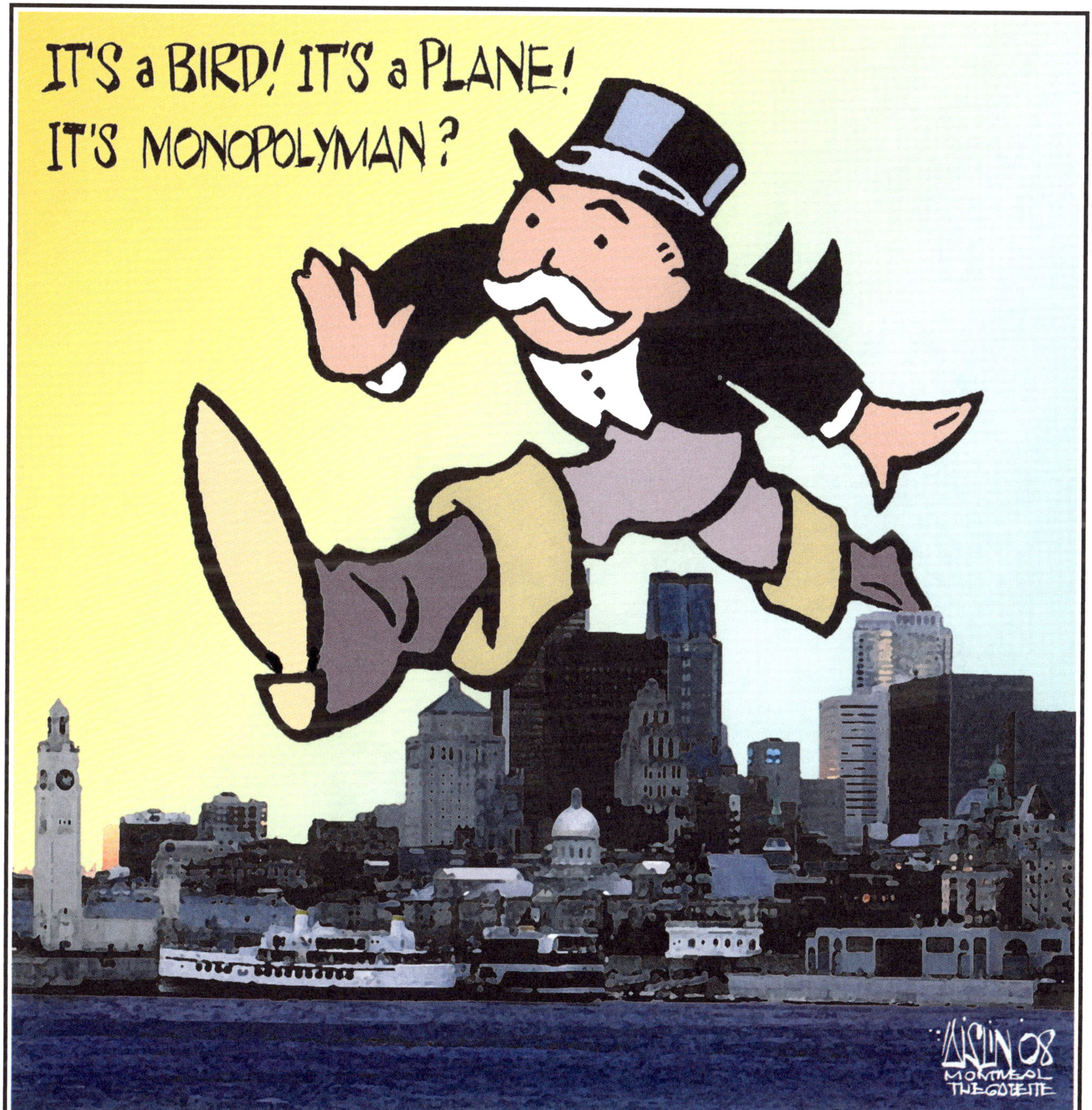
IT'S a BIRD! IT'S a PLANE!
IT'S MONOPOLYMAN?

Montreal becomes a property on international edition of Monopoly

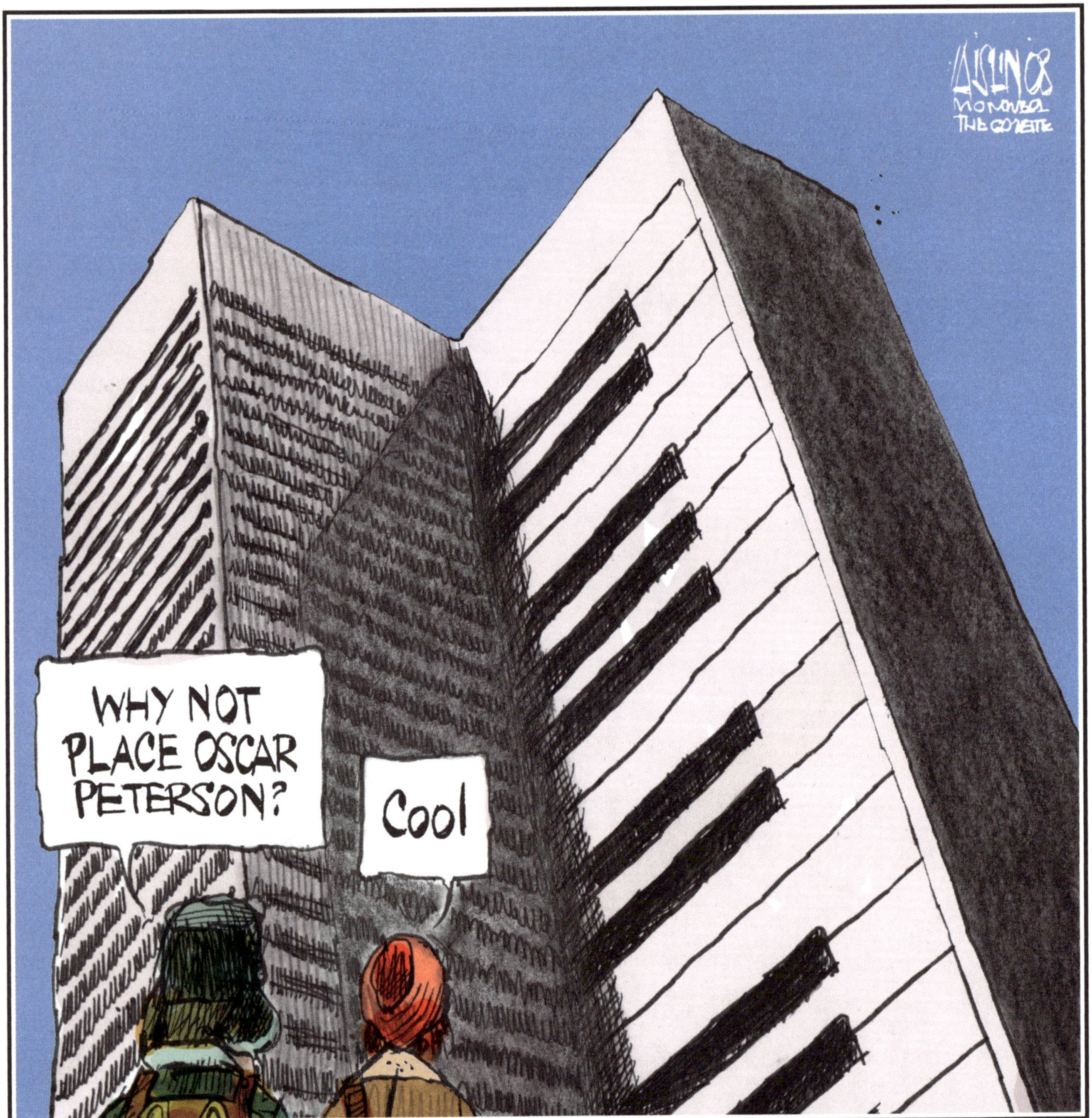
WHY NOT PLACE OSCAR PETERSON?
Cool

Oscar Peterson passes

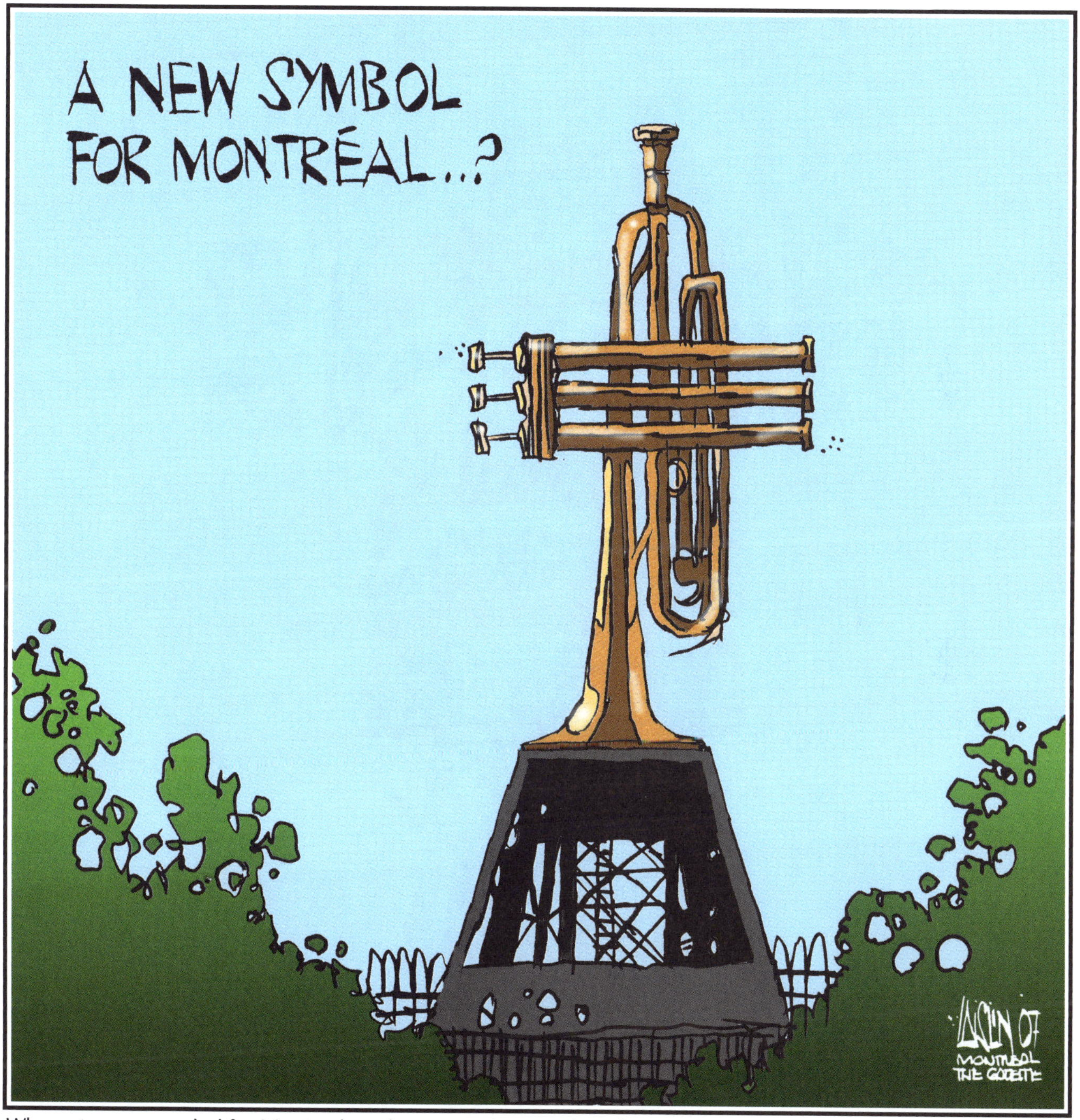
A NEW SYMBOL
FOR MONTRÉAL...?
MONTREAL
THE GAZETTE
Why not a new symbol for Montreal on the mountain to replace the cross?

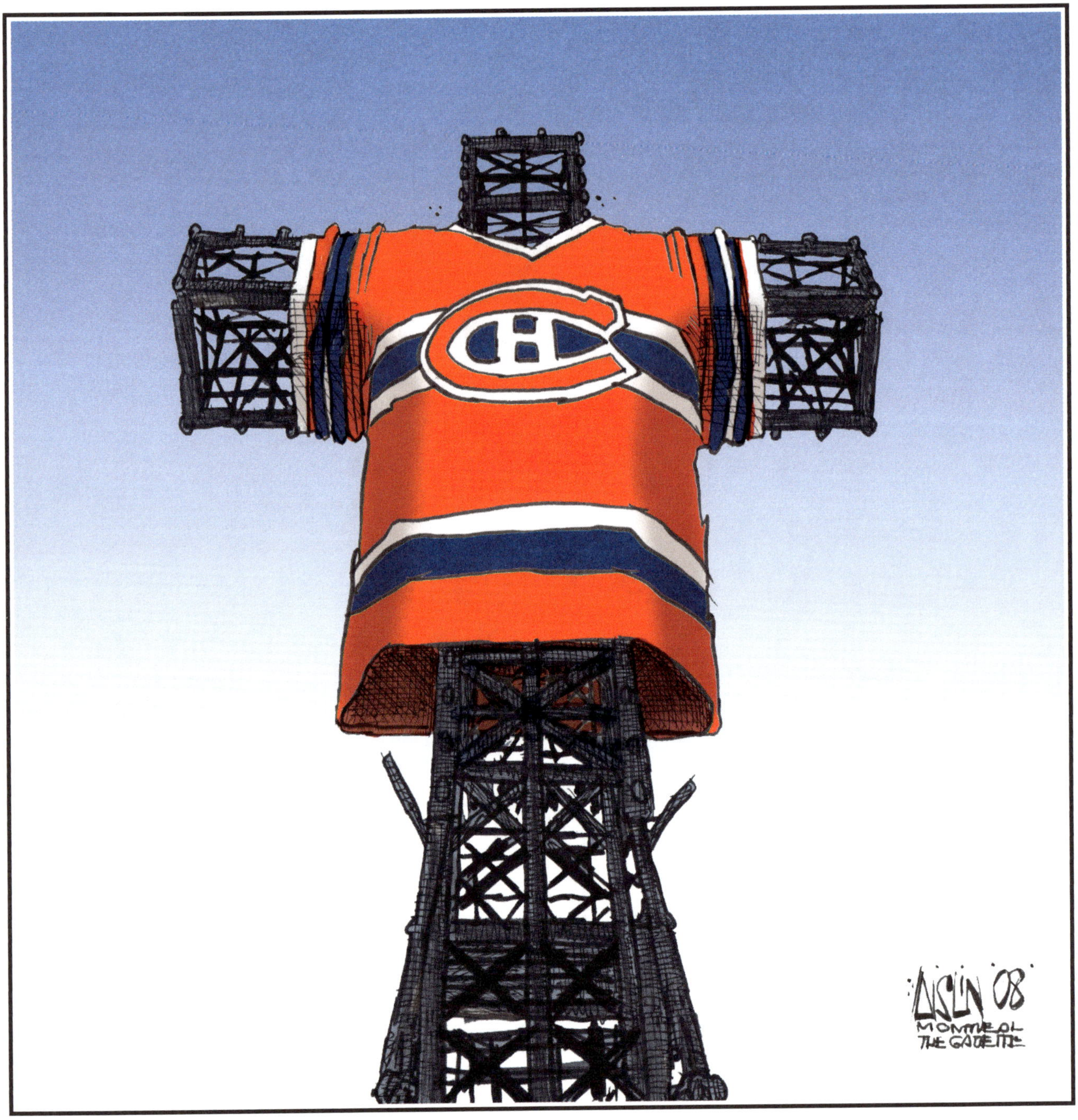
AISLIN '08
MONTREAL
THE GAZETTE
Or even better yet?

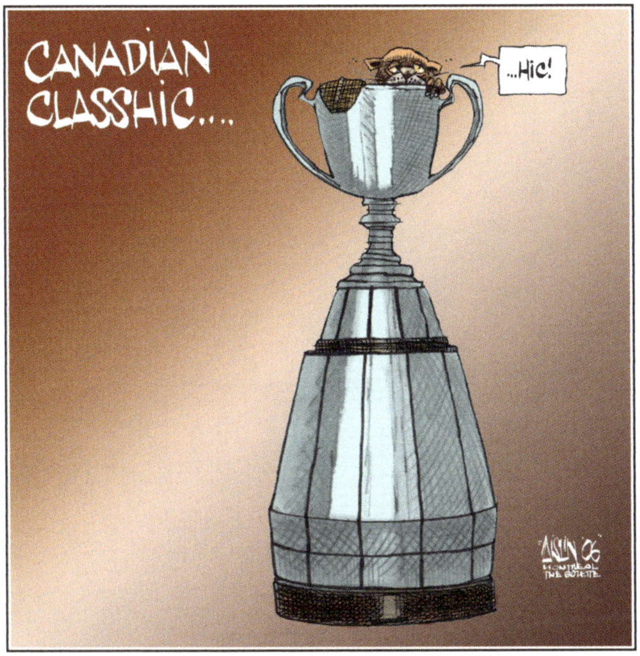
CANADIAN CLASSHIC....
...Hic!
AISLIN 08
MONTREAL
THE GAZETTE

Montrealers love all sports: Football…

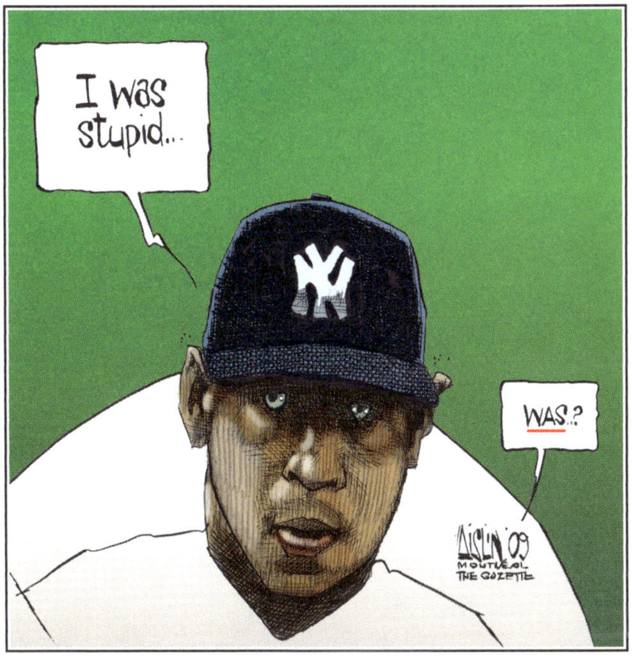
I was stupid...
WAS.?
AISLIN 09
MONTREAL
THE GAZETTE

…baseball…

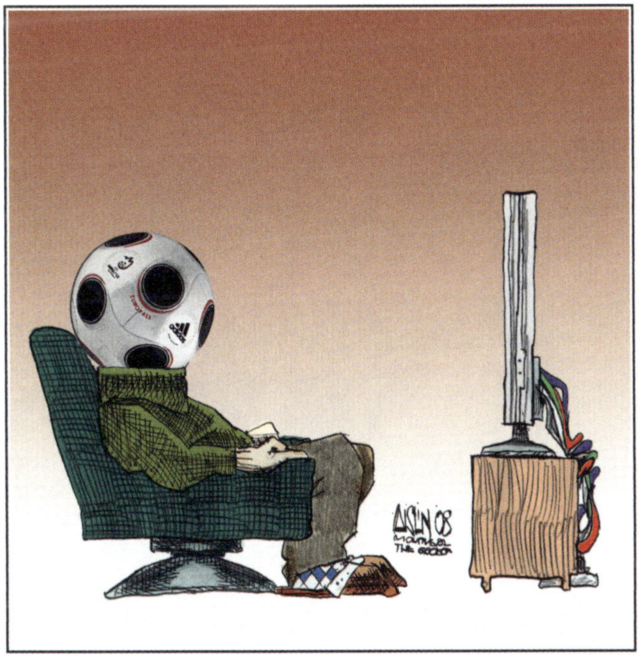
AISLIN 08

…soccer…

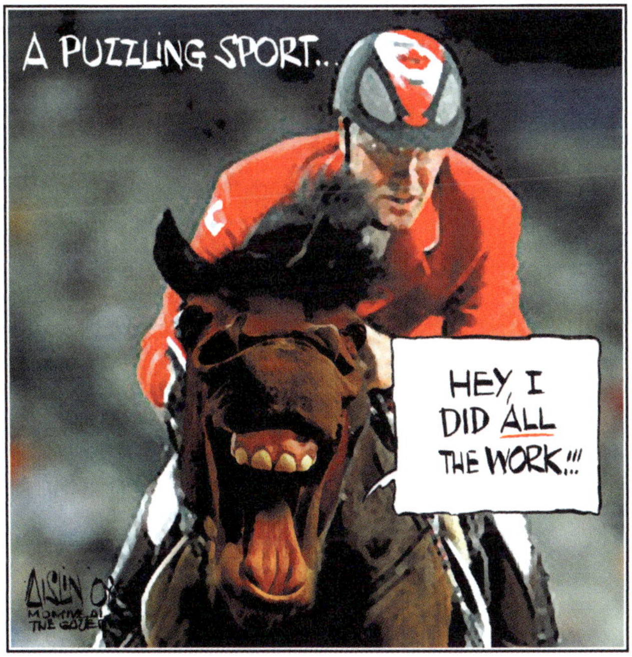
A PUZZLING SPORT...
HEY, I DID ALL THE WORK!!!

…the Olympics…

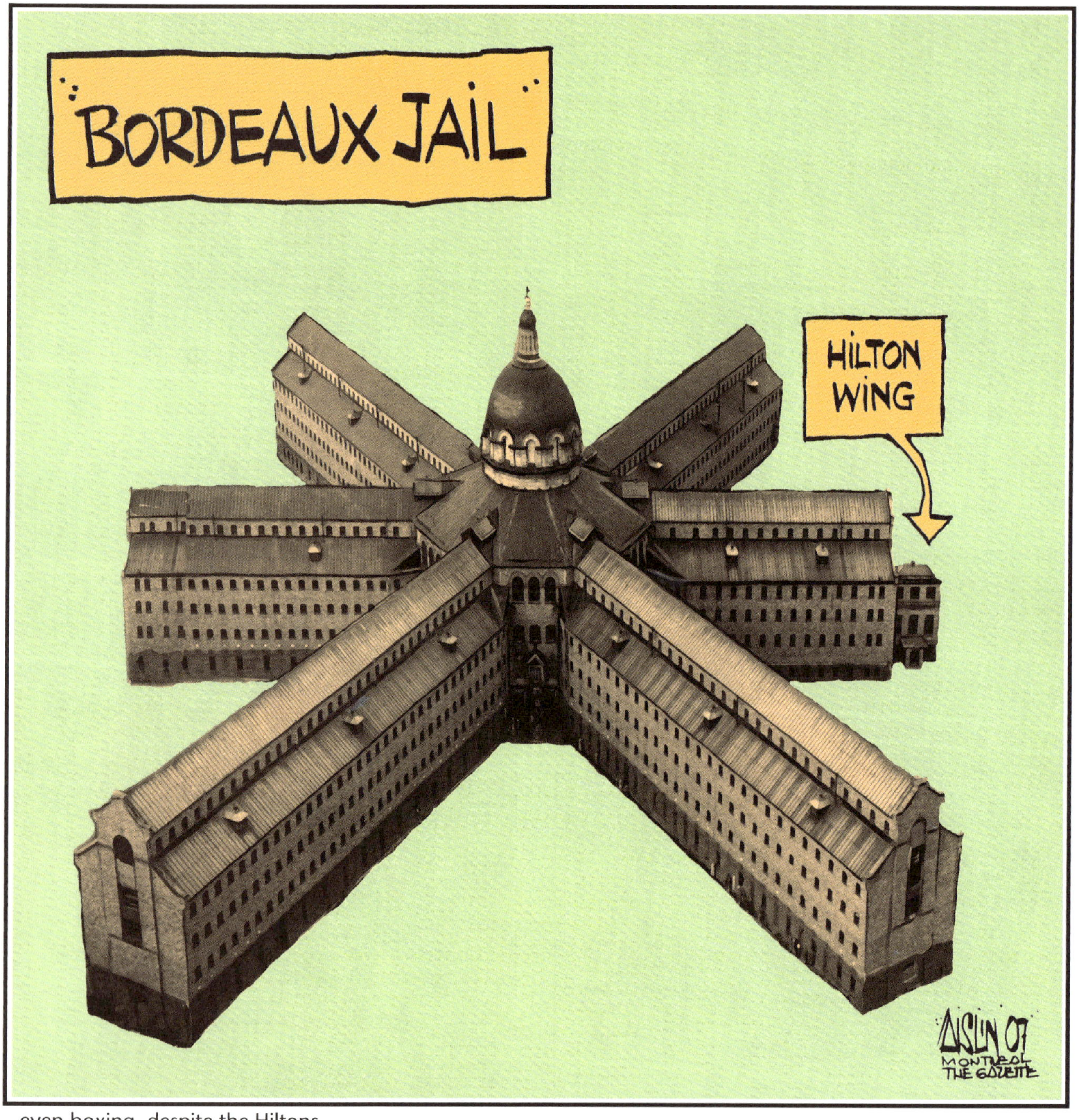
BORDEAUX JAIL
HILTON WING
AISLIN 07
MONTREAL THE GAZETTE
…even boxing, despite the Hiltons

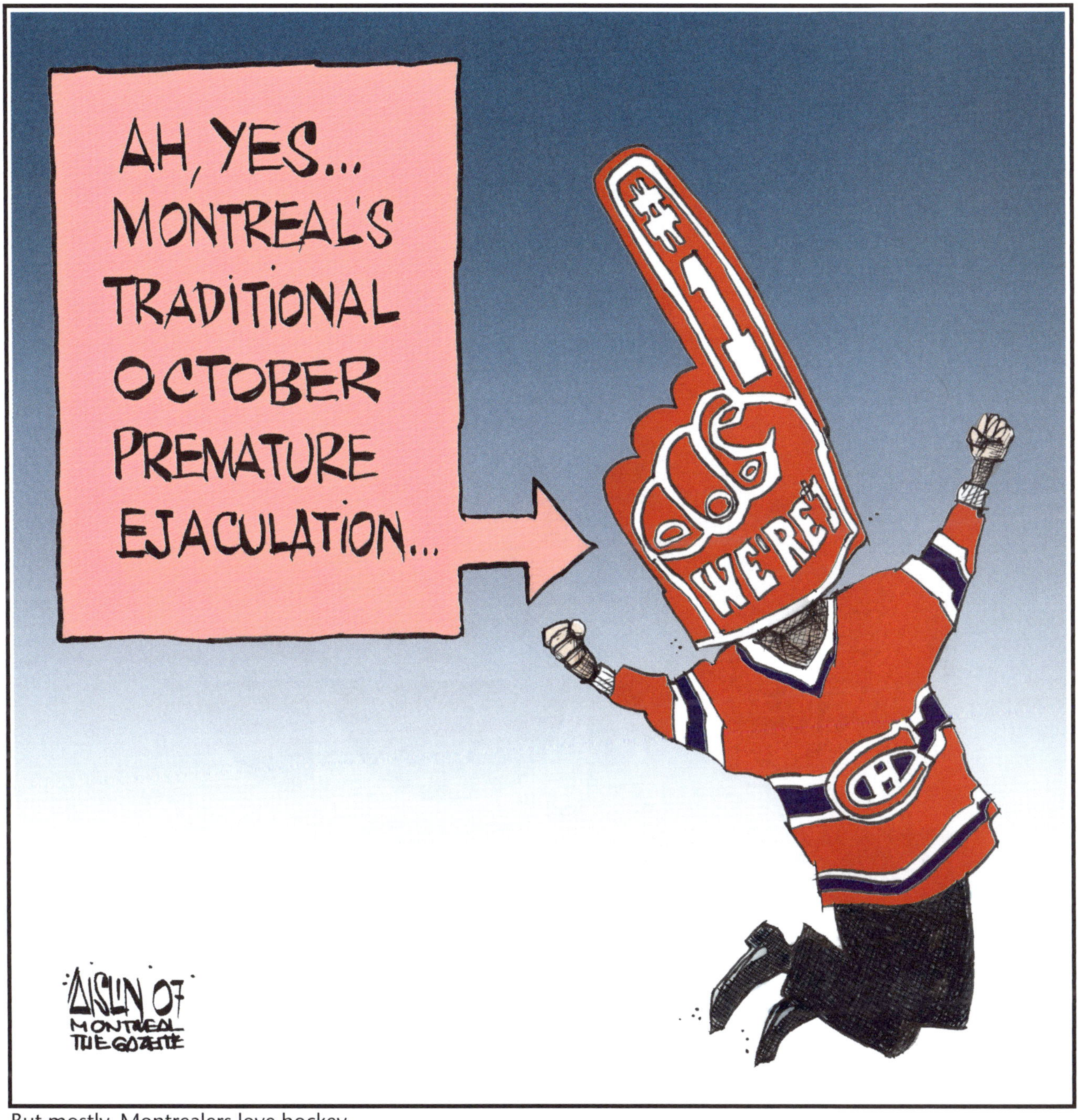
AH, YES...
MONTREAL'S
TRADITIONAL
OCTOBER
PREMATURE
EJACULATION...
#1
WE'RE
AISLIN 07
MONTREAL
THE GAZETTE

But mostly, Montrealers love hockey…

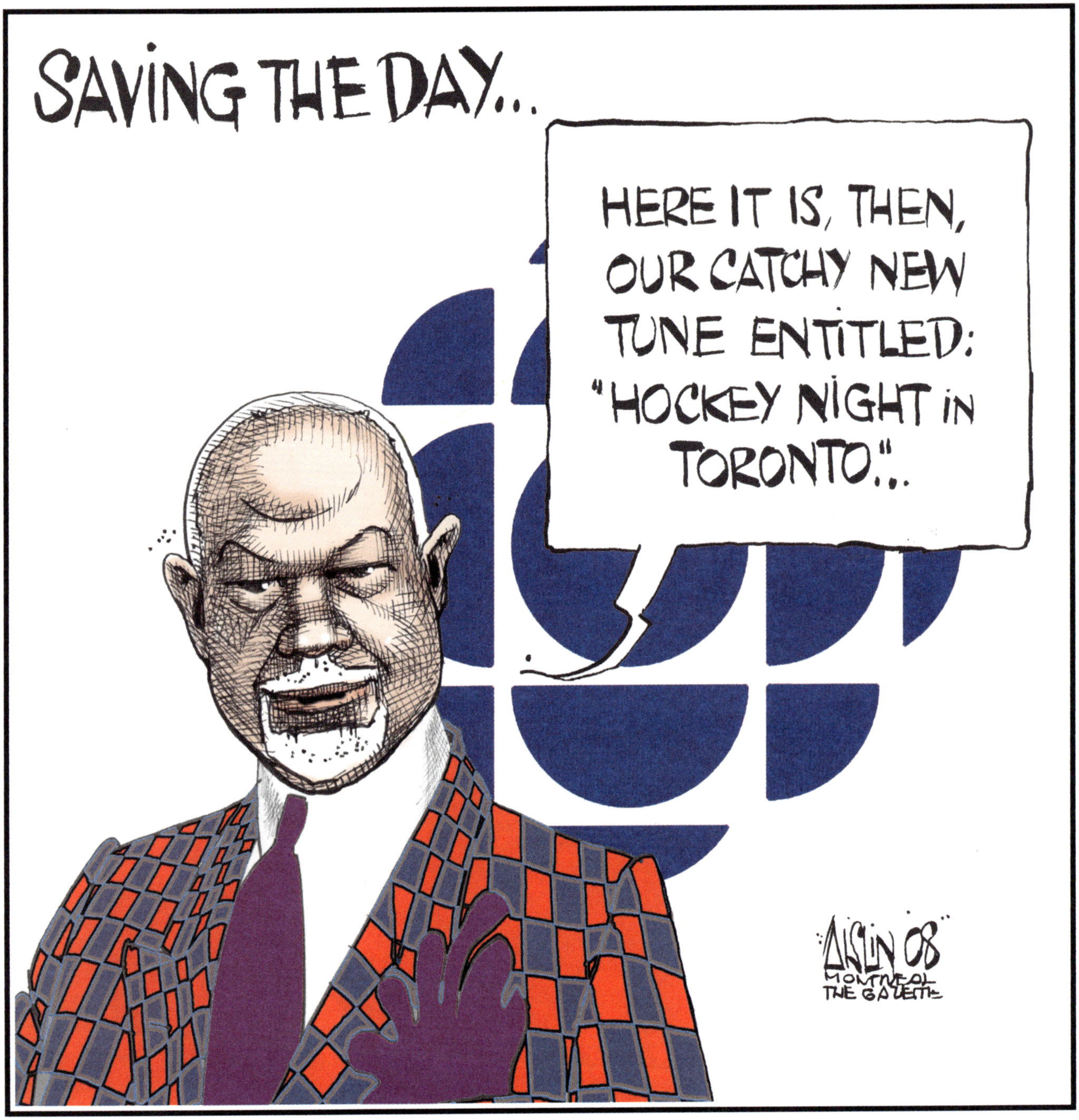
SAVING THE DAY...
HERE IT IS, THEN, OUR CATCHY NEW TUNE ENTITLED: "HOCKEY NIGHT IN TORONTO."..
AISLIN 08
MONTREAL THE GAZETTE

...and hating Toronto!

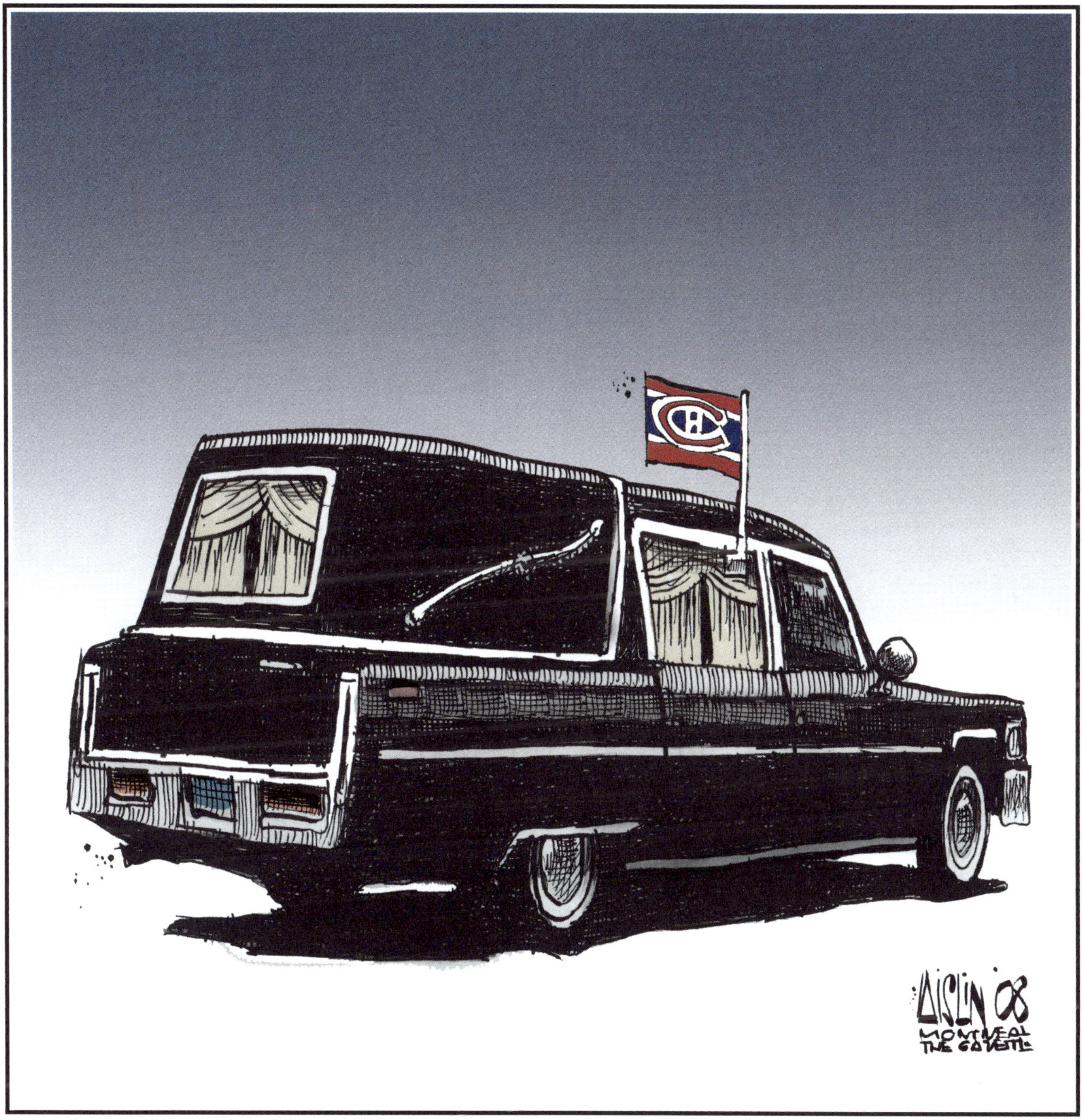
AISLIN '08
MONTREAL
THE GAZETTE
Habs eliminated from playoffs

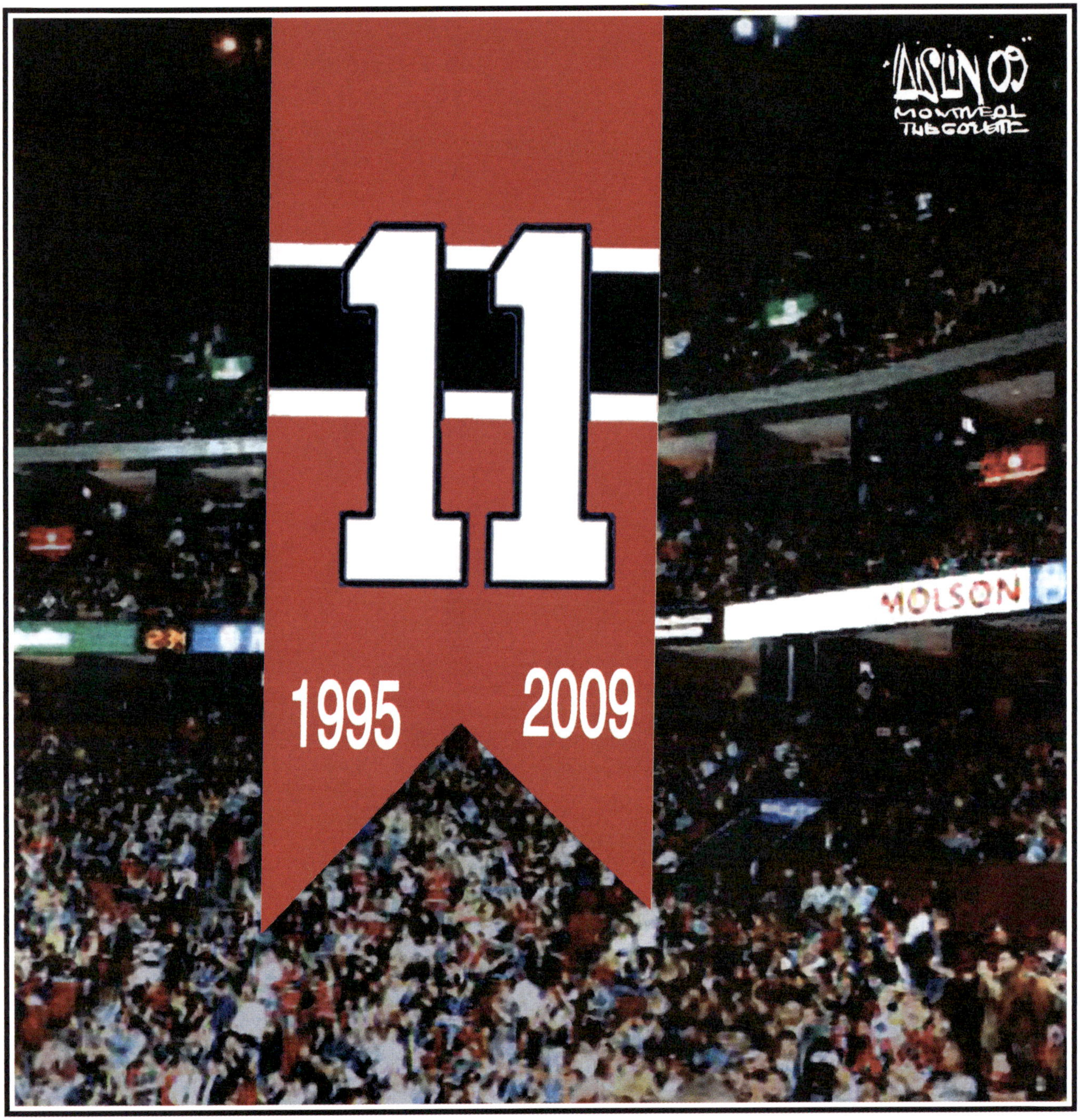
AISLIN 09
MONTREAL
THE GAZETTE
11
1995
2009
MOLSON

Popular Saku Koivu dropped by Habs

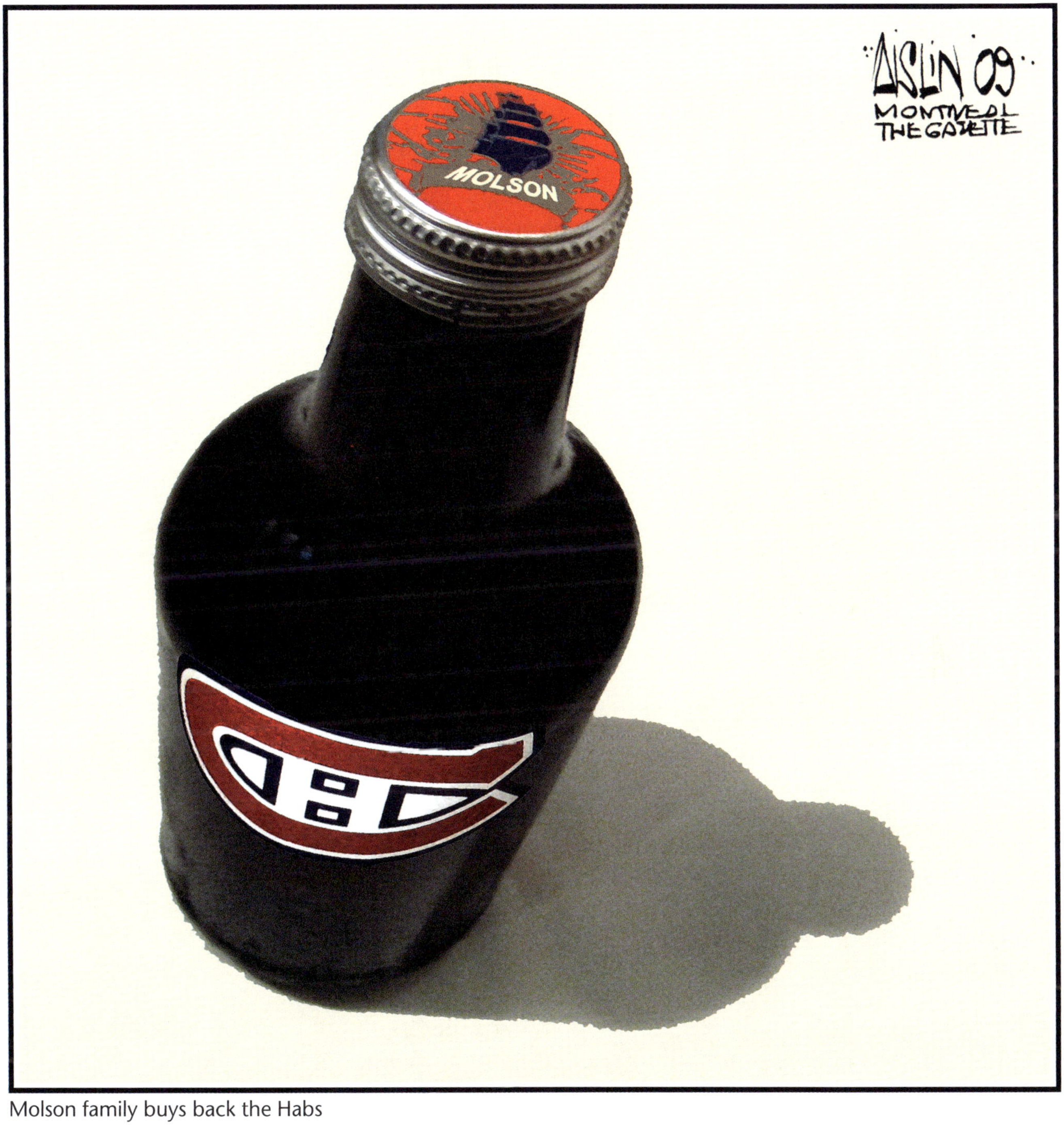
AISLIN 09
MONTREAL
THE GAZETTE
MOLSON

Molson family buys back the Habs

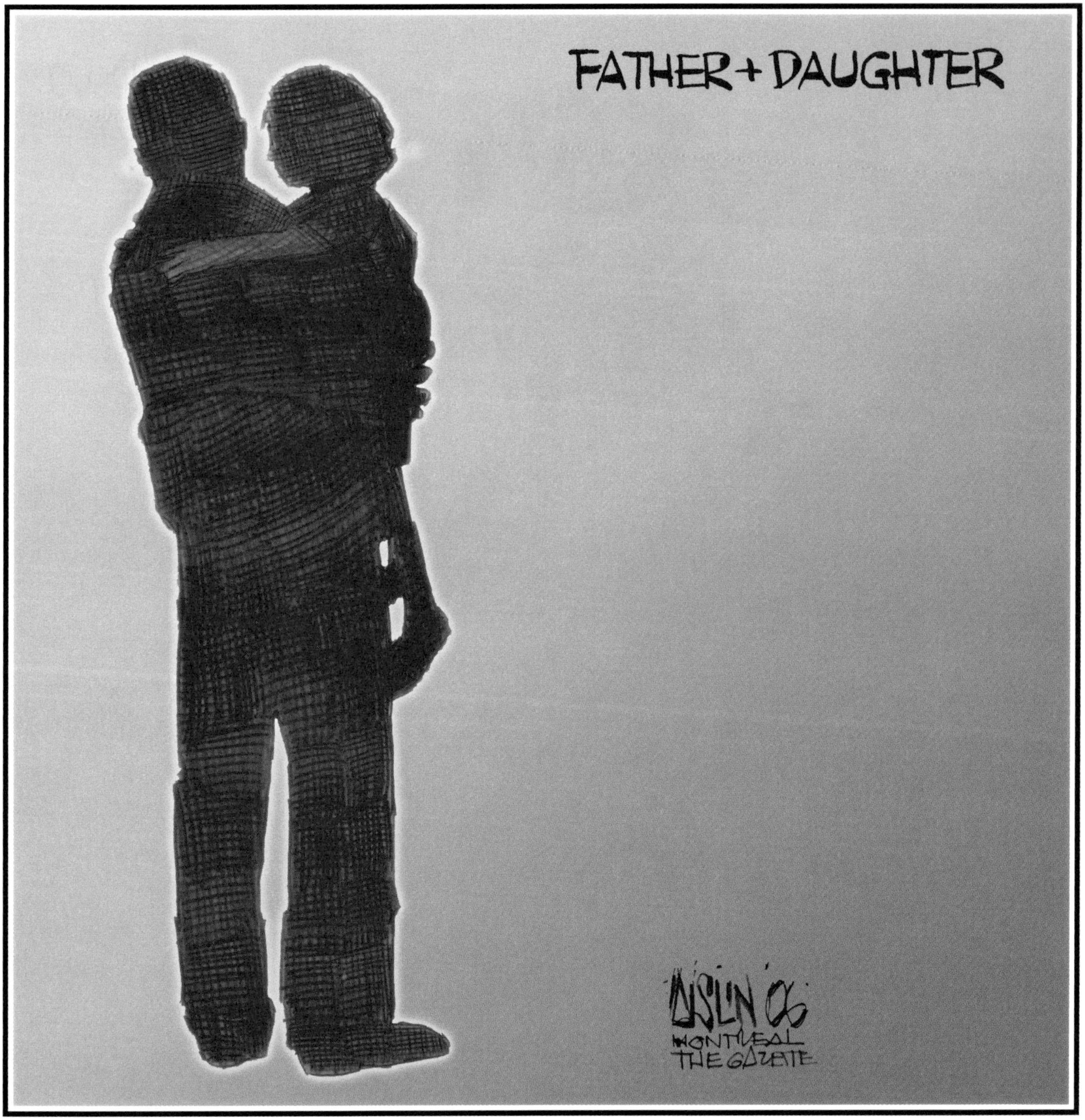
FATHER + DAUGHTER
AISLIN '06
MONTREAL
THE GAZETTE

CHAPTER 5

And So It Goes…

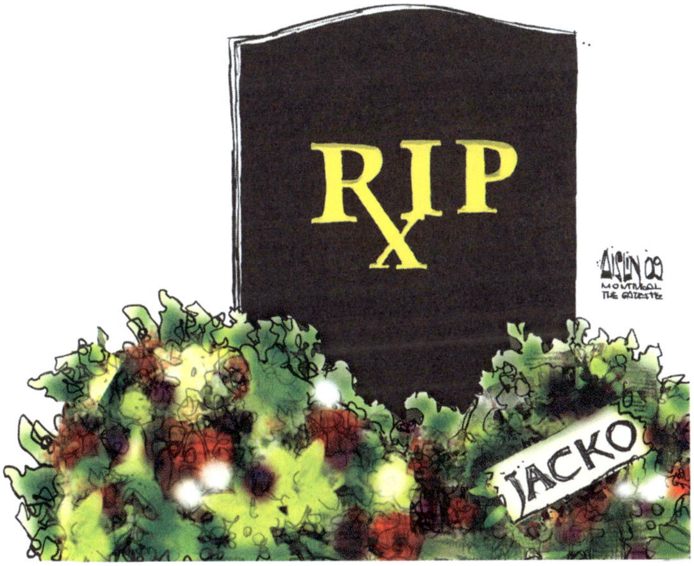
RIP
X
JACKO

Sometimes we're shaken by unexpected and sad events. Bob Gainey lost his daughter in a tragic boating accident at sea. Suddenly, the hockey seems trivial.

We were all riveted by the sudden death of Michael Jackson. No matter our feelings about him, we were affected by the passing of this eternal child, this Peter Pan.

The reach of the political cartoonist has grown in recent years. When I first started out, editorial page cartoons were expected to poke fun only at politics and politicians.

All that has changed. Today, the cartoonist must be aware of everything going around him or her: the world of finance, sports, the entertainment industry, health and environmental issues, technology and even the state of the media and the newspaper industry itself.

We live in a world where everything is intertwined, where even humour has gone global.

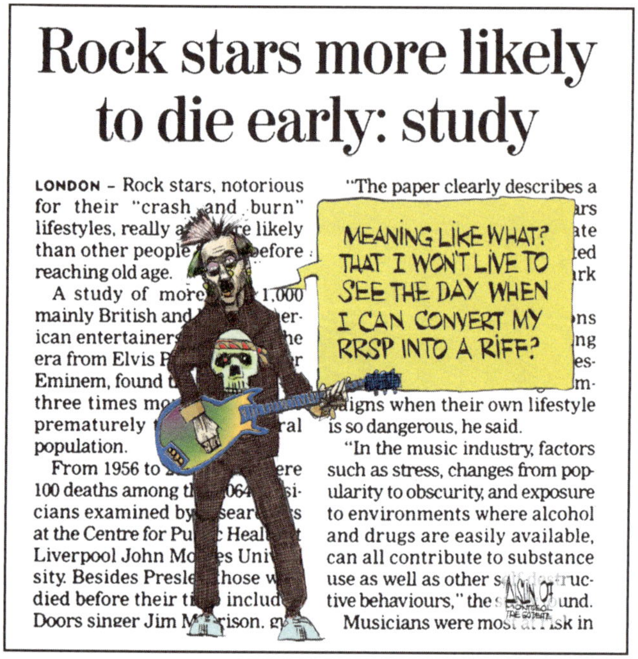
Rock stars more likely to die early: study
MEANING LIKE WHAT? THAT I WON'T LIVE TO SEE THE DAY WHEN I CAN CONVERT MY RRSP INTO A RIFF?

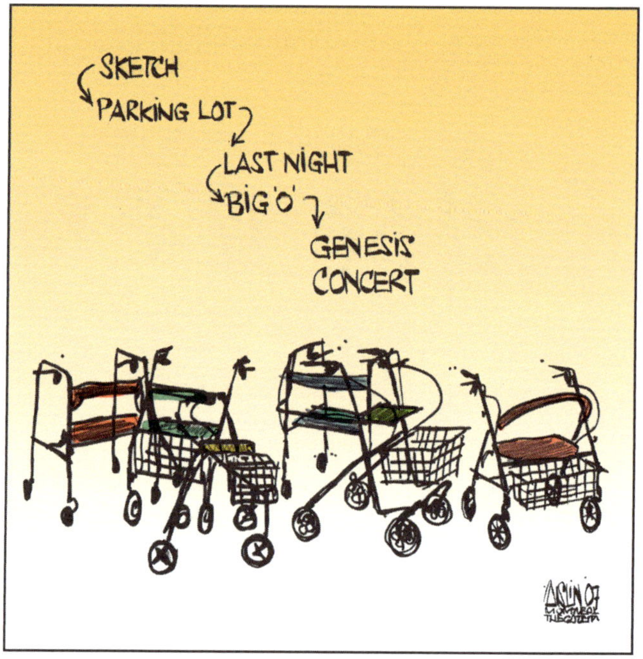
SKETCH
PARKING LOT
LAST NIGHT
BIG 'O'
GENESIS CONCERT

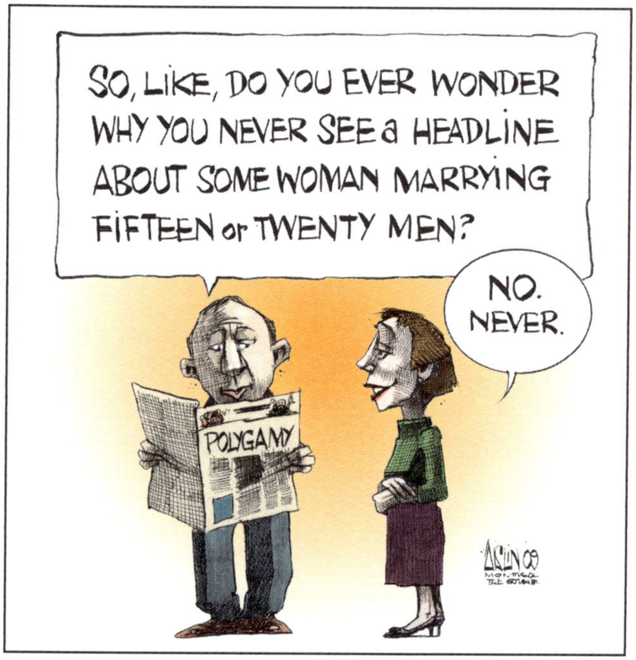
SO, LIKE, DO YOU EVER WONDER WHY YOU NEVER SEE a HEADLINE ABOUT SOME WOMAN MARRYING FIFTEEN or TWENTY MEN?
NO. NEVER.
POLYGAMY

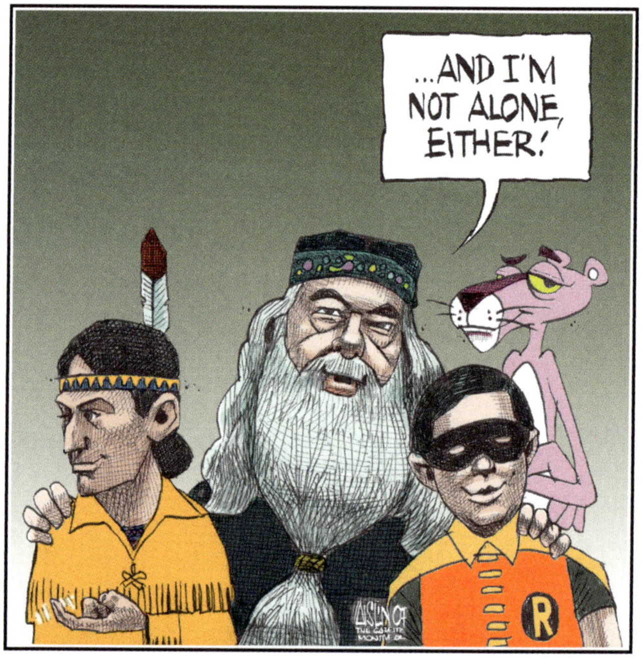
...AND I'M NOT ALONE, EITHER!

J. K. Rowling reveals that Dumbledore is gay

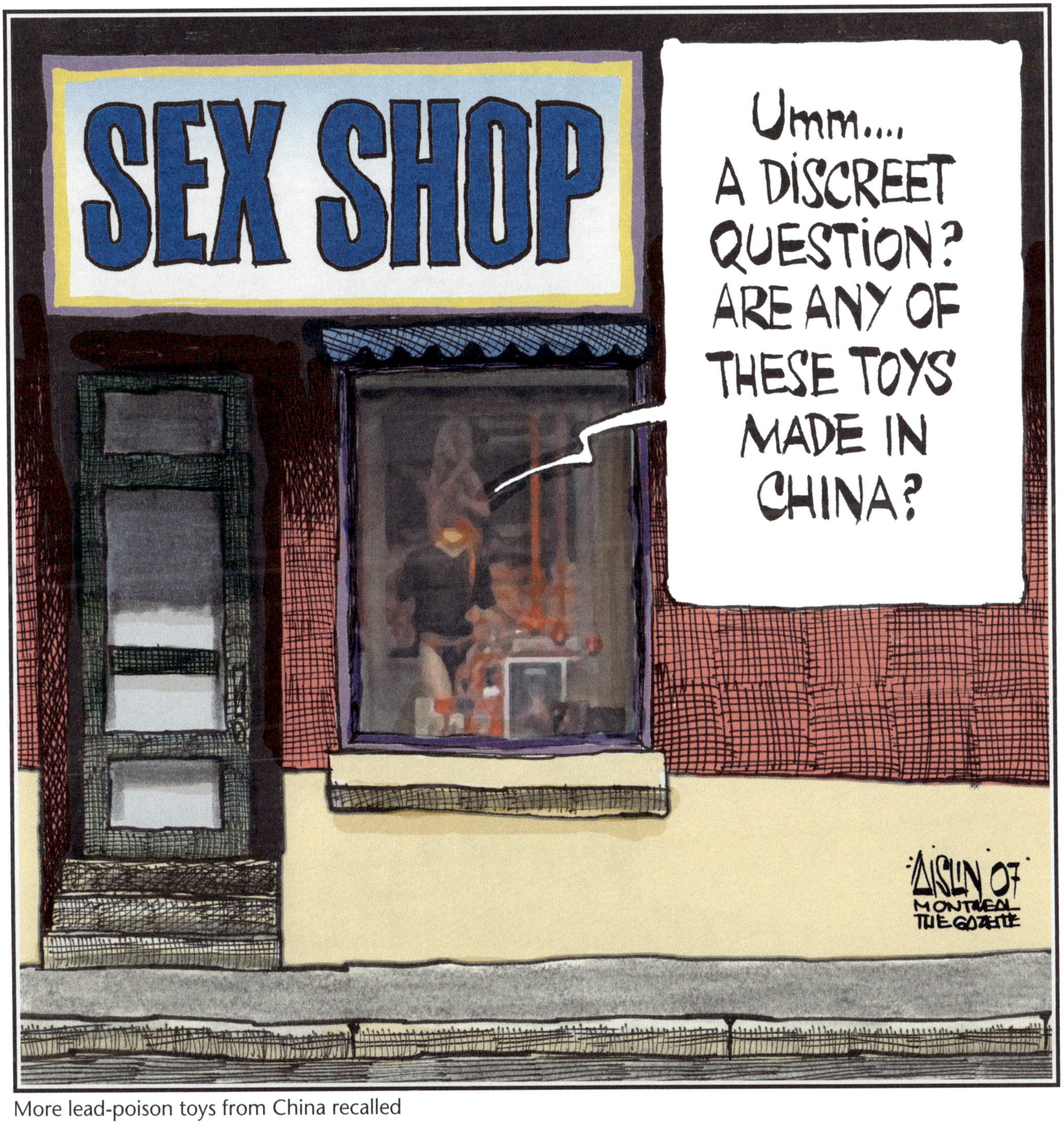
SEX SHOP
Umm.... A DISCREET QUESTION? ARE ANY OF THESE TOYS MADE IN CHINA?
AISLIN 07 MONTREAL THE GAZETTE

More lead-poison toys from China recalled

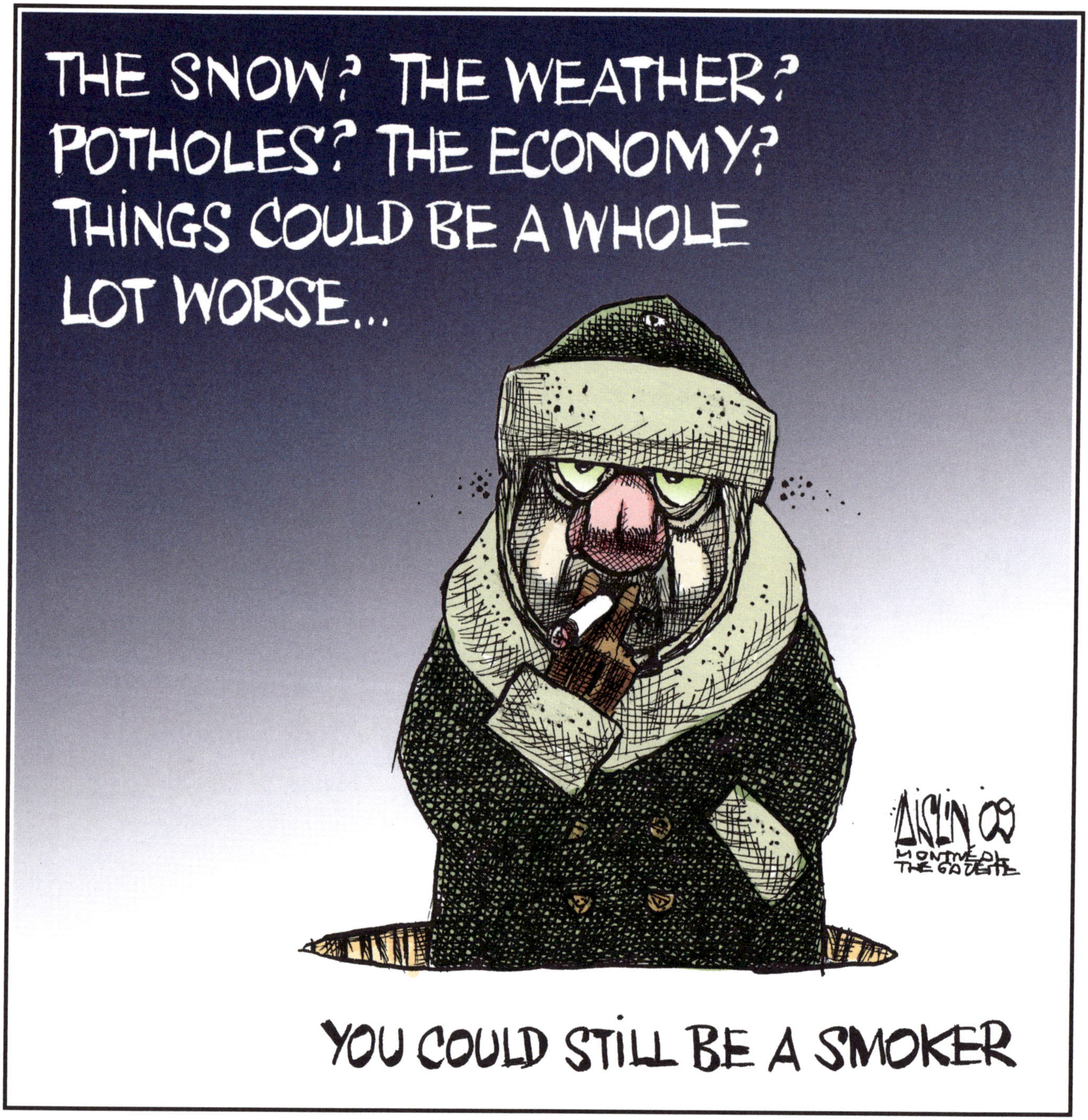
THE SNOW? THE WEATHER? POTHOLES? THE ECONOMY? THINGS COULD BE A WHOLE LOT WORSE...
YOU COULD STILL BE A SMOKER

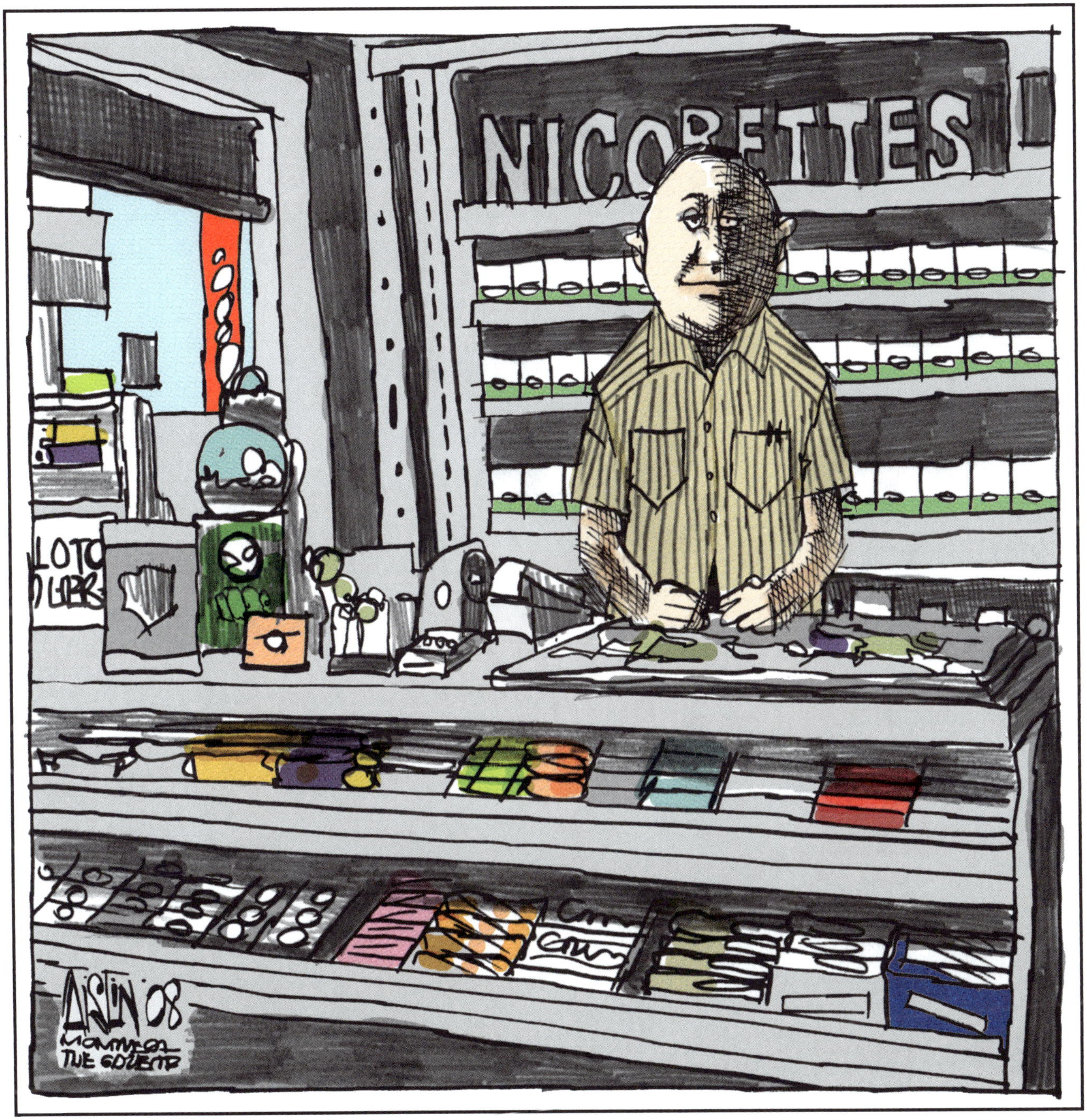
NICORETTES

Cigarettes may no longer be displayed in stores

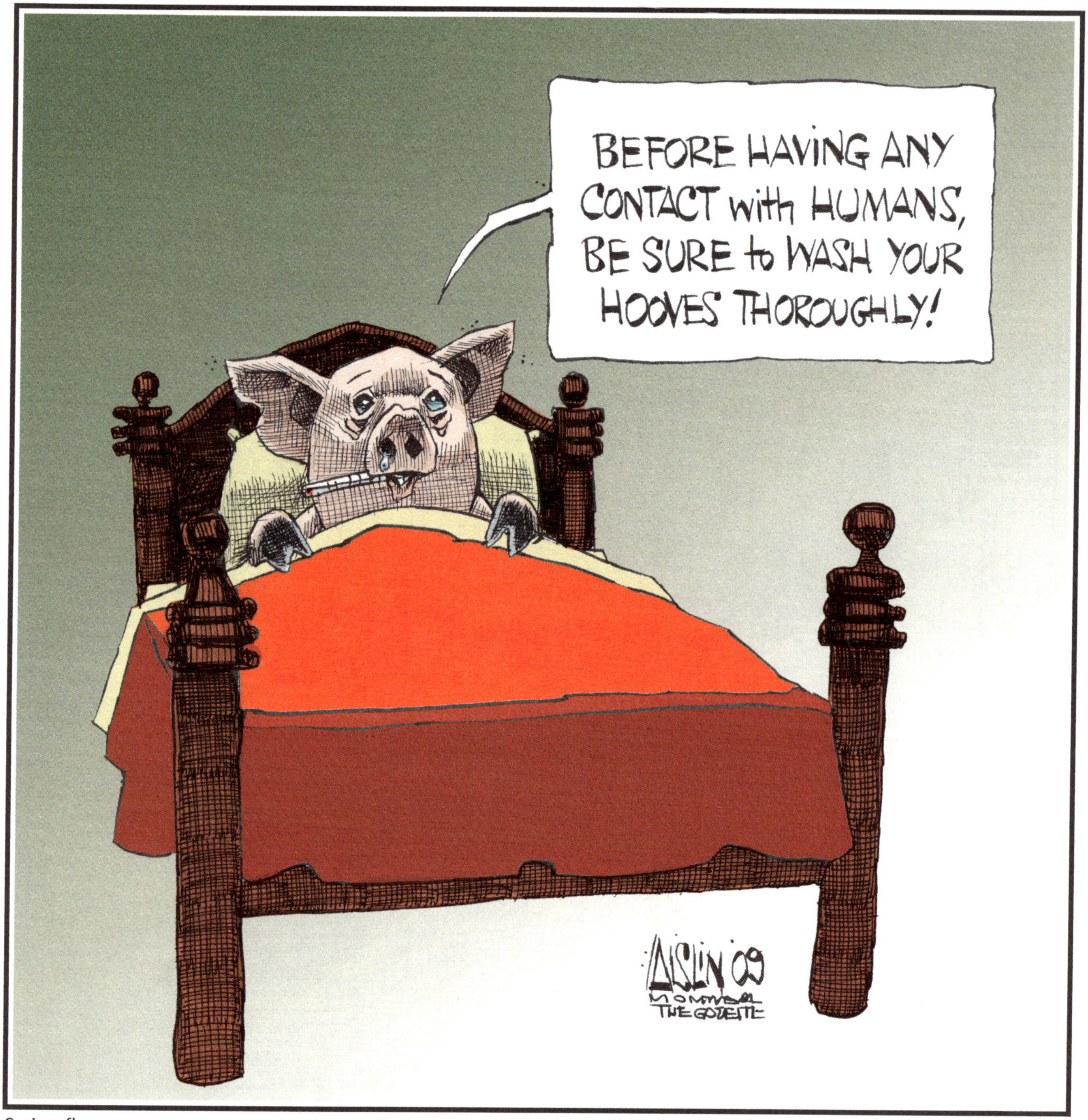
BEFORE HAVING ANY CONTACT with HUMANS, BE SURE to WASH YOUR HOOVES THOROUGHLY!
AISLIN '09
MONTREAL
THE GAZETTE

Swine flu

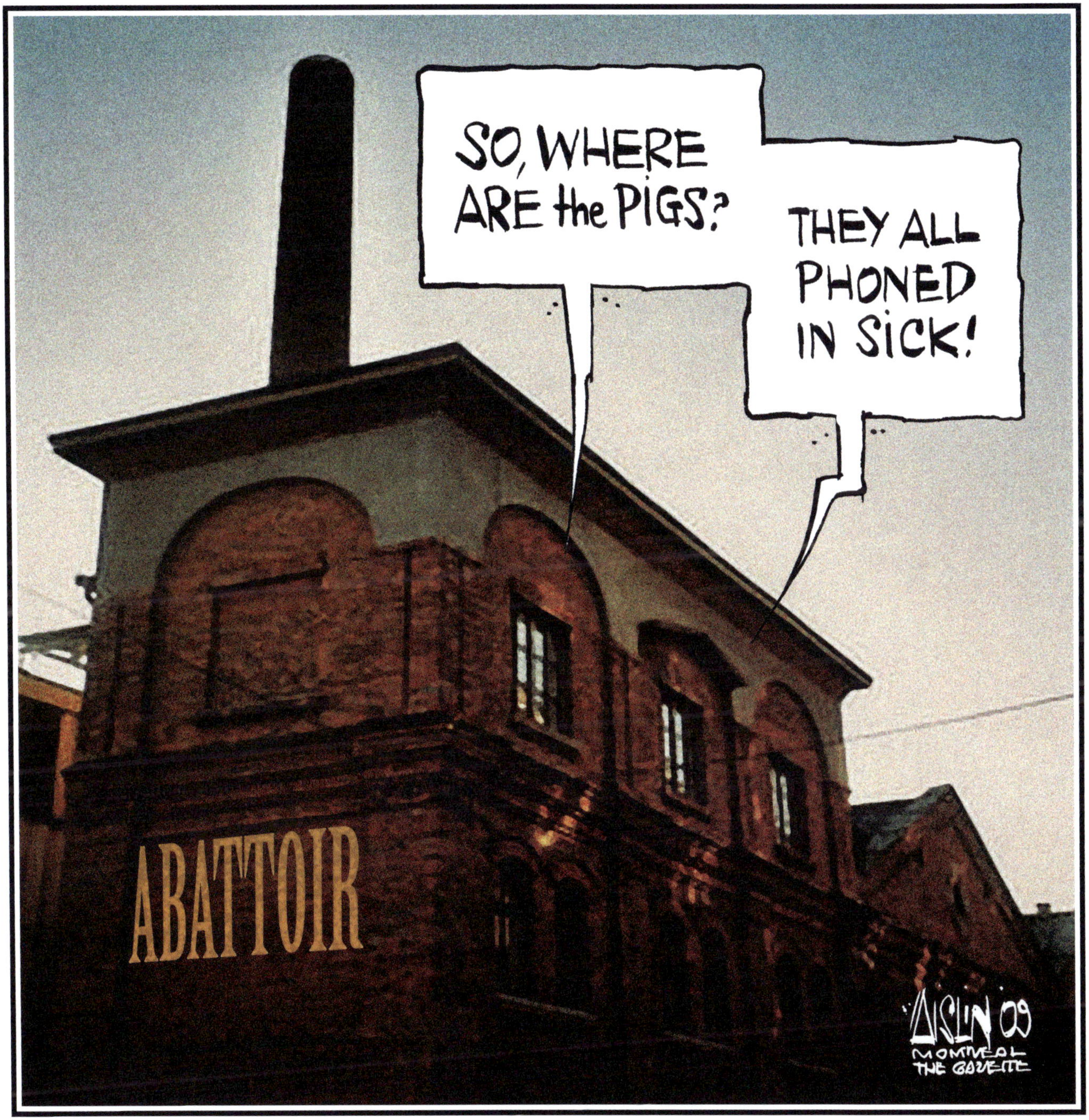
SO, WHERE ARE the PIGS?
THEY ALL PHONED IN SICK!
ABATTOIR
AISLIN '09
MONTREAL THE GAZETTE

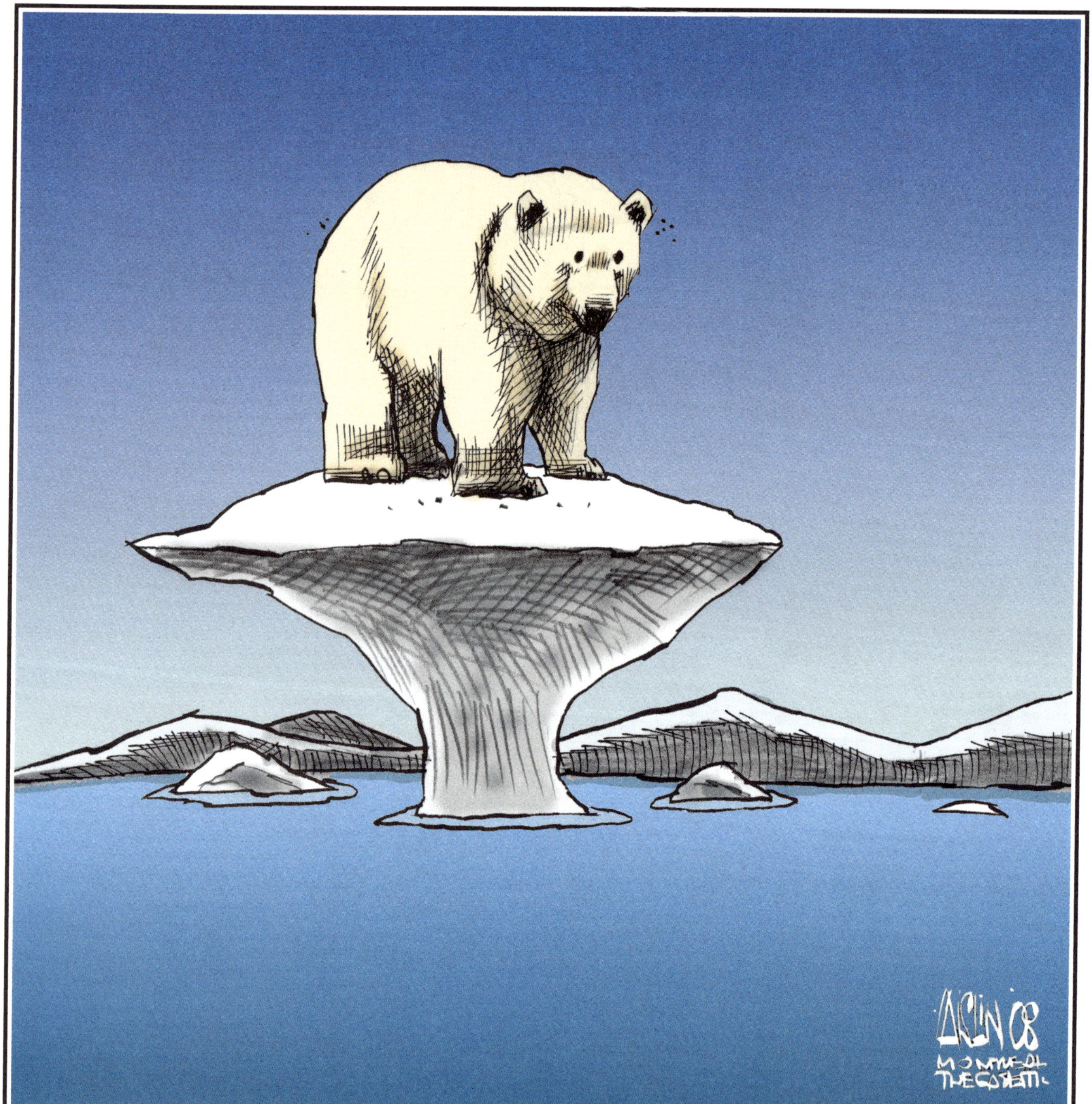
AISLIN 08

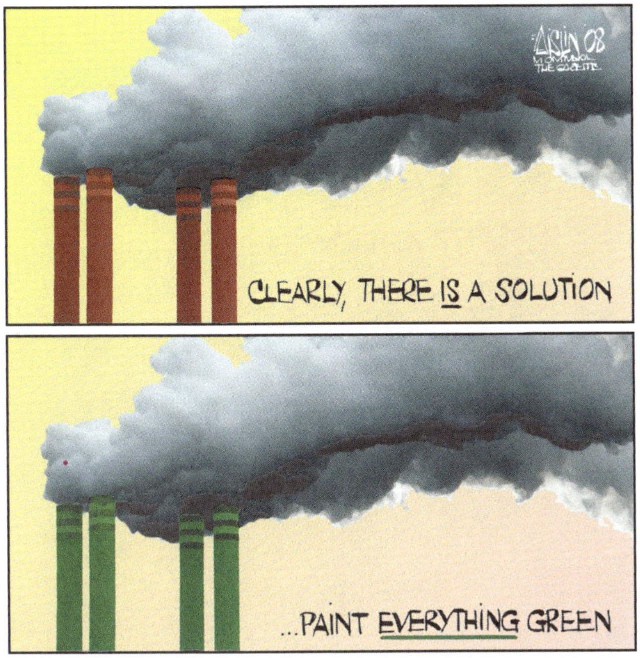
CLEARLY, THERE IS A SOLUTION
...PAINT EVERYTHING GREEN

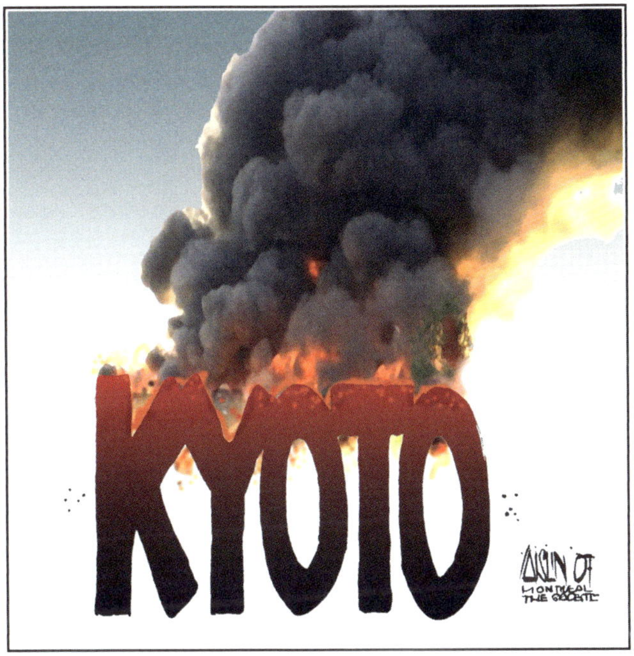
KYOTO

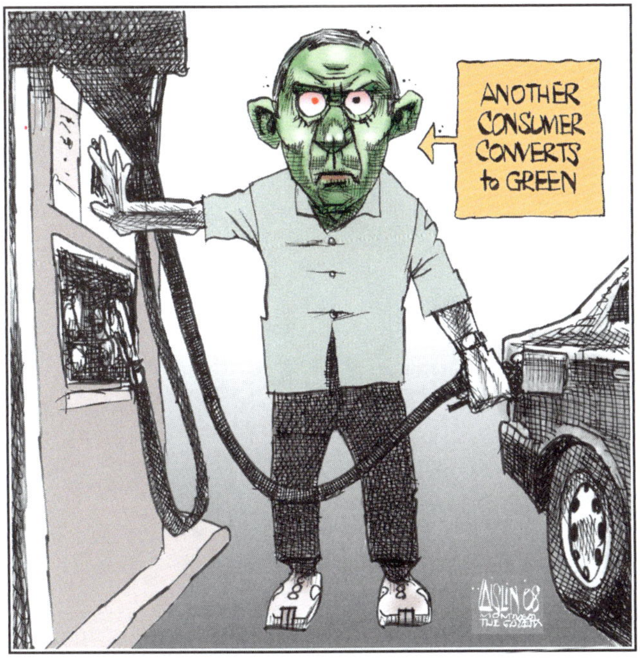
ANOTHER CONSUMER CONVERTS to GREEN

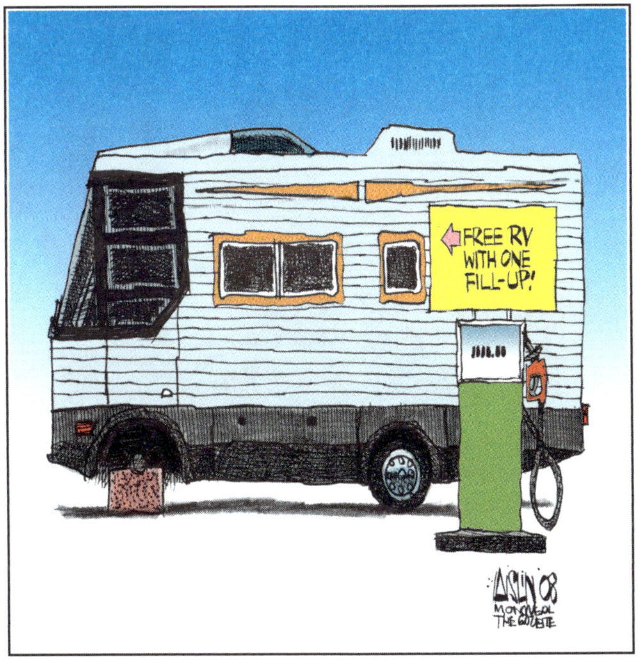
FREE RV WITH ONE FILL-UP!

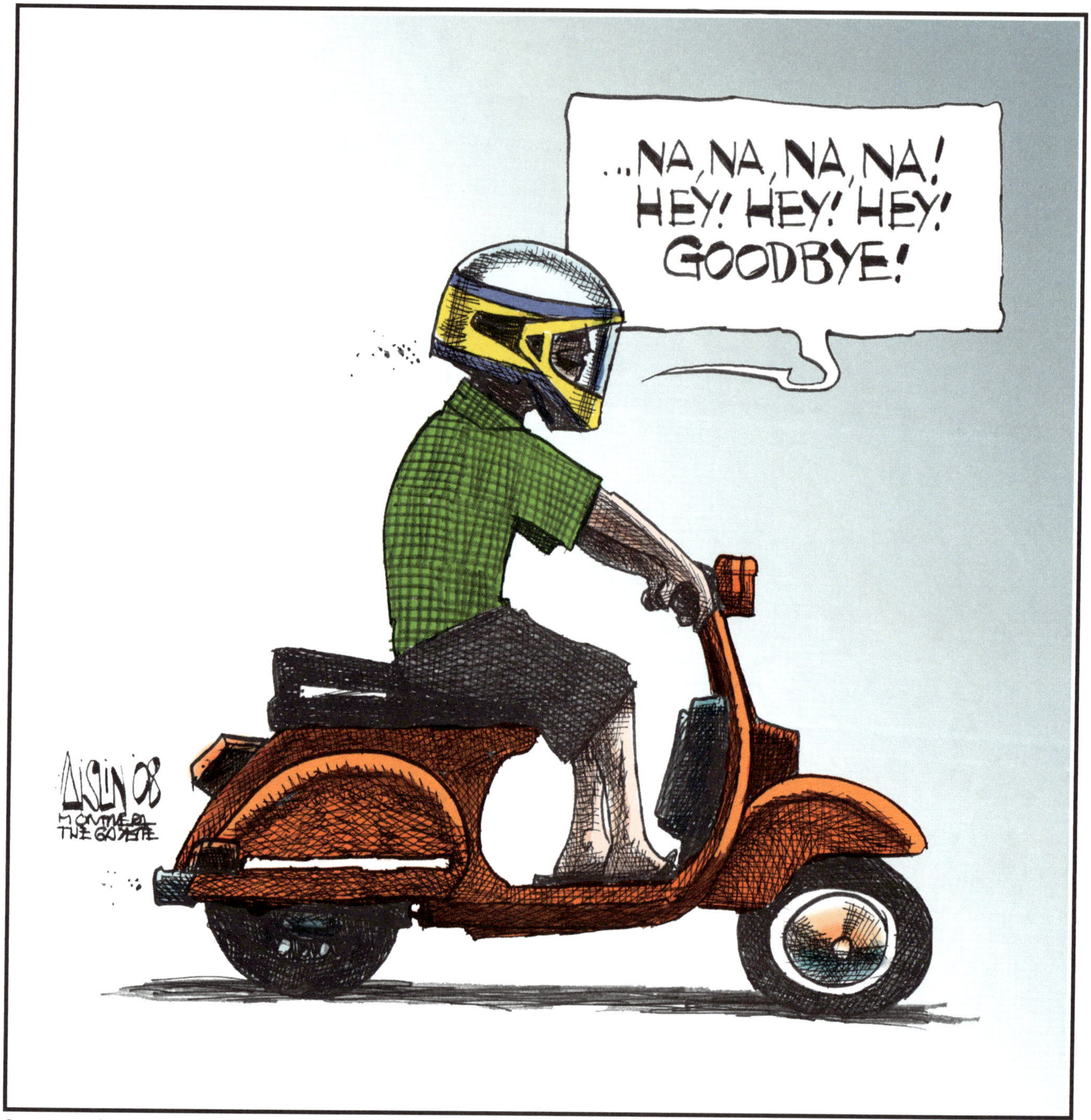
...NA, NA, NA, NA! HEY! HEY! HEY! GOODBYE!
AISLIN '08
MONTREAL THE GAZETTE

Scooter sales on the rise

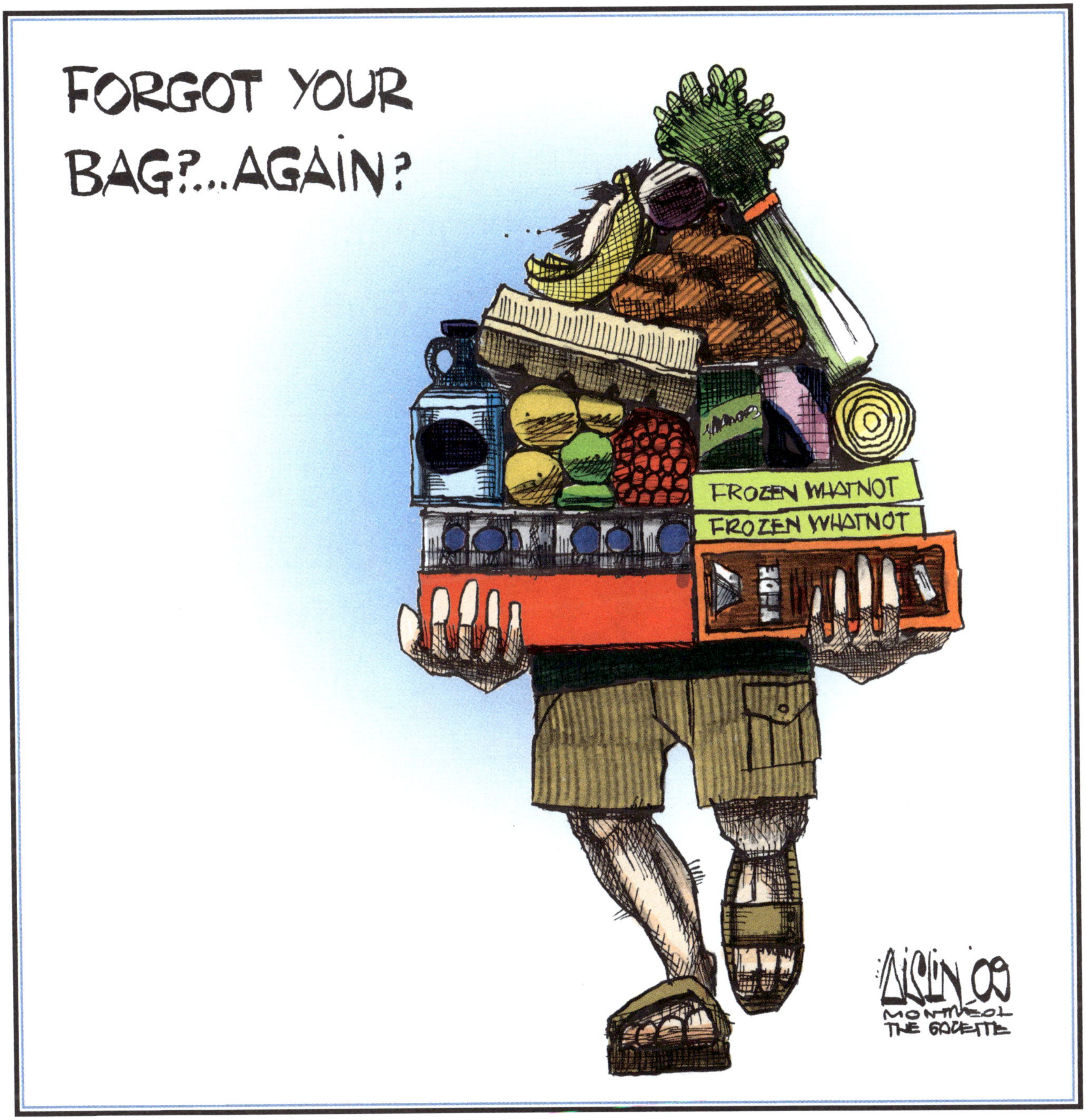
FORGOT YOUR BAG?...AGAIN?
FROZEN WHATNOT
FROZEN WHATNOT
AISLIN '09
MONTREAL THE GAZETTE

Grocery stores will no longer provide free shopping bags

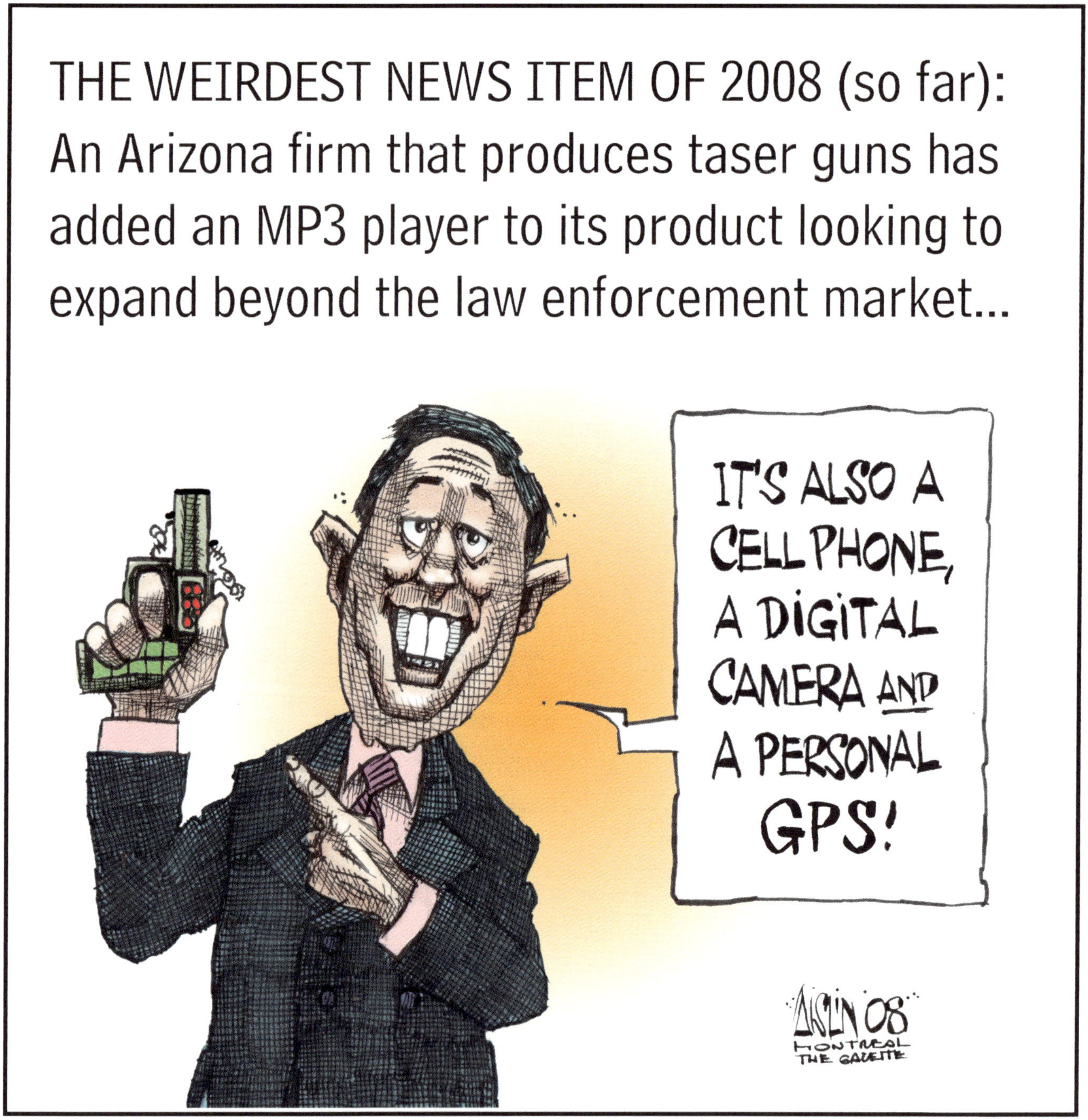
THE WEIRDEST NEWS ITEM OF 2008 (so far): An Arizona firm that produces taser guns has added an MP3 player to its product looking to expand beyond the law enforcement market...
IT'S ALSO A CELL PHONE, A DIGITAL CAMERA AND A PERSONAL GPS!
AISLIN 08
MONTREAL THE GAZETTE

Gadgetry overload

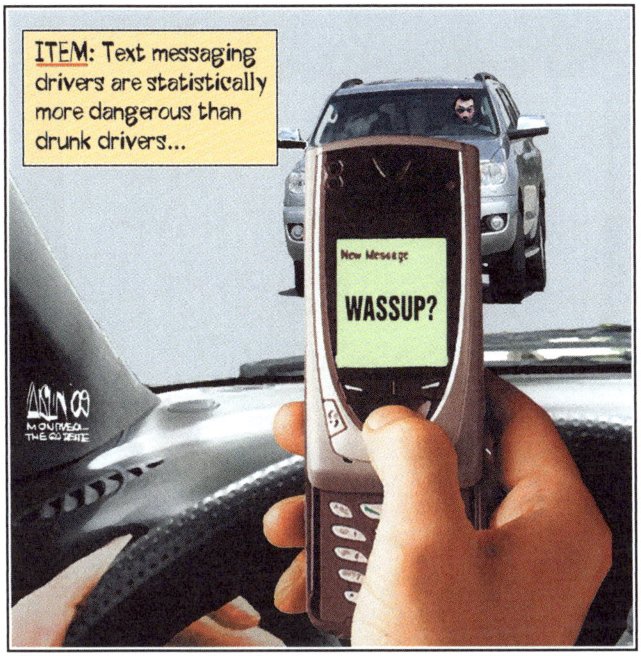
ITEM: Text messaging drivers are statistically more dangerous than drunk drivers...
New Message
WASSUP?
AISLIN 08
MONTREAL THE GAZETTE

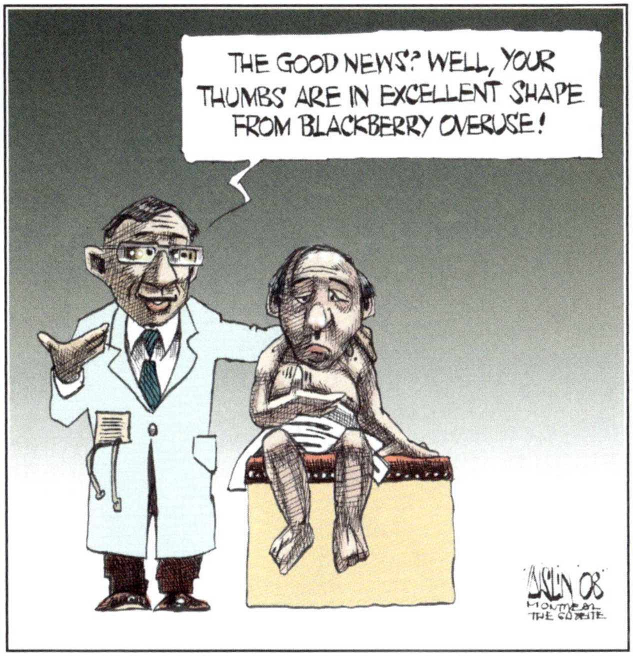
THE GOOD NEWS? WELL, YOUR THUMBS ARE IN EXCELLENT SHAPE FROM BLACKBERRY OVERUSE!
AISLIN 08
MONTREAL THE GAZETTE

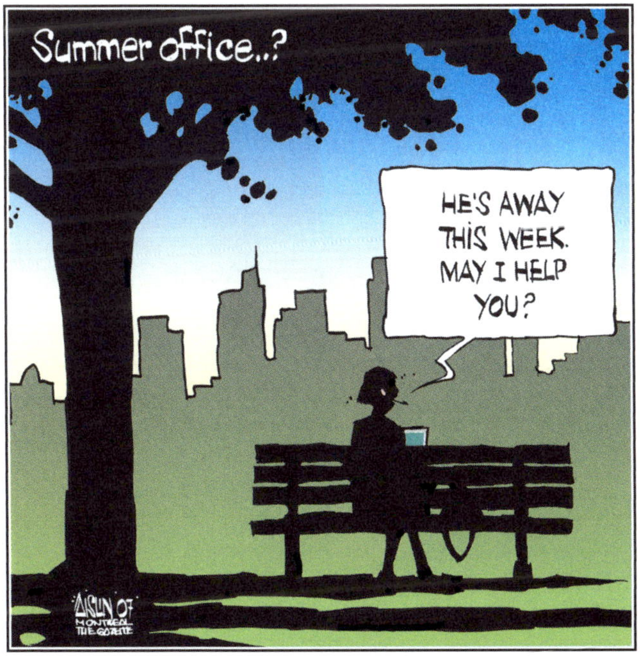
Summer office..?
HE'S AWAY THIS WEEK. MAY I HELP YOU?
AISLIN 07
MONTREAL THE GAZETTE

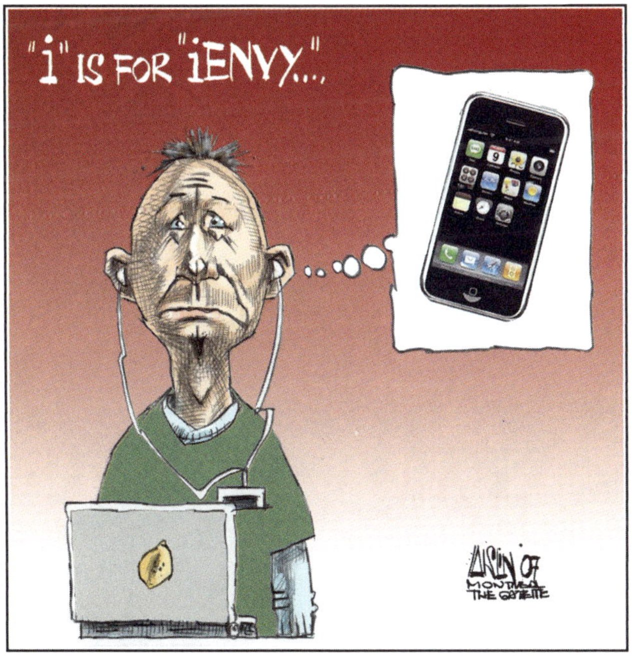
"i" IS FOR "iENVY."...
AISLIN 07
MONTREAL THE GAZETTE

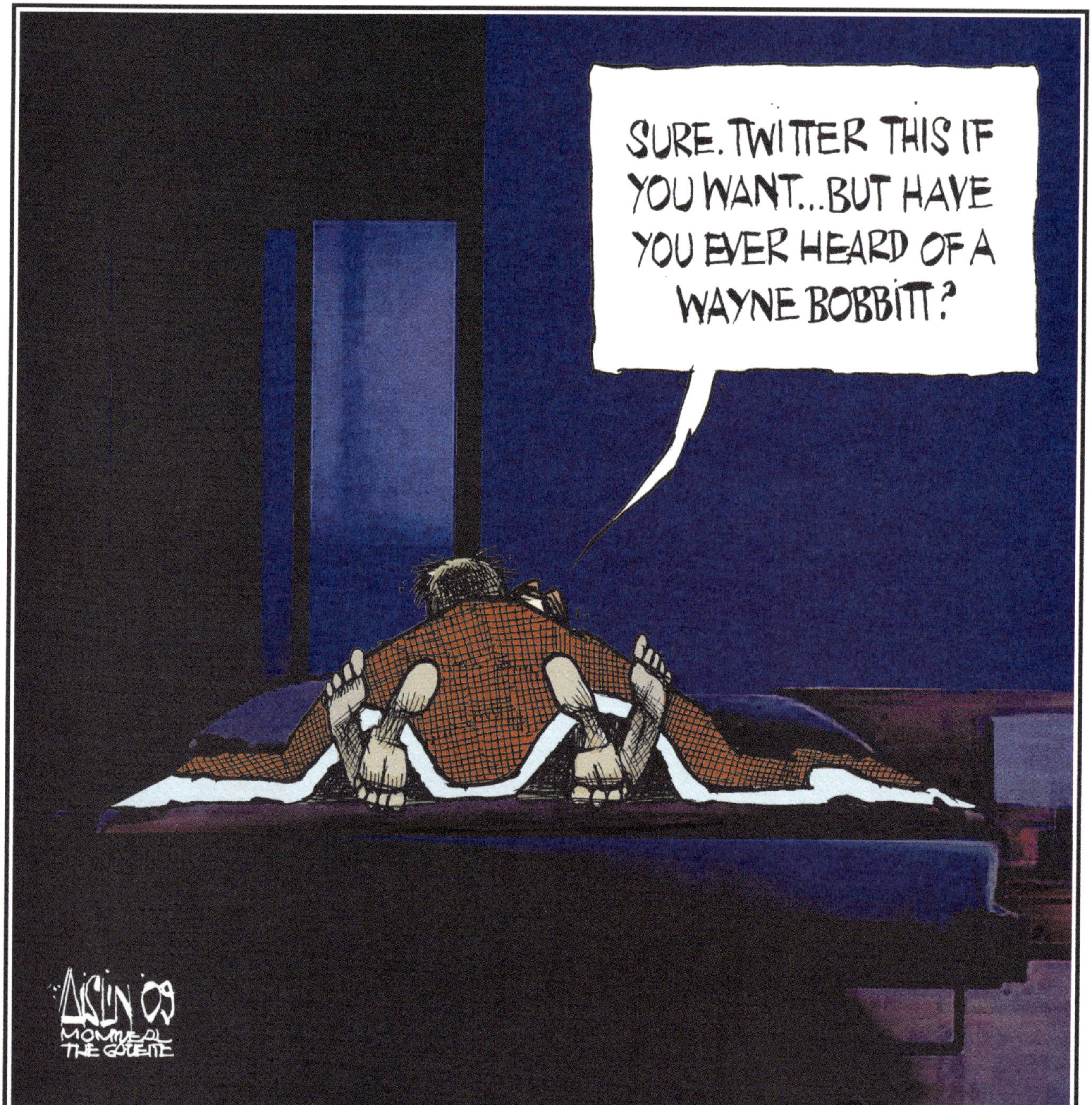
SURE. TWITTER THIS IF YOU WANT...BUT HAVE YOU EVER HEARD OF A WAYNE BOBBITT?
AISLIN 09
MONTREAL THE GAZETTE

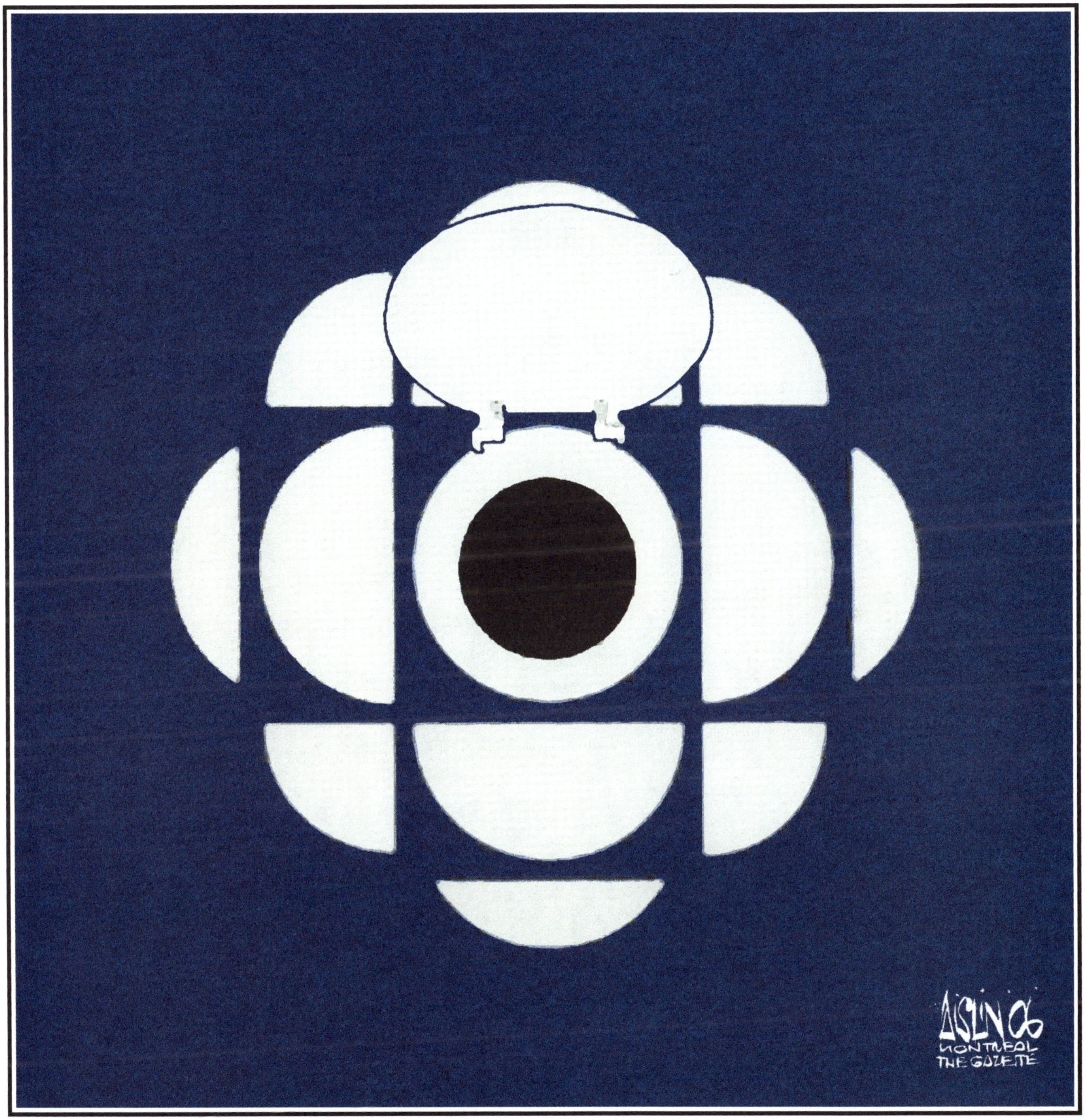
AISLIN 06
MONTREAL
THE GAZETTE

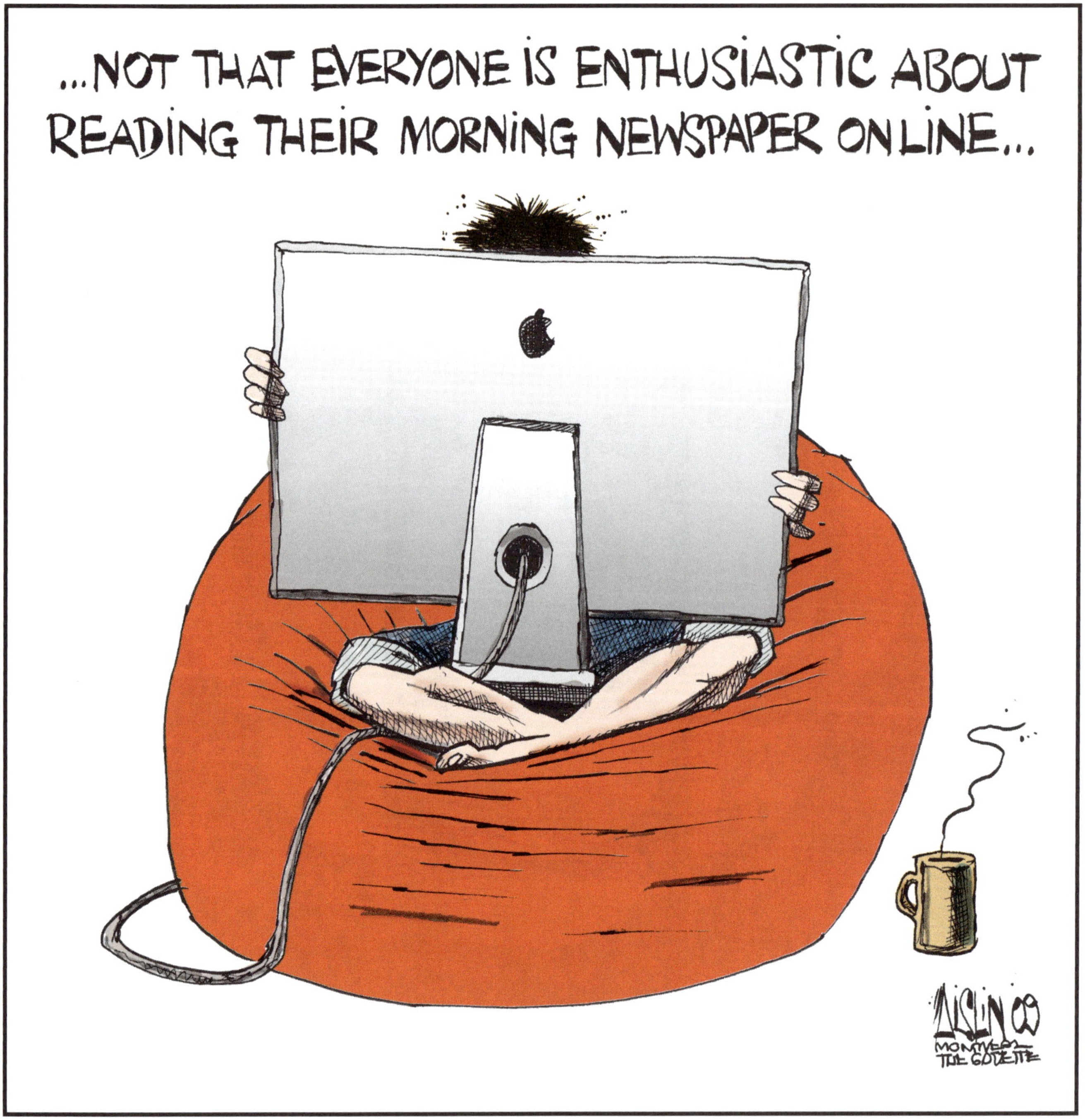
...NOT THAT EVERYONE IS ENTHUSIASTIC ABOUT READING THEIR MORNING NEWSPAPER ONLINE...

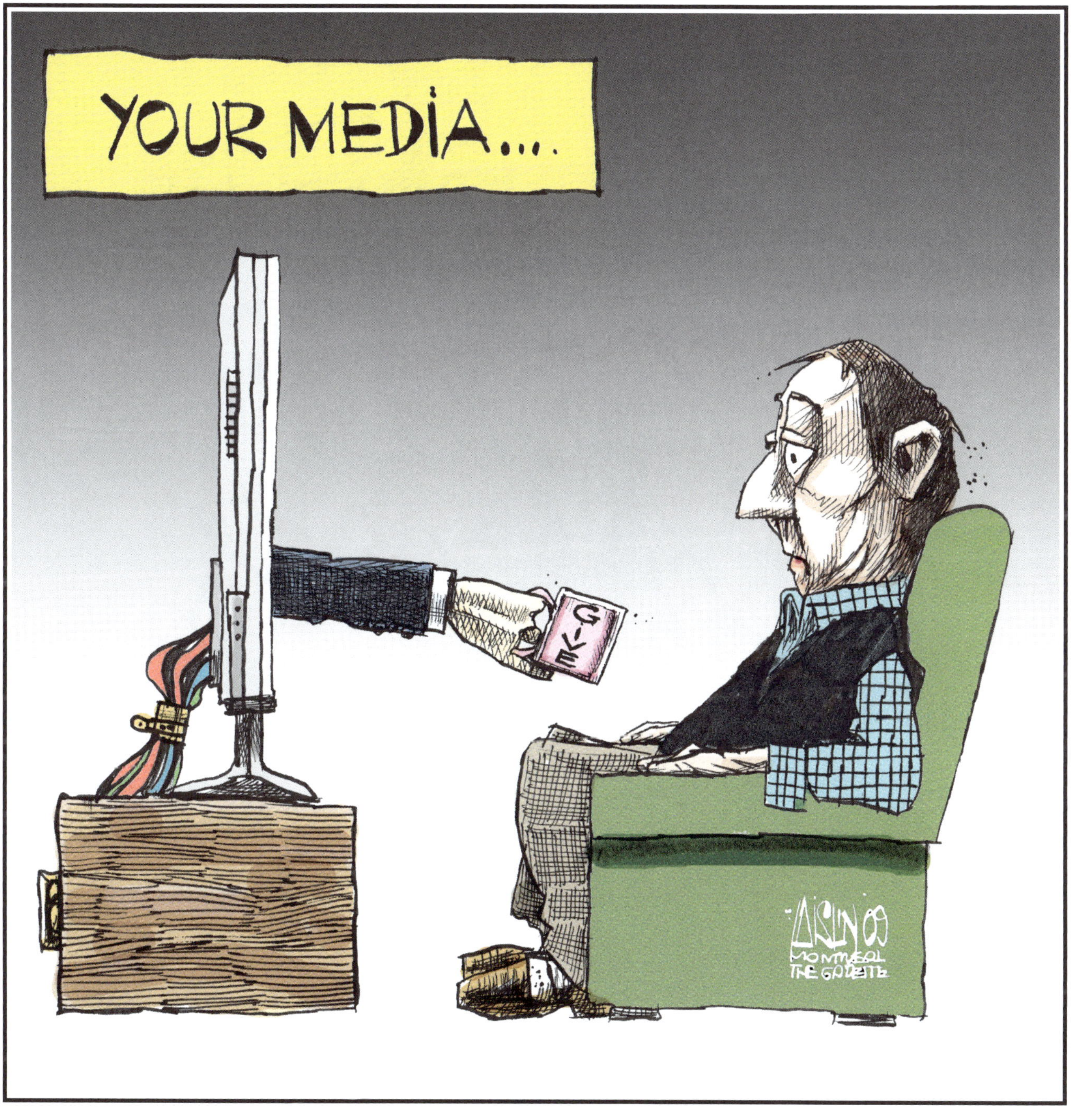
YOUR MEDIA....
GIVE
AISLIN 09
MONTREAL
THE GAZETTE

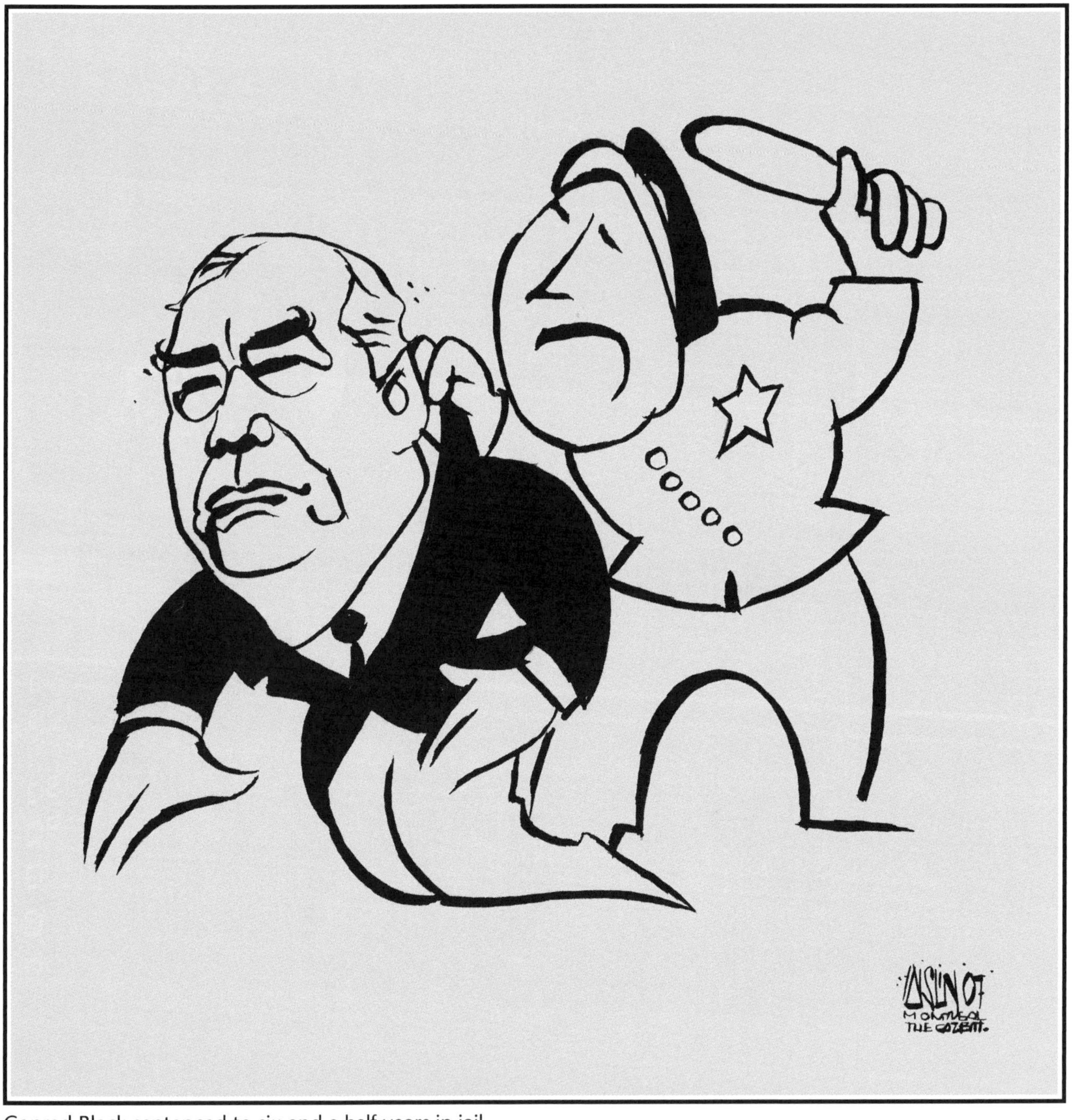
AISLIN 07
MONTREAL
THE GAZETTE.

Conrad Black sentenced to six and a half years in jail

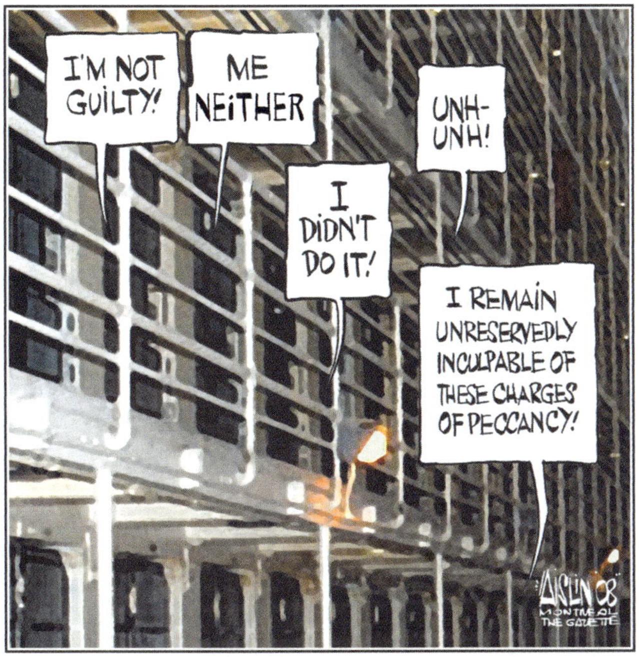

I'M NOT GUILTY!
ME NEITHER
UNH-UNH!
I DIDN'T DO IT!
I REMAIN UNRESERVEDLY INCULPABLE OF THESE CHARGES OF PECCANCY!
AISLIN 08
MONTREAL THE GAZETTE

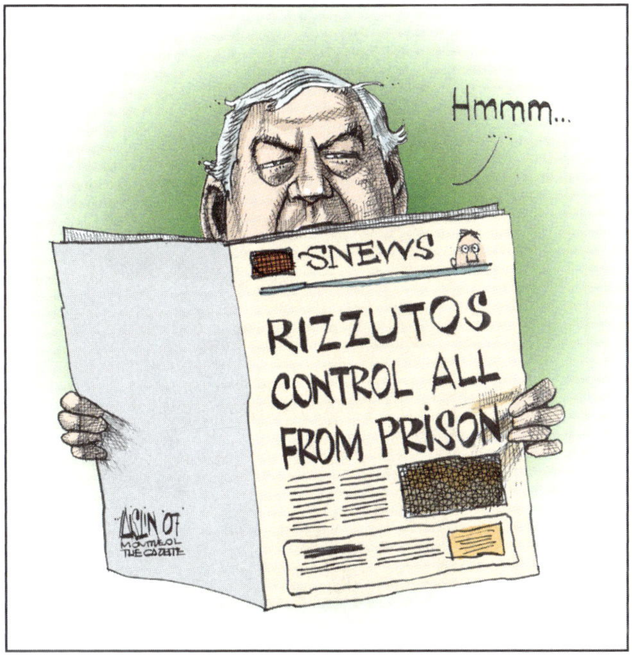

Hmmm...
NEWS
RIZZUTOS CONTROL ALL FROM PRISON
AISLIN 07
MONTREAL THE GAZETTE

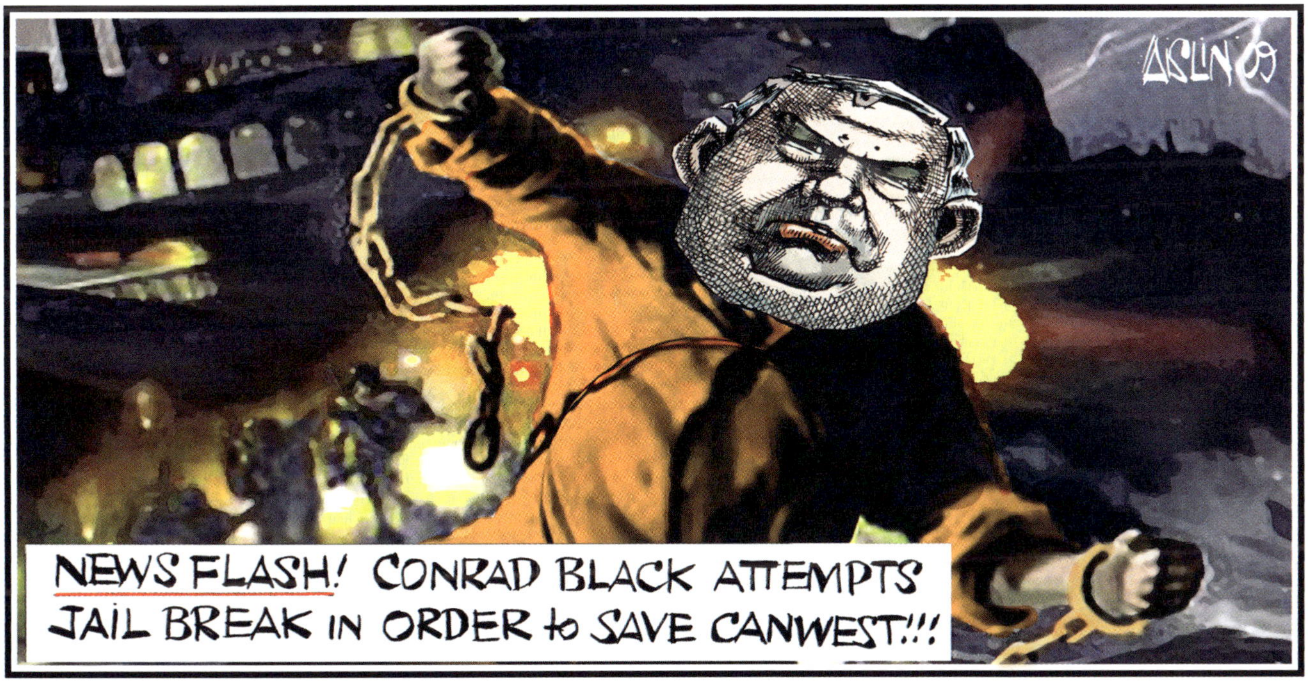

AISLIN 09
NEWS FLASH! CONRAD BLACK ATTEMPTS JAIL BREAK IN ORDER to SAVE CANWEST!!!

(Unpublished)

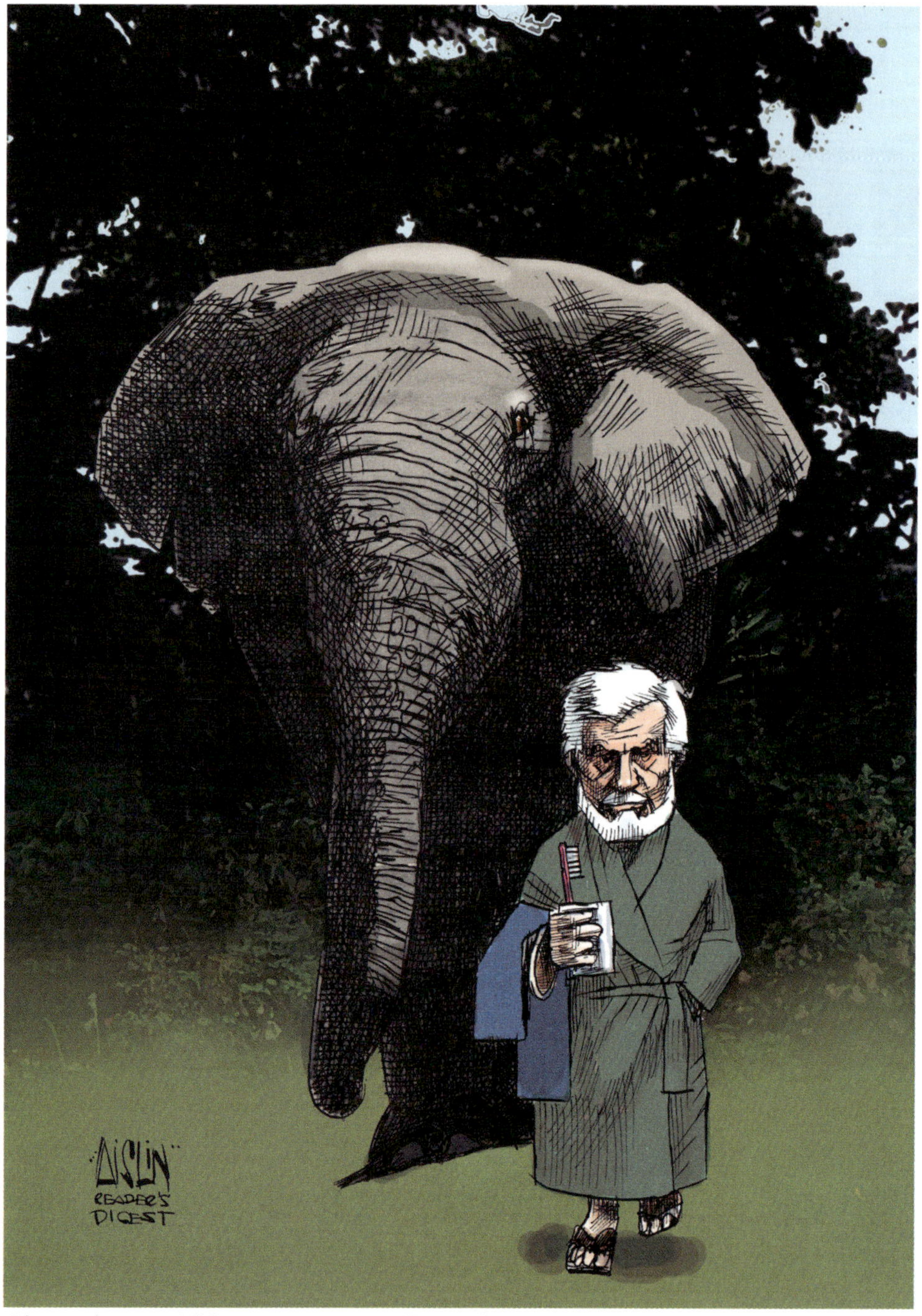
AISLIN
READER'S
DIGEST
After a shower: N'Gorongoro crater, Tanzania

CHAPTER 6

Aislin's Travels

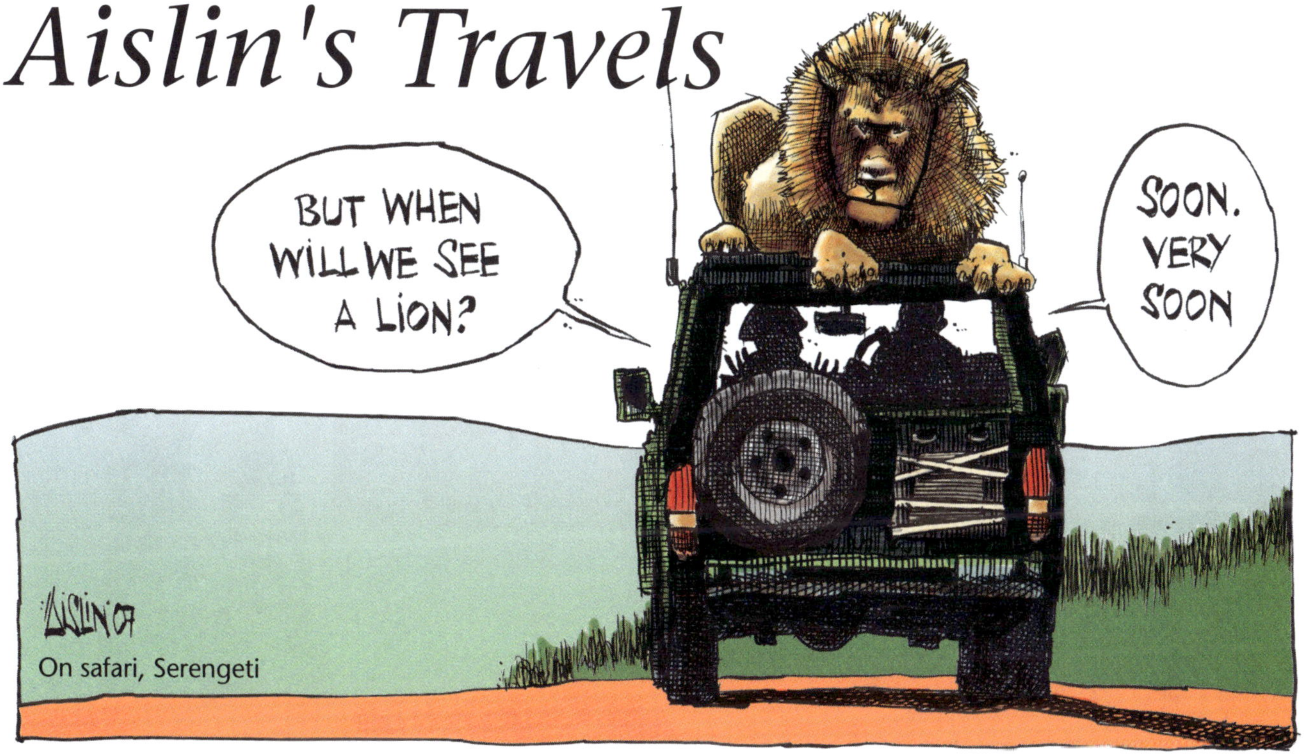
BUT WHEN WILL WE SEE A LION?
SOON. VERY SOON
On safari, Serengeti

For as long as I've been in the business of cartooning for publication, I've managed to coax various patrons into sending me here and there to draw sketchbooks for them. It might have been around the block – or around the world. I've enjoyed these trips immensely, not least because they give me a breather from the daily drama of parochial politics.

Most recently, I've been traveling four times a year for the Canadian edition of Reader's Digest, writing and drawing humorous travel pieces on Cuba, Ireland, Hawaii, Newfoundland, Tanzania, Mexico – even Jasper, Alberta.

As a teaser, here are some travel sketches from the past three years. These and many more from the last 35 years will be included in a forthcoming book from McArthur and Company entitled AISLIN'S TRAVELS.

Terry Mosher (Aislin)
Montreal, August 15, 2009

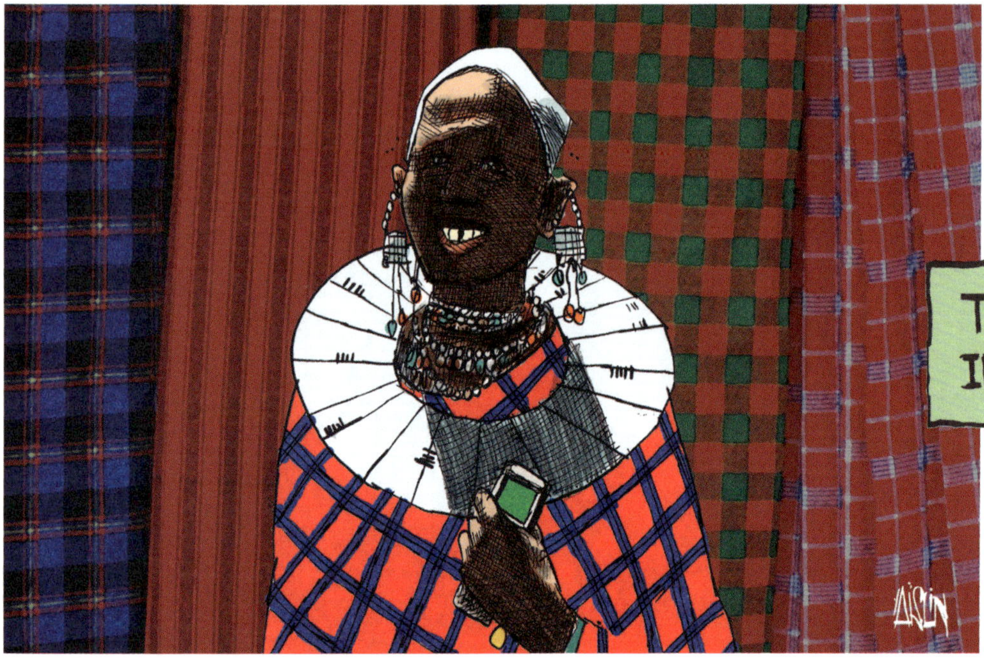

Maasai woman, Tanzania

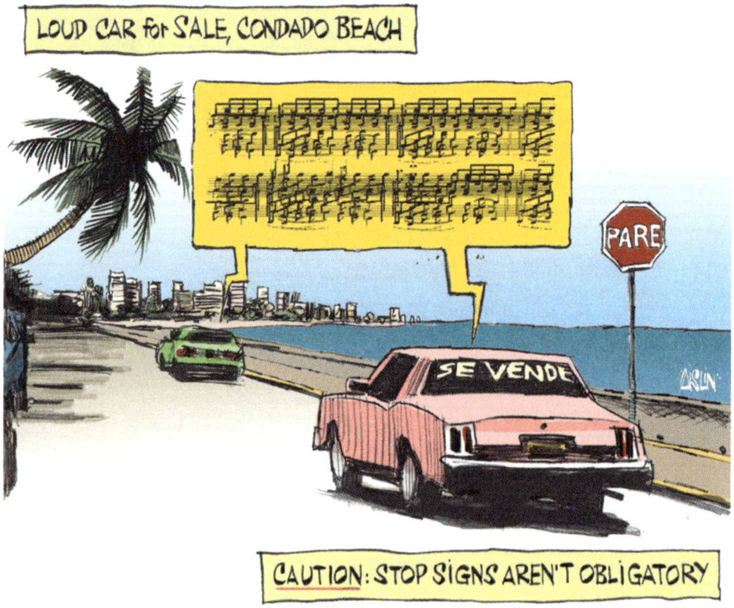
LOUD CAR for SALE, CONDADO BEACH
PARE
SE VENDE
CAUTION: STOP SIGNS AREN'T OBLIGATORY

San Juan, Puerto Rico

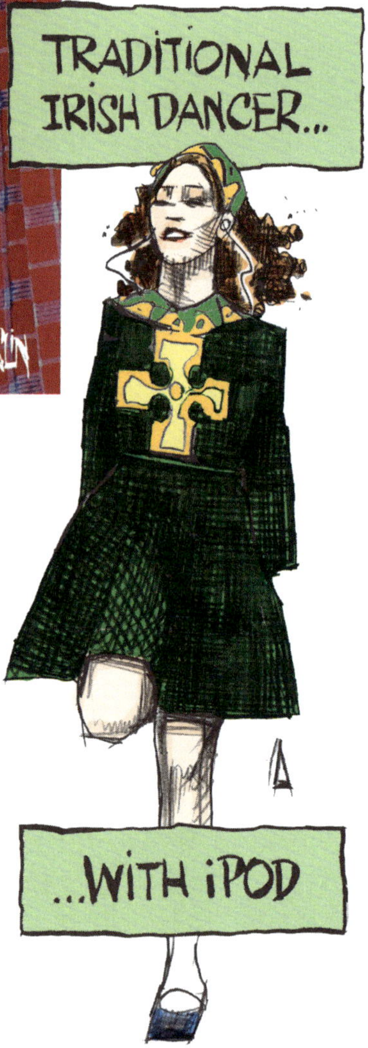
TRADITIONAL IRISH DANCER...
...WITH iPOD

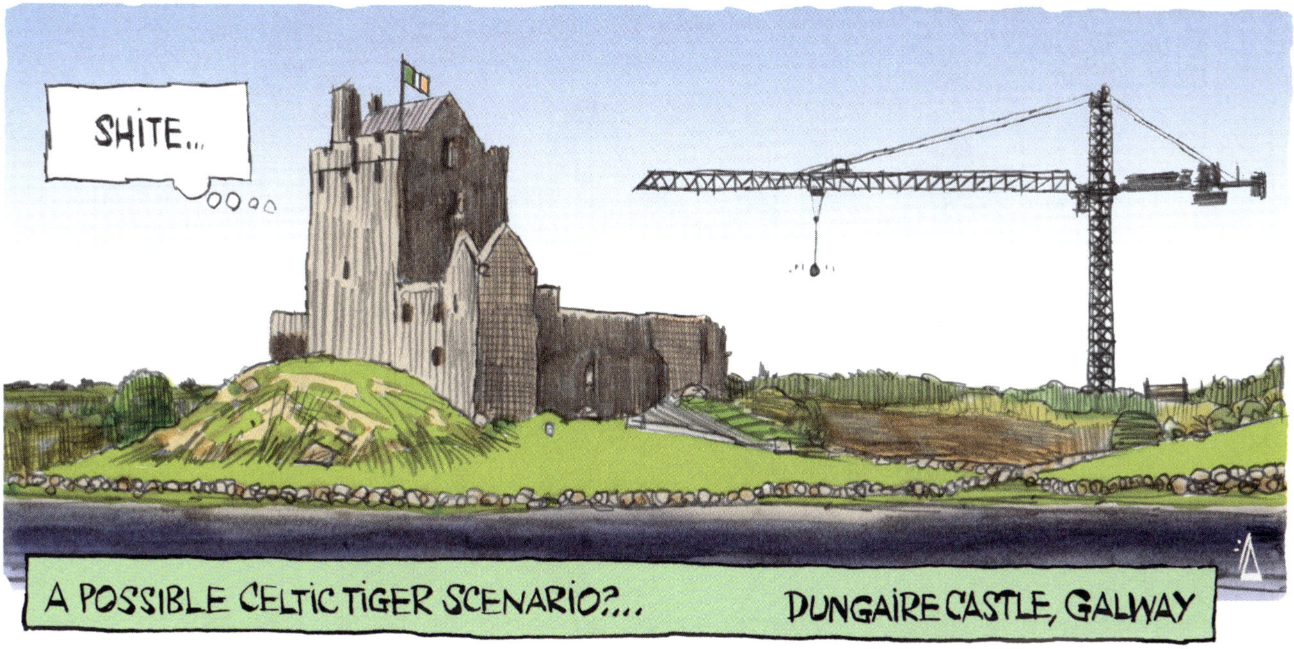
SHITE...
A POSSIBLE CELTIC TIGER SCENARIO?...
DUNGAIRE CASTLE, GALWAY

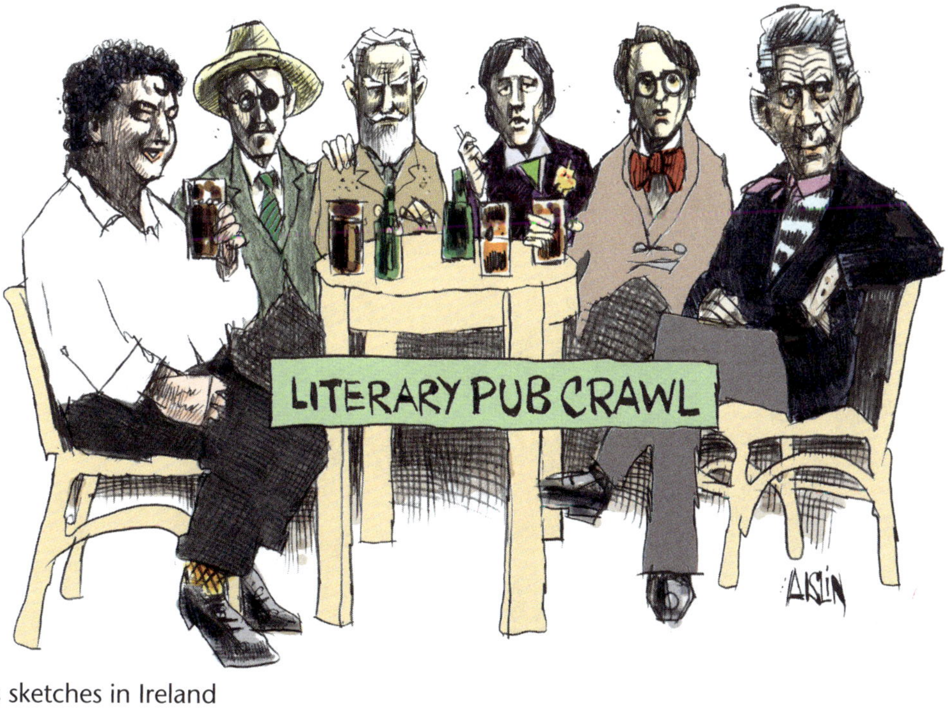
LITERARY PUB CRAWL
AISLIN

Miscellaneous sketches in Ireland

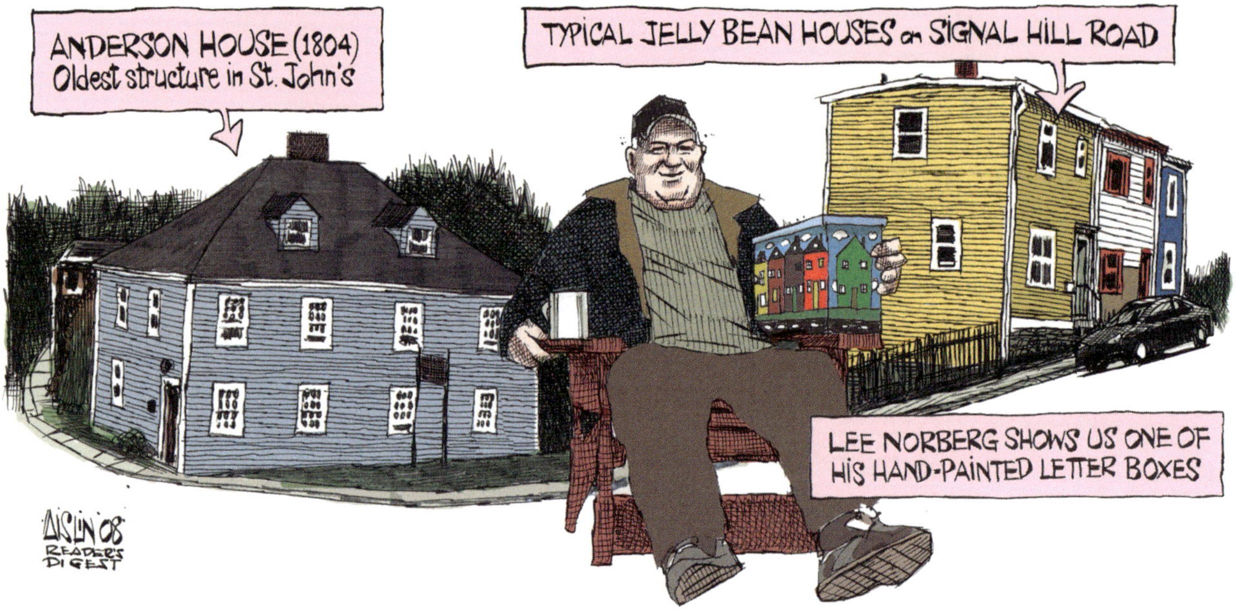
ANDERSON HOUSE (1804)
Oldest structure in St. John's
TYPICAL JELLY BEAN HOUSES on SIGNAL HILL ROAD
LEE NORBERG SHOWS US ONE OF HIS HAND-PAINTED LETTER BOXES
AISLIN '08
READER'S DIGEST

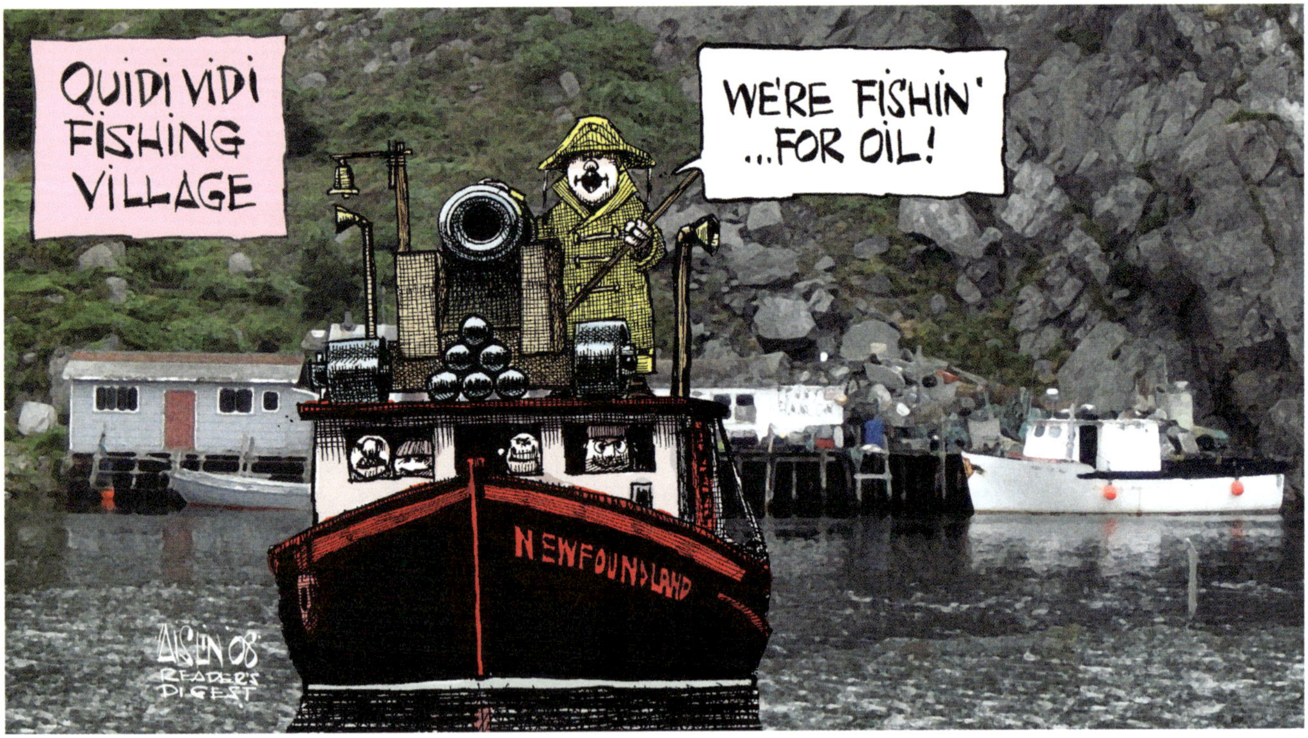
QUIDI VIDI FISHING VILLAGE
WE'RE FISHIN' ...FOR OIL!
NEWFOUNDLAND
AISLIN '08
READER'S DIGEST

St. John's, Newfoundland

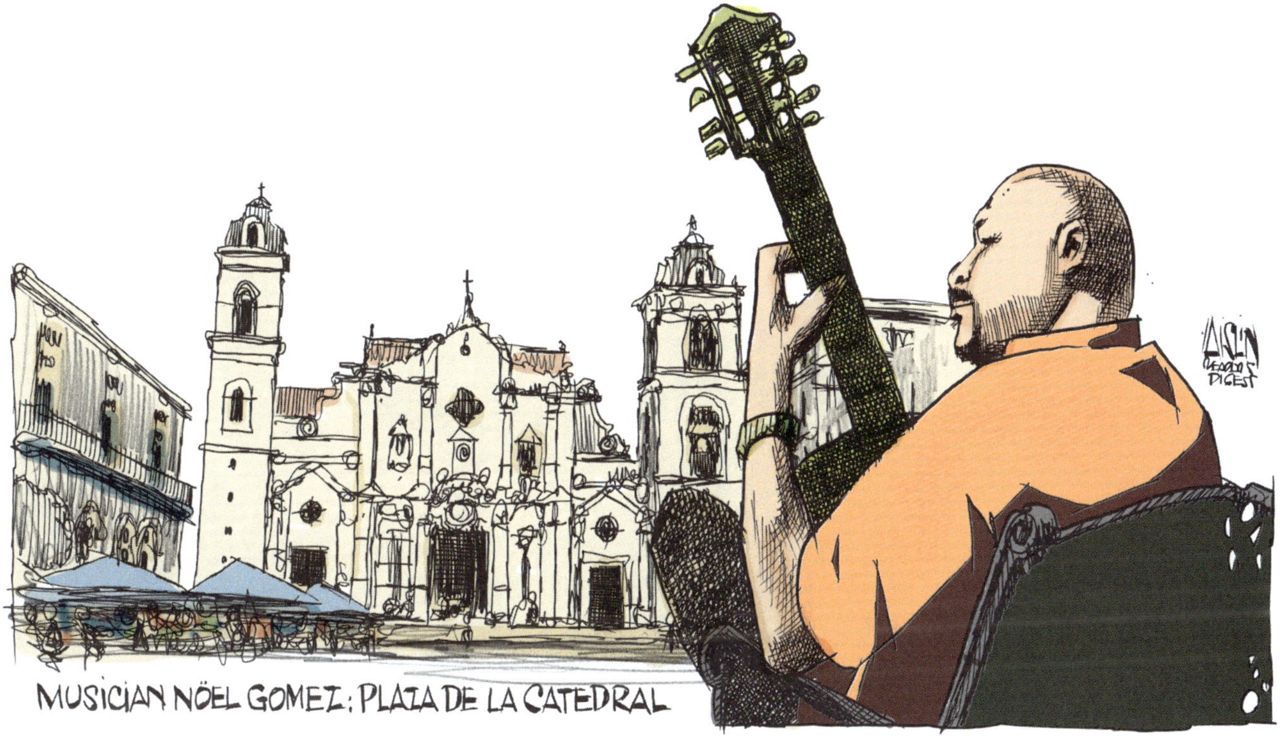
MUSICIAN NÖEL GOMEZ: PLAZA DE LA CATEDRAL

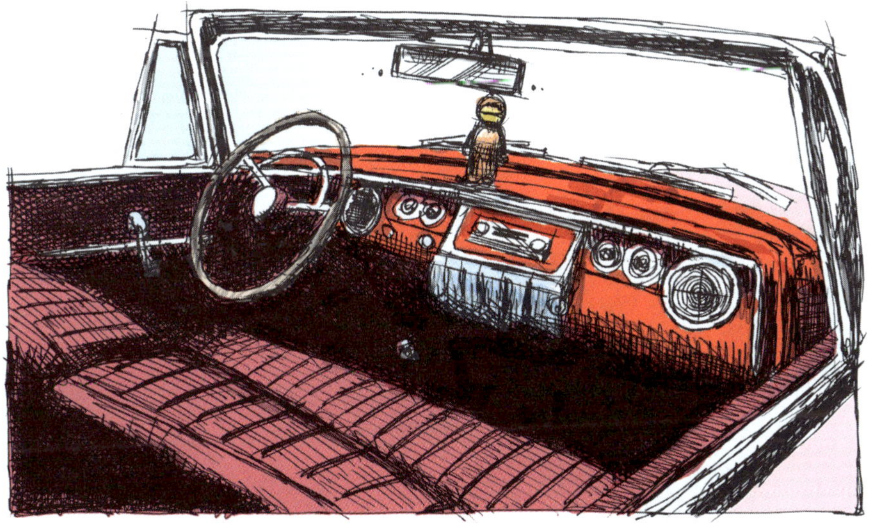

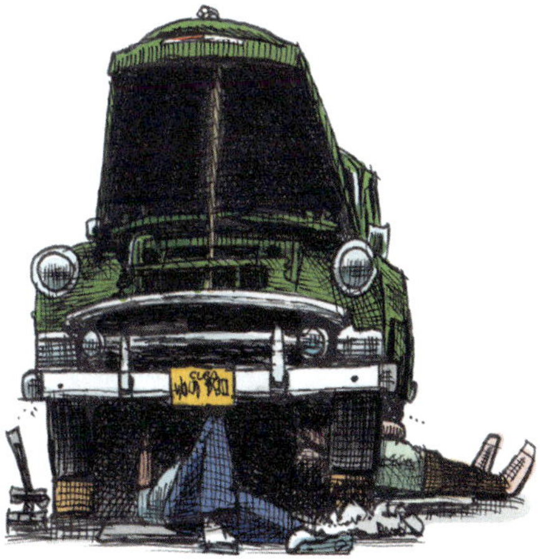

Havana, Cuba

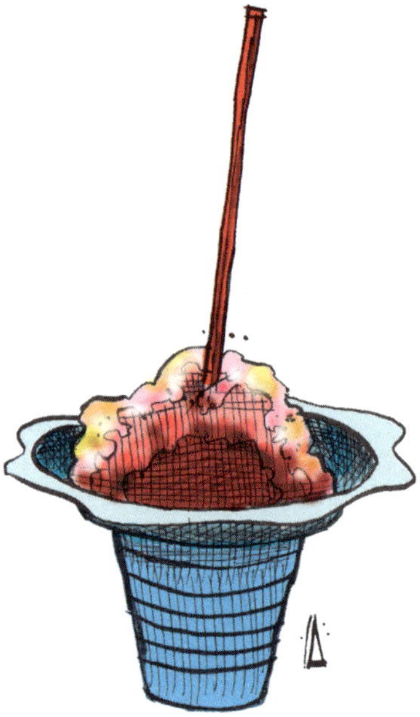

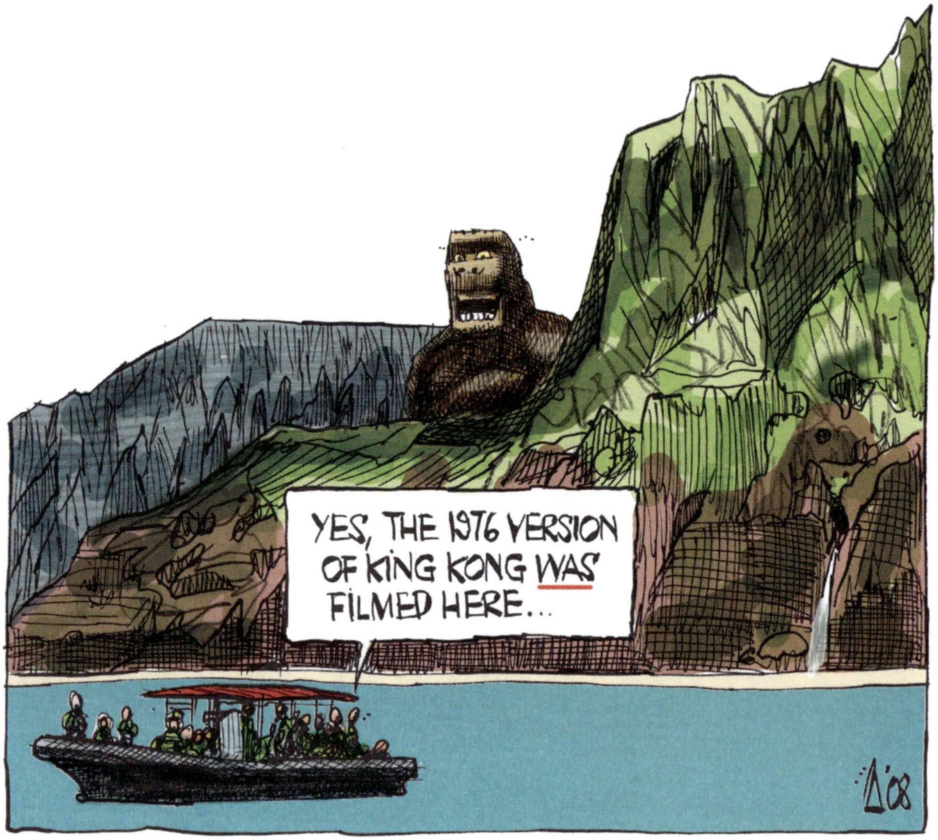
YES, THE 1976 VERSION OF KING KONG WAS FILMED HERE...

Kauai, Hawaii

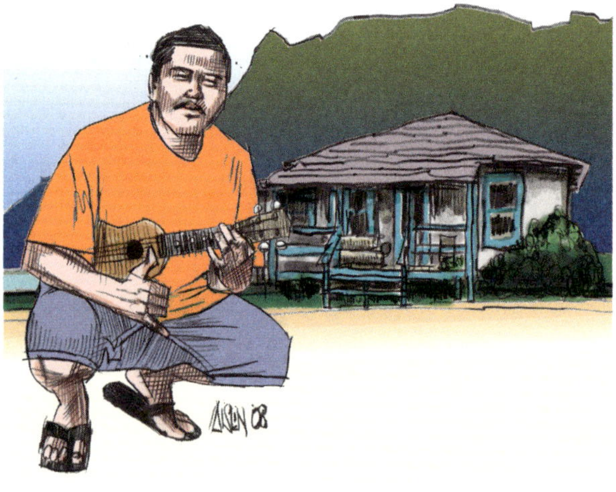

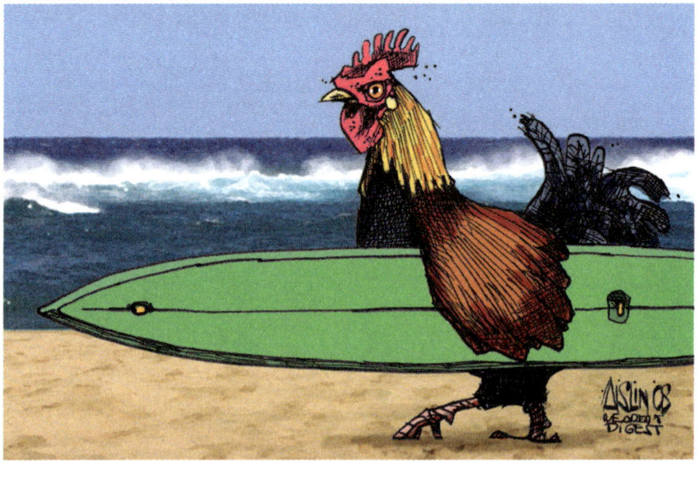

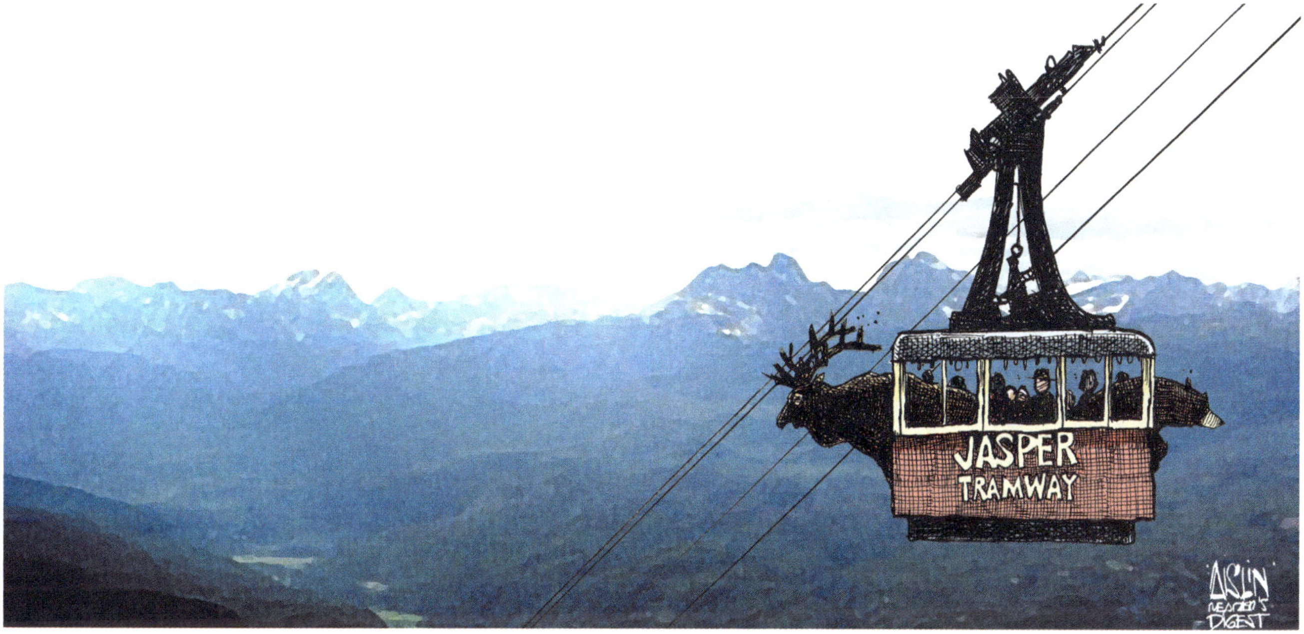
JASPER
TRAMWAY

Jasper, Alberta

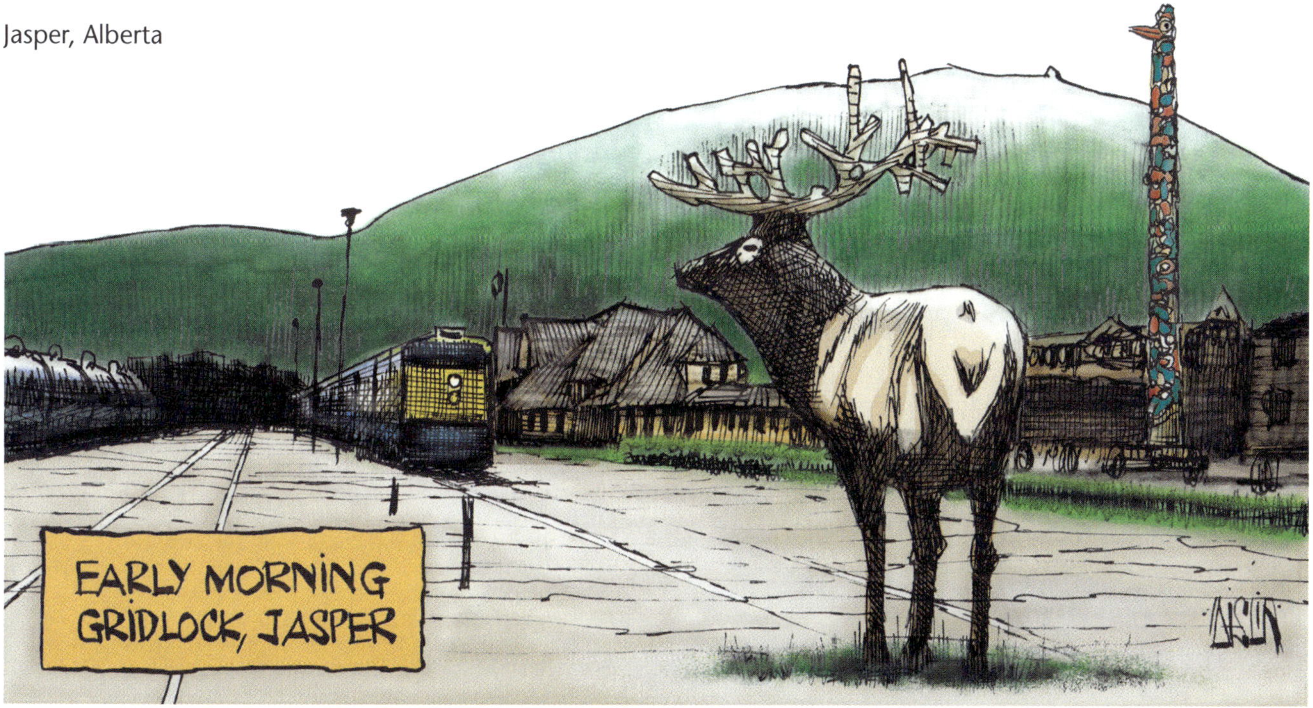
EARLY MORNING
GRIDLOCK, JASPER

PHOTO: Mary Hughson

Terry Mosher on assignment in New Bonaventure, Newfoundland.

AISLIN is the name of Terry Mosher's elder daughter and is the nom de plume that he has used for over thirty-five years as the political cartoonist for Montreal's English-language newspaper, The Gazette.

Over that period of time Aislin has also worked periodically for Maclean's Magazine, The Toronto Star and many other publications with his cartoons being syndicated internationally. Most recently, Mosher has been sharing his sketches and notes from his travels throughout Canada and around the world in the Canadian edition of Reader's Digest Magazine.

Film maker John Curtin won the Gemini for best biography documentary of 2007 for his Life and Times documentary on Terry Mosher entitled Dangerous When Provoked.

More information is available at: www.aislin.com

Other books by Aislin:

Aislin–100 Caricatures (1971)
Hockey Night in Moscow (1972, with Jack Ludwig)
Aislin–150 Caricatures (1973)
The Great Hockey Thaw (1974, with Jack Ludwig)
'Ello, Morgentaler? Aislin–150 Caricatures (1975)
O.K. Everybody Take a Valium! Aislin–150 Caricatures (1977)
L'Humour d'Aislin (1977)
The Retarded Giant (1977, with Bill Mann)
The Hecklers: A History of Canadian Political Cartooning
    (1979, with Peter Desbarats)
The Year The Expos Almost Won the Pennant
    (1979, with Brodie Snyder)
Did the Earth Move? Aislin–180 Caricatures (1980)
The Year The Expos Finally Won Something
    (1981, with Brodie Snyder)
The First Great Canadian Trivia Quiz
    (1981, with Brodie Snyder)
Stretchmarks (1982)
The Anglo Guide to Survival in Quebec
    (1983, with various Montreal writers)
Tootle: A Children's Story (1984, with Johan Sarrazin)
Where's the Trough? (1985)
Old Whores (1987)
What's the Big Deal? (1988, with Rick Salutin)
The Lawn Jockey (1989)
Parcel of Rogues (1990, with Maude Barlow)

Barbed Lyres, Canadian Venomous Verse
    (1990, with Margaret Atwood and other Canadian poets)
Drawing Bones–15 Years of Cartooning Brian Mulroney (1991)
Put Up & Shut Up! The 90s so far in Cartoons
    (1994, with Hubie Bauch)
Oh, Canadians! Hysterically Historical Rhymes
    (1996, with Gordon Snell)
One Oar in the Water: The Nasty 90s continued in cartoons (1997)
Oh, No! More Canadians! Hysterically Historical Rhymes (1998,
    with Gordon Snell)
Nick : A Montreal Life (1998, with Dave Bist, L. Ian Macdonald,
    Stephen Phizicky)
2000 Reasons to Hate the Millennium
    (1999, with Josh Freed and other contributors)
The Big Wind-Up! The final book of Nasty 90s cartoons (1999)
Yes! Even More Canadians! Hysterically Historical Rhymes
    (2000, with Gordon Snell)
The Oh, Canadians Omnibus (2001, with Gordon Snell)
In Your Face ... other recent cartoons (2001)
More Marvellous Canadians! (2002, with Gordon Snell)
The Illustrated Canadian Songbook, (2003, with Bowser & Blue)
Further Fabulous Canadians! (2004, with Gordon Snell)
OH,OH! ...and other recent cartoons (2004)
The Best Of OH! CANADIANS (2006, with Gordon Snell)
Mordecai Richler Was Here (2006, with Mordecai Richler)
What Next? ...and other recent cartoons by Aislin (2006)